THE BRITISH]
Forces and Chief Officer

CW00968128

2nd edition

MARTIN STALLION
Police History Society

DAVID S. WALL
University of Durham

Police history monograph number 7

POLICE HISTORY SOCIETY

First edition published in 1999 by the Police History Society
This edition first published in 2011 by the Police History Society,
c/o The Librarian, Bramshill House, Hook RG27 0JW

British Library Cataloguing in Publication Data
Stallion, Martin.
  The British police : forces and chief officers, 1829-2012.
  -- 2nd ed. -- (Police history monographs ; v. 7)
  1. Police--Great Britain--Directories. 2. Police--Great
  Britain--History--19th century. 3. Police--Great
  Britain--History--20th century. 4. Police chiefs--Great
  Britain--Directories. 5. Police chiefs--Great Britain--
  History--19th century. 6. Police chiefs--Great Britain--
  History--20th century.
  I. Title II. Series III. Wall, David, 1956- IV. Police
  History Society.
  363.2'0941'09-dc23
  ISBN-13: 9780951253861
  ISSN 0951-8800

Printed and bound in the UK by the MPG Books Group, Bodmin and
King's Lynn

Foreword to the 1st edition

It is with great pleasure that I write the foreword to this publication. I hope that it will be the first of a number of on-going, or living projects to be carried out by the Police History Society (PHS) which will be periodically updated to provide useful, if not essential, research tools and resources for its members and others who might hold an interest in the subject.

Like many police officers, I have often been surprised by the British Police Services' overall lack of a sense of its own history. It is, for example, only in recent times that organisations such as the PHS have emerged to assist and promote the interests of police historians.

Hitherto, a major hurdle for many British police historians has been the lack of the availability of consolidated information, even just a simple list, of the many British police forces that have existed over the years. A similar frustration lies in the lack of information about the people who commanded them. Hopefully this publication will address both issues in one fell swoop.

As Martin and David carefully observe in their preface and also in chapter 2, their own historical researches have revealed that the study of police history is not an exact science, moreover, it is often the case that sources of basic data can be contradictory. So, I encourage PHS members, and readers, to contact the authors with any suggestions for revisions, conflicting opinions about dates, force numbers, lacunae and so on, in order that they can be included in the next edition in five or so years' time. This is what I mean about living research.

I anticipate that this publication will provide us with one more milestone into our historical understanding of a service which has become such an important part of the British way of life.

Colin Bailey, QPM, LLB, Chief Constable, Nottinghamshire
Chairman of the Police History Society (1998-2001)

Foreword to the 2nd edition

The study of Police history can be utterly fascinating, absorbing and enjoyable. But it can also be an extremely frustrating activity. It is fascinating because the history of policing reflects so much of the history of our society. It captures and reflects social attitudes, cultural norms and the behaviours of the time. In the past two centuries the way British Policing has been structured, led and managed is a case study of the changing nature of organisations. The frustrations come about from the fragmented and often careless approach the service has towards preserving its history. The Police can tend to operate in the "here and now" and our rich history can pass through our hands without being preserved let alone treasured.

Thus, in the study of police history, a book such as this becomes an essential reference point. It provides a number of important hooks, especially dates and names, which can support further study. In a constantly changing landscape this book assists and enables researchers and interested parties to start homing in and focusing on further material drawn from the people and the times.

David Wall and Martin Stallion have done a superb job of making sense of many pieces of jigsaw and snippets of information to lay out for us, in this book, the landscape of policing. They have captured a range of changes and corrections from the first edition as well as bringing up to date the recent history of policing.

Looking through the book reminds us of the amount of change that policing has faced since the "new" police was established in the 1820s. Today the service is being urged and compelled to reform and, sometimes, it is suggested that the Police have not changed or reformed over the years. As can be seen in this book, such suggestions are wrong. Whatever the fresh reforms that are being promoted it behoves us all to reflect on the experiences of forces and Chief Constables over the past two centuries and consider the lessons they might be able to tell us about the way policing should be led, organised and delivered in the 21st century.

Rob Beckley, QPM, Deputy Chief Constable, Avon and Somerset
Chairman of the Police History Society (2007-)

Contents

Preface   *page*   6

Preface to the 2nd edition   7

1   The Organisation of Police 1829-2012   8

2   Collecting Historical Information about the Police   44

3   Some Explanatory Notes   47

4   Symbols and Abbreviations   51

5   British Police Forces 1829-2012   52

6   Index of Chief Police Officers 1829-2012   207

7   A Bibliography of British Police Force Histories   272

Preface

The study of police history has burgeoned during recent years and the Police History Society has provided an important focal point for that growth. In addition, we have also witnessed a growth of public interest in the subject through the increasing number of university courses in policing and related subjects. But, for many years a major hurdle for the police historian was to identify the many independent police forces that have existed since the 'new' police were introduced in the early 19th Century. Furthermore, police historians have been regularly frustrated by the lack of information about the individuals who were in charge of those forces. Such information is important as the fortunes of the forces were frequently tied up with the men (until 1995) who commanded them.

These lacunae seeded the origins of this book. Independently of each other we started compiling lists of police forces and the chief constables for our respective studies. We had both thought that the main source of data on chief constables would be *Who's Who*, but David found, when planning his socio-legal history of the chief constables of England and Wales, that only a minor percentage of all chief constables had entries. He further discovered that a comprehensive list of all chief constables since 1836 did not exist and that the borough chief constables were treated as a separate entity to their county colleagues. So, a major problem from the outset was a lack of information about the organisation of police forces and their chief officers. Therefore, one of the first tasks carried out for the quantitative study was to construct a list of all of the police forces that existed in England and Wales. The data collected formed the basis of his 1998 book *The Chief Constables of England and Wales*.

Quite independently Martin had been compiling information about all of the British police forces and their chief officers and had experienced very similar problems. As soon as we both found out about each other's project we decided to pool resources and this book is the product of those endeavours. We hope that this book will fill an important gap in the literature on police history and provide a reference point for many existing and future historians of the police. The events listed herein are accurate up until September 1999. As this is an ongoing project, we would be very grateful to be notified of any errors, omissions, changes, relevant references etc., for future editions.

David Wall, Leeds, and Martin Stallion, Braintree, September 1999

Preface to the 2nd edition

The success of the first edition has encouraged us to prepare this revised edition. It now includes over 500 forces and nearly 3000 chief officers. The main amendments are:

Chapter 1 has been extended to record developments in the last 12 years

Chapter 5 incorporates changes to chief officers etc over the same period, as well as numerous corrections and additions to earlier details, including a few 19th century forces that we had previously missed in our research. It also now shows the year when a borough achieved county borough or city status, which may help in dating documents, badges etc

Chapter 7 includes new and recently identified force histories and now has a total of some 750 entries

Acknowledgments
For additional information and suggestions: Mick Barry, Bernard Brown, Paddy Carpenter, Dr Bruce Durie, the late Reg Hale, the late Tom Madigan, the late John Mason, Brian Podmore, R A Wildblood, Len Woodley and the chief officers of many of the current forces listed. John C Green's book *Scottish insignia as used by old police forces* (2008, ISBN 978-0955310041) was particularly helpful with details of several Scottish forces of which we had previously been unaware

David Wall, Durham
Martin Stallion, Braintree
September 2011

Cover picture: Reproduced, with permission, from the National Archives: ref. HO45/10228/B36765

Cover layout Sophie Wall

1 The Organisation of Police 1829-2012[1]

David Wall

During the late 1820s and 1830s a 'new' policing system emerged to replace the previous inefficient and out-moded part-time voluntary 'old' system. This new system was characterised by local, independent, bureaucratically organised police forces of full-time paid constables.[2] So, the origins of the modern police are to be found not in mediaeval times, as the more 'orthodox' historians of the police would suggest, but in the police reforms of the late 1820s and 1830s and in subsequent legislation.[3] It was the case, however, that a number of characteristics of the old constables system came to be embodied in the 'new' police; the local nature of the organisation, the constable as the basic unit and the subordination of constables to justices. The 'new' police were both organisationally and conceptually different from their predecessor, but the major change was that the new police and other contemporary local reforms symbolised the beginning of a new era of bureaucratic public governance by excluding individuals and communities who were hitherto centrally involved in policing (Rawlings, 1995: 138; Shearing, 1996: 83). And yet, whilst these ideas of police were revolutionary, there is much evidence (Wall, 1998: Ch. 2) to suggest that the transition from one system to the other was far more incremental than radical.

---

[1] Please note that this essay mainly discusses the development of the police in England and Wales. Without wishing to understate any differences between the two jurisdictions, it is nevertheless the case that although the Scottish local administrative arrangements and legal system were different, the organisation of the police in Scotland developed largely in parallel to the police in England and Wales and experienced broadly similar legislative and organisational processes. A history of the Scottish police would make a very interesting project.

[2] Rawlings' detailed account of the history of the idea of police illustrates that the development of the 'new' police was in practice less radical and much more incremental than many historical accounts have suggested.

[3] For more complete, and sometimes quite different, accounts of the history of the police see Emsley (1983; 1996), Critchley (1978), Rawlings (1995; 1999), Radzinowicz (1956), Reiner (1992). For a specific history of the Metropolitan Police see Ascoli (1979). For specific accounts of the historical development of the police in Scotland and also Northern Ireland please see the bibliography of police forces at the end of this book.

The first major policy initiative for a full-time police organisation began in the aftermath of the Gordon riots of 1785 when Pitt introduced his Police Bill. Important here is the fact that the Bill was primarily driven by concerns about disorder rather than crime. The Bill failed to gain assent because of the considerable opposition that arose because of the prospective costs and also because of fears of the police developing into a repressive system of policing similar to that which operated in France. A decade or so after the failure of Pitt's Police Bill, Patrick Colquhoun, a London Magistrate, sought to persuade those opposed to the idea of a police force by conducting an evaluation of the potential effectiveness of a preventative police. Colquhoun's *Treatise on the Police of the Metropolis* (1797) estimated that a full-time, salaried force of police operating in the docklands of London would pay for itself by reducing theft from cargoes. It resulted in the creation of the Thames River Police in 1798, a private police force which was the first accredited full-time body of police. Colquhoun's 'experiment' was given further credence when, in the early 1800s, a number of local authorities successfully experimented with employing full-time watchmen under their city or borough improvement acts.

The driving force behind police reform, was the principle articulated by John Fielding fifty years previously, of crime prevention through "the certainty of ... speedy detection" (Fielding, 1768; Rawlings, 1995: 140; 1999). In 1811, over 200 offences carried the death penalty, yet the enforcement of the law was minimal in comparison to the incidence of crime and the severe sentences had little effect upon the level of crimes committed. Under the proposed system, a force of full-time police officers would perform the three-fold task of bringing law breakers to justice, suppressing disorder and deterring people from breaking the law. The idea of police reform gained further popularity shortly after the financial success of the Thames River police, and enabled the pro-police reformers to gain ground over their opposition. Nevertheless, subsequent attempts to reform the police during the first two decades of the nineteenth century failed. A Select Committee considered whether a full-time, centrally organised, police would be practicable in London[4] and decided against the proposal on the grounds that it would be a threat to personal liberty.

Yet, despite the opposition to the idea of police there were nine bodies in London which employed about four hundred people, in various ways, to

---

[4] Set up in the wake of the Queen Caroline affair of 1821, but also within recent memory of the Peterloo massacre of 1817.

perform police type functions (Gash, 1961:489). The main employers were the Bow Street Courts and the Thames River Police. By today's standards, however, it would be wrong to call them police as they were more of a cross between security guards and bounty hunters. The detection of crime was over and above their ordinary duties (Gash, 1961: 490). Gash argues that even before Peel went to the Home Office in 1822, it was beginning to assert itself over these police bodies. So, Peel's proposals for a full-time police were not wholly radical, especially as he had already tried out many of his ideas in Ireland (Walker, 1990), it was only the locus of control over the police that was controversial. In 1828, a Select Committee considered the possibility of introducing a full-time police force for London and accepted the idea. Within twenty months, and following remarkably little debate (Critchley, 1978: 50), the Metropolitan Police Bill passed through Parliament to become the Metropolitan Police Act 1829 (10 George IV, c.44). Shortly afterwards, on September 29, the first 'new' police officers stepped onto the streets.[5]

The introduction of the new police
The Metropolitan Police Act 1829 resulted from the effective parliamentary management and political entrepreneurship of Sir Robert Peel, the Home Secretary. It was the culmination of a humanitarian legislative programme by which Peel reformed the criminal law, reduced the overall number of capital offences from 221 to 10, and introduced a full-time police force to ensure that the new laws were impartially and effectively enforced. Peel shrewdly managed the debate over police reform by placating any opposition from the City of London by excluding it from the jurisdiction of the proposed Metropolitan police force.[6] He also reduced opposition from the Magistrature by placing them in managerial control of the force. Finally, Peel persuaded Parliament to place the Metropolitan Police Bill before the same Select Committee that had recommended its creation, thus ensuring that the bill received a sympathetic hearing (Gash, 1961: 497; Emsley, 1983: 60; 1996). The Metropolitan police subsequently provided a working model for the provincial forces, although not in terms of the mechanisms of accountability.

The organisation of the Metropolitan Police was not entirely original, as it merely brought together many tried and tested organisational and personnel practices that had existed during the past century in institutions, such as the

---

[5] The historical circumstances surrounding the build up to the police reforms of the 19th century are well documented elsewhere see for example Critchley, (1978) and Emsley, (1996).
[6] The City of London Police were formed in 1839, see Rumbelow's (1989) account of their formation.

army and the Irish police. But at a time when the idea of a full-time police was new, it provided a reference point, for future police organisations in terms of personnel and management. Regarding the latter point, the Metropolitan police model established the principle of excluding police officers from the executive management of the police. Generally speaking, the underlying philosophy and relatively low cost of the Metropolitan Police model made it a very attractive proposition for the many local authorities, who had to install a police force during the coming decade. In addition to cost, it was a politically advantageous alternative to the army for dealing with disorder, as had been demonstrated on a number of occasions since 1829. While the army were able to put down disorder, they were, because of their training, not very proficient at arresting rioters (*Hansard* 3rd Series, 1839, vol. 49: cols. 727-731; Smith, 1990: 5). Additionally, the Government were spared any political backlash, and internal discipline within the army was not affected, as so often was the case when they were called to police disorder.

Provincial police reforms
Before the County and Borough Police Act 1856 made the introduction of police forces compulsory in every borough and county, provincial police reforms were piecemeal, numerous and unfocused.[7] On the one hand, were the reforms promoted by central Government which took place within the general atmosphere of reform that existed during the 1830s: "when the flood tide of democracy, which followed the passing of the Reform Act, 1832, was still running strong" (*Police Review*, 1942: 173). Centred on the two main units of local government, the boroughs and the counties, the Municipal Corporations Act 1835 created the borough police, and the County Police Acts of 1839 and 1840 provided for the voluntary installation of the county police. On the other hand there were also attempts to revive, and improve the efficiency of, the old police system through the Lighting and Watching Acts of 1830 and 1833, the Special Constables Act 1831 and later through the Parish Constables Acts of 1842 and 1850. In addition, a number of cities and boroughs had passed individual improvement acts under which commissioners created separate night and day patrols of watchmen.

The lack of any co-ordinated structure in the policing of the provinces led to it being both confusing and inefficient. The Municipal Corporations Act

---

[7] In Scotland, the Police (Scotland) Act 1857 made the introduction of police forces compulsory. Prior to that date an act of 1833 enabled the Royal Burghs to install police forces, in 1847 this permission was extended to the Parliamentary Burghs and was later strengthened by the Burgh Police (Scotland) Act 1892. An act of 1839 had enabled the Scottish counties to create their own police forces.

1835 required each new chartered borough council to form a watch committee and, within three weeks of their first election, to employ a sufficient number of constables to preserve the peace within the borough (s. lxxvi.). Not all of the boroughs had their charters; legal difficulties with the charters of Manchester, Birmingham and Preston, three rapidly growing industrial towns, led to their police being placed under the temporary control of Home Office commissioners (Young and Haydock, 1956: 613). By 1842, all three had come under the provisions of the Municipal Corporations Act 1835. On finding themselves with an obligation to set up a police force at fairly short notice, many watch committees looked to see what was happening in other boroughs, many also approached the Commissioners of the Metropolitan Police for advice and help. The Commissioners responded to requests by sending advisers to the boroughs for a fee of 10 shillings per day, plus travel and accommodation (Mins. York WC, 25/8/1836).

The actual number of Metropolitan police that were sent to the provinces is open to debate. Reith (1943: 198, 213) found that 111 watch committees were lent men by the Metropolitan Police, but Hart (1955: 421/fn 1) argues that Reith over-estimated the extent of help by confusing loans to help set up a force with loans to help quell public disorder. The high charge made for the services of men loaned from the Metropolitan Police deterred many watch committees, particularly in the smaller boroughs, from seeking outside help. There does exist further evidence, however, to show that they frequently sought to recruit Metropolitan Police trained officers as chief officer (Wall, 1994, 1998).[8] However, whilst the personnel structure of the Metropolitan Police provided a practical working model for a force of full-time constables, the borough police reforms did not set out to imitate its management structure. Far from it, as one of the fundamental characteristics of the borough police was that they were not to be controlled by magistrates, rather by a local committee of elected people.[9] The watch committee was directed, under the Municipal Corporations Act 1835, to appoint, dismiss and discipline the members of its force. It also took control over local policing policy, and documentary evidence from the minutes of the various watch committees shows that they regularly exercised operational control over the policing operations of their forces.[10]

Under the 1835 Act, watch committees were vested with the same

---

[8] Interestingly, Peel's own valet, John Stephens, became the first chief constable of Newcastle-upon-Tyne in 1836.

[9] Eligibility to vote at the time was based upon property ownership.

[10] For example, in York, Devonport, Norwich and Southampton (Wall, 1998: chapter 3).

powers as the county chief constable under the County Police Act 1839. The consolidation of policing under one authority was quite a radical step for local government at the time, especially since, as stated earlier, it took powers away from the justices. The 1835 Act made no provision for a chief officer; it was probably assumed that the existing practice of designating one of the constables to be in charge would continue, as was the case with the various night and day patrols. It was certainly the case that there were few salaried officials in local government during the 1830s and therefore few precedents for appointing an officer with such a broad range of independent powers. The early borough chief officer was merely: "the superintending or executive officer of the watch committee."[11] Underpinning this arrangement was a broader political strategy of passing the responsibility for the policing of disorder from central to local government. The use of the army was an unpopular action which tended to be both expensive and politically divisive. Writing to Leeds council in 1855, the Home Secretary reminded members that: "military force should not be relied upon as a substitute for the police ... it should only act in support of the civil power."[12]

Although the position of borough chief officer was initially tenuous, it developed during the course of the nineteenth century to resemble, if not imitate, the office of county chief constable. Indeed, the common use of the title by all borough forces, excepting Liverpool[13], and the confusion it allegedly created for the delivery of mail caused the Home Secretary, in 1897, to allow them to use the title chief constable.[14] Initially called superintending constables, most borough chief officers subsequently became referred to as head constables and then chief constables. Some boroughs, however, always used the title as it had previously been used to describe the constable in charge of the old day or night watch. Leeds, for example, used the title of chief constable from the eighteenth century onwards to describe the constables in charge of their watch (Clay, 1974: 8).

The main reason for the independent development of the *de facto* office

---

[11] Chief Constable of Norfolk giving evidence to the 1855 Select Committee quoted by Critchley (1978: 143). Memorandum, October 29, 1858, HO 45/ 19774.

[12] Letter written on behalf of Sir George Grey to the Leeds Authorities, March 30, 1855 (Clay, 1974: 27).

[13] HO 45 9969/X26632/6

[14] The correspondence on this matter was typically from county chief constables who complained of the improper use of the term 'chief constable'. The letter from John Dunne, for example, suggests some considerable snobbery on the part of the county chief constables (HO 45 9969/X26632/3 - May 7, 1892) (See Wall, 1998: chapter 3).

of borough chief constable was the practicality of managing a police force
whose role developed in function, size and complexity. Quickly after their
introduction, most borough police forces acquired additional responsibilities
for the fire brigade and later the ambulance service.[15] These functions were
performed by constables and overseen by the chief officer.[16] A second,
though more minor reason, was that there tended to exist in most watch
committees a class divide between the middle and upper classes and the
working class police. Thus, the chief officer also acted as mediator between
the two, in much the same way as the visiting superintendent in the
Metropolitan Police (Wall, 1998). A third reason was that the regular turnover
of watch committee membership caused it to be reliant upon the borough
chief officer for local information about policing and also for continuity of
practice. So, the watch committee, being elected representatives with their
own livelihoods or interests to pursue, often had neither the time nor the
experience in police matters to manage their police force in the manner set
out by the 1835 Municipal Corporations Act: it was simply not practical for
them to do so. As the activities of the police became more complex, the
watch committees tended to devolve many of their powers to a specially
appointed chief officer. Importantly, as the watch committees delegated
their powers to a chief officer, they found it hard to regain them.[17] This was
because the broadening of the police role to include other aspects of
emergency services endeared chief officers and their constables to the
townsfolk, offsetting local opposition and often giving them considerable
personal legitimacy that was independent of the local council.
Consequently, in addition to becoming skilled managers of local emergency
services, borough chief officers also became important local individuals who
could court much local respect and political currency.[18]

The first provincial police forces were very different in appearance from
the Metropolitan Police; their uniforms were often designed locally and varied
in both colour and style between the counties and boroughs. In the 1840s, for
example, the borough police in Manchester[19] wore different coloured tunics to

---

[15] Activities that made the police into an all purpose emergency service and which also
led to the establishment of the English Policing image (Reiner, 1992: chapter 2).
[16] See the various local histories of the police, for example, Clay (1974), Swift (1988),
Smith (1973), Richer (1990). Also Bridgeman and Emsley (1989) and Stallion (1997).
[17] The minutes of York Watch Committee, for example, clearly show that the
operational orders decreased during the second half of the nineteenth century and
issues discussed came to relate to conditions of service etc.
[18] This tended to depend upon the individual.
[19] Formed under the Manchester Police Act 1839 until 1842.

those of the County of Lancashire police who were stationed in the same town. The organisation of borough forces also tended to vary considerably between boroughs as they were designed around local models of management (Steedman, 1974). Many watch committees, such as York and Leeds (Swift, 1988; Clay, 1974), found themselves involved in local political controversies over the cost and format of the police and simply merged their existing night and day patrols to form their 'new' police force.

The provisions of the Municipal Corporations Act of 1835 and the County Police Act of 1839 for the installation of police forces were not taken up immediately by some provincial police authorities, even though the former was compulsory. There is, however, some controversy over the immediacy of take up, especially in the boroughs. Hart, for example, used Parliamentary records to argue that many boroughs were guilty of a "dilatoriness in fulfilling their statutory obligations" (1955: 415) and therefore the borough police reforms were slowly implemented (*HC Papers* 1847, xivii and 1854, liii). Wall, on the other hand, found that the discrepancies between accounts of the number of forces were likely to have resulted from the fact that watch committees simply omitted to supply details of their arrangements to the Home Office (Wall, 1998). Moreover, Wall's findings suggest that resistance ot the idea of police was not as great as previously indicated because many boroughs were already operating some form of day or night patrol.

County police reforms. The county police reforms, like those in the boroughs, were also driven by the need to maintain order rather than prevent crime. However the government's first stumbling block was the fact that the idea of police reform in the counties was initially rejected by most of the Quarter Sessions who were responsible for the administration of the counties. Only a few of the Quarter Sessions were willing to accept the idea of an independent, full-time, and paid police force in their county because of the high cost. Nevertheless, the imminent threat of unrest by the Chartist movement led to the introduction of county police reforms[20] on a voluntary basis. The County Police and District Constabulary Act 1839[21] empowered, but did not compel, justices in Quarter Sessions to establish a police force for all or part of their county. Whilst some of the ideas put forward in the *Report of the Royal Commission on Establishing an Efficient Constabulary Force in the Counties* in 1839 were retained, the idea of a centrally organised national police force

---

[20] He also increased the size of the army by 5000.
[21] Often referred to as the County Police Act 1839 and elsewhere as the Rural Police Act.

was ignored, as was the idea to part-fund it from the Treasury.

In contrast to the comparative vagueness of the Municipal Corporations Act 1835, the County Police and District Constabulary Act 1839 was quite specific about the structure and management of county police forces. Executive control over the police would rest with a specially appointed chief officer of police called a chief constable (Para IV) who would be appointed by the Quarter Sessions. This chief constable would be responsible for appointing, dismissing and disciplining the constables in the force. The prescribed minimum wage of the chief constable was more than six times greater than the constable's minimum wage and the maximum wage was nine times greater.[22] The differential in pay was to be instrumental in determining the type of people who filled the posts (as in the Metropolitan police) and the first county police officers were drawn from the labouring classes because it was assumed that they possessed the physical characteristics required for the job. More importantly, they had a clear knowledge of their place in the local social hierarchy and did not question it (Steedman, 1984). It would, however, be wrong to assume that they were agricultural workers as many historical accounts suggest, but were drawn from a variety occupations; so varied, in fact, that Emsley and Clapson warn against too much generalisation from single local experiences (1994: 269). However, like the first Metropolitan police officers, they were a very unstable occupational group. Most either resigned from the police or were dismissed within a short time of joining. The chief constables were drawn from very different social and occupational backgrounds to the constables under their command.

In comparison to the installation of the borough police forces, the implementation of the (voluntary) County Police Act 1839 was slow. Just under half (27) of the 57[23] counties in England and Wales had fully installed forces before the Act of 1856 came into force. There were a number of very practical reasons why police reforms in the provinces were slow to take effect. An important deciding factor, Emsley observes, was the overall level of unrest within the country (Emsley, 1996: 40-41), and the counties in which there was much unrest tended to implement the Act. However, in the counties where the threat of unrest was not so imminent, three issues came to the fore to delay implementation.[24] Firstly, the intensity of crime and disorder was not

---

[22] Today a chief constable's salary is approximately three to four times greater than that of a constable.

[23] Including the Liberty of Peterborough.

[24] For an interesting account of the establishment of a county force see Smith (1990: 3-23).

perceived in the provinces to the same degree as it was in London. Next, there was some evidence of apathy on the part of local authorities to implement the police reforms, especially in the counties where there was little unrest. The Quarter Sessions either felt that a police force was unnecessary for their county or that the cost would be excessive. In some counties, the Quarter Sessions chose to reform their police by expanding the existing network of constables and high constables under the Parish Constables Acts of 1842 and 1850. Finally, some local authorities simply could not reach a decision because of irreconcilable differences of opinion, thus adding fuel to the Marquis of Normanby's view that it was a "serious and almost fatal error" that the new county police were not more closely under government control (Critchley, 1978: 80).

Making the police compulsory in England and Wales
In 1853, the Select Committee on Police in the Counties and Boroughs examined the effectiveness of policing arrangements in England and Wales and sought to rationalise the organisation of the police. It found that crime had decreased where forces complying with the police reform acts were in operation and the police had efficiently replaced the army in controlling disorder. The Committee also found that the attempts to revitalise the old system had largely failed[25] and that the County Police Act of 1839 exceeded expectations, despite its piecemeal application (*Second Report of the Select Committee on Police in the Counties and Boroughs*, 1852-53: 163-164). The subsequent Police Bill of 1854 was designed to increase central control over all forces whilst preserving local control over management. All forces in small boroughs with a population of less than 20,000 people were to amalgamate with adjoining counties, and the Home Secretary's rules for the government, pay, clothing etc., for police would also become applicable to the boroughs. Most of the watch committee's powers of control over their force were to be transferred to the officer in charge.

In the face of considerable hostility from the boroughs, who felt that their powers were being threatened, Palmerston's Police Bill was rejected by Parliament. An amended version suffered the same fate the following year. In 1855 Palmerston became Prime Minister, with Sir George Grey as Home Secretary. Grey successfully introduced a third Bill in 1855 which omitted the

---

[25] Although the remnants of the old system remained operative for a number of years after the County and Borough Police Act of 1856, the office of High Constable remained on the statute books until it was abolished by the High Constables Act, 1869 (32 & 33 Victoria c.47).

proposal to abolish the smaller borough forces[26], and it became the County and Borough Police Act of 1856. The Act compelled all Quarter Sessions to establish police forces under the County Police Act of 1839; gave county police officers the same jurisdiction in boroughs as the borough police had in the counties; empowered the Crown to appoint three HM Inspectors of Constabulary[27] to assess the efficiency of each force and present annual reports of their inspections before Parliament; gave a Treasury grant to all forces certified by the Inspectorate as efficient to cover one quarter of the costs of clothing and salaries;[28] forced the small boroughs, with a population under 5,000, to make a choice between amalgamating with adjoining counties or paying the full cost incurred by their force; requested all police authorities to submit annual records of crimes, committed and solved in their area, to the Home Secretary. The Select Committee's plans to impose direct central control over policing were not realised. However, the Act did give central government a co-ordinating role and laid down a constitutional basis for increasing central control over policing which was to gain importance in early twentieth century police reforms.

The borough forces were split into three categories: large forces in boroughs with populations of over 20,000; medium forces in boroughs of between 5,000 and 20,000; and small forces in boroughs with less than 5,000. The 65 small boroughs were not entitled to a grant and were not inspected. About half of the medium sized borough forces were not certified as efficient in 1857; but by 1870 only 19 (25 per cent) were still found to be inefficient. All of the 57 large borough forces, except one, were certified as efficient. Gateshead, Sunderland and Southampton resisted the County and Borough Police Act, but they were, nevertheless, inspected and of the three only Gateshead was found to be inefficient. Sunderland and Southampton rejected the grant that was offered to them but eventually succumbed to the lure of the government purse (Critchley, 1978).

---

[26] One of the motivating factors behind the third police bill was the anticipation of thousands of displaced unemployed soldiers returning from the Crimean war.

[27] Of the first three Inspectors, only Maj General Cartwright had no prior police force experience. Lt Colonel John Woodford had previously been chief constable of the Lancashire Constabulary and Captain Edward Willis had previously been chief constable of the Manchester City Police.

[28] This, and a number of the other proposals, had previously been suggested by the Royal Commission on Establishing an Efficient Constabulary Force in the Counties of England and Wales, 1839, [169]XIX.1, but were rejected on the basis that they constituted unnecessary interference in the running of the county.

The County and Borough Police Act of 1856 laid down an organisational structure within which the administration of the police took place during the next century. The Act introduced elements of central control over policing and laid the foundations for the future standardisation of police. It also recognised the need for a chief officer in the borough forces for the first time, although it did not give them any statutory powers. From 1856 onwards, the police organisation has been shaped by four key processes: standardisation, centralisation, unification and, more recently, corporatisation.[29] Whilst each of the above processes has been present to varying degrees since the introduction of the new police, each can be identified with a specific period in its development.

Towards the standardisation of the police organisational structure 1856 - 1918
Following the County and Borough Police Act 1856, a series of minor legislation, mainly concerned with fine tuning the provisions of the Act, sought to standardise some of the idiosyncrasies in the organisation of policing. The rationale behind these attempts to standardise the police arose, initially, out of the bureaucratic inefficiency of having so many independent police forces. Many of which did not feel obliged to respond to the Home Office's statutory requests for information under s. 86 of the Municipal Corporations Act 1835.[30] There were also a number of problems arising from the varying administrative and policing practices which occurred within police forces, to which the Home Office would have to respond.

One of these problems was the common practice of watch committees making operational decisions (see earlier). Part of the problem here was that, not only did the legislation give such wide ranging powers to the local authority, or chief constable in the county forces (Troup, 1928: 11), but the Home Office, whether it be the Home Secretary or Permanent Under-Secretary, did not appear to have particularly strong views about the police until the turn of the century. In fact, successive Home Secretaries seemed reluctant to incur the political wrath of the formidable group of MPs who represented the many boroughs with independent forces by proposing to

---

[29] Although these discussions largely focus upon the provincial police of England and Wales, the processes described here also apply, or applied, to all of the main police forces in the UK.

[30] The Home Office were constantly frustrated by the reluctance of many forces to respond to their requests for statistics and information about their composition and activities (HO 158/1 March 5 1855). The many annotations to the files (HO 45 and HO 158) at the Public Record Office illustrate this point.

change existing arrangements. In addition, officials lacked an independence of thought and were reluctant to engage without guidance from their political masters (Pellew, 1982: 5-33, Wall, 1998).

The Home Office managed to make some headway on reducing the numbers of very small forces three years later, when the Municipal Corporations (New Charters) Act 1877 prohibited boroughs with populations of fewer than 20,000 from forming new police forces. The main reason was that the representatives of the small boroughs were concerned only with protecting their existing interests, so they did not object so strongly to the new provisions. The debate over the small borough forces continued until the Local Government Act 1888 forced all boroughs with populations of less than 20,000 to amalgamate with their adjoining county force. The number of independent borough forces fell from 220 to 181,[31] although the overall figure rose again slightly to 185 by the First World War as new boroughs were created.

Around the turn of the century there was a "quiet revolution" at the Home Office as strong personalities like Edward Troup, later Sir Edward Troup,[32] joined the Home Office through the civil service open competition and started to make their strong views about policing known to Government. Troup later became the Permanent Under-Secretary of State. One product of this quiet revolution was the Police Act 1890. It was an important piece of legislation, which gave police officers the right to a pension after twenty-five years' service, or after fifteen years' service and with discharge on medical grounds. This was a significant development in the autonomy of the police officer, because prior to the Act, the decision to award a pension rested with the chief constable in the counties and the watch committee in the boroughs. Until the Act, pensions were sometimes denied to police officers, even though they may have contributed to the force superannuation fund throughout their working life. Another function of the Police Act 1890 was to introduce a facility for providing mutual aid between police forces in times of emergency. It was a provision that was to gain renewed importance during the Miners' Strikes of the 1970s and 1980s. If a police force was found to be understaffed

---

[31] The amalgamated forces were so small that most did not have a formally appointed chief officer, they tended to be run by superintending constables. These forces disappeared after the Local Government Act 1888. Also in a number of situations, one of which was Cumberland and Westmorland, two forces were commanded by one chief constable.

[32] Permanent Under-Secretary for State at the Home Department between 1908 and 1922.

during an emergency situation, such as a public disorder, then a chief officer could call upon the chief officer of another force to provide reinforcements.[33]

An equally important event in police history was the debate leading up to the Police Weekly Rest Day Act of 1910. Until 1910, being a police officer was a seven-day-a-week occupation and, although most constables were given one day off work every one or two weeks, leave was granted at the discretion of the chief constable. The Police Weekly Rest Day Act of 1910 granted police officers a statutory weekly rest day. It was the evidence that was presented to the Select Committee on the Police Weekly Rest Day Bill in 1908 that was, perhaps, more important in the long-term than the Act itself. It was the first time that policing issues, normally the domain of the individual chief constable or police authority, were discussed before Parliament. Whilst responding to a question from the floor of the House, the Home Secretary displayed considerable ignorance of the occupational or social origins of the chief constables of England and Wales.

By the end of the First World War, grievances which had been building up for some time, over police leadership and representation, were brought to a head by the extra demands placed upon policing by the First World War. First, the number of laws that required police intervention was increasing and placed many new duties upon the police. Between 1900 and 1908, for example, sixteen such laws were passed.[34] Secondly, the incidents of public unrest around the turn of the century placed many new demands on police resources. The increase in the number of suffragettes who were arrested following demonstrations highlighted a general lack of provision for dealing with women offenders. Furthermore, the first decades of the century had also been witness to a series of industrial strikes. The miners' strike of 1910 was the most remembered of these strikes, because of the infamous Tonypandy Riot where the police, supported by the army, were used to quell the disorders. Thirdly, the rising popularity of the automobile created logistic problems for a foot-patrol based policing system by placing extra demands on police resources to enforce traffic regulations and match the mobility of

---

[33] See HO 158/6-8 for copies of the agreements. Also provided to chief officers were lists of forces that they could draw upon, plus some guidance on how to go about it.

[34] It was a small number when compared with the large number of laws requiring police intervention that were passed in later decades. Between 1960 and 1976, 160 laws were passed that required the intervention of the police (Whittaker, 1978). The number of new offences jumped to just under 500 under the Conservative Thatcher and Major Governments 1979-1997. During their first nine years in office, the New Labour Government introduced 3,023 offences (Morris, 2006).

motorised criminals (Critchley, 1978: 176). It also brought the police into contact, and conflict, with the middle and upper classes for the first time as they were the only people who could afford such luxuries.[35] Finally, the (First World) War-time emergency powers placed many new duties upon the shoulders of the police, such as arresting aliens, performing air-raid duties, guarding vulnerable locations, and enforcing lighting restrictions. These additional duties were not popular and forced war-time police officers to work longer hours and sacrifice their rest days and holidays. Moreover, many regular police officers had left their forces to join the war effort thus creating a personnel shortage and extra workloads for those who were left (*Police Review*, 1915: 633). The war also enticed a number of (mainly county) chief constables back to their old regiments, leaving their forces without proper leadership. Mischievously, the *Police Review* could not resist the temptation, to ask, as part of its campaign to promote a policy of appointing chief officers from within the police service, whether chief constables were actually necessary.[36] Their proposition was based upon the observation that most of the forces which had lost their chief constables to the war effort ran perfectly well without them (1918: 229).

Each complaint arose out of the inadequacy of the police organisation to deal with the rising demands made of it since the latter half of the previous century. The manner in which policing in England and Wales was organised was the root cause of most of the problems that were experienced by police forces. Little communication and virtually no co-ordination existed between the borough, county and the Metropolitan forces and it was only during the war that a serious effort was made to encourage such co-ordination. The Home Office established a series of chief constables' district conferences, which were the first occasion that borough and county chief constables had met within an official framework to exchange views and opinions (*Report three of the Committee of Inquiry on the Police, 1979*: Appendix II: 106-109). Previously, both borough and county chief constables' associations had existed since 1858 and 1896, respectively, to encourage social intercourse between chief constables (*idem*: 106. para 1). Little more than gentlemen's clubs, they were nevertheless forums for chief officers to meet and share ideas and experiences. However, the two bodies remained quite separate as the

---

[35] *Punch* cartoons regularly featured the poorly educated police officer in encounters with the motoring upper classes.

[36] See Wall, (1998) for a description of the role played by the *Police Review* in the development of a collective police mentality.

county chief constables regarded the borough chiefs as their inferiors.[37]

Towards uniformity: centralising police policy 1919 - 1964

The policing crisis at the end of the First World War was brought to a head in 1918 and 1919 by two police strikes.[38] In response, a committee was appointed, chaired by Lord Desborough to advise the Home Secretary on police pay and conditions of service. Its official brief was to consider: "and report whether any, and what, changes should be made in the method of recruiting for, the conditions of service of, and the rates of pay, pensions and allowances of the police forces of England, Wales and Scotland."[39] The urgency of the matter was apparent in a personal note by the Home Secretary to Lord Desborough. Edward Shortt stated that he was "desirable that the Committee should report at as early a date as possible and for that reason should meet frequently".[40] Towards the middle of May 1919, the Committee indicated to the Home Secretary that it would be recommending a substantial rise in pay, to be standardised throughout all forces and a mechanism through which representations could be made to the Home Secretary. In July 1919, the Home Secretary pre-empted the Committee's report by introducing a Police Bill that would, amongst other things, legislate to prevent police officers from joining a trade union and to set up an alternative form of representation that would not take the form of a union. Prompted by fears of Bolshevism within the police ranks, the Bill became the Police Act of 1919 the following month. It prohibited police officers from entering into any trade union activity and proposed the formation of a Police Federation to represent the interests of the ranks of inspector and below (ss. 1-3). In addition, a Police Council was to act as a consultative body for the Home Secretary on police matters (s. 4(2)) and finally, the Home Secretary was to be given the power to regulate the police pay and conditions of service of all police officers (s. 4(1)). It was the latter proposal that was to have an important and lasting effect on the relationship between the Home Office, police authority and the police. Most of the Desborough Committee's recommendations were subsequently enforced through these regulations.

---

[37] See for example the acrimonious exchange between Col. Anson the Chief Constable of Staffordshire and David Webster, Chief Constable of Wolverhampton (*Police Review* 1922: 8).

[38] In August 1918 and July 1919 (see Critchley, 1978).

[39] HO 45 15605, minute signed by Edward Shortt, dated March 1 1919. Also to be found in the front of the *Report of the Committee on the Police Service of England, Wales and Scotland*, pt. 1, 1920).

[40] Letter from Edward Shortt, Home Sec., to Lord Desborough, Feb. 21, 1919 (HO 45/15605).

The Desborough Committee's first report, published in July 1919, recommended that police pay and conditions of service should be improved, standardised and centrally determined by the Home Secretary. It also recommended a substantial increase in police pay, and for the first time since the Metropolitan Police Act of 1829 police pay ceased to be comparable with that of an agricultural labourer. The Committee's second report, published in January 1920, made recommendations on police recruitment, training, promotion, discipline, control over policing, the merging of small borough forces and the appointment of chief constables.[41]

The Desborough Committee's recommendations symbolised a change in the official perception of policing towards the idea of a standardised police service. It also symbolised the beginning of the decline of the effective powers of police authorities and an increase in the respective powers of the Home Secretary and chief constables. It is perhaps slightly ironic that a suggestion made during the hearing of evidence, that the police should become a national police force, was rejected on the premise that would prejudice the intimate relations between the police and their localities, and yet the Committee sought to standardise, and centralise, many aspects of the police, a process which effectively led to a decrease in the powers of the police authority. Perhaps a greater irony is that these views were at the centre of the debates that took place three-quarters of a century later, during the early 1990s, over the reform of the police (see later). The reforms proposed by the Desborough Committee created four groups of influential legal and bureaucratic mechanisms which altered the balance of what later became known as the tripartite relationship.

An increase in the role of the Home Office in formulating central policing policy. The Police Act 1919 extended the Home Secretary's powers to regulate the pay and conditions of service of the borough police. The Home Secretary's influence therefore increased considerably through his ability to make rules and regulate police pay and conditions for the whole of the police.[42] Not only did the Home Office now have a clarity of vision about the role of the police, but the use of rules and regulations was made even more effective by the increased use of the circular.

A revision of the philosophy behind the police personnel structure. The

---

[41] For a more detailed overview of the Desborough Committee see Critchley (1978: 190-198) and Morgan (1987: 84-87).

[42] The Police Regulations of the 20th August 1920 made by the Secretary of State under section 4 of the Police Act 1919 (Statutory Rules and Orders 1920, No. 1484).

Desborough Committee's greatest impact, from the point of view of this study, was its revision of the police personnel structure. It envisaged that a new type of police officer, a "scientifically" trained police officer, would staff the new integrated police service (*Police Review*, 1919: 181). Furthermore, the managers of the new style police service would have extensive experience as professional police officers and, preferably, have served as constable. This idea of internal recruitment had gained momentum during the past two decades (Wall, 1994, 1998). At the time, a handful of borough, compared with almost all county chief constables, were recruited directly from outside the police.

A change in the status of borough chief constables. Whilst the proposal to place borough chief constables on a similar statutory footing to that of county chief constables failed because of opposition from local municipal authorities (Morgan, 1987: 87), their position was nevertheless strengthened by the increased influence of the Home Office over the police and the formalisation of the title of chief constable for all borough chief officers in 1897.

The development of police representative machinery. The development of police representative machinery during the 1920s introduced a forum through which the ideas and views of police officers on policing could be voiced. Whilst the Police Act prevented police officers from joining a trade union, it did provide for the formation of organisations to represent the interests of police officers on the negotiating table. The Police Council, replaced in 1964 by the Police Advisory Board, was a central advisory body to the Home Secretary and comprises of representatives of police authorities and all ranks of the police.

In order to support the new centralised approach towards policing policy, legal theory was introduced into the debate over the constitutional position of the police (Morgan, 1987: 87). The legal officers of the Home Office had on a number of occasions been called to decide upon the legal position of the borough chief constable,[43] and from the time of Desborough onwards, the Home Office began to "popularise the theme that the keeping of the King's Peace was a 'Royal prerogative as old as the monarchy itself'" (Morgan, 1987: 87)[44]. This ideology of constabulary independence was to be

---

[43] With regard to Devonport, Newport, Norwich and Southampton in 1901 See HO 45/17278.

[44] See the evidence of Leonard Dunning to the Desborough Committee. *Report of the Committee on the Police Service of England, Wales and Scotland.* Part II, p. 665 (Morgan, 1987: 88, fn 46).

later strengthened by case law (see Lustgarten, 1986: 62) and in years to come especially by the case of *R v. Metropolitan Police Commissioner, ex parte Blackburn* [1968][45].

During the years between the two World Wars, which is an important but under-documented period in the development of the police, the recommendations of the Desborough Committee effectively placed existing police practices on a statutory footing and brought police legislation up to date. In doing so, they provided a framework for the creation of a uniform police service with a high degree of central co-ordination.

The impact of the Second World War upon the police organisation
The Desborough Committee's ambitions to create a framework for increasing the standardisation of many aspects of police work were not quickly realised, because the legislators had underestimated the extent of local government resistance to change, particularly with regard to the new policy of only recruiting chief constables with prior police experience. The county police authorities continued to appoint chief constables because of their social rather than policing qualifications. This resistance remained until the regulations of the Emergency Powers (Defence) Act 1939[46] gave the Home Secretary control over the appointment of provincial chief constables and police authorities "in the interests of public safety, the defence of the realm, the maintenance of public order and the efficient prosecution of war". Regulation 39(1), for example, specifically empowered the Home Secretary to instruct chief officers to assist other police forces where necessary. By increasing central control over the police, the Defence Regulations acted as the catalyst for a number of organisational and administrative changes. Firstly, they led to the weakening of the traditional powers held by local police authorities over the police and permanently changed the relationship between local and central government. Secondly, the war-time Defence Regulations also, formally, strengthened the link between the Home Secretary and the chief constables, increasing the power of the former over the latter. So, the war-time regulations not only reinforced the concept of a nationally co-ordinated police service, but they also changed the culture which underpinned the bureaucracy of policing. Consequently, they resulted in new working practices which

---

[45] Lustgarten argues that Lord Denning's statement in *R. v. Metropolitan Police Commissioner, ex parte Blackburn*, [1968] (1 All E.R. 763, Lord Denning, M.R.) was *obiter dicta* on *obiter dicta* and contained six errors of logic which call into question the strength it gives to the doctrine of constabulary independence (1986: p. 64). See further Stenning (2007)
[46] The Defence (General) Regulations, 1939 (Statutory Rules and Orders, No. 927).

reduced the possibility of returning to the pre-war arrangements.

In 1944, Herbert Morrison, the Home Secretary, set up a committee to discuss the Post-War reconstruction of the police service and prepare it to deal with the problems of policing a Post-War society. The Post-War Reconstruction Committee was composed of representatives of the chief constables and Home Office officials and was briefed to look into the organisation of local police forces; particularly with regard to training, promotion, management, buildings and communications. The Committee produced four reports which formed the basis for the Police Act of 1946. The first considered higher training and recommended that a new police college be created to improve the quality of command. The remainder dealt with the organisation of the police, buildings and welfare, the responsibilities of the higher ranks and the organisation of the special constabulary. These proposals formed the basis of future legislation.

Whilst the Police Act of 1946 solved some of the problems that were emerging in the organisation of the police, such as abolishing the 47 non county-borough forces,[47] it did little to quell the disquiet amongst police officers over pay and conditions, a scenario reminiscent of the pre-Desborough era. A pay increase was awarded in 1946 with the promise of a review in 1950, but rising inflation devalued the pay rise within two years. To prevent a repetition of the events of 1918 and 1919, the government brought forward the promised review and in 1948 the Oaksey Committee was appointed to:

> consider in the light of the need for the recruitment and retention of an adequate number of suitable men and women for the police forces in England, Wales and Scotland, and to report on pay, emoluments, allowances, pensions, promotion, methods of representation and negotiation, and other conditions of service (*Report of the Committee on Police Conditions of Service*, 1948-9: pt. 11: 379).

The Committee produced two reports. The first, published in April 1949, dealt with police pay, pensions and various other conditions of service. The second, produced seven months later, dealt with a variety of issues that ranged from the appointment, training, promotion and discipline of police officers, to police housing, amenities and the establishment of negotiating machinery to replace the consultative framework established by Desborough. The police did not get the increase in pay they had hoped for on the premise that a large rise would contravene the government's pay policy. Rather, the Oaksey Committee hoped that improved conditions of service and other changes in

---

[47] With the exception of Peterborough which had a population of over 50, 000.

the occupation would dampen down the disquiet over pay levels. Police wages increased over the next seven years, but always fell behind the levels set by Desborough. The low level of police pay reduced the attractiveness of the police as an occupation and police forces found difficulty in finding the suitable recruits to fill their vacancies. Some forces lowered their height limits in order to increase the pool of potential recruits. In 1954, the Police Council for Great Britain, whose authority had been increased by the Oaksey Committee, became a negotiating body. It raised wages, but failed to keep up with inflation.

The failure of the Oaksey Committee to resolve the dispute over low pay was not the only problem faced by the police during the late 1940s and early 1950s. A noticeable divide was growing between the police and the public, especially the affluent young. New policing initiatives were introduced to win back public support and re-legitimise the police - team policing methods were brought in to make policing more efficient and a national crime prevention campaign was launched. In addition, new supposedly realistic, media images of the police were being presented to the public such as George Dixon, the star of the television programme *Dixon of Dock Green*. Dixon and his colleagues were modern Bobbies who combined modern policing techniques with the traditional role of the police officer (Reiner, 1992: Ch. 2). The programme made the public aware of the functions performed by the police and presented to the public a particular image of police work that conveniently hid both the problematic constitutional position of the police and also the inadequacy of police organisation to cope with the demands made of the police in the 1950s.

The effect of this and other new "re-legitimisation" strategies were soon negated by a series of public scandals, during the 1950s and 60s, which involved a number of chief constables. In 1956, disciplinary action was taken against the chief constable of Cardiganshire after it was alleged that his force was not being properly administered (Critchley, 1978: 270). During the following year the chief constable and other senior members of the Brighton force were charged with corruption. The chief constable was acquitted, although he was later dismissed from office, and two of his senior officers were imprisoned. His appeal against dismissal was later upheld by the House of Lords on the grounds that natural justice had not been done (*Ridge v. Baldwin*). Later in that year, the chief constable of Worcester was convicted of fraud and sent to prison (Critchley, 1978: 270). These scandals, and others in the Scottish police, served to worsen relations between the police and the public by lowering public confidence in both the police and also in the office of chief constable. However, it was the constitutional implications of two further public scandals which were more influential in bringing about demands for a large-scale reform of the police.

The first case illustrated uncertainty about the constitutional position of the chief constable. It involved a dispute between the chief constable of Nottingham, Captain Athelstan Popkess, and his watch committee (see Critchley, 1978, Wall, 1998). Popkess was suspended by the watch committee on the grounds that he was unfit for office, the Home Secretary intervened in the dispute and argued that the maintenance of law and order was the chief constable's responsibility and not that of the watch committee and therefore the watch committee had acted wrongly. Popkess was reinstated but retired at the end of the year. The Popkess affair illustrated the changes that had taken place over the years in the constitutional position of the police, a constitutional position that was perceived to be quite different from that envisaged in the original legislation passed a century earlier. The respective roles of the chief constable and Home Secretary in the governance of the police had gradually become more prominent, at the expense of the police authority.

The second scandal, in 1959, involved the stopping of Brian Rix, the actor, by a P.C. Eastmond for a possible motoring offence. A third party became involved and was allegedly assaulted by P.C. Eastmond. The third party sued the Metropolitan Commissioner for the assault and received damages out of court. During a House of Commons debate which followed, MPs were angered at their inability to raise questions about the Metropolitan Police from the floor of the House. The incidents led to the Royal Commission on the Police in 1960 whose purpose was "sufficiently wide ranging to require it to examine afresh the fundamental principles on which the service always relied" (Critchley, 1978: 267).

Unifying the organisation of police 1964 - 1973

The terms of reference of the 1960 Royal Commission on the Police were: to review the constitutional position of the police throughout Great Britain, the arrangements for their control and administration. They were to consider: the constitution and functions of local police authorities; the status and accountability of members of police forces, including chief officers of police; the relationship of the police with the public and the means of ensuring that complaints by the public against the police are effectively dealt with; and the broad principles which should govern the remuneration of the constable, having regard to the nature and extent of police duties and responsibilities and also the need to attract and retain an adequate number of recruits with proper qualifications (*Final Report of the Royal Commission on the Police*, 1962: para. 140).

The Royal Commission was the first time that the principles, organisation and constitutional position of the police had all been examined publicly. It was a watershed in police history as it revised many of the existing principles of policing and brought them into line with current practices. The main report, published in 1962[48], sought to secure: a system of control over the police that achieved maximum efficiency and the best use of manpower; adequate means of bringing the police to account; and proper arrangements for dealing with complaints (*ibid*). The Commission did not think that the present system achieved the first two objectives and that dissatisfaction existed with the third. Whilst it felt that no fundamental disturbance of the existing system was necessary, the Commission thought that the main problem was that the local forces needed to be brought under more effective central control (*idem*: para. 22).

All of the Royal Commission's recommendations were based upon three fundamental conclusions reached by the Commission about the nature of policing. Whilst it was not without its critics and controversies, for example, Hart criticised its lack of concern for particularities, its "verbiage and hollow phrases" and its excessive respect for the past (Hart, 1963), nevertheless it became an influential document. First, the Commission decided somewhat controversially that, constitutionally, the constable was an office whose authority is original, and not delegated, and whose powers were therefore exercised by virtue of that office.[49] Secondly, the Commission favoured the retention of a system of local forces, but with increased central co-ordination.[50] The Commission proposed to increase the size of forces and reduce the overall number of forces to allow for a more efficient administration at local level. Thirdly, and importantly, it recognised that the

---

[48] There had been an interim report in 1960 to recommend an increase in pay etc.

[49] This has been debated by Marshall (1965), Jefferson and Grimshaw (1984) and Lustgarten (1986). The Royal Commission based their observation that the constable was neither a servant of the Crown nor of his police authority on examples of case law (see Lustgarten, 1986) and did not consider the occupational reality of being a police officer, the effects of bureaucratic control or occupational culture on the exercise of the powers of the constable.

[50] One of the Royal Commission members, Dr A.L. Goodhart, believed that a national police force would be more politically accountable and issued a memorandum of dissent which was published as part of the report.

problem of controlling the police was the problem of controlling chief constables.

The Royal Commission's report underpinned the Police Act 1964, which still determines the structure of the police service today, although it was consolidated by the Police Act 1996. The 1964 Act faithfully followed most of the Commission's recommendations and brought the legislation into line with existing practices. The first part dealt with the organisation of police forces and replaced the old borough and county police authorities, the standing joint and watch committees, with police authorities whose composition included two-thirds elected representatives and one-third magistrates.[51] The powers of the new police authorities were far inferior to those of their predecessors, particularly in the boroughs, where, as stated earlier, the watch committees used to exercise considerable control over their forces.

The 1964 Act placed a duty upon the police authority to maintain an efficient police force for its area, but gave the authority no operational powers over the force. Whilst the police authority did retain a responsibility for appointing the senior officers, the chief, deputy and assistant chief constables[52], from a Home Office approved shortlist and also retained a power to force their chief constable to retire in the interests of efficiency; both powers also required the approval of the Home Secretary. Similarly, the Act gave the police authority the power to request a report, separate from the chief constable's annual report, on matters relating to policing in their area, but then it gave the chief constable the right to refuse such a request if he or she believed that disclosure of the information was not in the public interest. In this, the chief constable effectively became the guardian of the public's interests. In cases of stalemate between a police authority and a chief constable, the Home Secretary was to make the final decision.

Part II of the Police Act 1964 defined the functions of the Home Secretary. The Act gave the Home Secretary a duty to promote the efficiency of the police (section 28) through a new range of powers which would enable this duty to be carried out. Many of these powers were already exercised in a limited form under the original police legislation, but the new Act widened and extended them to cover all forces. They fell into two categories: powers

---

[51] Elected by the Quarter sessions in the counties and local board of justices in the boroughs.

[52] The latter in consultation with the chief constable.

over the chief constable and powers to regulate the government, administration and conditions of service of the police service. Under the Police Act, the Home Secretary had, and still has, to approve a police authority's choice of chief constable[53] and can require a chief constable to retire in the interests of efficiency or suspend him/ her pending the outcome of an inquiry. The Home Secretary could, and still can, also request a report from chief constables on policing matters, has the right to make grants for expenses incurred for police purposes and can institute a local inquiry into the policing of an area. Furthermore, the Home Secretary, as has been the practice since 1856, appoints the HM Inspectors of Constabulary who have the responsibility to report on all matters concerning the police. They inspect each police force and, once certified as efficient, its police authority then receives a treasury grant to cover two thirds of the total cost of policing for its area. The Police Act effectively rearranged the distribution of power within the tripartite arrangement of control over policing to make the Home Secretary and chief constables the dominant partners and the Police Authorities the subordinates.[54]

The most visible effects of the Police Act 1964 upon the police organisation were the force amalgamations, which reduced the number of independent provincial forces from 116 in 1965 to 44 in 1969. Just as the force reorganisations were being finalised, the Local Government Act of 1972 re-defined local authority boundaries and caused a number of police areas to be redrawn and some forces to be reorganised. The Local Government Act created seven metropolitan police areas and the large city police forces that survived the first wave of amalgamations became part of the new metropolitan police forces. The overall number of independent provincial police forces fell from 44 to 41, the number that exists today.[55]

Centralising police policy and corporatising the police: 1974-2000
Whilst the number of independent provincial police forces remains much the same as it did in 1974, the police organisation, the police, and indeed, police

---

[53] The police authority now chooses their chief constable from a Home Office approved list of candidates. See *Chief Officer Appointments in the Police Service: Guide-lines on Selection Procedures* which accompanies HOC 52/96 - Chief Officer Appointments in the Police Service, 2 December 1996.

[54] The third part of the Police Act 1964 dealt with representative organisations and the fourth dealt with complaints against the police.

[55] In addition are the Metropolitan and City of London Forces, eight Scottish Forces, the Police Service of Northern Ireland, two Channel Islands forces and the Isle of Man Police - total 55.

officers have undergone considerable change. The public police model today is somewhat contradictory because not only has it become increasingly pluralistic, especially through the expansion of the private police,[56] but police policy, and also the police organisation, have become increasingly centralised. Furthermore, the formal levers of power over the police have also been placed in more hands, such as the customers of police services and to some extent, the reconstituted police authorities. Yet, the impact of this diversity is contestable, as we have also experienced the re-configuring and the structuring of the central police policy making process, which, in the 1990s, has shown signs of an increased corporatisation. It will be argued, that as we reach the next millennium, this corporatisation will increasingly come to mark the next era of the public police.

In the late 1970s and early 1980s, the police became an integral part of Conservative law and order policy. The increased resources, made available to the police through the Edmund Davies agreement, increased police wages and against the backdrop of rising unemployment had the effect of attracting officers from a broader social background. This contrasted with the limited social origins, mainly skilled working class (Reiner, 1978), of their predecessors. In addition to the increased resources was a series of legislation which impacted considerably upon the police by not only centralising police and police policy, but also laying the foundations for the new police corporatisation mentioned above.

The Police and Criminal Evidence Act 1984 (PACE) increased police powers over search, entry and seizure, and arrest and detention following arrest. To balance this increase of powers, PACE also increased the rights of the suspect against the abuse of police power. It increased formal police accountability by creating a new independent body to deal with police complaints - the Police Complaints Authority. More importantly, PACE impacted upon police management by transferring some supervisory roles from the ACPO ranks to inspectors and sergeants, further removing the responsibility for operational police work from the higher ranks and placing effective operational power in the hands of the middle management and front-line supervisors. It was one of a series of legislation passed in the 1980s and 1990s which sought to structure and make police decision making more transparent. Two years later, the Public Order Act 1986 gave police officers greater control over policing unrest. At street level officers have greater

---

[56] Not discussed here, but see Johnston (1992); Shearing and Stenning (1981); Jones and Newburn (1998).

powers of arrest where behaviour is unruly. The Public Order Act also gave the senior ranks greater powers to supervise public gatherings forcing them to make political decisions and increasing the political profile of the police. In the early 1990s, the Criminal Justice Acts 1991 and 1992, whilst not addressing police organisation directly, placed increased pressure on the police role as gatekeeper to the criminal justice system by formalising contents of Home Office circular 60/1990 which encouraged the police to caution offenders and thus divert them away from the courts.

Other legislation impacted upon the internal structure of the police organisation, some in minor ways and others more significantly. The Prosecution of Offences Act 1985 removed the power of prosecution from the police and passed it on to the independent Crown Prosecution Service.[57] The responsibility for prosecution had previously rested with the chief constable. Police officers who prosecuted offenders did so on behalf of their chief constable. This broke the practice, conducted since the late 19th century, of the police carrying out their own prosecutions, although in practice, the police still make recommendations as to whether or not they think that a person should be prosecuted following their investigations.

During the 1990s, the Royal Commission on Criminal Justice (1993), *White Paper on Police Reform* (1993) and the Sheehy Report (1993), followed by the Police and Magistrates' Courts Act 1994 (PMCA), have been the most influential engines of recent change to the police structure.[58] The PMCA compacted the rank structure by reducing the overall number of police ranks and it placed senior (ACPO rank) officers on fixed term contracts. It also restructured police authorities by almost halving their size[59] and by introducing lay representatives who are appointed locally from a Home Office approved shortlist[60].

---

[57] In Scotland, this power had always rested with an independent public office, the Procurator Fiscal. Although during the 19th and early 20th centuries it was not unusual for the chief constable, or other police officers, also to hold this appointment.

[58] Also of considerable importance were the influential reports of the Audit Commission and reviews of core police skills and competencies. N.B. The legislation relating to the police organisation was consolidated under the Police Act 1996

[59] Although the size of police authorities varied, most had between 30 and 40 members.

[60] Following the PMCA Act 1994, advertisements for lay representatives were placed locally by police authorities and centrally by the Home Office. Local police authorities drew up shortlists of a maximum of 20 and submitted the names to the Home Office who then reduced the list by half. The local police authority then selected its members

The cumulative effect of both the debate and also the legislation has been to centralise both the police and, in the case of that legislation which calls for the (central) issue of codes of practice, also policing policy. But, this final move towards the centralisation of police is not just legislative as it has been accompanied by an important, cultural, change in the overall philosophy, even rationale, behind police management. The urban unrest of the early to mid-1980s, combined with the miners' strike, led to the development and operation of the centrally controlled national reporting centre which co-ordinated policing actions nationally. Secondly, underlying the legislative changes since the late 1970s and early 1980s has been the growing influence of new public management, or new police management (Leishman *et al.*, 1995: 11). This is a social market philosophy (Loveday, 1995: 281) which seeks to make public organisations more economic, efficient and effective. It impacted upon the police through Home Office circular 114/1983 and was subsequently articulated through a series of Audit Commission reports (1996, 1993, 1989) and through the introduction of Financial Management Initiatives which have led to quite a large scale internal restructuring of police organisations. The Audit Commission's main impact has been to rationalise the bureaucracy of the police and has led to uniformity in the delivery of many previously local functions. Another of its impacts has been to civilianize many, and privatise a few, of the hitherto state police functions (Johnston, 1992). The combination of strict financial controls, increased consumerism and targeted resources has created a hybrid style of management which presents a service style of policing which is not only very legalistic in approach (Reiner, 1992), but is also increasingly specialised. Consequently, by the late-1980s and early 1990s, both police and policing were centralised to a point at which we had a *de facto*, although not a *de jure* national police force (Reiner, 1995).[61] During the 1990s and 2000s, however, four centralising processes took place within police policy that led to the development of what effectively became a *de jure* national police force

The first was the foundation of a process that led to the formation of a national police agency with a national policing function. Initially there was a rationalisation of the various regional crime squads following the setting

---

from the 'short' shortlist. Although there were allegations of party political interference, it is not correct to say that these are central appointees (Jones and Newburn, 1997).

[61] Newburn places a slightly different spin on this argument. Whilst he does not dispute the power and influence of ACPO in the 'steering' of the police, he does argue that the level of 'steering' varies from force to force (correspondence with Tim Newburn, March 1998).

up of the National Criminal Intelligence Service (NCIS) in 1991 - NCIS later became formally defined by the Police Act 1997 (pt. I). This was followed by the creation of the operational National Crime Squad (NCS) following the Police Act 1997 (pt. II).

The second was the actual process that led to the formation of a national policing organisation, the National Policing Agency (with effect from 2013). In April 2006, the Serious Organised Crime and Police Act 2005 joined together the NCS and NCIS with the drug trafficking investigation and intelligence branches of Customs and Excise, and the organised immigration crime component of the Immigration Service to form the Serious Organised Crime Agency (SOCA). In 2013 SOCA combines with parts of the National Policing Improvement Agency and part of the UK Border Agency to form the National Crime Agency.

The third was the broadening of the role of the security services by the Security Service Act 1996, which amended the Security Service Act 1989 to allow the Security Service (MI5) to gather intelligence about serious crimes in order to assist the police. The Foreign Office also announced their intentions to draw upon the Intelligence Services Act 1994 in order to extend the role of Secret Intelligence Service (MI6) to support the police by gathering intelligence about serious crimes.[62] The 9/11 (2001) and 7/7 (2005) terrorist attacks brought the work of intelligence community and policing services closer together

The fourth was the restructuring of ACPO as the central police policy making organisation. This development arose from the expressed preference by central government during the late 1980s for a single voice on issues relating to police and policing policy. ACPO has subsequently become the main forum for the articulation and formation of police policy. In 1997, ACPO was restructured and its representative function was passed to the Chief Police Officers Staff Association (CPOSA). Today, ACPO (now incorporated as a private company limited by guarantee) has become an independent police-led strategic body with the express purpose of leading and coordinating the development of the English, Welsh and Northern Ireland police services. A separate ACPO exists for Scotland with a similar function.

---

[62] Speech by Foreign Secretary, Robin Cook, to the Malaysia Institute of Diplomacy and Foreign Relations, Kuala Lumpur, August 28, 1997.

The role of the chief constable and the organisation of police

Once a multi-purpose emergency service, the police of today have become much more narrow in focus and yet more complex in function. All this is set against the backdrop of a broader public policing model, which has become multi-tiered and pluralistic. Nowhere is this increasing complexity more apparent than in the quality and quantity of the decisions that have to be made by the chief constable. Consequently, senior police managers now make their decisions in a professional decision-making environment which requires a very different type of decision-maker from that of old (Wall, 1998). In the 1990s, the chief constables' work mainly involves the management of resources, the making of general policy decisions and, importantly, the management of the appearance of law enforcement within their police area.[63] At the head of a professionally trained management team of senior officers, chief constables are now professionally trained police managers whose art lies in their application of management skills - a stark contrast to their predecessors who were judged upon their abilities to lead their force from the front.

As both police forces sizes and also their administrative complexity have grown, chief constables have progressively become removed from operational police work. Their managerial role has transformed from that of warrior leader, to manager leader, to the chief executive of today. However, the notion of the chief constable as a professional manager, trained in management and with an ability to manage any organisation, runs counter to the police occupational culture which requires chief constables to have risen through the ranks of the police service (the ideology of internal recruitment, Wall, 1998). The existence of fast track promotion schemes culminating in the strategic command course (and its predecessors at the Police Staff College in Bramshill) bridged the gap between these contradictions.

As chief executives at the head of the management team of a large bureaucratic public service organisation, today's chief constables are mainly account-givers rather than account-takers and are therefore not wholly accountable for their actions in the conventional obedient and subordinate way (Reiner 1995: 81) as were their predecessors. Following the PMCA 1994 and other changes in policing during the early 1990s such as, the introduction of fixed-term contracts for chief constables and the

---

[63] The former and serving chief constables who were interviewed for Wall (1998) were asked about this function. Some thought that this was a cynical view of the chief constable's role but they nevertheless conceded that it was *one* of the many roles performed by the chief constable.

establishment of performance indicators, it was anticipated that the existing explanatory, or account giving, form of accountability would be replaced by a more calculative or contractual form (Reiner 1995: 92). By the late 1990s there were few signs that this was happening (Jones and Newburn, 1997) as chief constables continued to be comparatively free from any stringent formal accountability, although, importantly, they were subject to a number of forms of informal or semi-formal accountability. By the late 2010s, however, a number of cases had occurred during the previous decade where chief constables had, for a range of professional transgressions, been subject to formal (and informal) accountability - in some cases being forced out of post.

The rigorous selection procedures and lengthy socialisation period prior to appointment, however, probably creates the most effective form of accountability that chief officers experience - to their peers (the police they manage and work with). Without such peer recognition, for example, it is unlikely that they would rise to a position from which they could be appointed as chief constable. However, whilst this informal accountability provides some protection against the appointment of extremely politically motivated or even dangerous individuals, it nevertheless raises further concerns. Most specifically, it could also be argued that chief officers have effectively become a conforming self-selecting élite and one which, through ACPO, has a direct link into the police policy-making process. In practice a balance between local innovation and adherence to national police policy has to be achieved.

As the corporatising police structure has developed past the first decade of the millennium, chief officers have emerged more as directors of local, or regional, police services rather than as chief executives of large policing organisations. Their (police) estates have expanded with the introduction of Police Community Support Officers and also the increase in non-police aides to police officers (e.g. forensics). This begs the question over whether chief police officers still need to have served as police officers and why could they not be recruited from outside the police service? This issue was raised publicly in 2010/11 during the debate over the failed (at the time of writing in May 2011) Police Reform and Social Responsibility Bill 2010-11[64] which proposed the introduction of elected Police Commissioners for each police force.

---

[64] Police Reform and Social Responsibility Bill 2010-11, HL Bill 62, http://www.publications.parliament.uk/pa/ld201011/ldbills/062/11062.i-v.html

All the current evidence suggests that the particular function of the British Police as a rather unique public service organisation dictates that the current model of chief officer recruitment should probably remain intact for the foreseeable future at least (Wall, 1998: 310). There are five main arguments to support this statement. Firstly. there is the need for constabulary independence in operational decisions as the chief constable is highest holder of office of constable in their force. Secondly, there is a need to maintain informal structures of accountability within management teams. Thirdly, the symbolic importance of the office of chief constable and the impact upon police morale were outsiders to be appointed. Fourthly, career police officers have the essential experience required to manage the complexities of a police organisation and also the office of chief constable. Finally, the incumbents' own experience (and peer respect) is important when dealing with problems arising from the closed nature of police, especially national security issues (Wall, 1998: 310).

Conclusion
The police organisation has changed considerably over the past 160 years. Until just after the First World War the police were still very localised, indeed before that time the Home Office did not hold particularly strong views about the police. But the historical development of police since the First World War has taken place against the political backdrop of the struggle between central and local government. The "Victorian bric a brac" described by Critchley (1978: 176) of small independent forces run locally by a local police authority has now developed into a centrally co-ordinated set of fairly uniform police organisations. However, the history of the growth in centralised control over police is not a simply a centralisation argument. Rather any centralisation that has occurred is an outcome that has arisen through four quite distinct processes which have themselves resulted from the desire to minimise local political influence over the police. Initially, there were the moves to *standardise* many aspects of police, followed by the *centralisation* of police policy. These two processes continued whilst the various policing traditions were *unified*. More recently we have witnessed an increasing uniformity of police and an emerging *corporatisation* of the public police model. These processes have mainly taken place in the absence of a formal statutory framework and have largely been policy driven.

The police organisations have changed from a set of small local autocracies, to a series of large regional bureaucracies, in so far as most police areas now have little local meaning, either in the old borough or traditional county sense. This essay has demonstrated that the history of the police in England and Wales has been neither a process of linear development, as many of the orthodox interpretations would have us believe, nor has it been particularly rational. Rather, it has been characterised by a number of distinctive historical-administrative processes rather than radical events.

References
Ascoli, D. (1979) *The Queen's Peace: The Origins and Development of the Metropolitan Police 1829-1979*, London: Hamish Hamilton.
Audit Commission (1996) *Tackling Crime Effectively Volume 2*, London: Audit Commission.
Audit Commission (1993) *Helping with Enquiries: tackling crime effectively*, London: Audit Commission.
Audit Commission (1989) *Police Paper Number Four*, London: HMSO.
Bridgeman, I. and Emsley, C. (1989) *A Guide to the Archives of the Police Forces of England and Wales*, Milton Keynes: Police History Society
Cale, M. (1996) *Law and Society: an introduction to sources for criminal and legal history from 1800*, London: Public Record Office Publications.
Clay, E.W. (ed) (1974) *The Leeds Police 1836-1974*, Leeds: Leeds City Police.
Colquhoun, P. (1797) *A Treatise on the Police of the Metropolis.*
Critchley, T.A. (1978) *A History of the Police in England and Wales*, London: Constable.
Emsley, C. (1996) *The English Police: A political and social history*, Second edition, London: Longman.
Emsley, C. (1983) *Policing and its Context 1750-1870*, London: Macmillan.
Emsley, C. and Clapson. M. (1994) "Recruiting the English policeman c. 1840-1940", *Policing and Society*, vol. 4, pp. 269-286.
Fielding, J. (1768) *Extracts from such of the penal laws, as particularly relate to the peace and good order of this Metropolis* (new edition), London.
Gash, N. (1961) *Mr Secretary Peel: the life of Sir Robert Peel to 1830*, London: Longmans.
Hart, J. (1963) "Some Reflections on the report of the Royal Commission on the Police, *Public Law,* pp. 283-298.
Hart, J. (1955) "Reform of the borough police, 1835-1856", *English Historical Review*, July, pp. 411-427.
Jefferson, T. and Grimshaw. R. (1984) *Controlling the Constable*, London: Frederick Muller.
Johnston, L. (1992) *The Rebirth of Private Policing*, London: Routledge.

Jones, T. and Newburn, T. (1998) *Private Security and Public Policing*, Oxford: Clarendon Press.
Jones, T. and Newburn, T. (1997) *Policing after the Act: police governance after the Police and Magistrates' Courts Act 1994*, London: Policy Studies Institute
Leishman, F., Savage, S. and Loveday, B. (1996) *Core Issues in Policing*, London: Longman.
Loveday, B. (1995) "Contemporary Challenges to Police Management in England and Wales: Developing Strategies for Effective Service Delivery," *Policing and Society*, vol. 5, pp. 281-303.
Lustgarten, L. (1986) *The Governance of the Police*, London: Sweet and Maxwell.
Marshall, G. (1979) "Police Accountability Revisited," in Butler, D. and Halsey, A. (eds) *Policy and Politics*, London: Macmillan.
Marshall, G. (1965) *Police and Government*, London: Methuen.
Manning, P.K. (1979) "The Social Control of Police Work", in Holdaway, S. (ed) *The British Police*, London: Edward Arnold.
Morgan, J. (1987) *Conflict and Order: The police and labour disputes in England and Wales, 1900-1939*, Oxford: Clarendon Press.
Morris, N. (2006) "Blair's 'frenzied law-making': a new offence for every day spent in office", *Independent*, 16 August, http://www.independent.co.uk/news/uk/politics/blairs-frenzied-law-making-a-new-offence-for-every-day-spent-in-office-412072/html
Pellew, J. (1982) *The Home Office 1848-1914: from clerks to bureaucrats*, London: Heinemann Educational.
Radzinowicz, L. (1956) *A History of English Criminal Law and its Administration from 1750*, Vol. 3, London: Sweet and Maxwell.
Rawlings, P. (1995) "The Idea of Policing: a history", *Policing and Society*, vol. 5, no. 2, pp. 129-149.
Rawlings, P. (1999) *Crime and Power: A history of Criminal Justice*, London: Longman.
Reith, C. (1943) *The British Police and the Democratic Ideal*, Oxford: Oxford University Press.
Reiner, R. (1995a) "Counting the Coppers: antinomies of accountability in policing", in Stenning, P. (ed) *Accountability for Criminal Justice: Selected Essays*, Toronto: University of Toronto Press, pp. 74-92.
Reiner, R. (1992) *The Politics of the Police*, Second edition, London: Harvester Wheatsheaf.
Reiner, R. (1978) *The Blue Coated Worker*, Cambridge: Cambridge University Press.

Richer, A.F. (1990) *Bedfordshire Police 1840-1990*, Bedford: Hooley and Associates.

Rumbelow, D. (1989) *I Spy Blue: Police and Crime in the City of London from Elizabeth 1 to Victoria*, London: Macmillan.

Savage, S. and Charman, S. (1996) "In favour of compliance", *Policing Today*, vol. 2., no. 1, pp. 10-17.

Shearing, C. (1996) "Public and Private Policing", in Saulsbury, W., Mott, J. and Newburn, T. (eds) *Themes in Contemporary Policing*, London: Independent Committee of Inquiry into the role and responsibilities of the police, pp. 83-95.

Shearing, C. and Stenning, P. (1981) "Modern Private Security" in Tonry, M. and Morris, N. (eds) *Crime and Justice: An Annual Review of Research*, Chicago: University of Chicago Press.

Smith, D.J. (1990) "The establishment and development of the Worcestershire County Constabulary 1839-1843", *Journal of the Police History Society*, vol. 5, pp. 3-23.

Stallion, M.R. (1997) *British Police Force Histories: a Bibliography*, Leigh-on-Sea: M.R. Stallion.

Steedman., C. (1984) *Policing The Victorian Community*, London: Routledge, Kegan and Paul.

Stenning, P. (2007) 'The idea of the political "independence" of the police: international interpretations and experiences', pp. 183-256 in M. Beare and T. Murray (eds) Police and Government Relations, University of Toronto Press.

Swift, R. (1988) *Police Reform in Early Victorian York*, 1835-1856, York: Borthwick Papers No. 73, p. 6.

Troup, Sir E. (1928) "Police Administration, Local and National", *Police Journal*, vol. 1, pp. 5-18.

Walker, C.P. (1990) "Police and Community in Northern Ireland," *Northern Ireland Law Quarterly*, vol. 41, no. 2, p. 105.

Wall, D.S. (1998), *The Chief Constables of England and Wales: The Socio-legal History of a Criminal Justice Elite,* Aldershot: Dartmouth.

Wall, D.S. (1994) "The Ideology of Internal Recruitment: the selection of chief constables within the tripartite arrangement", *British Journal of Criminology*, vol. 34, no. 3, pp. 322-338.

Webb, S. and B. (1906) *The Parish and the County*, London: Longmans.

Whittaker, B. (1979) *The Police In Society*, London: Eyre Methuen.

Young, G.M. and Haydock, W.D. (eds) (1956) *English Historical Documents*, London: Eyre and Spottiswode.

Parliamentary papers

Royal Commission on County Rates, 1836: XXVII, (Young and Haydock, 1956: 630)

Report of the Royal Commission on Establishing an Efficient Constabulary Force in the Counties of England and Wales, 1839, [169]XIX.1

Report of the Committee on the Police Service of England, Wales and Scotland. Part 1; HC 1919 Cmd.253 xxvii. 708: Part II; HC 1920 Cmd.574 xxii. 539: Evidence; HC 1920 Cmd.974 xxvii. 573.

Report of the Committee on Police Conditions of Service, Part 1; HC 1948-49 Cmd. xix. 251: Part II; HC 1948-49 Cmd 7831 xix. 379.

Final Report of the Royal Commission on the Police, 1962, HC, Cmnd. 1728, xx. 515.

Report three of the Committee of Inquiry on the Police (1979), July, Cmnd 7633.

Sheehy (1993) *Inquiry Into Police Responsibilities*, London: HMSO.

White Paper (1993), *Police Reform: A Police Service for the 21st Century, White Paper, The Government's Proposals for the Police Service of England and Wales*. Cm 2281, HMSO

Police Reform and Social Responsibility Bill 2010-11, HL Bill 62, http://www.publications.parliament.uk/pa/ld201011/ldbills/062/11062.i-v.html

2 Collecting Historical Information about the Police

The compilation of neither of the following lists of police forces or chief constables was wholly straightforward (Wall, 1998: Ch.1). Indeed, the compilation of what were apparently straightforward events was beset by problems of definition and interpretation. Here, we outline some of those problems.

Firstly, there was little or no information about many of the smaller borough forces. Some forces consisted of no more than one or two individuals, whilst in other cases there were uncertainties as to whether the force had ever existed.

Secondly, some forces had only one chief officer between them. These arrangements ranged from the permanent linking of Cumberland and Westmorland to the ephemeral connection of East and West Suffolk. In other similar circumstances forces such as Herefordshire and Hereford, a county and a borough force, were also commanded by the same chief officer, whereas a number of forces, were under joint command, for example, Birkenhead, between 1841 and 1843.[65] This problem was compounded by the non-statutory nature of the early borough chief constable. Further complications arose from the fact that during the Second World War many of the south coast borough forces, typically in Kent and Sussex, combined with their county forces because of the threat of invasion. The chief constables of these forces became assistant chief constables of the combined forces. To complicate matters further they returned to their prior posts upon dis-amalgamation at the end of hostilities.[66] Such idiosyncrasies provide an explanation for any differences between the numbers of forces given in this book and those given in any one year by other commentators who have derived their figures from Parliamentary returns, many of which were incomplete. One of the Home Office's earliest bugbears was that independent police forces did not regularly make their statistical returns (Wall, 1998: Ch. 2).

---

[65] Under the joint command of Supt. Boughey (1839-1844) and Supt. Porter (1841-1843).

[66] Only to be recombined later as the result of the various amalgamation programmes that took place after the Police Acts of 1946 and 1964 and the Local Government Act 1972.

Thirdly, a number of practical problems arose from the competing versions of events that can be found in different sources. Some sources were subsequently found to lack precise accuracy, particularly with regard to dates of appointment and leaving. Aside from human error, there was a genuine problem in identifying the precise date an appointment actually took effect and when it ceased. More specifically, it was often the case that different sources would give different dates for appointment to, or departure from, office. Some represented the date that the individual was appointed, whilst others were the date upon which they took up office. There was a similar confusion over dates of resignation and the individual's departure from office. Collectively, this meant that there would sometimes appear to be an overlap where a chief constable left one force and started another. In the majority of cases the dates given are believed to be correct within a year.

Fourthly, of particular concern were problems of continuity and reliability arising from the fact that the data set was derived from published sources. The data was second or third hand. In practice, these anticipated problems rarely materialised because more than one source tended to be used and, wherever possible, the data were cross-checked to ensure a greater degree of reliability. Two important sources of information about chief constables' backgrounds were *Who's Who* and until about the 1930s, *Kelly's Handbook of the Official and Titled Classes*. Initially, it was feared that these directories would only contain a select group of chief constables, and this fear was borne out in practice because it was quite clear that until quite recently chief constables were included because of their personal social standing. Today chief constables are included because of their standing as senior police officers (see Wall, 1998: Ch. 9). In addition to directories of élites, the many force histories gave details of their early chief constables, as did the *Police Review* following its introduction in 1893. The *Police Review* regularly featured biographical details of newly appointed and retiring, chief constables, and thus spanned a considerable period of time, for example, a chief constable retiring in the mid-1890s might have been appointed as early as the 1850s. Other sources also provided some data, for example, *The Police Chronicle,* the annual reports of the *Inspectorate of Constabulary* and the many painstakingly descriptive biographical accounts that have appeared in the *Journal of the Police History Society* since 1986. Next, a number of the orthodox, and not so orthodox, histories of the police, whilst limited in analysis, were also a good source of information and data. Together, these sources provided a broad range of information about the many chief constables and their forces.

It is estimated that the data contained in this book represents over 99 per cent of all appointments as chief officer. However, the information is weakest during the 1840s, but this is hardly surprising given the aforementioned non-statutory status of the borough chief and also the fact that almost two thirds of borough forces in 1865 had an establishment of less than 15 officers (many had between one and five, including the chief officer). Part of the problem here was that many watch committees assumed most of the functions of a chief officer and therefore did not declare a chief officer when/if they provided information to the Home Office.

3 Some Explanatory Notes

The forces included in this book
Although we have titled this volume *The British Police,* it also includes the police forces in Northern Ireland and also the British Islands. It does not however, include specialist police forces, such as the parks police, MOD, Atomic Energy Authority etc. It also excludes the national policing agencies, such as the Serious Organised Crime Agency and Child Exploitation and Online Protection Centre (which will be merged into the National Crime Agency in 2013)

Force names
For the sake of simplicity, names in the following lists which changed temporarily to include a merged borough force within the county, for example, Essex and Southend-on-Sea, have not been listed separately, but are recorded in the notes.

The force names do not include the term Borough, City or County etc., except to distinguish otherwise identical names, eg Durham City and Durham County.

No attempt has been made to record changes from Xshire Constabulary to Xshire Police or X County Constabulary etc. In earlier days, some variants appear to have existed at the whim of the chief constable.

Force strength
This is the total number of police officers, including the Chief Officer, that was authorised by the watch committee, standing joint committee or the Home Office to be appointed. In practice, the actual number in post could be lower, particularly when recruiting was difficult or restricted for reasons of economy. If we have been unable to trace the initial strength, we have given the earliest figure appearing in the *Police and constabulary almanac,* followed by the date in [ ]

The final police force strength is usually that which was recorded when the force demised. In some cases, it is taken from the *Police and constabulary almanac* of the year before abolition but, as the Home Office/Scottish Office would probably not sanction an increase for a force about to be merged, the figure is likely to be fairly accurate.

The figures for current strength are the latest available (31 Mar 2011 for England, Wales, Scotland and Northern Ireland)

City and county borough status

To help users to date documents, badges etc, we have now included symbols and dates to show when a borough became a county borough and/or a city. Obviously, we have not included this information if it occurred after the borough/city force ceased to exist. Where it is shown, it must be used with caution, as stationery and uniforms with the old status may well have remained in use for some years after the change

Chief officers' dates of appointment, military titles, forenames etc.

Dates of appointment and departure are actual working dates if they are known. In the case of the first chief constable of a newly established force, the date of appointment is often the date on which the Watch/Standing Joint Committee selected a candidate: it is sometimes impossible to say when that CC took up office, as he often had to find and appoint his own constables.

In a number of early cases, dates of appointment and resignation shown as a year only are taken from *General police and constabulary list 1844, Police and constabulary almanac,* or other published sources, such as force histories, and are not exact, they merely indicate that the officer was in post at that date.

As far as possible, titles and military ranks are shown as at date of appointment. Later changes are in [ ]. Military ranks are only given where apparently used during police service. Unused first forenames or initials are shown in ( ).

Appointments of *Acting Chief Constable* are not normally noted, *except* at the end of a force's existence where, for completeness, it was felt desirable to record the name of the last person in command.

Chief officers' titles

Our original plan had been to include the formal designation (Chief constable, Head constable etc) of each chief officer in each force and the date on which any change took place. Some force histories do contain such detail, but others make it clear that the local records are incomplete and sometimes conflicting, with the head of the force being referred to as, say, Chief constable in one police authority document and Superintendent in another (see Ch. 1). In other cases, it appears that chief officers assumed a title without seeking the authority's approval. Printed directories such as the *Police and constabulary almanac* show similar inconsistencies and we reluctantly decided to omit chief officers' designations. The following notes indicate the range of titles used in the past for chief officers' posts.

Provincial forces: chief officers' titles (also see chapter 1)
All forces in England (outside London), Wales and Scotland are now headed by a *Chief Constable* and this has been the practice since the Home Secretary's Rules (1920) under the Police Act 1919, when ranks were standardised nationally. The general practice before then was that the head of a county force was designated *Chief Constable* and that of a city or borough, *Superintendent* or *Chief Superintendent* (see earlier). However, this was not invariable as some city and borough forces (eg, Leeds) had always used the title *Chief Constable*. Conversely, a number of counties, especially in Scotland, had, at some time, a *Superintendent* in charge. Other designations used for chief officers include:
Captain of the Night Watch [eg Birkenhead]
Chief captain [Bath]
Chief inspector [Reading]
Chief of police [Southwold]
Chief officer [Guernsey, Middlesbrough]
Chief officer of police [Jersey]
Chief police officer [Scarborough]
Chief surveyor [Marine Police]
District constable [Thurso]
Head constable [Abingdon, Liverpool]
Head police officer [Oswestry]
High constable [Canterbury]
Inspector [Cheltenham, Deal]
Inspector of watchmen [Deal]
Master of Police [Glasgow, Gorbals]
Sergeant [Droitwich, Tewkesbury]
Sheriff officer [Hawick]
Superintending constable [Bradnich, Pontefract]
Superior officer [Dunbartonshire]
Watch sergeant [Colchester]
In some cases, various combinations of these titles were used, eg *Chief Superintendent and High Constable* at Gloucester.

In the very smallest forces, consisting sometimes of only 2 or 3 men, there was often no chief officer at all, each constable reporting individually to the Watch Committee. Five of the designations noted above (*Chief inspector*, *Chief superintendent*, *Inspector*, *Sergeant* and *Superintendent*) are, or were, used in many forces for intermediate ranks.

Metropolitan and City of London Police: chief officers' title

In both these forces, the chief officer is, and always has been, designated *Commissioner*, except for the first few years of the Metropolitan Police's existence, when the joint chief officers were called *Justices* due to their status as ex-*officio* Justice of the Peace. Confusingly, from about 1880 until the 1950s, the Met. had a rank of *Chief Constable*, so-called because they were the highest ranking officers who were actually sworn police officers, the Commissioner and Assistant Commissioners being ex-*officio* Justices of the Peace.

Royal Irish Constabulary and Royal Ulster Constabulary: chief officers' title

Until 1970, the RUC had a different rank structure to forces elsewhere in the UK. Since 1970, the rank structure has been identical to that in other UK provincial forces, with a *Chief Constable* as chief officer. Previously, the head of the force was designated *Inspector General*. The RIC and RUC both had an intermediate rank of *Head Constable*, equivalent to *Sergeant* or *Station Sergeant* and until 1839, the RIC had a rank of *Chief Constable* immediately above *Head Constable*.

Main published sources used

Dictionary of national biography on CD-ROM. OUP, 1995

Hallett, H V D. (1975) *Survey of the present and former police forces of England, Wales and the Channel Islands*. London: International Police Association.

General police and constabulary list 1844. (1990) Police History Society Reprint

Police and constabulary almanac (Annually from 1858) London: R. Hazell

Taylor, M.B. *and* Wilkinson, V.L. (1990) *Badges of office*. London: R Hazell

Who's Who 1897-1996. (1996) CD-ROM. OUP

Individual force histories

Individual chief officers' memoirs and biographies. For a list, see Stallion, Martin. (2002) *A life of crime: a bibliography of British police officers' memoirs and biographies*. 2nd ed. Braintree: M R Stallion

Police Review, formerly *Police Review and Parade Gossip: Organ of the British Constabulary*

4   Symbols and Abbreviations

📖   Published history of the force, not necessarily for the whole area or period of its existence

🗀   No separate history, but some information included in a history of its successor force

For details of all these published histories, see chapter 7

●   County Borough

🏰   City

These two symbols are followed by the year in which that status was conferred. H indicates an historic city for no specific date is known

♱   Died in office

CC   Chief Constable
Const   Constable
HC   Head Constable
Insp   Inspector
Sgt   Sergeant
Supt   Superintendent

5 British Police Forces 1829-2012

Aberdeen	1818-1975	📖

Formed: 1 Jun 1818
Abolished: 16 May 1975. Became part of Grampian
Strength: *Initial* 8   *Final* 415   🏭 1891
Chief Officer:

1818 (1 Jun)	1822 (Mar)	Charles Baird
1822 (4 May)	1830 (2 Oct)	Robert Chapman
1830 (18 Oct)	1835 (4 Dec)	John Fyfe
1836 (4 Apr)	1839 (30 Nov)	Robert Alexander
1839 (1 Dec)	1854 (29 Mar)	Robert Barclay ✠
1854 (14 Apr)	1861 (24 Apr)	John Watson ✠
1861 (5 Aug)	1868 (21 Sep)	James Duthie ✠
1868 (1 Dec)	1879 (14 Dec)	John Swanson
1880 (27 Jan)	1902 (23 Dec)	Thomas Wyness ✠
1903 (8 Jan)	1932 (23 Dec)	William Anderson
1933 (30 Jan)	1955 (23 Jan)	James McConnach ✠
1955 (4 Jul)	1963 (14 Mar)	Alexander J Matheson ✠
1963 (1 Sep)	1970 (30 Jun)	William M Smith
1970 (1 Nov)	1975 (15 May)	Alexander Morrison

Notes:
Absorbed Aberdeen Harbour, 1854

Aberdeen Harbour	-1854	

Formed: Not known
Abolished: 1854. Became part of Aberdeen
Strength: *Initial* ?   *Final ca*7
Chief Officer: Not known

Aberdeenshire	1840-1949	📁

Formed: 21 Apr 1840
Abolished: 16 May 1949. Became part of Scottish North-eastern Counties
Strength: *Initial* 19   *Final* 228
Chief Officer:

1840 (2 Feb)	1858 (14 Mar)	*Lt [Capt]* William Anderson
1858 (15 Mar)	1863 (15 Jan)	Robert T Barnes
1863 (11 Mar)	1892 (28 Nov)	*Major* John Ross ✠
1893 (28 Nov)	1920 (30 Sep)	*Major* Duncan F Gordon ✠
1920 (1 Nov)	1946 (15 May)	John Gauld
1946 (16 May?)	1949 (15 May)	Alexander Hunter

Notes:
The force was established and run as a mounted constabulary, 1840-1843

Anderson was also CC and Supt of the Great North of Scotland Railway and the Turiff Junction Railway police
Absorbed Fraserburgh Burgh, 1 Jan 1867

Abergavenny	**1854 1857**	📂

Formed: 1854
Abolished: 23 Mar 1857. Became part of Monmouthshire
Strength: *Initial* 4　　　　　*Final* 4?
Chief Officer: Not known

Aberystwyth	**1837-1857**	📂

Formed: 1837
Abolished: 30 Jun 1857. Became part of Cardiganshire
Strength: *Initial* 2　　　　　*Final* 4?
Chief Officer: Not known

Abingdon	**1836-1889**	📖

Formed: 1 Apr 1836
Abolished: 1 Apr 1889. Became part of Berkshire
Strength: *Initial* 8　　　　　*Final* 6
Chief Officer:

1853	1872	Alfred Rawlins
1872	1876 (Jan?)	George Barratt
1877	1881	J F Brabner
1881	1889 (31 Mar)	Oliver Robotham

Notes:
Barratt was convicted of theft from a fellow railway passenger, 21 Dec 1875

Accrington	**1882-1947**	📖

Formed: 1 Jan 1882, from part of Lancashire
Abolished: 1 Apr 1947. Became part of Lancashire
Strength: *Initial* 32　　　　　*Final* 62
Chief Officer:

1882 (1 Jan)	1884 (17 Dec)	Joseph Walker ♰
1884 (Dec)	1903 (Oct)	James Beattie
1903 (13 Oct)	1928 (21 Oct)	George Sinclair
1928 (Oct?)	1936	Ernest H Holmes
1936	1940	Charles H Walters
1940 (Jun)	1947 (31 Mar)	*Lt-Col* William J H Palfrey

Notes:
Palfrey served with the British Control Commission in Europe, Jan 1944-Mar 1947.
Nathan Todd was Acting CC

Airdrie		1822-1967

Formed: 1822
Abolished: 16 Aug 1967. Became part of Lanarkshire
Strength: *Initial* 11 [1859]   *Final* 66
Chief Officer:

1838		James Gillies
1859	1881	Nisbet Sinclair
1882	1883	J C Neilson
1884	1891	Alexander Hynd
1891	1909	George Burt
1909	1933	Alexander W Christie
1933	1951	James Turner
1951 (16 Apr)	1967	Robert M Clark

Alloa		1854-1930

Formed: 1854
Abolished: 16 May 1930. Became part of Clackmannanshire
Strength: *Initial* 4 [1858]   *Final* 15
Chief Officer:

1858	1859?	W Pennycook
1862	1865	Thomas Anderson
1866	1869	John MacLeod
1870	1872?	John Ross
1873	1875?	Archibald Carmichael
1876	1881?	John Macdonald
1881	1883	John Henderson
1883	1906	Thomas Nicol
1906	1930 (15 May)	John Johnston

Anderston		1824-1846

Formed: 1824
Abolished: 27 Jul 1846. Became part of Glasgow City
Strength: *Initial* ?   *Final* 28
Chief Officer:

1828	1829	John Wilson
1830	1832	*Not known*
1832	1836	David McKenzie
1836	1836	George Lamb
1836	1837	Daniel McLean
1837	1840	Alexander Findlater
1840	1844	Archibald Wilson
1844	1846 (26 Jul)	George McKay

Andover	1836-1846

Formed: 1836
Abolished: 1846. Became part of Hampshire
Strength: *Initial* 5   *Final* ?
Chief Officer: Not known

Anglesey	1857-1950	📖

Formed: 20 Apr 1857
Abolished: 1 Oct 1950. Became part of Gwynedd
Strength: *Initial* 16   *Final* 65
Chief Officer:

1857 (20 Apr)	1876 (24 Nov)	*Capt* David W Griffith ✝
1877 (3 Jan)	1877 (4 Jul)	*Capt* George W Bulkeley Hughes ✝
1877 (13 Nov)	1894 (May)	*Col* William H Thomas
1894 (27 Sep)	1919 (Jan)	Lewis Prothero
1919 (16 Jan)	1949 (12 Dec)	Robert H Prothero ✝
1950 (16 Feb)	1950 (30 Sep)	Gilbert W Brown (*Acting CC*)

Notes:
Robert Prothero was the son of Lewis and had been his Deputy CC
Absorbed Beaumaris Borough, 1860

Angus	1928-1975

Formed: 1928 by re-naming of Forfarshire
Abolished: 16 May 1975. Became part of Tayside
Strength: *Initial* 52   *Final* 203
Chief Officer:

1928	1929	Robert T Birnie
1930(1 Jan)	1939	David C Christie
1939 (20 Mar)	1949 (15 May)	Robert R K Ogilvie
1949 (16 May)	1955	Andrew Meldrum
1955 (7 Nov)	1966	John J Dingwall
1966 (1 Nov)	1975 (15 May)	John Farquharson

Notes:
Absorbed Brechin City, Montrose Burgh and Forfar Burgh, 16 May 1930
Absorbed Arbroath Burgh, 16 May 1949. Ogilvie had been CC of both forces since 1946

Annan	1858?-1881

Formed: 1858?
Abolished: 27 Jun 1881. Became part of Dumfries-shire
Strength: *Initial* 2 [1859]   *Final* 2
Chief Officer:

1859		John Foster
1861		E Beattie

1866	1881	David Gibson

Arbroath	**1836-1949**

Formed: 1836
Abolished: 16 May 1949. Became part of Angus
Strength: *Initial* 8   *Final* 23
Chief Officer:

1836 (11 Oct)	1836 (6 Dec)	David Keddie
1836	1837	James Innes
1837	1840	David O Stewart
1840	1850	Donald McPherson
1850	1854	James McDougall
1854	1855	Angus Mackay
1855	1865	James Charles
1865	1884	John Milne
1884	1914	Duncan MacNeill
1914	1946	James Macdonald
1946	1949 (15 May)	Robert R K Ogilvie

Ardrossan	**1859-1878**

Formed: 1859
Abolished: 1878. Became part of Ayrshire
Strength: *Initial* 1 [1870]   *Final* ?
Chief Officer: Not known

Argyllshire	**1840-1975**

Formed: 16 Jul 1840
Abolished: 16 May 1975. Became part of Strathclyde
Strength: *Initial* 55 [1859]   *Final* 156
Chief Officer:

1840	1840	Hugh Mackay
1840 (16 Jul)	1850	Angus Mackay
1850	1864	James Fraser
1864 (29 Apr)	1889	Colin Mackay
1889 (Oct)	1913	James Fraser
1913 (1 Jun)	1920	[*Lt Col Sir*] Hugh S Turnbull
1920 (1 Oct)	1927	*Lt Col* William D Allan
1927 (1 Sep)	1961	Donald A Ross
1961 (29 Jun)	1975	Kenneth Mackinnon

Notes:
Absorbed Campbeltown Burgh, 1863/64

Arundel	**1836-1889**	🗁

Formed: 10 Feb 1836

Abolished: 1 Apr 1889. Became part of West Sussex
Strength: *Initial* 9?   *Final 3*
Chief Officer:

1836 (10 Feb)	1860	Robert Redwood
1860	1864	John Peacock
1865	1868	Thomas Stevens
1869		James H Linvell
1870	1875	Daniel Smith
1875	1889 (31 Mar)	James Robertson

Ashford	1840-1857 ?	📖

Formed: 1840
Abolished: 1857? Became part of Kent
Strength: *Initial* 1   *Final 4*
Chief officer:

1840	1842	Walter Smith
*ca*1855	1857	Fawcett

Ashton-under-Lyne	1848-1947	📖

Formed: 1848
Abolished: 1 Apr 1947. Became part of Lancashire
Strength: *Initial* 13   *Final 63*
Chief Officer:

1848	1858?	Robert Newton
1858	1860	M Buckley
1860	1888	George Dalgliesh
1888	1913	John Snell
1914 (1 Jan)	1932	Henry A Tolson
1932 (25 Jul)	1937	Harry Gregson
1937 (1 Aug)	1947	Henry Diston

Avon and Somerset	1974	📖

Formed: 1 Apr 1974, by merger of Somerset and Bath, Bristol and part of Gloucestershire
Strength: *Initial* 2868   *Current 3196*
Chief Officer:

1974 (1 Apr)	1979	Kenneth W L Steele
1979 (1 Sep)	1983	Brian Weigh
1983 (Aug)	1989	R F Broome
1989	1998 (15 Feb)	David J Shattock
1998 (16 Feb)	2005 (26 Jan)	Stephen Pilkington
2005 (27 Jan)		Colin Port

Ayr	1845-1968

Formed: 1845
Abolished: 16 May 1968. Became part of Ayrshire
Strength: *Initial* 9 [1858]   *Final* 112
Chief Officer:

1845	1885	Donald MacDonald
1885	1902	William MacKay
1902	1950	J Lowdon
1950	1951	Robert Adamson
1951	1962	John S R Muir
1962	1968 (15 May)	Charles L Jack

Ayrshire	1839-1975

Formed: 1839
Abolished: 16 May 1975. Became part of Strathclyde
Strength: *Initial* 55 [1859]   *Final* 662
Chief Officer:

1839	1876	*Capt* James Young
1876 (16 Nov)	1907	*Cmdr* [*Capt*] Hardy McHardy
1911 (1 May)	1919	C C Robertson-Glasgow
1919 (6 Mar)	1928	*Major* Ernest R Cockburn
1929	1951	*Capt* Horace F M Munro
1951	1968	Robert Adamson
1968	1975	Quintin C Wilson

Notes:
Absorbed Maybole Burgh, 1860/61
Absorbed Ardrossan Burgh, 1878/79
Absorbed Ayr and Kilmarnock Burghs, 16 May 1968

Bacup	1887-1947	📖

Formed: 1 Aug 1887, from part of Lancashire
Abolished: 1 Apr 1947. Became part of Lancashire
Strength: *Initial* 26   *Final* 28
Chief Officer:

1887	1891 (Jul)	James T Cumming
1891 (9 Aug?)	1914 (Aug)	John Harland
1914 (Sep)	1920 (5 May)	James N Campbell
1920 (1 Sep)	1938 (Jul)	Ernest W Sturt
1938 (Jul)	1946 (4 May)	Robert W Priest ✟
1946 (22 May)	1947 (31 Mar)	John Spencer (*Acting CC*)

Banbury	1836-1925	📖

Formed: Mar 1836
Abolished: 1 Oct 1925. Became part of Oxfordshire

Strength: *Initial* 12　　　　　*Final* 17
Chief Officer:

1836 (25 Jan)	1875 (19 Aug)	William Thompson
1875 (15 Nov)	1900 (4 Feb)	Daniel Preston
1900 (15 Feb)	1913 (21 Jun)	Frank H L Hatcher ♁
1914 (1 Aug)	1925 (30 Jun)	Fred Wilson

Banff	**1859-1886**

Formed: 1859
Abolished: 20 Mar 1886. Became part of Banffshire
Strength: *Initial* 4　　　　　*Final* 6
Chief Officer:

1859	1886	George Mearns

Banffshire	**1840-1949**	🗀

Formed: 15 Apr 1840
Abolished: 16 May 1949. Became part of Scottish North-eastern Counties
Strength: *Initial* 7　　　　　*Final* 51
Chief Officer:

1840	1841	*Lt [Capt]* William Anderson
1842	1843	John Bremner ♁
1843	1844	William Cormie
1844 (Aug)	1885 (Sep)	Neil Robertson
1885 (Oct)	1898 (May)	David Haig
1898 (Jun)	1903	James T Gordon
1904 (1 Mar)	1931	William Hope ♁
1931 (10 Nov)	1949 (15 May)	George I Strath

Notes:
Originally merged with Aberdeenshire, with Anderson as Supt of both forces
Absorbed Cullen Burgh, *ca*1861
Absorbed Macduff Burgh, 17 May 1870
Absorbed Banff Burgh, 20 Mar 1886

Barnsley	**1896-1968**	📖

Formed: 16 Oct 1896, from part of West Riding
Abolished: 1 Oct 1968. Became part of West Yorkshire
Strength: *Initial* 40　　　　　*Final* 177　　　　🛡 1913
Chief Officer:

1896 (15 Jul)	1898 (10 May)	David H Turner
1898 (11 May)	1939 (30 Sep)	George H Butler
1939 (5 Oct)	1944 (31 Jul)	Henry T Williams
1944 (1 Nov)	1966 (2 Sep)	*[Sir]* George Parfitt
1966 (9 Sep)	1968 (30 Sep)	William L Brown (*Acting CC*)

Barnstaple	1836-1921	📁

Formed: 1836
Abolished: 1 Oct 1921. Became part of Devon
Strength: *Initial* 2   *Final* 15
Chief Officer:

1836	1836 (Nov?)	John Evans
1836 (26 Dec)		William Chanter
1839		David Steel
1847		Joseph Gibbin
1848		Byron Oldham
1854	1862	Matthew Moran
1862	1872	Thomas Blanchard
1872	1893	George Songhurst
1893 (Jul)	1905	Richard Eddy
1905 (Mar)	1921 (30 Sep)	Richard S Eddy

Notes:
Richard S Eddy was the son of Richard Eddy

Barrow-in-Furness	1881-1969	

Formed: 31 Jul 1881
Abolished: 1 Apr 1969. Became part of Lancashire
Strength: *Initial* 48   *Final* 158   ♥ 1889
Chief Officer:

1881	1907	*Capt* R N C Foll
1907 (Jul)	1939	John Berry
1940 (1 Jan)	1944	Norman W Goodchild
1944 (25 Sep)	1961	Sidney Ballance
1961 (13 Dec)	1969	Jack Aston

Basingstoke	1836-1889	

Formed: 1836
Abolished: 1 Apr 1889. Became part of Hampshire
Strength: *Initial* 4   *Final* 8
Chief Officer:

1853	1861	Stephen Franklin
1862	1889	Mark Hibbert

Bath	1836-1967	📖

Formed: 6 Feb 1836
Abolished: 1 Jan 1967. Became part of Somerset
Strength: *Initial* 112   *Final* 162   🏭 1590
Chief Officer:

1836 (6 Feb)	1849	*Capt* [*Admiral*] William Carroll
1849	1852	W Oakley

1852	1868	Alfred Hughes
1869	1874	G A Muttlebury
1874	1882	*Major* C B Wilkinson
1883	1900	*Col* Reginald T Gwyn
1900	1902	Charles de C Parry
1902 (Sep)	1931	(J) Vaughan Phillipps
1931 (Apr)	1933	*Capt* [*Sir*] (F R) Jonathan Peel
1933 (May)	1937	Nelson Ashton
1937 (Nov)	1957	H P Hind
1957 (Feb)	1967	G E T Nichols

Notes:
Absorbed Walcot Parish, 1836

| **Beaumaris** | **1836-1860** |

Formed: 1836
Abolished: 1860. Became part of Anglesey
Strength: *Initial* ?   *Final* 8?
Chief Officer:

| 1856 | 1860 | William Williams |

| **Beccles** | **1840-1857** |

Formed: 1840
Abolished: Aug 1857. Became part of East Suffolk
Strength: *Initial* ?   *Final* ?
Chief Officer:

| 1844 | 1857 | John Hatton |

Notes:
Hatton was also CC of East Suffolk

| **Bedford** | **1836-1947** | 📖 |

Formed: 1 Jan 1836
Abolished: 1 Apr 1947. Became part of Bedfordshire
Strength: *Initial* 7   *Final* 79
Chief Officer:

1836 (14 Jan)	1852 (5 Apr)	William Coombs
1852 (22 Apr)	1869 (17 Aug)	Richard Stennett
1869 (1 Nov)	1871 (3 Feb)	*Capt* John W Arrowsmith
1871 (28 Feb)	1884 (10 Jan)	*Capt* Charles Verey
1884 (10 Jan)	1887 (25 Feb)	Frank Meredyth
1887 (25 Feb)	1906 (16 Oct)	Harry Thody
1907 (1 Feb)	1909 (9 Dec)	Arthur E Danby
1910 (1 Jan)	1930 (31 Oct)	Francis Timbrell
1930	1947 (31 Mar)	Edward N Christie

Notes:

Coombs and Danby were dismissed

Bedfordshire	1840	📖

Formed: 21 Mar 1840
Strength: *Initial* 47   *Current* 1196
Chief Officer:

1840 (18 Feb)	1871 (Jan)	*Capt* Edward M Boultbee
1871 (16 Jan)	1879 (29 Nov)	*Major* Ashton C Warner ✝
1880 (21 Feb)	1910 (8 Oct)	*Lt Col* Frederick J Josselyn ✝
1910 (22 Oct)	1939 (16 Oct)	*Maj* [*Lt Col Sir*] Frank AD Stevens ✝
1940 (8 Apr)	1953 (31 Jul?)	*Cmdr* William J A Willis
1953 (Oct)	1971 (17 Jul)	Henry R Pratt
1971 (4 Jun)	1979 (11 Nov)	Anthony Armstrong
1979 (12 Nov)	1983 (12 Jun?)	[*Sir*] William G M Sutherland
1983 (12 Jul)	1985	[*Sir*] Andrew K Sloan
1985 (1 Sep)	1995	Alan Dyer
1995	2001 (3 Jan)	Michael O'Byrne
2001 (1 Apr)	2005 (19 Jun)	Paul D Hancock
2005 (4 Jul)	2009 (22 Dec)	Gillian Parker
2010 (4 Jan)		Alfred Hitchcock

Notes:
Dunstable set up separate force, 19 Sep 1865
Luton set up separate force, 30 Sep 1876
Absorbed Dunstable, 1 Apr 1889
Lt Cmdr Richard Coleridge appointed CC, 30 Dec 1939, but not approved by Home Office
Absorbed Bedford and Luton, 1 Apr 1947
Luton re-formed, 1 Apr 1964-31 Mar 1966
Re-absorbed Luton, 1 Apr 1966
Named Bedfordshire and Luton, 1966-74

Belfast	1816-1865	📖

Formed: Sep 1816
Abolished: 31 Aug 1865. Became part of Royal Irish   🏰 1888
Strength: *Initial* 4   *Final* ca 160
Chief Officer:

1816 (16 Oct)	1826 (Dec)	William H Ferrar
	1833	Cortland M Skinner
1833	1840	*Capt* Arthur M Skinner
1840?	1843 (Jun)	R D Coulson
1843?	1849(Jan)	Thomas Verner
1852	1860	Adam Hill
1860 (Jun)	1861 (Aug)	*Capt* [*Sir*] Eyre M Shaw

Notes:
Force reorganised, Jul 1845

Arthur Skinner was the son of Cortland Skinner
There was no Supt from 1861-65 but Thomas Green was the most senior officer and
effectively in command

Berkshire		1856-1968	📖

Formed: 9 Feb 1856
Abolished: 1 Apr 1968. Became part of Thames Valley
Strength: *Initial* 94   *Final* 905
Chief Officer:

1856 (9 Feb)	1863 (29 Jun)	*Col [Sir]* James Fraser
1863 (19 Oct)	1902 (1 Oct)	*Lt Col* Adam Blandy
1902 (2 Oct)	1932 (30 Jun)	*Major [Lt Col]* Arthur F Poulton
1932 (1 Jul)	1954 (31 Mar)	*Cmdr the Hon* Humphry Legge [later *Earl of Dartmouth*]
1954 (1 Apr)	1958	*[Sir]* John L Waldron
1958	1968 (31 Mar)	Thomas C B Hodgson

Notes:
Absorbed Wantage Borough, 9 Feb 1856
Absorbed Wallingford Borough, 28 Jul 1856
Absorbed Newbury Borough, 26 Mar 1875
Absorbed Abingdon Borough and Maidenhead Borough, 1 Apr 1889
Poulton served as Asst Administrator, War Office Forage Dept, 28 Aug 1915-31
Aug 1918. *Col* Francis C Ricardo was Acting CC from 16 Oct 1915-28 Aug 1918
Absorbed Windsor Borough, 1 Apr 1947

Berwick Roxburgh and Selkirk	1948-1975	📁

Formed: 16 May 1948, by merger of Berwickshire, Roxburghshire and Selkirkshire
Abolished: 16 May 1975. Became part of Lothian and Borders
Strength: *Initial* 119   *Final* 182
Chief Officer:

1948 (16 May)	1952	David W S Brown
1952	1958	*[Sir]* John A Willison
1958 (8 Apr)	1975 (15 May)	Thomas B V McCallum

Berwick-upon-Tweed	1835-1921	📁

Formed: 1835
Abolished: 1 Apr 1921. Became part of Northumberland
Strength: *Initial* 1   *Final* 15
Chief Officer:

1835		William Proudfoot
1865	1872	A Ronaldson
1872	1899	John Garden
1899 (Apr)	1920	William Nicholson ✝

Berwickshire		1850-1948	📂

Formed: 1850
Abolished: 16 May 1948. became part of Berwick, Roxburgh and Selkirk
Strength: *Initial* 16 [1859]   *Final* 32
Chief Officer:

1850		Stephen Underhill
1858 (Mar)	1861	Robert Gifford
1862	1893 (31 Dec)	George H List
1893	1909	Alexander Porter
1909 (!6 Nov)	1933	John Morren
1933	1948 (15 May)	David W S Brown

Notes:
List was also CC of Haddingtonshire (*ie* East Lothian)
Porter was also CC of Roxburghshire and (from 1904) CC of Selkirkshire
Morren and Brown were also CC of Roxburghshire and Selkirkshire

Beverley		1836-1928	📖

Formed: 1 Jan 1836
Abolished: 1 Apr 1928. Became part of East Riding
Strength: *Initial* 26   *Final* 19
Chief Officer:

1836	1855	William Nicholls
1855	1857	John H Holden
1857	1861 (Dec)	Daniel Dove
1861	1865	*Capt* William Pattison
1865	1870	George Hopkinson
1870 (Oct)	1877	Henry Knight
1877	1912	George H Knight
1912 (Jul)	1917	*Capt* John W Moore
1918 (1 Jan)	1928	James E Carpenter

Notes:
George Knight was the son of Henry Knight

Bewdley	1836-1882

Formed: 1836
Abolished: Apr 1882. Became part of Worcestershire
Strength: *Initial* 2 [1858]   *Final* 1
Chief Officer:

	1861	Benjamin Jeffries
1861	1868	P D Maynerds
1869	1882	James Fisher

Bideford		1836-1889	📂

Formed: 22 Aug 1836

Abolished: 19 May 1889. Became part of Devon
Strength: *Initial* 2 [1858]   *Final* 6
Chief Officer:

1836 (22 Aug)		Elias Palmer
1853	1873	William Vanstone
1873	1877	John Cole
1878	1883	R Chapman
1883 (Sep)	1889 (31 Mar)	David Morgan

Birkenhead	**1833-1967**	📖

Formed: 10 Jun 1833
Abolished: 1 Jul 1967. Became part of Cheshire
Strength: *Initial* 5   *Final* 372   ● 1889
Chief Officer:

1837	1839	T C Griffiths
1837	1839	Gleave (*Capt of the Night Watch*)
1839	1844	Boughey
1841	1843	Porter
1844	1855	McHarg
1855	1863	James Birnie
1863	1869	*Major* F Beswick
1869	1875 (6 Dec)	R H Kinchant
1876	1898	*Major* J B Barker
1898	1912	Walter S Davies
1913 (10 Mar)	1923 (Mar)	Edward Parker
1923 (30 Apr)	1942 (Aug)	*Capt* A C Dawson
1942 (1 Sep)	1958	Henry J Vann
1958 (1 Oct)	1967 (30 Jan)	*Major* Sydney J Harvey

Notes:
From 1841 to 1843, Boughey was Supt of the Night Watch and Porter Supt of the Day Watch

Birmingham	**1839-1974**	📖

Formed: 20 Nov 1839
Abolished: 1 Apr 1974. Became part of West Midlands
Strength: *Initial* 260   *Final* 3029   ● 🏭 1889
Chief Officer:

1839 (23 Sep)	1842 (30 Sep)	*Capt* Francis Burgess
1842 (2 Dec)	1860 (24 Jan)	Richard A Stephens
1860 (Feb)	1876 (30 Jun)	George Glossop
1876 (1 Jul)	1881 (27 Dec)	*Major* Edwin Bond
1882 (14 Feb)	1899 (Jul)	Joseph Farndale
1899 (6 Aug)	1935 (23 Aug)	*Sir* Charles H Rafter ✝
1935 (1 Sep)	1941 (4 Sep)	Cecil C H Moriarty

1941 (5 Sep)	1945 (30 Sep)	[*Sir*] William C Johnson
1945 (1 Oct)	1963 (1 Sep)	[*Sir*] Edward J Dodd
1963 (2 Sep)	1974 (31 Mar)	[*Sir*] (William) Derrick Capper

Blackburn 1852-1969 📖

Formed: 1 Mar 1852, from part of Lancashire
Abolished: 1 Apr 1969. Became part of Lancashire
Strength: *Initial* 12   *Final* 243   ♥ 1889
Chief Officer:

1852		Thomas Marshall
1854		William Laverty
1863	1878?	Joseph Potts
1878 (6 Oct)	1880?	*Major* Herbert W Showbridge
1881		James Jervis
1882	1886?	William Ward
1887 (26 Sep)	1914	Isaac G Lewis
1914 (Jan)	1931	Christopher Hodson
1932 (Apr)	1958	Cornelius G Looms
1958 (Oct)	1969 (31 Mar)	Richard R Bibby

Blackpool 1887-1969 📖

Formed: 1 Jul 1887, from part of Lancashire
Abolished: 1 Apr 1969. Became part of Lancashire
Strength: *Initial* 23   *Final* 356   ♥ 1904
Chief Officer:

1887 (3 Jun)	1911	John C Derham ⚓
1912 (Jan)	1919	W J Pringle
1919	1935	Herbert E Derham
1936	1942	Ernest H Holmes
1942	1958	Harry Barnes
1958 (26 Sep)	1962	Henry E Sanders
1962	1967	Stanley Parr
1967	1969 (31 Mar)	A Rydeheard (*Acting CC*)

Notes:
Herbert Derham was the son of John Derham

Blairgowrie 1842?-1875 🗁

Formed: before 1842
Abolished: 1875. Became part of Perthshire
Strength: *Initial* 1   *Final* 2
Chief Officer:

1842?	1848	Alexander Reid
[*ca*1859]		James Young

Notes:

The sole officer was designated Town Officer. The strength was doubled *ca*1860

Blandford	1835-1889	

Formed: 1 Feb 1836
Abolished: 1 Apr 1889 Became part of Dorset
Strength: *Initial* 4?   *Final* 3
Chief Officer:

1838 (10 Sep)	1859	George Davis
1859	1868	Peter Southey
1868	1887	James Moore
1887	1889	Thomas F Cole

Bodmin	1836-1865

Formed: 1836
Abolished: 22 Oct 1865. Became part of Cornwall
Strength: *Initial* 3 [1858]   *Final* 3
Chief Officer:

1859	1865	William Bray

Bolton	1839-1969	📖

Formed: 18 Feb 1839
Abolished: 1 Apr 1969. Became part of Lancashire
Strength: *Initial* 12   *Final* 398   ♥ 1889
Chief Officer:

1839 (9 Jan)		Simpton ✝
1839		Frederick M Baker
1839 (25 Oct)	1842 (7 Dec)	Boyd
1843 (6 Sep)	1867 (14 Oct)	James Harris
1867	1877 (25 Jan)	Thomas Beech
1877	1911 (1 Aug)	John Holgate
1911 (Aug)	1930 (4 Oct)	Frederick W Mullineux ✝
1931 (12 Jan)	1957 (21 Jul)	William J Howard
1957	1964	Edward Barker
1964	1969 (31 Mar)	John W Moody

Bootle	1887-1967

Formed: 1 Jul 1887
Abolished: 1 Apr 1967. Became part of Liverpool and Bootle
Strength: *Initial* 47   *Final* 203   ♥ 1889
Chief Officer:

1887	1888	*Capt* James P Arrowsmith
1888	1890	Adrien D'Espiney
1891	1905	James T Cumming
1906 (Jan)	1919	John Stewart

1919 (17 Feb)	1920	*Lt Col* William D Allan
1920 (7 Oct)	1926	*Capt* Philip T B Browne
1926 (17 Mar)	1949	T Bell
1949 (1 May)	1953	William E Pitts
1953 (1 Aug)	1967 (31 Mar)	Harold E Legg

Boston	**1836-1947**	🗁

Formed: 6 Feb 1836
Abolished: 1 Apr 1947. Became part of Lincolnshire
Strength: *Initial* 11   *Final* 35
Chief Officer:

1836 (6 Feb)	1839 (24 Sep)	Henry Drake
1839 (1 Nov)	1845 (22 Sep)	Benjamin H Cheney
1845 (1 Nov)	1850 (14 Oct)	James Wilson
1850 (11 Nov)	1855 (27 Sep)	Edward Hambleton
1855 (5 Oct)	1875 (28 Aug)	George Waghorn
1875 (15 Sep)	1894 (26 Oct)	Henry Bellamy
1894 (26 Oct)	1900 (May)	John W D Wyse
1900 (30 May)	1918 (31 Dec)	Alfred Adcock
1919 (1 Jan)	1922 (Jan)	Joseph A Burnett
1922 (21 Jan)	1944 (Jul)	Leonard Johnson
1944 (1 Aug)	1947 (31 Mar)	Norman Frost

Bournemouth	**1948-1967**	📖

Formed: 1 Apr 1948, from part of Hampshire
Abolished: 1 Oct 1967. Became part of Dorset and Bournemouth
Strength: *Initial* 205   *Final* 358   ♥ 1900
Chief Officer:

1948 (1 Apr)	1958 (12 Jan)	Sydney Bennett
1958 (13 Jan)	1967	Donald Lockett

Bradford	**1848-1974**	📖

Formed: 1 Jan 1848
Abolished: 1 Apr 1974. Became part of West Yorkshire
Strength: *Initial* 64   *Final* 761   ♥ 1889 🏭 1897
Chief Officer:

1847 (27 Nov)	1859 (31 Jul)	William Leverett
1859	1874 (4 Oct?)	Frederick W Granhan
1874 (25 Nov)	1894 (22 Oct)	James Withers
1894	1898	Charles J Paul
1898 (7 Sep)	1900	Roderick Ross
1900 (Aug)	1931 (1 Jan)	Joseph Farndale
1931 (21 Mar)	1940 (30 Jun)	*Capt* Thomas Rawson
1940 (18 Jul)	1957 (30 Nov)	Herbert S Price

| 1957 (1 Dec) | 1973 (Jun) | Harry Ambler |
| 1973 | 1974 (31 Mar) | Harry Kitching (*Acting CC*) |

Notes:
Farndale was the nephew of Joseph Farndale, CC of Birmingham.

| **Bradninch** | **1836-1865** | 📂 |

Formed: 1836
Abolished: 1865. Became part of Devon
Strength: *Initial* 2 [1858]   *Final* 1
Chief Officer:

| 1853 | 1863 | Richard Haydon |
| 1864 | 1865 | Robert Swain |

| **Brechin** | **1859-1930** | |

Formed: 1859
Abolished: 16 May 1930. Became part of Angus
Strength: *Initial* 9 [1859]   *Final* 9   🏭 H
Chief Officer:

1859		John Dodds
1864		Neil Campbell
1873	1883	Angus Stuart
1884	1891	Lewis Gordon
1891	1920	David Smart
1920	1930	Robert Bruce

| **Brecon** | **1829-1889** | 📂 |

Formed: 1829
Abolished: 1 Apr 1889. Became part of Breconshire
Strength: *Initial* 1   *Final* 6
Chief Officer:

1839		Thomas Bradford
1836		Jonas Williams
1842 or 3	1860	Joseph F J Stephens *or* Stevens
1861	1871	H Lee
1872	1880	S A Webb
1880	1887	J Watkins
1887	1889	Philip S Clay

| **Breconshire** | **1857-1948** | 📖 |

Formed: 6 Jan 1857
Abolished: 1 Apr 1948. Became part of Mid-Wales
Strength: *Initial* 29   *Final* 65
Chief Officer:

| 1857 (Apr) | 1905 | Edmund R Gwynne *or* Gwyn |

1905	1907	*Capt* (W) Morgan Thomas ✞
1907 (14 Jun)	1911	*Capt* Arthur S Williams
1912 (14 Sep)	1947 (Jun)	*Lt Col* Claud G Cole-Hamilton
1947 (1 Jun)	1948	*Major* William Ronnie

Notes:
Absorbed Brecon Borough, 1 Apr 1889

Bridgend		*ca*1838-1841	🗁

Formed: *ca*1838
Abolished: 1841. Became part of Glamorgan
Strength: *Initial 1?*   *Final* 1
Chief Officer:

*ca*1838	1841	John Loosmore

Notes:
Loosmore transferred to the county force

Bridgnorth		1836-1850	🗁

Formed: 8 Jan 1836
Abolished: Jul 1850. Became part of Shropshire
Strength: *Initial* 12   *Final* 2
Chief Officer:

1836 (1 Jan)	1836 (19 May)	Edward Goodall ✞
1836 (7 Oct)		George Evans
1840 (3 Feb)	1841 (6 Aug)	Luke Edwards
1841 (3 Sep)	1850 (Jul)	Richard Evans

Notes:
Force originally included 3 night constables, employed only in the winter months

---

Bridgnorth		1855-1889	🗁

Re-formed: 1 Jul 1855, from part of Shropshire
Abolished: 1 Apr 1889. Became part of Shropshire
Strength: *Initial* 2   *Final* 5
Chief Officer:

1855 (8 Jun)	1857 (29 Jan)	George Ross
1857 (13 Feb)	1887 (10 Oct)	John Cole
1887 (11 Oct)	1889 (31 Mar)	Charles Childs

Notes:
Uniform was rifle green

Bridgwater		1839-1940	📖

Formed: 10 Nov 1839
Abolished: Oct 1940. Became part of Somerset
Strength: *Initial* 2   *Final* 20
Chief Officer:

1839 (10 Oct)	1861	John Hill
1862	1893	Thomas M Lear
1893	1909	G A Barnett
1909 (Jul)	1922	William J Davey
1922 (Oct)	1940	Frederick W Pearce

Bridport   1836-1858

Formed: 18 Feb 1836
Abolished: Jan 1858. Became part of Dorset
Strength: *Initial* 5   *Final* ?
Chief Officer: Not known

Brighton   1838-1943   ▢

Formed: May 1838
Abolished: 1 Apr 1943. Became part of Sussex Combined
Strength: *Initial* 31   *Final* 224   ● 1889
Chief Officer:

1838 (18 May)	1844 (Mar)	Henry Solomon ☗
1844 (22 May)	1853	Thomas H Chase
1853 (21 Dec)	1876	George White ☗
1876 (7 Dec)	1877	Owen Crowhurst ☗
1877 (8 Aug)	1881 (Apr)	Isaiah Barnden
1881 (6 Apr)	1894	James Terry
1894 (27 Jan)	1901	Thomas Carter
1901 (26 Sep)	1920	[*Sir*] William B Gentle
1920 (5 Jun)	1933	Charles Griffin
1933 (1 Dec)	1943 (31 Mar)	*Capt* William J Hutchinson

Notes:
Solomon was murdered by a prisoner at the police station

Brighton   1947-1968   ▢

Re-formed: 1 Apr 1947, from part of Sussex Combined
Abolished: 1 Jan 1968. Became part of Sussex
Strength: *Initial* 227   *Final* 424
Chief Officer:

1947 (1 Apr)	1956	*Capt* William J Hutchinson
1956 (1 Jul)	1957	Charles F W Ridge
1957 (28 Oct)	1963	Albert E Rowsell
1963 (8 Oct)	1967 (31 Dec)	William T Cavey

Notes:
Ridge was dismissed after being acquitted of conspiracy
Rowsell was appointed Acting CC and confirmed in office 11 Jul 1958

Bristol	1836-1974	📖

Formed: 22 Jun 1836
Abolished: 1 Apr 1974. Became part of Avon and Somerset
Strength: *Initial* 228-233   *Final* 1167   ♥ 1889 ⚒ 1373
Chief Officer:

1836 (20 May)	1838 (5 May)	Joseph Bishop
1838 (30 May)	1856 (21 Jun)	*Lt* Henry Fisher
1856 (22 Jun)	1876 (4 Mar)	John S Handcock
1876 (8 Mar)	1894 (27 Jun)	Edwin W Coathupe
1894 (11 Sep)	1906 (19 Sep)	Henry Allbutt
1906 (24 Sep)	1914 (23 Sep)	James Cann
1914 (28 Oct)	1930 (5 Mar)	John H Watson
1930 (2 Jul)	1954 (4 Sep)	*Sir* Charles G Maby
1954 (5 Sep)	1964 (15 Mar)	Norman Frost
1964 (16 Mar)	1974 (31 Mar)	George Twist

Broughty Ferry	1888-1913	📁

Formed: 15 May 1888
Abolished: 4 Nov 1913. Became part of Dundee
Strength: *Initial* 8   *Final* 11
Chief Officer:

1889		William Cameron
1893		James Brechin
1909 (Mar)	1913	J H Sempill

Buckingham	1836-1889	📖

Formed: Jan 1836
Abolished: 1 Apr 1889. Became part of Buckinghamshire
Strength: *Initial* 3   *Final* 4
Chief Officer:

1836	1866	William Giles
1866	1878	John Howe
1878	1881	Job Denson
1881	1889 (31 Mar)	John Nobes

Buckinghamshire	1857-1968	📖

Formed: 6 Feb 1857
Abolished: 1 Apr 1968. Became part of Thames Valley
Strength: *Initial* 102   *Final* 1042
Chief Officer:

1857 (6 Feb)	1867 (31 Oct)	*Capt* Willoughby H Carter
1867 (1 Nov)	1896	*Capt* John C Tyrwhitt Drake
1896 (5 Aug)	1928 (9 Sep)	*Major* Otway Mayne
1928 (10 Sep)	1953 (15 Oct)	*Col* [*Sir*] Thomas R P Warren

1953 (15 Oct)   1967   *Brig* John N Cheney
Notes:
Absorbed Buckingham Borough, 1 Apr 1889
Absorbed Wycombe Borough, 1 Apr 1947

Burnley	**1887-1969**	📖

Formed: 1 Jul 1887, from part of Lancashire
Abolished: 1 Apr 1969. Became part of Lancashire
Strength: *Initial* 70   *Final* 186   ● 1889
Chief Officer:

1887	1901 (29 Jul)	Joseph Harrop
1901	1905 (20 Mar)	Henry C Rawle
1905 (12 May)	1924 (Oct)	William H Smith
1924 (7 Nov)	1937	W Fairclough
1937 (1 Apr)	1939	Alfred E Edwards
1939 (1 Apr)	1942	Harry Barnes
1942 (1 Oct)	1948	William Green
1948	1960	R A Noble
1960	1962	L Massey
1962	1968	J H Thompson
1968	1969	N Greenwood (*Acting CC*)

Notes:
Harrop was dismissed for financial irregularities

Burntisland	**1854?-1861/62**	🗀

Formed: 1854?
Abolished: 1861/62. Became part of Fife
Strength: *Initial* 1   *Final* 1
Chief Officer:

1854?	1861/2?	William Toshack?

Notes:
This force may not have existed. The burgh was policed by Fife County until the end of 1853 but the Council did not agree to continue paying for an officer in the town, leaving 1 (county) man to police the piers only. This was probably Toshack

Bury St Edmunds	**1836-1857**	📖

Formed: Mar 1836
Abolished: 1 Jan 1857. Became part of West Suffolk
Strength: *Initial* 13   *Final* 15
Chief Officer:

1836 (Mar)	after 1845	Richard Caney
1846?		John Hockett

Bute	1858-1949

Formed: 1858
Abolished: 16 May 1949. Became part of Renfrew and Bute
Strength: *Initial* 7 [1859]   *Final* 23
Chief Officer:

1858 (Apr)	1898	John MacKay
1898 (16 Jul)	1925	*Capt* Charles Harding
1925 (16 Nov)	1949 (15 May)	John Robertson

Notes:
Harding was also CC of Renfrewshire, 1887-1925, and of Kinning Park, 1892-1905
Absorbed Rothesay Burgh, 1923
Robertson was also CC of Renfrewshire

Caernarvonshire	1857-1950	📖

Formed: 9 Apr 1857
Abolished: 1 Oct 1950. Became part of Gwynedd
Strength: *Initial* 37   *Final* 176
Chief Officer:

1857 (9 Apr)	1870 (May?)	Thomas P Williams Ellis
1870 (Jun?)	1879	*Capt* Charles Pearson
1879 (28 Jun)	1886	*Major* James M Clayton ✝
1886 (12 Jun)	1912	*Lt Col* Arthur A Ruck
1912 (13 Jun)	1923	John Griffith ✝
1923 (26 Apr)	1939	Edward Williams
1939 (1 Aug)	1945	Thomas J Pritchard
1946 (11 May)	1950 (30 Sep)	*Lt Col* [*Sir*] William J Williams

Notes:
Force commenced duty 20 Jul 1857
Pearson resigned after becoming bankrupt
Absorbed Pwllheli Borough, Jul 1879

Caithness-shire	1841-1969

Formed: 1841
Abolished: 16 May 1969. Became part of Northern
Strength: *Initial* 11 [1859]   *Final* 54
Chief Officer:

1858		John Miller
1859 (Feb)	1884	Alexander Mitchell
1884 (27 Jun)	1912	Thomas Sinclair
1912 (4 May)	1952	William K Cormack
1952 (21 Dec)	1969	John W Georgeson

Notes:
Absorbed Thurso and Wick Burghs, 1858
Wick re-formed 1863

Re-absorbed Wick, 1873
Absorbed Pulteneytown, 2 Dec 1902

Calton	1819-1846

Formed: 1819
Abolished: 27 Jul 1846. Became part of Glasgow City
Strength: *Initial* ?   *Final* 21
Chief Officer:

1819	1833	John Hamilton
1833	1834	Bryce Smith
1834	1835	John Gilliland
1835	1846	James Smart

Cambridge	1836-1965	📖

Formed: 21 Jan 1836
Abolished: 1 Apr 1965. Became part of Mid-Anglia
Strength: *Initial* 31   *Final* 201   📊 1951
Chief Officer:

1842 (19 Sep)	1853	*Capt* Charles C Bailey
1856	1857 ?	W Jaggard
1858 (Jan)	1889	William G Turrall
1889	1894	(C E) Septimus Innes
1894 (May)	1918	Charles E Holland
1919 (1 Nov)	1944	Robert J Pearson
1944 (28 Feb)	1963	(Bernard) Nicolas Bebbington
1964	1965 (31 Mar)	Frederick Drayton Porter

Cambridgeshire	1851-1965	📖

Formed: 25 Nov 1851
Abolished: 1 Apr 1965. Became part of Mid-Anglia
Strength: *Initial* 70   *Final* 156
Chief Officer:

1851 (3 Dec)	1876	*Capt* [*Vice-Admiral*] George Davies
1877	1888	*Capt* [*Major*] Reginald Calvert
1888	1915	Charles J D Stretten
1915	1919	*Lt Col* Alan G Chichester
1919	1935	William V Webb
1935	1941	William Winter
1941	1945	William H Edwards
1948	1963	Donald C J Arnold
1963	1965 (31 Mar)	Frederick Drayton Porter

Notes:
CC appointed jointly with Huntingdonshire but forces administered separately, 1857-77

Chichester was also CC of Huntingdonshire
Arnold had been Acting CC since 1946

Cambridgeshire		1974
Formed: 1 Apr 1974, by re-naming of Mid-Anglia		
Strength: *Initial* 1022		*Current* 1394
Chief Officer:		
1974 (1 Apr)	1977	Frederick Drayton Porter
1977 (1 Jul)	1981	Victor L Gilbert
1981 (1 Oct)	1993 (31 Dec)	Ian H Kane
1994 (1 Jan)	2002 (30 Jun)	Dennis G Gunn
2002 (1 Jul)	2005 (1 Jun)	Tom Lloyd
2005 (9 Dec)	2010 (5 Sep)	Julie Spence
2010 (6 Sep)		Simon Parr

Campbeltown	1858-1863
Formed: 1858	
Abolished: 1863. Became part of Argyllshire	
Strength: *Initial* ?	*Final* ?
Chief Officer: Not known	

Canterbury	1836-1943	📖
Formed: 7 Mar 1836		
Abolished: 1 Apr 1943. Became part of Kent		
Strength: *Initial* 18	*Final* 40	♥ 1889 🏭 1189
Chief Officer:		
1836 (7 Mar)	1860	John Clements
1860 (14 May)	1881	Robert P Davies
1881	1888 (Mar)	James McBean
1888	1892	[*Sir*] Robert Peacock
1892 (Mar)	1907	John W Farmery
1907 (Mar)	1913	L T Dunk
1913 (Apr)	1917	John H Dain
1917 (Jul)	1923	Benjamin H A Carlton
1923 (1 Aug)	1930	*Capt* J A McDonnell
1930 (1 Jun)	1943	George T Hall

Cardiff	1836-1969
Formed: Jan 1836	
Abolished: 1 Jun 1969. Became part of South Wales	
Strength: *Initial* 5	*Final* 750 🏭 1905
Chief Officer:	
1836 (Jan)	1870	J Box Stockdale
1870	1873	John Freeman

1874	1876	*Major* Edwin Bond
1876 (5 Jul)	1889	Walter Hemingway
1889	1912	William Mackenzie
1912	1920	David Williams
1920	1946	[*Sir*] James A Wilson
1946	1954	William J Price
1954 (1 Oct)	1963	William F Thomas
1963 (Dec)	1969 (31 May)	[*Sir*] (Thomas) Gwilym Morris

Cardiganshire	**1844-1958**	📖

Formed: 5 Mar 1844
Abolished: 1 Jul 1958. Became part of Carmarthenshire and Cardiganshire
Strength: *Initial* 18   *Final* 75
Chief Officer:

1844 (5 Mar)	1876 (4 Jan)	*Capt* William C Freeman
1876 (4 Jan)	1890 (30 Jun)	*Capt* [*Major*] Charles B Lewis
1890 (12 Jul)	1890 (6 Oct)	David Evans ♰
1890 (19 Nov)	1903 (Aug)	Howell Evans ♰
1903		Richard Jones
1904 (14 Jan)	1922	Edward Williams
1922 (1 Jan)	1939	Steven Jones
1939 (3 May)	1943 (Jul)	*Major* John J Lloyd-Williams
1944 (16 Jan)	1957 (Nov)	William J Jones

Notes:
Absorbed Aberystwyth Borough, 30 Jun 1857
Lewis was dismissed from office
The appointments of David Evans and Richard Jones were not approved by the Home Office

Carlisle	**1827-1963**	📖

Formed: 13 Jul 1827
Abolished: 1 Sep 1963. Became part of Cumberland Westmorland and Carlisle
Strength: *Initial* 22   *Final* 133   ♥1914 🏭 1189
Chief Officer:

1827 (3 Feb)	1831 (9 Mar)	Benjamin Batty
1831 (10 Mar)	1839 (16 Oct)	Robert Brown
1839 (17 Oct)	1844 (26 Sep)	John Graham
1844 (27 Sep)	1857 (21 Jan)	John H Sabbage
1857 (22 Jan)	1873 (17 Jul)	George E Bent
1873 (21 Aug)	1876 (3 Aug)	Walter Hemingway
1876 (19 Aug)	1904 (11 Aug)	George Mackay
1904 (12 Aug)	1913 (7 Jan)	George Hill
1913 (2 May)	1928 (30 Nov)	Eric H De Schmid [*later* Spence]
1928 (1 Dec)	1929 (30 Nov)	Archibald K Wilson

1929 (1 Dec)	1938 (31 Aug)	Andrew A Johnston
1938 (1 Sep)	1961 (15 Nov)	William H Lakeman
1961 (16 Nov)	1963 (31 Aug)	Frank E Williamson

Notes:
Batty's appointment in Feb 1827 was temporary, pending a local statute

---

Carmarthen	**1827-1947**	

Formed: 16 Feb 1827
Abolished: 31 Mar 1947. Became part of Carmarthenshire
Strength: *Initial* 5   *Final* 17
Chief Officer:

1827 (16 Feb)	1832	James Evans
1832	1836 (4 Jan)	John Lazenby
1836 (4 Jan)	1836 (Sep)	Joseph *or* John Morris
1836 (Sep)		John Hall
1837 (Nov)	1843	John Pugh
1843 (Aug)	1844 (Apr?)	Henry Westlake
1844	1847	Edwin Young
1847	1848	James H George
1848	1870 (Dec)	Samuel Kentish
1871	1876	*Capt* D I Browne-Edwardes
1876	1877?	Frank D Lewis
1877 (Aug)	1887	George James ✟
1887	1911	Thomas Smith
1912 (Feb)	1917	Arthur K Mayall
1918	1918	Herbert Hilton
1918 (10 Jan)	1947 (31 Mar)	William Howell Evans

Notes:
Lazenby was dismissed by the newly-elected Whig Watch Committee for having gaoled Whig party rioters in 1831
Pugh was dismissed for the inefficiency of the force (5 men) in dealing with 4000 Rebecca rioters

---

Carmarthenshire	**1843-1958**	

Formed: 25 Jul 1843
Abolished: 1 Jul 1958. Became part of Carmarthenshire and Cardiganshire
Strength: *Initial* 57   *Final* 228
Chief Officer:

1843 (10 Aug)	1875 (Mar)	*Capt* [*Lt Col*] Richard A Scott ✟
1875 (8 Apr)	1908 (19 May)	William Philipps ✟
1908 (1 Jul)	1940 (1 Jul)	(William) Picton Philipps
1940 (14 Oct)	1958 (30 Jun)	(Thomas) Hubert Lewis

Notes:
Absorbed Kidwelly Borough, Sep 1858
The Philipps were father and son

Absorbed Carmarthen Borough, 1 Apr 1947

Carmarthenshire and Cardiganshire 1958-1968

Formed: 1 Jul 1958, by merger of Cardiganshire and Carmarthenshire
Abolished: 1 Apr 1968. Became part of Dyfed Powys
Strength: *Initial* 309   *Final* 371
Chief Officer:

1958	1960	(Thomas) Hubert Lewis
1960 (1 Jul)	1968 (31 Mar)	(John) Ronald Jones

Central Scotland   1975

Formed: 16 May 1975, from Stirling and Clackmannan and parts of Perth and Kinross, and Lothians and Peebles
Strength: *Initial* 493   *Current* 871
Chief Officer:

1975 (16 May)	1979 (Nov)	Edward Frizzell
1979	1990 (Nov)	*Dr* Ian T Oliver
1990	2000 (31 Mar)	William J M Wilson
2000 (1 Aug)	2008 (30 Sep)	Andrew Cameron
2008 (1 Oct)		Kevin Smith

Chard   1839-1889

Formed: 1839
Abolished: 1 Apr 1889. Became part of Somerset
Strength: *Initial* 4 [1858]   *Final* 2
Chief Officer:

1861	1886	James Player
1886	1889	Henry W Hutchings

Cheltenham   1831-1839

Formed: 1831
Abolished: 1839
Strength: *Initial* 21 or 26   *Final* 21
Chief Officer: Not known

Chepping Wycombe   *see* Wycombe

Cheshire   1857   📖

Formed: 20 Apr 1857
Strength: *Initial* 173   *Current* 2050
Chief Officer:

1857 (5 Jan)	1877 (28 Nov)	*Capt* Thomas J Smith ✝
1878 (19 Feb)	1881 (18 Jun)	*Capt* John W Arrowsmith ✝

1881 (4 Aug)	1910 (29 Sep)	*Col* John H Hamersley
1910 (30 Sep)	1934 (30 Apr)	*Major* [*Lt Col*] Pulteney Malcolm
1934 (1 May)	1935 (30 Sep)	*Capt* [*Sir*] Archibald F Hordern
1935 (1 Oct)	1946 (30 Sep)	*Major* [*Sir*] Jack Becke
1946 (1 Oct)	1963 (30 Aug)	Godwin E Banwell
1963 (1 Sep)	1974 (14 Oct)	Henry Watson
1974 (15 Oct)	1977 (4 Dec)	William Kelsall
1977 (5 Dec)	1984 (31 Jan)	G E Fenn
1984 (1 Feb)	1993	David J Graham
1994?	1997 (31 Aug)	(J) Mervyn Jones
1997(8 Dec)	2002 (Dec)	Nigel Burgess
2002 (Dec)	2008 (31 Oct)	Peter Fahy
2008 (1 Dec)		Dave Whatton

Notes:
Hyde set up separate force, 1 Apr 1899
Wallasey set up separate force, 1 Apr 1913
Absorbed Congleton, Hyde, Macclesfield and Stalybridge Boroughs, 1 Apr 1947
Absorbed Chester City, 1 Apr 1949
Absorbed Birkenhead, Stockport and Wallasey Boroughs, 1 Jul 1967
Parts of area transferred to Derbyshire, Greater Manchester and Merseyside, 1 Apr 1974

Chester	1836-1949	🗁

Formed: 1 Jan 1836
Abolished: 1 Apr 1949. Became part of Cheshire
Strength: *Initial* 5   *Final* 70   ♥ 1889 🏭 1506
Chief Officer:

1836	1864	John Hill
1864	1898	George L Fenwick
1898	1920	John H Laybourne
1920	1949 (31 Mar)	Thomas C Griffiths

Chesterfield	1836-1947

Formed: 7 Jan 1836
Abolished: 1 Apr 1947. Became part of Derbyshire
Strength: *Initial* 7   *Final* 90
Chief Officer:

1836	1853	S Hollingsworth
1859	1864	J Radford
1864 (19 Feb)	1869	Samuel Stevens
1870	1871	Joseph Farndale
1872	1876	Thomas Horne
1876	1882	John Else
1883	1900	Edward Emery
1900	1923	Robert Kilpatrick

1923 (1 May)	1925 (19 Feb)	*Capt* [*Sir*] Percy J Sillitoe
1925	1931	*Major* F S James
1932 (Jan)	1941	Thomas Wells
1941 (Nov)	1947	Lawrence Milner

| Chichester | 1836-1889 | 📖 |

Formed: 1836
Abolished: 1 Apr 1889. Became part of West Sussex
Strength: *Initial* 9   *Final* 9   🏭 1189
Chief Officer:

1850		Richard Greene
1853	1859	J Green
1859	1867	Charles Everett
1867 (25 Nov)	1889 (31 Mar)	Arthur A Pratt

| Chipping Norton | 1836-1857 | 📖 |

Formed: 6 Sep 1836
Abolished: 20 May 1857. Became part of Oxfordshire
Strength: *Initial* 2   *Final* 2
Chief Officer:

1836 (6 Sep)	1846 (9 Mar)	Charles Knott
1845 (24 Dec)	1846 (Jan)	William Barton
1846 (1 Feb)	1847 (9 Nov)	James Williams
1847 (9 Nov)	1851 (Jan)	Charles Yates
1851 (Jan)	1856?	David Smith

Notes:
Knott was dismissed after being acquitted of killing a prisoner
Barton was appointed while Knott was still awaiting trial and was dismissed for negligence
Yates was still a constable in 1857 and transferred to Oxfordshire

| City of London | 1839 | 📖 |

Formed: Nov 1839
Strength: *Initial* 500   *Current* 873   🏭 1189
Chief Officer:

1839 (11 Nov)	1863 (27 Feb)	Daniel Whittle Harvey ⚜
1863	1890 (26 Jun)	*Col* [*Sir*] James Fraser
1890	1901 (Dec)	*Lt Col* [*Sir*]Henry Smith
1902 (21 Mar)	1925 (Sep)	[*Sir*] (John) William Nott-Bower
1925	1950	*Lt Col* [*Sir*] Hugh S Turnbull
1950	1971	*Col* [*Sir*] Arthur E Young
1971	1977	(Charles) James Page
1977	1985	Peter Marshall
1985	1993	Owen Kelly

1994	1998 (1 May)	William Taylor
1998 (24 Jun)	2002 (23 Jun)	Perry Nove
2002 (24 Jun)	2006 (23 Jun)	James Hart
2007 (Jan)	2010 (30 Dec?)	Mike Bowron
2010 (31 Dec)		Adrian Leppard

Notes:
Young was seconded as CC, Royal Ulster, 1969-70

Clackmannanshire	**1850-1949**	

Formed: 1850
Abolished: 16 May 1949. Became part of Stirling and Clackmannan
Strength: *Initial* 7 [1859]   *Final* 37
Chief Officer:

1850		Thomas Berkins
1859	1868	George Gordon
1868 (11 Nov)	1897	John White
1897 (8 Feb)	1932	John Scott
1932 (29 Oct)	1949	David Robertson

Notes:
Gordon was also CC of Kinross-shire and Perthshire
Absorbed Alloa Burgh, 16 May 1930

Cleveland	**1974**	📖

Formed: 1 Apr 1974, from Teesside, part of Durham and part of York and North East Yorkshire
Strength: *Initial* 1410   *Current* 1444
Chief Officer:

1974 (1 Apr)	1976 (30 Jun)	Ralph Davison
1976 (1 Jul)	1990	Christopher F Payne
1990	1993 (31 Jan)	Keith Hellawell
1993 (5 Apr)	2003 (16 Mar)	Barry D D Shaw
2003 (31 Mar)		Sean Price

Clitheroe	**1887-1947**	📖

Formed: 1 Jul 1887, from part of Lancashire
Abolished: 1 Apr 1947. Became part of Lancashire
Strength: *Initial* 9   *Final* 15
Chief Officer:

1887	1893	John Edwards
1893 (Jan)	1913	Walter Clayton
1913 (25 Mar)	1914	James N Campbell
1914 (8 Jul)	1917 (7 May)	Charles Griffin
1917 (7 May)	1934	John C Huxtable
1934 (1 Nov)	1937	William M Thompson

1937 (1 Jul)　　　1947　　　　　　Frank K Exelby

Clyde River	1858-1867

Formed: 1858
Abolished: 1867. Became part of Glasgow
Strength: *Initial*?　　　　　　*Final*?
Chief Officer: Not known

Coatbridge	1886-1967

Formed: 1886, from part of Lanarkshire
Abolished: 16 Aug 1967. Became part of Lanarkshire
Strength: *Initial* 33 [1897]　　　　*Final* 102
Chief Officer:

1886	1893	John Dods
1893	1911	John Anderson
1911	1931	William McDonald
1931	1938	James Irving
1938 (14 Nov)	1957	Daniel M McLauchlan
1957 (16 Apr)	1966	Charles A McIntosh
1966	1967	James E G Lockhart (*Acting CC*)

Colchester	1836-1947	

Formed: 25 Feb 1836
Abolished: 1 Apr 1947. Became part of Essex
Strength: *Initial* 20　　　　　*Final* 77
Chief Officer:

1836 (15 Feb)	1837 (30 Dec)	James A Neville
1837 (29 Dec)	1841 (21 Apr)	William Rand
1841 (17 Jun)	1853 (6 Dec)	Abraham Kent
1854 (25 Jan)	1857 (14 Dec)	James Dunn
1858 (11 Jan)	1858 (25 Nov)	William G Turrall
1858 (25 Nov)	1873 (28 Sep)	Obadiah Downes ♱
1873 (27 Oct)	1883 (28 Feb)	George Mercer
1883 (25 Mar)	1902 (Jun/Jul?)	Richard O Coombs
1902 (1 Jul?)	1912 (15 Nov)	Samuel R Midgley
1913 (Feb)	1947 (31 Mar)	*Capt* [*Lt Col*] Hugh C Stockwell

Notes:
Edward M Showers was Acting CC from 19 May 1915 to Apr? 1919

Congleton	1836-1947	

Formed: Feb 1836
Abolished: 1 Apr 1947. Became part of Cheshire
Strength: *Initial* 1　　　　　*Final* 18
Chief Officer:

1853	1877	John Bohanna
1877	1902	Jonathan Hall
1902 (Apr)	1908	John H Watson
1908 (Apr)	1912	Henry Ingles ✞
1912 (1 Sep)	1914	Thomas Danby
1915 (10 May)	1923	Thomas Nuttall ✞
1923 (16 Jul)	1930	Edward N Christie
1930 (1 Nov)	1932	George S Lowe
1932	1934	J A Kelsall (*Acting CC*)
1934 (18 Feb)	1947 (31 Mar)	R W James

Cornwall	1857-1967	📖

Formed: 6 Jan 1857
Abolished: 1 Jun 1967. Became part of Devon and Cornwall
Strength: *Initial* 179   *Final* 478
Chief Officer:

1857 (6 Jan)	1896 (17 Oct)	*Col* Walter R Gilbert ✞
1896 (21 Dec)	1909 (15 Oct)	Richard Middleton Hill
1909 (16 Oct)	1935 (31 Mar)	*Major* [*Lt Col Sir*] Hugh B Protheroe-Smith
1935 (18 Apr)	1956 (30 Aug)	*Major* Edgar Hare
1956 (1 Sep)	1964	Richard B Matthews
1964 (18 Feb)	1967 (31 May)	K M Wherly

Notes:
Absorbed Wolborough Borough, *ca*1859
Absorbed Bodmin Borough, 22 Oct 1865
Absorbed Liskeard Borough, 16 Jul 1877
Absorbed Launceston Borough, Jan 1883
Absorbed Falmouth, Helston, Penryn and St Ives Boroughs, 1 Apr 1889
Absorbed Truro City, 1 Mar 1921
Absorbed Penzance Borough and Scilly Isles, 1 Apr 1947

Coventry	1836-1969	📖

Formed: 7 Mar 1836
Abolished: 1 Oct 1969. Became part of Warwickshire and Coventry
Strength: *Initial* 23   *Final* 670   ♥ 1889 🏭 1345
Chief Officer:

1836 (20 Apr)	1857 (9 Sep)	Thomas H Prosser
1857 (Sep)	1861 (Nov)	Thomas Skermer
1862 (14 Apr)	1890	John Norris
1890	1899	Alexander Gray
1899 (7 Aug)	1918 (31 Oct)	Charles C Charsley
1918 (Nov)	1927	William Imber
1927 (May)	1946	*Capt* Stanley A Hector
1946 (1 Nov)	1948	George S Jackson
1948 (Jun)	1969	Edward W C Pendleton

Notes: Prosser had been appointed High Constable under the old system in 1832
Skermer absconded and Prosser acted as CC from Nov 1861-Mar 1862

Cromarty Burgh	1859-1868

Formed: 1859
Abolished: 1868. Became part of Cromarty
Strength: *Initial* ?   *Final* ?
Chief Officer: Not known

Cromarty County	1859-1889

Formed: 1859
Abolished: 29 Aug 1889. Became part of Ross and Cromarty
Strength: *Initial* 3 [1870]   *Final* 3
Chief Officer:
1867	1889	Donald Munro
1889	1889 (28 Aug)	James Gordon

Notes:
Absorbed Cromarty Burgh, 1868
Munro and Gordon were also CC of Ross

Croydon	1829-1840	📖

Formed: 12 Sep 1829
Abolished: 13 Jan 1840. Became part of the Metropolitan Police
Strength: *Initial* 5   *Final* 10
Chief officers:
1829 (28 Sep)	1839 (9 Jan)	William Smith
1838	1840 (12 Jan)	John Callingham (*Acting Supt*)

Cullen	1840-1861?

Formed: 1840
Abolished: *ca*1861. Became part of Banffshire
Strength: *Initial* 1 [1859]   *Final* 1
Chief Officer:
1852	1859	James Gordon
1859	1861	John Goodbrand

Cumberland	1857-1963

Formed: 6 Jan 1857
Abolished: 1 Sep 1963. Became part of Cumberland, Westmorland and Carlisle
Strength: *Initial* 60   *Final* 374
Chief Officer:
1857	1902	[*Sir*] John Dunne
1902 (1 Sep)	1920	Charles de C Parry

1920 (1 Aug)	1925	*Lt Col* [*Sir*] Hugh S Turnbull
1926 (4 Mar)	1951	*Capt* Philip T B Browne
1952	1959	John S H Gaskain
1959	1963	Henry Watson

Notes:
Absorbed Derwent Division, 6 Jan 1857?
CC appointed jointly with Westmorland but forces administered separately

Cumberland Westmorland and Carlisle	1963-1967

Formed: 1 Sep 1963, by merger of Cumberland, Westmorland and Carlisle City
Abolished: 1 Apr 1967. Became part of Cumbria
Strength: *Initial* 613   *Final* 688
Chief Officer:

1963 (1 Sep)	1967 (31 Mar)	Frank E Williamson

Notes:
Legally, the force was an integration of the three constituents, not an amalgamation

Cumbria	1967

Formed: 1 Apr 1967, from Cumberland Westmorland and Carlisle, parts of Lancashire and West Yorkshire
Strength: *Initial* 688   *Current* 1162
Chief Officer:

1968 (1 Jan)	1980	William T Cavey
1980	1987	Barry D K Price
1988	1991	[*Sir*] Leslie Sharp
1991	1997 (Mar)	Alan G Elliott
1997	2001 (9 Oct)	Colin Phillips
2001 (26 Nov)	2007 (30 Jun)	Michael Baxter
2007 (17 Sep)		Craig Mackey

Cupar	1858-1862	📁

Formed: 22 Feb 1858, from part of Fife
Abolished: Feb 1862. Became part of Fife
Strength: *Initial* 4   *Final* 3
Chief Officer:

1858 (22 Feb)	1862	Thomas H Simpson

Dalkeith	18??-18??

Formed: ?
Abolished: Became part of Mid Lothian
Strength: *Initial* ?   *Final* ?
Chief Officer: Not known
Notes:
In existence in the mid-19th century

Daventry		1835-1889	🗀

Formed: 1835
Abolished: 1 Apr 1889. Became part of Northamptonshire
Strength: *Initial* 3   *Final* 2
Chief Officer:

	1842 (Feb)	Richard Coles ✝
1842 (Feb?)		Thomas Farley
1866	1868	William Edmunds
1869	1889	George Foster

Deal		1836-1889	📖

Formed: 18 Jan 1836
Abolished: 1 Apr 1889. Became part of Kent
Strength: *Initial* 6   *Final* 9
Chief Officer:

1836 (Jan)	1848	George Hoile
1848	1850	Boyd
1850	1858	Henry Redsull ✝
1858	1874	Thomas Parker ✝
1874 (Dec)	1877	William T Parker
1877	1889 (31 Mar)	Hilder B Capps

Notes:
William Parker was the son of Thomas Parker

Denbigh	?-1858

Formed: Not known
Abolished: Jan 1858. Became part of Denbighshire
Strength: *Initial* ?   *Final* ?
Chief Officer: Not known

Denbighshire		1840-1967	📖

Formed: May 1840
Abolished: 1 Oct 1967. Became part of Gwynedd
Strength: *Initial* 28   *Final* 379
Chief Officer:

1840 (May)	1850	John Denman
1850	1857	G M King *and* J Bradshaw
1857 (17 Feb)	1877 (20 Feb)	John Denman
1877 (20 Feb)	1878 (Aug)	*Capt* Augustus W Price
1878 (1 Nov)	1911 (Dec)	*Major* Thomas J Leadbetter
1912 (1 Jan)	1921	Edward Jones
1921 (1 Jul)	1946	George T Guest
1946 (1 Jul)	1957	Philip Tomkins
1957 (1 Apr)	1964	Arthur M Rees

1964 (1 Dec)   1967   [*Sir*] Walter Stansfield
Notes:
Richard M Wynne appointed as first CC but not approved by Home Office
Force reorganised in 1850 as two Divisions each under a Supt, with no CC
Post of CC re-established 1856
Absorbed Denbigh Borough, Jan 1858

Derby	1836-1967	📖

Formed: 10 Feb 1836
Abolished: 1 Apr 1967. Became part of Derbyshire
Strength: *Initial* 10   *Final* 328   ♥ 1889
Chief Officer:

1859	1876	George Hilton
1876	1898	*Lt Col* W A Delacombe
1898 (Mar)	1926	*Capt* H M Haywood
1926 (8 May)	1956	*Capt* [*Lt Col*] H Rawlings
1956	1959	Eric V Staines
1959	1960	R A Noble
1961	1967	Francis G Hulme

Derbyshire	1857	📖

Formed: 17 Mar 1857
Strength: *Initial* 154 or 156   *Current* 2005
Chief Officer:

1857	1873	*Capt* Willoughby G Fox
1873 (29 Apr)	1892	*Capt* Francis J Parry
1892 (1 May)	1897	*Major* G A Godfrey
1897 (1 Sep)	1916 (3 May)	*Capt* Herbert C Holland ♱
1918 (1 Jun)	1941	*Major* F R Anley
1941 (1 Apr)	1951	*Major* J M Garrow
1951	1952	Willis Clarke ♱
1953	1967	William E Pitts
1967	1979	[*Sir*] Walter Stansfield
1979	1981 (10 Mar)	James Fryer ♱
1981	1985 (5 Nov?)	Alfred S Parrish
1985	1989	Alan O Smith
1990	2000	John F Newing
2001 (1 Jan)	2007 (30 Sep)	David F Coleman
2007 (1 Oct)		Mike Creedon

Notes:
Uniform was originally bottle green
Glossop set up separate force, 1882
Absorbed Chesterfield and Glossop Boroughs, 1 Apr 1947
Absorbed Derby Borough, 1 Apr 1967
Named Derby County and Borough, 1967-74

Parrish was compulsorily retired after allegations of unauthorised spending

Derwent Division	1839-1857

Formed: 31 Dec 1839
Abolished: 6 Jan 1857? Became part of Cumberland
Strength: *Initial* ?　　　　　　　*Final* ?
Chief Officer:
1840 (16 Oct)　　　　　　　Robert Brown

Devon	1857-1967

Formed: 6 Jan 1857
Abolished: 1 Jun 1967. Became part of Devon and Cornwall
Strength: *Initial* 300　　　　　　*Final* 2584
Chief Officer:

1856 (25 Nov)	1891 (31 Dec)	Gerald de Courcy Hamilton
1892 (1 Jan)	1907 (31 Mar)	Francis R C Coleridge
1907 (1 Apr)	1931 (1 Apr)	*Capt* Herbert R Vyvyan
1931 (2 Apr)	1946 (7 Nov)	*Major* Lyndon H Morris ✝
1947 (1 Apr)	1961	*Lt Col* [*Sir*] Ranulph R M Bacon
1961 (1 Dec)	1967 (31 May)	*Lt Col* Ronald B Greenwood

Notes:
Absorbed Okehampton Borough, 1860
Absorbed Bradninch Borough, 1865
Absorbed Torquay Borough, 1870
Absorbed Torrington Borough, Oct 1870
Absorbed South Molton Borough, 16 Oct 1877
Torrington set up separate force, 1878
Absorbed Totnes Borough, 1 Jul 1884
Re-absorbed Torrington Borough, 1 Apr 1889
Absorbed Bideford Borough, 19 May 1889
The force wore bush or slouch hats instead of helmets 1903-8
Absorbed Barnstaple Borough, 1 Oct 1921
Absorbed Tiverton Borough, 1 Jan 1943
Absorbed Exeter City, 1 Apr 1966
Named Devon and Exeter Joint, 1966-67

Devon and Cornwall	1967

Formed: 1 Jun 1967, by merger of Cornwall, Devon and Exeter Joint and Plymouth City
Strength: *Initial* 2480　　　　　　*Current* 3440
Chief Officer:

1967 (1 Jun)	1973	*Lt Col* Ronald B Greenwood
1973 (20 Nov)	1982	John C Alderson
1982	1983	David A East

1984 (1 Mar)	1988 (18 Sep)	Donald Elliott
1989 (1 Jan)	2002 (30 Jun)	[*Sir*] John S Evans
2002	2006 (26 Jul)	Maria Wallis
2007 (15 Jan)		Stephen Otter

Devonport   1836-1914

Formed: 1836
Abolished: 9 Nov 1914. Became part of Plymouth City
Strength: *Initial* 30 [1859]   *Final* 92   ● 1889
Chief Officer:

1854	1859	Robert Hitchman
1860	1863	James Edwards
1863	1889	John Lynn
1889	1893	Samuel Evans
1893	1908	John Matters
1908	1914	John H Watson

Dewsbury   1863-1968

Formed: 1 Jan 1863
Abolished: 1 Oct 1968. Became part of West Yorkshire
Strength: *Initial* 9   *Final* 122   ● 1913
Chief Officer:

1862 (Oct)	1865 (Jul)	John Thomas
1865 (Jul)	1885	Alexander Millar
1885 (13 Mar)	1887	James P Arrowsmith
1887	1890	*Cmdr* Charles T Scott
1890	1893	T Weatherald
1893	1896	*Capt* Herbert J Despard
1896	1911	Henry M Shore
1911	1914	Henry M Kerslake
1914 (Jan)	1930	Sam Barraclough
1930 (Apr)	1950	Frederick E Pritchard
1950 (15 Nov)	1954	Richard W Walker
1954 (1 Oct)	1959	Arthur Iveson
1959 (1 Jun)	1961	Francis G Hulme
1961 (1 Jul)	1968 (30 Sep)	Roy Harrison

Dingwall   1859-1865

Formed: 1859
Abolished: 1865. Became part of Ross
Strength: *Initial* 2 [1859]   *Final* 2
Chief Officer: Not known

Doncaster	1836-1968	📖

Formed: 1836
Abolished: 1 Oct 1968. Became part of West Yorkshire
Strength: *Initial* 5   *Final* 198   ● 1927
Chief Officer:

1837	1841	Thomas Tymms
1841 (Jan)	1861	Williamson Etches
1861	1889	Isaac Gregory ♔
1889	1912	George Lister
1912 (Jul)	1926	William Adams
1926 (Nov)	1940	James Clayton ♔
1940 (Sep)	1949	Thomas W Enfield ♔
1949 (Nov)	1957	Albert E Needham
1957 (Mar)	1968	William T Davis
1968		R Coggan (*Acting CC*)

Dorchester	1836-1889	🗀

Formed: 29 Jan 1836
Abolished: 1 Apr 1889. Became part of Dorset
Strength: *Initial* 8   *Final* 8
Chief Officer:

1842 (1 Jan)	1853	William Russell
1853	1871	T S Pouncy
1871 (May)	1889	Charles Coward

Dorset	1856-1967	📖

Formed: 2 Dec 1856
Abolished: 1 Oct 1967. Became part of Dorset and Bournemouth
Strength: *Initial* 110   *Final* 522
Chief Officer:

1856 (14 Oct)	1867	*Lt Col* Samuel S Cox
1867 (Oct)	1898 (12 Feb)	*Capt* Amyatt Brown
1898 (16 Apr)	1924 (18 Apr)	*Capt* Dennis Granville
1924 (19 Apr)	1955 (28 Feb)	*Major* Lionel W Peel Yates
1955 (Apr)	1961	*Lt Col* Ronald B Greenwood
1962 (1 Jan)	1967 (30 Sep)	Arthur Hambleton

Notes:
Absorbed Bridport Borough, Jan 1858
Absorbed Lyme Regis Borough, 3 Apr 1860
Absorbed Blandford and Dorchester Boroughs, 1 Apr 1889
Absorbed Poole Town and County, 11 Nov 1891
Grey uniform and helmet introduced for summer use (so that dust from unsurfaced roads would not show), 1907, but not approved by Home Office and discontinued
Absorbed Weymouth Borough, 1921

Dorset	1974	📖

Formed: 1 Apr 1974, by renaming of Dorset and Bournemouth
Strength: *Initial* 1088   *Current* 1430
Chief Officer:

1974 (1 Apr)	1980 (29 Feb)	Arthur Hambleton
1980 (1 Mar)	1982 (31 Mar)	David Owen
1982 (1 Jun)	1994	Brian H Weight
1995	1999 (May)	Dirk W Aldous
1999	2004 (31 Oct)	Jane Stichbury
2005 (1 Jan)		Martin Baker

Dorset and Bournemouth	1967-1974	📁

Formed: 1 Oct 1967, by merger of Dorset and Bournemouth
Abolished: 1 Apr 1974. Renamed Dorset
Strength: *Initial* 963   *Final* 1088
Chief Officer:

1967 (1 Oct)	1974 (31 Mar)	Arthur Hambleton

Notes:
Bournemouth was in the administrative county of Hampshire until 1974, when it was transferred to Dorset

Dover	1836-1943	📖

Formed: 20 Jan 1836
Abolished: 1 Apr 1943. Became part of Kent
Strength: *Initial* 15   *Final* 65
Chief Officer:

1836 (20 Jan)		(*Three Sgts*)
1836 (Feb)		Henry Crosoer
1839 (Mar)	1847	Edward Correll
1847	1850	Laker
1850	1851	John Rofe
1851 (Apr)	1872	John Coram
1872	1901	Thomas O Sanders
1901 (Mar)	1908 (May)	H N Knox Knott
1908 (May)	1920	David H Fox
1920 (1 Jul)	1924	Charles Green
1924 (1 Dec)	1935	Alexander M Bond
1935 (2 Dec)	1941	Marshall H Bolt
1941	1943 (31 Mar)	H A Saddleton (*Acting CC*)

Dowlais	1832-1841	📁

Formed: 1832
Abolished: 1841. Became part of Glamorgan
Strength: *Initial* 1   *Final* 1

Chief Officer:
1832?   1841 (23 Oct*)   Evan Davies * or 6 Nov
Notes:
Force paid for from a fund voluntarily contributed by wealthy inhabitants

Droitwich	1836-1881

Formed: 1836
Abolished: 1 Aug 1881. Became part of Worcestershire
Strength: *Initial* ?   *Final* 2
Chief Officer:
1853   1867   Thomas Harris
1868   1874   Alfred Stait
1874   1881   John Colley

Dublin Metropolitan	1836-1925	📖

Formed: 4 Jul 1836
Abolished: 5 Apr 1925. Became part of Garda Siochana
Strength: *Initial* 820   *Final* 1145   🔨 1171
Chief Officer:
1836 (6 Aug)   1871   John L More-O'Ferrall
1836 (6 Aug)   1837 (Jun)   *Lt Col* Augustus Cuyler ✝
1837 (1 Jul)   1858   *Major* George B Browne
1871   1877   *Col Sir* Henry A Lake
1877   1883 (9 Jan)   *Capt* George Talbot
1883 (9 Jan)   1893 (28 Jan)   *Sir* David Harrel
1893 (28 Jan)   1901 (17 Jan)   John J C Jones
1901 (20 Jan)   1914 (5 Aug)   *Lt Col Sir* John F G Ross of Bladenburg
1915 (14 Jan)   1923 (30 Apr)   *Lt Col Sir* Walter Edgeworth-Johnstone
1923 (7 May)   1925 (3 Apr)   *Major Gen* William R E Murphy
Notes: The force actually commenced duty on 1 January 1838
The force had two chief officers as Joint Commissioners, 1836-58

Dudley	1920-1966	📖

Formed: 6 May 1920, from part of Worcestershire
Abolished: 1 Apr 1966. Became part of West Midlands
Strength: *Initial* 55   *Final* 125   🛡 1889
Chief Officer:
1920 (1 Apr)   1946   John N Campbell
1946   1966   C W Johnson

Dumfries	1788-1932	📖

Formed: 1788
Abolished: 16 May 1932. Became part of Dumfries-shire

Strength: *Initial* 6 [1833]   *Final* 26
Chief Officer:

1843	1849	John Jones
1849 (5 Oct)	1855 (2 Feb)	William McNab
1855 (30 Mar)	1858 (Jul)	George Ingram
1858	1859 (Jun)	David Anderson ✝
1859 (1 Jul)	1866 (Jan)	William Mitchell
1866 (23 Feb)	1903 (16 Mar)	John Malcolm ✝
1903 (24 Mar)	1909 (7 Jan)	George S Lipp ✝
1909 (4 Mar)	1932 (15 May)	William Black

Notes:
Jones was also CC Dumfries-shire

Dumfries and Galloway	**1948-**	📖

Formed: 16 Feb 1948, by merger of Dumfries-shire, Kirkcudbrightshire and Wigtownshire
Strength: *Initial* 145   *Current* 503
Chief Officer:

1948 (16 Feb)	1965	Sydney A Berry
1965	1984	Alexander Campbell
1984	1989	John M Boyd
1989	1994	George A Esson
1996	1996	[*Sir*] (Hugh) Roy G Cameron
1996	2001 (30 Jun)	[*Sir*] William Rae
2001 (1 Jul)	2007 (28 Mar?)	David J R Strang
2007 (14 May)		Patrick Shearer

Dumfries-shire	**1840-1948**	📖

Formed: 6 Oct 1840
Abolished: 16 Feb 1948. Became part of Dumfries and Galloway
Strength: *Initial* 14   *Final* 88
Chief Officer:

1840 (18 Nov)	1841 (31 Dec)	William Mitchell
1841	1843	*Sheriff Depute Sir* Thomas Kirkpatrick
1843 (16 Nov)	1891	John Jones
1891 (15 May)	1932 (15 May)	William Gordon
1932 (16 May)	1948 (15 Feb)	William Black

Notes:
Absorbed Langholm Burgh, 15 May 1893
Kirkpatrick had no formal designation
Jones was also CC Dumfries Burgh, 1843-49
Absorbed Dumfries Burgh, 16 May 1932

Dunbar	1844?-1869

Formed: *ca*1844
Abolished: 1869. Became part of East Lothian
Strength: *Initial* 2 [1858]   *Final* 4
Chief Officer:

1844		Alexander Robertson
1858	1861	Robert Shiells
1862	1869	William Urquhart

Dunbarton	1855-1949	🗀

Formed: Nov 1855
Abolished: 15 May 1949. Became part of Dunbartonshire
Strength: *Initial* 7   *Final* 46
Chief Officer:

1855 (16 Nov)	1876	Adam McKay
1876	1882	Thomas Cumming ✝
1882 (22 Sep)	1910	John Henderson ✝
1911 (11 Jan)	1921	Alexander Cruickshank
1921 (30 Aug)	1939 (Aug)	William Fraser
1939 (1 Sep)	1949 (14 May)	Alexander MacLeod

Notes:
Also known as Dumbarton

Dunbartonshire	1840-1975	📖

Formed: 26 May 1840
Abolished: 16 May 1975. Became part of Strathclyde
Strength: *Initial* 13   *Final* 464
Chief Officer:

1840	1844	Edward Pond
1844 (4 Jun)	1850 (8 Apr)	James McDougall
1850	1858 (14 Mar)	Thomas Dunbar
1858 (15 Mar)	1859 (20 May)	Charles Riddell
1859 (2 Jun)	1884 (12 Sep)	Joseph Jenkins
1884 (30 Sep)	1914 (26 Feb)	Charles McHardy ✝
1914 (23 Mar)	1934 (17 Apr)	Neil McLennan
1934 (1 Jun)	1956 (8 Mar)	Arthur J McIntosh ✝
1956 (1 Jun)	1973	William Kerr
1973 (1 Dec)	1975 (15 May)	Robert F P McNeill

Notes:
Also known as Dumbartonshire
Riddell was required to resign when found to be an undischarged bankrupt at the time of his appointment
Absorbed Kirkintilloch Burgh, 15 Jan 1872
Absorbed Helensburgh Burgh, 1875

Absorbed Dunbarton Burgh, 16 May 1949

Dundee	1824-1975	📖

Formed: 1824
Abolished: 16 May 1975. Became part of Tayside
Strength: *Initial* 100 [1858]   *Final* 453   🏭 1892
Chief Officer:

1824		John Low
1824	1825 (May)	Alexander Downie
1825	1834 (21 Feb)	John Home
1834	1839 (Oct)	*Sgt Major* James Drummond
1839	1844	David Corstorphan
1844	1844	William Mackison
1844	1876	Donald W MacKay
1876 (Oct)	1909	David Dewar
1909	1931 (4 Aug)	John Carmichael ✝
1931 (8 Oct)	1936	John McDonald
1936 (10 Mar)	1945	Joseph Neilans
1945	1960	James C Pattison
1960	1968 (Sep?)	[*Sir*] John H Orr
1968	1975 (15 May)	John R Little

Notes:
Drummond resigned on being caught breaking into a shop
Within 3 weeks of appointment, Mackison was arrested for fraud and embezzlement in Yorkshire
Absorbed Broughty Ferry Burgh, 4 Nov 1913

Dunfermline	1811?-1949	🗁

Formed: 1811?
Abolished: 16 May 1949. Became part of Fife
Strength: *Initial* 3 [1842]   *Final* 62   🏭 H
Chief Officer:

1832	1835?	William Cunning
1835	1842	James Simpson ✝
1842	1846 (Oct)	John Livingston[e]
1847	1854	Thomas Lambert
1854	1884	George Stuart
1884	1901 (Nov)	William Forbes ✝
1902	1927 (27 Nov)	George Bruce
1927	1942 (Nov)	Robert Stronach
1943	1949 (15 May)	[*Sir*] John R Inch

Dunstable	1865-1889	📖

Formed: 19 Sep 1865, from part of Bedfordshire

Abolished: 1 Apr 1889. Became part of Bedfordshire
Strength: *Initial* 2   *Final* 3
Chief Officer:
1865 (1 Aug)   1889 (31 Mar)   Benjamin George

Durham City	**1836-1921**	📖

Formed: 2 Feb 1836
Abolished: 1 Apr 1921. Became part of Durham County
Strength: *Initial* 5   *Final* 24   🏭 1189
Chief Officer:

1853	1859	C Reeves
1859	1860	George Morris
1861	1868	William Beard
1869	1874	James Wilson
1876		Robert Dodds
1876 (14 Nov)	1882	James Duns
1882 (20 Mar)	1907	John Smith
1907 (10 May)	1911	Henry M Kerslake
1911 (1 Jun)	1921	W Dunn

Durham County	**1840**	📖

Formed: 1 Mar 1840
Strength: *Initial* 66   *Current* 1402
Chief Officer:

1839 (10 Dec)	1848 (23 Sep)	*Major* James Wemyss ✝
1848 (7 Nov)	1892 (31 Mar)	*Major* [*Lt Col*] George F White
1892	1902 (26 Feb)	*Lt Col* John H Eden
1902 (15 Dec)	1922 (30 Apr)	William G Morant
1922 (1 Oct)	1942 (13 Oct)	[*Sir*] George Morley ✝
1943 (Feb)	1944 (Aug)	*Capt* [*Sir*] Henry Studdy
1945 (1 Jan)	1950 (30 Sep)	*Col* [*Sir*] (Thomas) Eric St Johnston
1950 (4 Nov)	1970 (1 Oct)	Alec A Muir
1970 (1 Oct)	1981 (30 Sep)	Arthur G Puckering
1981 (12 Nov)	1988 (31 Mar)	Eldred J Boothby
1988 (1 Apr)	1997 (14 Jul)	Frank W Taylor
1997 (12 Sep)	2002 (30 Sep)	George E Hedges
2002	2005 (11 Dec)	Paul Garvin
2005 (12 Dec)	2007	Jon Stoddart

Notes:
Hartlepool set up separate force, 1851
Absorbed Durham City, 1 Apr 1921
Absorbed Hartlepool Borough, 1 Apr 1947
Absorbed Sunderland Borough, 1 Apr 1967
Part of area transferred to Teesside, 1 Apr 1968

Absorbed Gateshead and South Shields Boroughs, 1 Oct 1968
Parts of area transferred to Cleveland and Northumbria, 1 Apr 1974

Dyfed-Powys	1968	📖

Formed: 1 Apr 1968, by merger of Carmarthenshire and Cardiganshire, Mid Wales and Pembrokeshire
Strength: *Initial* 820   *Current* 1134
Chief Officer:

1968 (1 Apr)	1975	(John) Ronald Jones
1975	1986	Richard B Thomas
1986	1989	David J Shattock
1989	2000 (5 Mar)	Raymond White
2000 (27 Mar)	2007 (19 Nov)	Terence Grange
2008 (8 Jun)		Ian B Arundale

Notes:
Parts of area transferred to Gwent and South Wales, 1 Apr 1974
Grange retired following allegations of financial and other irregularities

Dysart	1858-1859?	🗁

Formed: 1858
Abolished: 1859? Became part of Fife
Strength: *Initial* ?   *Final* ?
Chief Officer: Not known
Notes:
This force may not have existed. The Burgh had been paying Fife County for police services since 1844 and this appears to have continued after the Police Act of 1857

East Lothian	1832-1950	📖

Formed: 1832
Abolished: 16 May 1950. Became part of Lothians and Peebles
Strength: *Initial* 8   *Final* 53
Chief Officer:

1832 (16 Oct)	1840	Alfred J List
1840 (Jan)	1893 (10 Nov)	George H List
1894 (19 Jan)	1914 (6 Oct)	*Lt Col* Alexander Borthwick ✟
1914 (8 Dec)	1950 (15 May)	*Major* Sholto W Douglas

Notes:
Force orginally named Haddingtonshire
Alfred and George List were brothers
Absorbed Musselburgh Burgh, *ca*1841?
Absorbed North Berwick, 1857/8
George List was also CC of Berwickshire, 1862-93
Absorbed Dunbar Burgh, 1869
Absorbed Haddington Burgh, 1874

From 1894 to 1950, the same CC administered four forces: East Lothian, Mid Lothian, Peebles-shire and West Lothian

East Riding	1857-1968	📖

Formed: 6 Jan 1857
Abolished: 1 Jul 1968. Became part of York and North East Yorkshire
Strength: *Initial* 61   *Final* 410
Chief Officer:

1856 (26 Nov)	1872	*Lt Col* Bernard Granville Layard
1872 (1 Nov)	1899	*Major* H J Bower
1899 (1 Sep)	1924 (28 Nov)	*Major* William H Dunlop ✝
1925 (19 Feb)	1926	*Capt* [*Sir*] Percy J Sillitoe
1926 (1 May)	1934	*Capt* [*Sir*] Archibald F Hordern
1934 (1 May)	1939	J E Ryall
1939 (28 Aug)	1942	[*Sir*] (Richard) Dawnay Lemon
1942 (1 Jul)	1946	Godwin E Banwell
1946 (15 Oct)	1953	*Brig* John N Cheney
1953 (15 Oct)	1968	J W P Blenkin

Notes:
Absorbed Hedon Borough, 1859
Absorbed Beverley Borough, 1 Apr 1928

East Suffolk	1840-1967	📖

Formed: 12 May 1840
Abolished: 1 Apr 1967. Became part of Suffolk
Strength: *Initial* 64   *Final* 434
Chief Officer:

1840 (1 Apr)	1842 (Dec)	John Hayes Hatton
1843 (24 Jan)	1869 (Feb)	John Hatton
1869 (2 Jun)	1898 (2 Dec)	*Major* Clement H J Heigham ✝
1899 (3 Mar)	1933 (May)	*Capt* Jasper G Mayne
1933 (1 Jun)	1942 (Mar)	George S Staunton
1942 (1 Apr)	1957 (Apr)	*Lt Col* Arthur F Senior ✝
1957 (1 Oct)	1963 (Apr)	Edwin P B White
1963	1965	Arthur Long (*Acting CC*)
1965 (1 May)	1967 (31 Mar)	[*Sir*] Peter J Matthews

Notes:
The two Hattons were *not* related but were both from the same area of Ireland
John Hatton resigned on being made bankrupt
Heigham commanded both East Suffolk and West Suffolk from 1869 to 1899
Absorbed Beccles Borough, Aug 1857
Absorbed Eye Borough, Nov 1857
Absorbed Orford Borough, Jul 1860
Absorbed Southwold Borough, 1 Apr 1889

East Sussex	1840-1943	📖

Formed: 9 Oct 1840
Abolished: 1 Apr 1943. Became part of Sussex Combined
Strength: *Initial* 26   *Final* 299
Chief Officer:

1840 (16 Nov)	1881 (26 Jun)	*Capt [Lt Col]* Henry F Mackay
1881 (27 Jun)	1894 (25 Mar)	*Major* George B Luxford ✟
1894 (24 Jun)	1920 (24 Jun)	*Capt [Major]* Hugh G Lang
1920 (25 Jun)	1936 (18 May)	*Lt Col* George M Ormerod ✟
1936 (12 Aug)	1943 (31 Mar)	Reginald E Breffit

Notes:
The initial strength included a Sgt and 3 parish constables at Lewes, merged with the county with the proviso that *they were not to be employed away from Lewes except in the most pressing emergency*. In addition, there were 120 local constables, paid but not uniformed, who were not compelled to serve outside their area
Hove set up separate force, 1858
Absorbed Rye Borough, 1 Apr 1889
Eastbourne set up separate force, 6 Apr 1891

East Sussex	1947-1967	📖

Re-formed: 1 Apr 1947, from part of Sussex Combined
Abolished: 1 Jan 1968. Became part of Sussex
Strength: *Initial* 402   *Final* 785
Chief Officer:

1947 (1 Apr)	1965	Reginald E Breffit
1965	1967 (31 Dec)	*[Sir]* George W R Terry

Eastbourne	1891-1943	📖

Formed: 6 Apr 1891, from part of East Sussex
Abolished: 1 Apr 1943. Became part of Sussex Combined
Strength: *Initial* 38   *Final* 114   ● 1911
Chief Officer:

1891 (Feb?)	1893 (Mar)	John G Fraser
1893 (Mar)	1900	Harry Plumb
1900	1918	*Major* Edward J J Teale
1918	1943 (31 Mar)	William H Smith

Eastbourne	1947-1967	📖

Re-formed: 1 Apr 1947, from part of Sussex Combined
Abolished: 1 Jan 1968. Became part of Sussex
Strength: *Initial* 123   *Final* 146
Chief Officer:

1947 (1 Apr)	1954	Norman Frost
1954 (Oct)	1967 (31 Dec)	Richard W Walker

Easter Ross	1850-1853

Formed: 1850
Abolished: 1853. Became part of Ross
Strength: *Initial* ?   *Final* ?
Chief Officer: Not known

Edinburgh	1805-1975	📖

Formed: 1805
Abolished: 16 May 1975. Became part of Lothian and Borders
Strength: *Initial* 324 [1858]   *Final* 1280   🏛 1329
Chief Officer:

1805	1812	John Tait
1812	1822	James Brown
1822	1828	*Capt* Robertson
1828	1842	*Capt* James Stewart
1842 (Dec)	1848	William Haining
1848	1851	Richard J Moxey
1851	1878	Thomas Linton
1878	1900	William Henderson
1900	1935	Roderick Ross
1935	1955	[*Sir*] William B R Morren
1955 (Sep)	1975 (15 May)	[*Sir*] John R Inch

Notes:
Absorbed Leith Burgh, 2 Nov 1920

Edinburghshire	*see* Mid Lothian

Elgin	1850-1893	🗀

Formed: 1850
Abolished: 1 Mar 1893. Became part of Morayshire
Strength: *Initial* 5 [1859]   *Final* 7   🏛 H
Chief Officer:

1850	1854	John Sutherland
1854	1856	*Sgt* MacLennan [*Deputy*]
1856	1865	Peter Grant
1865	1872	Thomas Wyness
1872	1889 (23 Jan)	Alexander Matthew ✟
1890	1892	John B Mair
1892 (Jan)	1893	Alexander Morrison (*Acting CC*)

Elginshire	1844-1890	🗀

Formed: 1844
Abolished: 1890. Re-named Morayshire

Strength: *Initial* 13 [1858]   *Final* 19
Chief Officer:
1840   1844 (17 Jan)   John Munn ✝
1844   1870   William Hay
1870 (10 Mar)   1890   James Pirie
Notes:
Absorbed Forres Burgh, 1 Jun 1866

Essex	1840	📖

Formed: 11 Feb 1840
Strength: *Initial* 116   *Current* 3587
Chief Officer:
1840 (11 Feb)   1881 (31 Oct)   *Capt [Admiral]* John B B McHardy
1881 (1 Nov)   1887 (2 Jul)   William H Poyntz
1888 (3 Jul)   1915 (30 Apr)   Edward M Showers
1915 (8 May)   1932 (6 Dec)   *Capt* John A Unett ✝
1933 (1 May)   1962 (9 Dec)   *Capt [Sir]* (F R) Jonathan Peel
1962 (10 Oct)   1978 (30 Jun)   *[Sir]* John C Nightingale
1978 (1 Jul)   1987 (31 Dec)   *[Sir]* Robert S Bunyard
1988 (1 Feb)   1998 (30 Jun)   John H Burrow
1998 (1 Jul)   2005 (30 Jun)   David F Stevens
2005 (1 Jul)   2009 (5 Jul)   Roger Baker
2009 (8 Sep)   Jim Barker-McCardle
Notes:
Absorbed Harwich Borough, 1 Feb 1857
Absorbed Saffron Walden Borough, 1 Nov 1857
Absorbed Maldon Borough, 1 Apr 1889
Southend-on-Sea set up separate force, 1914
Absorbed Colchester Borough, 1 Apr 1947
Part of area transferred to Metropolitan, 1 Apr 1965
Absorbed Southend-on-Sea Borough, 1 Apr 1969
Named Essex and Southend-on-Sea Joint, 1969-74
Part of area transferred from Metropolitan, 1 Apr 2000

Evesham	1836-1850	

Formed: 12 Jan 1836
Abolished: 14 Oct 1850. Became part of Worcestershire
Strength: *Initial* ?   *Final* 3
Chief Officer:
1836 (Jan)   1850   William Arton

Exeter	1836-1966	📖

Formed: 18 Jan 1836
Abolished: 1 Apr 1966. Became part of Devon and Exeter

Strength: *Initial* 26   *Final* 174   ♥ 1889 ⛏ 1189
Chief Officer:

1836	1847 (31 Aug)	Hugh Cumming
1847 (1 Sep)	1873	David Steel
1873	1886	*Capt* Thomas Bent
1886	1888	Edward M Showers
1888	1893	H B Le Mesurier
1893	1901	John Short
1901 (Jun)	1911	R L Williams
1912 (1 Jan)	1913	Eric H De Schmid [*later* Spence]
1913 (May)	1930	Arthur F Nicholson
1930	1940 (Dec)	Frederick T Tarry
1941	1958	Albert E Rowsell
1958	1967	K E Steer

Eye	1840-1857

Formed: 1840
Abolished: Nov 1857. Became part of East Suffolk
Strength: *Initial* ?   *Final* 2
Chief Officer: Not known

Falmouth	1836-1889

Formed: 1836
Abolished: 1 Apr 1889. Became part of Cornwall
Strength: *Initial* 8 [1858]   *Final* 4
Chief Officer:

1853	1874	George Julyan
1874	1889	Robert Borne

Faversham	1839-1889	🗁

Formed: 21 Oct 1839
Abolished: 1 Apr 1889. Became part of Kent
Strength: *Initial* 17   *Final* 9
Chief Officer:

1853	1861	Thomas Burrough
1862	1871	Charles White
1872	1889	M Breary

Fife	1840	📖

Formed: 4 Aug 1840
Strength: *Initial* 37   *Current* 1107
Chief Officer:

1839 (May)	1860	Robert Adamson
1860	1863	William Bell

1863	1903	*Capt* James F Bremner
1903 (8 Dec)	1934	James T Gordon
1935 (11 Feb)	1949	Victor G Savi
1949 (16 May)	1955	[*Sir*] John R Inch
1955 (3 Nov)	1965	Andrew Meldrum
1965 (1 Jun)	1983	Robert F Murison
1984	1996	William McD Moodie
1996 (Sep)	2001 (16 Jan)	John P Hamilton
2001 (16 Apr)	2008 (28? May)	Peter M Wilson
2008 (Jul)		Norma Graham

Notes:

Absorbed Kirkcaldy Burgh, 25 Nov 1845

Cupar set up separate force, 22 Feb 1858

Absorbed Dysart and St Andrews Burghs [if they existed], *ca*1859?

Absorbed Burntisland Burgh [if it existed], 1861

Absorbed Cupar Burgh, 1862

Absorbed Newburgh Burgh, 1869

Kirkcaldy Burgh re-formed, 11 Nov 1877

Absorbed Inverkeithing Burgh, 1885

CC was also CC of Kinross-shire, 1891-1930

Absorbed Dunfermline City and re-absorbed Kirkcaldy Burgh, 16 May 1949

Mrs Graham was the first woman CC in Scotland

Flint	**1835?-1864**	🗁

Formed: *ca*1835?

Abolished: 1 May 1864. Became part of Flintshire

Strength: *Initial* 1 [1857]   *Final* 1

Chief Officer:

1859	1864	Levi Toothill

Flintshire	**1856-1967**	📖

Formed: Nov 1856

Abolished: 1 Oct 1967. Became part of Gwynedd

Strength: *Initial* 28   *Final* 280

Chief Officer:

1857 (15 Jan)	1888 (15 Nov)	Peter Browne
1888 (Dec?)	1909 (Aug)	*Major* Robert T Webber ✞
1909 (Aug)	1918 (26 Jan)	(John) Ivor Davies ✞
1918 (6 Feb)	1942 (21 Jan)	Robert Yarnell Davies ✞
1942 (1 Mar)	1947 (20 May)	Albert E Lindsay ✞
1947 (1 Dec)	1959	John F Roberts
1959 (1 Feb)	1967	R Atkins

Notes:

The force became operational on 21 Mar 1857

Absorbed Mold Borough, date unknown

Absorbed Flint Borough, 1 May 1864

Folkestone		1836-1943	📖

Formed: 1836
Abolished: 1 Apr 1943. Became part of Kent
Strength: *Initial* 2   *Final* 9
Chief Officer:

1850	1857 (16 Jul)	James Steer
1857	1872 (28 Dec)	W Martin ♱
1873	1880 (Jul)	John M Wilshere ♱
1880 (Oct)	1883	Samuel Rutter
1883	1899	John Taylor
1899 (Mar)	1922	Harry Reeve
1923 (1 Apr)	1941	Alfred S Beesley
1941	1943 (31 Mar)	Robert C M Jenkins

Forfar	1857-1930

Formed: 1857
Abolished: 16 May 1930. Became part of Angus
Strength: *Initial* 5 [1858]   *Final* 11
Chief Officer:

1859	1865	George Cooper
1866		Donald Munro
1867	1903	James Stirling
1903 (May)	1903 (Dec)	William Spense
1904	1930	James Thomson

Forfarshire	1840-1928

Formed: 1840
Abolished: 1928. Re-named Angus
Strength: *Initial* 29 [1858]   *Final* 52
Chief Officer:

1840	1856	Henry Williams
1856	1863	Michael Hinchey
1863 (23 Sep)	1886	William Keith
1886 (27 Sep)	1900	Robert Adamson
1900 (26 Sep)	1928	Robert T Birnie

Forres	1858-1866

Formed: 1858
Abolished: 1 Jun 1866. Became part of Elginshire
Strength: *Initial* 4 [1859]   *Final* 4
Chief Officer:

1858 (4 Jan)	1861 (16 Jan)	William Rae

1861 (13 May)   1866 (1 Jun)   John MacFarlane

Fraserburgh	1859-1867

Formed: 1859
Abolished: 1 Jan 1867. Became part of Aberdeenshire
Strength: *Initial*?   *Final*?
Chief Officer: Not known

Galashiels	1850-1930	🗁

Formed: 1850
Abolished: 16 May 1930. Became part of Selkirk
Strength: *Initial* 6 [1870]   *Final* 12
Chief Officer:

1850	1864	James McBean
1864	1872	James Beaton
1872	1880	William MacKay
1880	1905	Andrew Sutherland
1905	1922	Alexander Noble
1923	1924	John Scott
1924	1930	Henry J Wallace

Gateshead	1836-1968	📖

Formed: 1 Oct 1836
Abolished: 1 Oct 1968. Became part of Durham County
Strength: *Initial* 9   *Final* 214   ♥ 1889
Chief Officer:

1836	1842 (27 Jun)	John Usher
1842	1845 (29 Mar)	Charles C Rudd
1845	1863 (1 Mar)	William H Schorey
1863	1891 (30 Jun)	John Elliott
1891	1892	Edward Harris
1892 (1 Jul)	1917 (Feb)	James Trotter
1917 (1 Mar)	1937 (31 Oct)	Richard Ogle
1937 (1 Nov)	1958 (1 Nov)	Edward Bainbridge
1958 (1 Nov)	1962 (4 Jul)	Robert W Walton
1962 (1 Dec)	1968 (30 Sep)	John A Hallett

Gilling West Division	1840-1856?

Formed: 9 Jan 1840
Abolished: 14 Oct 1856? Became part of North Riding
Strength: *Initial*?   *Final*?
Chief Officer:
1842   Ralph L Snowden

Glamorgan	**1839-1969**	📖

Formed: Dec 1839
Abolished: 1 Jun 1969. Became part of South Wales
Strength: *Initial* 7   *Final* 1300
Chief Officer:

1839 (Dec)	1841	Thomas M Lewis
1841 (11 Aug)	1867 (11 Jan)	*Capt* Charles F Napier ✝
1867 (Mar?)	1891	*Lt Col* Henry G Lindsay
1891 (7 Feb)	1937	*Capt* [*Major*] Lionel A Lindsay
1937 (8 Mar)	1951	Joseph Jones
1951	1963	Cecil H Watkins
1963	1969 (31 May)	Melbourne Thomas

Notes:
The force initially only covered Miskin and Caerphilly petty sessional divisions, with 1 supt and 6 PCs. It was extended to the whole county, 1841
Lewis remained in the force as a supt until 1845
Absorbed Bridgend, Dowlais and Merthyr Tydfil parishes, 1841
The Lindsays were father and son
Merthyr Tydfil set up separate force, 1 Oct 1908
Absorbed Neath Borough, 1 Apr 1947

Glasgow	**1800-1975**	📖

Formed: 1800
Abolished: 16 May 1975. Became part of Strathclyde
Strength: *Initial* 78   *Final* 3141   ⛏ 1451
Chief Officer:

1800 (29 Sep)	1803 (5 Sep)	John Stenhouse
1803 (5 Sep)	1805 (2 Sep)	Walter Graham
1805 (2 Sep)	1821 (5 Jul)	James Mitchell
1821 (5 Jul)	1825 (21 Jul)	James Hardie
1825 (21 Jul)	1832 (1 Mar)	John Graham
1832 (1 Mar)	1833 (24 Jan)	F G Denovan
1833 (24 Jan)	1836 (10 Apr)	John Watson
1836 (10 Apr)	1847 (5 Apr)	Henry Miller
1847 (5 Apr)	1848 (10 Apr)	William Pearce
1848(10 Apr)	1848 (18 Dec)	Henry Miller
1848 (18 Dec)	1870 (7 Jun)	James Smart
1870 (7 Jun)	1888 (5 Apr)	Alexander McCall
1888 (5 Apr)	1902 (2 Apr)	John Boyd
1902 (2 Apr)	1922 (1 Apr)	James V Stevenson
1922 (1 Apr)	1931 (1 Dec)	Andrew D Smith
1931 (1 Dec)	1943 (1 Mar)	*Capt* [*Sir*] Percy J Sillitoe
1943 (1 Mar)	1943 (29 May)	David Warnock ✝
1943 (1 Sep)	1959 (31 Dec)	[*Sir*] Malcolm M McCulloch
1960 (1 Jan)	1971 (6 Apr)	[*Sir*] James A Robertson

1971 (7 Apr)   1975 (15 May)   [*Sir*] David B McNee
Notes:
Absorbed Anderston, Calton and Gorbals Burghs, 27 Jul 1846
Absorbed Clyde River, 1867
Absorbed Maryhill Burgh, 7 Jul 1891
Absorbed Kinning Park Burgh, 29 Nov 1905
Absorbed Govan and Partick Burghs, 5 Nov 1912

Glasgow Airport	1966-1975

Formed: 1966
Abolished: 16 May 1975. Became part of Strathclyde
Strength: *Initial* 39   *Final* ?
Chief Officer: Not known

Glastonbury	?-1856

Formed: before 1856
Abolished: 21 May 1856. Became part of Somerset
Strength: *Initial* ?   *Final* ?
Chief Officer: Not known

Glossop	1867-1947

Formed: 9 Apr 1867
Abolished: 1 Apr 1947. Became part of Derbyshire
Strength: *Initial* 8   *Final* 32
Chief Officer:

1868	1870	Samuel Kershaw
1871	1873	William Beard
1874	1875	Henry Hilton
1876	1899	W H Hodgson
1899 (Feb)	1922	John G Hodgson
1922 (Feb)	1929	William R Wilkie
1929 (15 Apr)	1941	Robert C Greensmith
1941 (1 Jun)	1947	Percy Hawkins

Gloucester	1836-1859

Formed: 26 Feb 1836
Abolished: 1 May 1859. Became part of Gloucestershire
Strength: *Initial* 15? or 25   *Final* 20   🏭 1541
Chief Officer:

1836	1838	John Marsh
1838?	1846	George Williams
1846	1859	Edmund Estcourt

Gloucestershire	1839	📖

Formed: 18 Nov 1839
Strength: *Initial* 250   *Current* 1266
Chief Officer:

1839 (18 Nov)	1865 (1 Jul)	Anthony T Lefroy
1865 (1 Jul)	1910 (2 May)	*Admiral* Henry Christian
1910 (3 May)	1917 (30 Aug)	*Major* [*Lt Col*] Richard C Chester-Master ✞
1918 (1 Jan)	1937 (30 Apr)	*Major* Frederick L Stanley-Clarke
1937 (1 May)	1959 (8 Apr)	*Col* William F Henn
1959 (9 Apr)	1962 (18 Dec)	John S H Gaskain
1963 (8 Apr)	1975 (30 Jun)	Edwin P B White
1975 (1 Jul)	1979 (31 Aug)	Brian Weigh
1979 (1 Sep)	1987	Leonard A G Soper
1987	1993	Albert H Pacey
1993	2001 (1 Apr)	Anthony J P Butler
2001 (2 Apr)	2010 (2 Jan)	*Dr* Tim Brain
2010 (3 Jan)		Tony Melville

Notes:
Chester-Master rejoined the Army in 1915 and was killed in action
M W Colchester-Wemyss, Chairman of the Standing Joint Committee, was Acting CC (unpaid) during Chester-Master's absence

Godalming	1836-1851	📖

Formed: 1836
Abolished: 1 Jan 1851. Became part of Surrey
Strength: *Initial* 2   *Final* ?
Chief Officer:

1841	1850 (31 Dec)	William H Biddlecombe

Godalming	1857-1889	📖

Re-formed: 1 Apr 1857, from part of Surrey
Abolished: 1 Apr 1889. Became part of Surrey
Strength: *Initial* 2   *Final* 3
Chief Officer:

1857	1859	Charles Everett
1859	1860	James Wheller
1860	1865	Thomas High
1865	1868	John H Burt
1870	1879	Thomas High
1880	1889	George Turner

Godmanchester	?-1857	📁

Formed: ?
Abolished: June 1857. Became part of Huntingdonshire

Strength: *Initial*?   *Final*?
Chief Officer: Not known

Gorbals	1808-1846

Formed: 1808
Abolished: 27 Jul 1846. Became part of Glasgow
Strength: *Initial*?   *Final* 48
Chief Officer:

1808	1815	Robert McHendry
1815	1825	Donald McKenzie
1825	1833	John Clark
1833	1839	George Jaffray
1839	1840	Andrew McKerrow
1840	1846	James Richardson

Govan	1864-1912

Formed: 1864
Abolished: 5 Nov 1912. Became part of Glasgow
Strength: *Initial* 14   *Final* 122
Chief Officer:

1864	1883 (15 Oct)	David Young
1883 (15 Oct)	1901	William Hamilton
1901	1912	James S Whitecross

Grampian	1975

Formed: 16 May 1975, from Aberdeen and Scottish North-eastern Counties
Strength: *Initial* 882   *Current* 1516
Chief Officer:

1975 (16 May)	1983	Alexander Morrison
1983 (6 Dec)	1990 (3 Sep)	Alistair G Lynn
1990 (10 Sep)	1998 (24 May)	Dr Ian T Oliver
1998 (Jun)	2004	Andrew G Brown
2004 (12 Apr)		Colin McKerracher

Grantham	1836-1947

Formed: 9 Feb 1836
Abolished: 1 Apr 1947. Became part of Lincolnshire
Strength: *Initial* 5   *Final* 32
Chief Officer:

1836 (9 Feb)	1846 (30 Jun)	Charles Churchill
1846 (1 Jul)	1863 (12 Aug)	John Howard
1863 (13 Aug)	1865 (11 Apr)	James Strugnell
1865 (17 Apr)	1873 (26 Feb)	John Rudkin
1873 (12 Mar)	1876 (6 Oct)	Charles Pole

1876 (12 Oct)	1887 (18 Feb)	John Pemberton
1887 (18 Jun)	1891 (8 Aug)	John Harland
1891 (9 Oct)	1894 (29 Jun)	Charles E Holland
1894 (7 Aug)	1898 (1 Oct)	William B Jones
1898 (Nov)	1937 (Sep)	John R Cashurn
1937 (1 Oct)	1947 (31 Mar)	William Weatherhogg

Notes:
Pemberton was required to resign for losing a prisoner

Gravesend	**1836-1943**	📖

Formed: 1836
Abolished: 1 Apr 1943. Became part of Kent
Strength: *Initial* 11   *Final* 59
Chief Officer:

1836	1851	Will North
1851 (1 Apr)	1873	Frederick White
1873	1892	George Berry
1892	1912	Walter Thornton
1912 (Jun)	1923	Harry F Thurley
1923 (Jul)	1930	Arthur G Martin
1930 (Dec)	1934 (31 Aug)	Frank L Bunn
1934 (Oct)	1943 (31 Mar)	Keith Webster

Great Yarmouth	**1836-1968**	🗁

Formed: Jan 1836
Abolished: 1 Jan 1968. Became part of Norfolk
Strength: *Initial* 18   *Final* 132   ♥ 1889
Chief Officer:

1836	1857	*Capt* Benjamin L Love
1857	1878	George Tewsley
1878	1881	Joseph Ogden
1881	1894 (Nov)	William Brogden
1894 (Nov)	1918	William H Parker
1918 (Sep)	1940 (13 May)	Ben W Smith ♱
1940 (May)	1947	Charles G Box
1947 (Apr)	1967 (31 Dec)	Charles F Jelliff

Greater Manchester	**1974**	📖

Formed: 1 Apr 1974, by merger of Manchester and Salford with parts of Cheshire, Lancashire and West Yorkshire
Strength: *Initial* 5532   *Current* 7606
Chief Officer:

1974 (1 Apr)	1976	William J Richards
1976 (1 Jul)	1991 (30 Jun)	[*Sir*] (Cyril) James Anderton

1991 (1 Jul)	2002 (30 Sep)	[*Sir*] David Wilmot
2002 (1 Oct)	2008 (10 Mar)	Michael Todd ♱
2008 (1 Nov)		Peter Fahy

Greenock	**1800-1967**	📖

Formed: 1800
Abolished: 16 Aug 1967. Became part of Renfrew and Bute
Strength: *Initial* 4   *Final* 189
Chief Officer:

1800	1815	Nathaniel Wilson
1815	1822	John Lennox
1822	1832	John McIlwraith
1832	1838	Robert Lyle
1838	1858	Alexander Mann
1858	1863	William Newham
1863	1876	*Capt* David Dewar
1876	1886	*Capt* James Orr
1886	1913	*Capt* John W Angus
1913	1945	James Christie
1945	1955	William M McKechnie
1955	1958	David Gray
1958	1967 (15 Aug)	David Williamson

Notes:
Absorbed Greenock Harbour, 1822
Greenock Harbour re-formed 1825-1843
McIlwraith was jailed in 1825 at the instance of his creditors but later reinstated

Greenock Harbour	**1817-1822**

Formed: 1817
Abolished: 1822. Became part of Greenock Burgh
Strength: *Initial* ?   *Final* ?
Chief Officer: Not known

Greenock Harbour	**1825-1843**

Re-formed: 1825, from part of Greenock Burgh
Abolished: 1843. Became part of Greenock Burgh
Strength: *Initial* ?   *Final* ?
Chief Officer:

| 1825 | 1843 | *Lt* Duncan Blair ♱ |

Grimsby	**1846-1967**	📖

Formed: 27 Apr 1846
Abolished: 1 Apr 1967. Became part of Lincolnshire
Strength: *Initial* 4   *Final* 237   ♥ 1889

Chief Officer:

1846	1853	*Not known*
1853	1859	Isaac [*or* John] Anson
1860	1879	John Campbell
1879	1891	Job Waldram
1891	1899	Henry Pickersgill
1899	1901	John Fisher ✞
1901 (Aug)	1930 (28 Jul)	John Stirling
1930 (Aug)	1934	Charles Tarttelin ✞
1934 (1 Sep)	1936 (31 Aug)	Frank L Bunn
1936 (Nov)	1962	Charles E Butler
1962 (Aug)	1967 (31 Mar)	James Angus

Notes:
The whole force was dismissed in 1859

Guernsey	**1853**	📖

Formed: 28 May 1853
Strength: *Initial* 4   *Current* 177
Chief Officer:

1853 (28 May)		(*4 assistant constables*)
1915 (10 Jan)	1930 (14 Oct)	Edwin A Green
1930 (15 Oct)	1946 (23 Jan)	William R Sculpher
1946 (23 Jan)	1965 (30 Apr)	Albert P Lamy
1965 (1 May)	1966 (31 Mar)	Eric A Howard
1966	1976 (30 Sep)	Cyril D Eley
1976	1982 (5 Nov)	Arthur R Bailey
1982 (11 Oct)	1984 (10 Oct)	Alfred D G Wallen
1984 (11 Oct)	1996 (25 Apr)	Michael Le Moignan
1997 (1 Feb)	2003	Michael H Wyeth
2003 (1 Sep)	2010 (30 Jul)	George Le Page
2010 (10 Aug)		Patrick Rice

Notes:
Established as St Peter Port Paid Police
Separate Island Police Force created *for the duration of the War*, 14 Mar 1915
Became Guernsey Island Police Force, 10 Apr 1920, absorbing St Peter Port and other parish constables
Sculpher was suspended by the German Military Command, 5 Mar 1942 and deported until 9 Aug 1945. A Langmead was appointed Acting Chief Officer until 30 Jul 1942, when he was replaced by Albert Lamy

---

Guildford	**1836-1851**	📖

Formed: 20 Jan 1836
Abolished: 17 Feb 1851. Became part of Surrey
Strength: *Initial* 3   *Final* ?
Chief Officer:

1836 (18 Jan)		Richard Jarlett
1841 (28 Sep)	1850	Charles Hollington

Guildford	1854-1943	📖

Re-formed: 16 Oct 1854, from part of Surrey
Abolished: 1 Feb 1943. Became part of Surrey
Strength: *Initial* 5 *Final* 63
Chief Officer:

1854	1854 (31 Dec)	Goff ☫
1855	1863 (30 Nov)	George Vickers ☫
1863 (Dec)	1887	John H Law
1887?	1892	William Berry
1892 (Oct)	1909	William A Worlock ☫
1910 (Jan)	1929 (May)	William V Nicholas ☫
1929 (May)	1943 (31 Jan)	Walter Oliver

Gwent	1967	📖

Formed: 1 Apr 1967, by merger of Monmouthshire and Newport
Strength: *Initial* 836 *Current* 1479
Chief Officer:

1967	1980	W Farley
1980	1993	John E Over
1993	1995	[*Sir*] Anthony T Burden
1996	1999 (16 Apr)	Francis L Wilkinson
1999 (16 Apr)	2003	Keith Turner
2004 (1 Apr)	2008 (3 Sep)	Michael Tonge
2008 (4 Sep)	2011 (31 Mar)	Mick Giannasi
2011 (1 Apr)		Carmel Napier

Notes:
Part of area transferred to South Wales, 1 Apr 1974

Gwynedd	1950-1974	🗁

Formed: 1 Oct 1950, by merger of Anglesey, Caernarvonshire and Merionethshire
Abolished: 1 Apr 1974. Re-named North Wales
Strength: *Initial* 293 *Final* 1156
Chief Officer:

1950 (1 Oct)	1970	Lt Col [*Sir*] William J Williams
1970	1974 (31 Mar)	[*Sir*] Philip A Myers

Notes:
Absorbed Denbighshire and Flintshire, 1 Oct 1967

Haddington	*ca*1844-1874	

Formed: *ca*1844
Abolished: 1874. Became part of East Lothian

Strength: *Initial* 2 [1858]   *Final* 3
Chief Officer:
1844   James Gillies
1858   1873 William Bain

Haddingtonshire	*see* **East Lothian**

Halifax	**1848-1968**	📖

Formed: 7 Jul 1848
Abolished: 1 Oct 1968. Became part of West Yorkshire
Strength: *Initial* 25   *Final* 214   ● 1889
Chief Officer:
1844 (7 Jul)   1851   Thomas Spiers
1851   1872   John Pearson
1872 (6 Aug)   1876   Charles T Clarkson
1876   1903   Charles Pole
1903   1943 (31 Oct) Alfred H Richardson
1944 (1 Jan)   1968   Gerald F Goodman

Hamilton	**1855-1949**

Formed: 1855
Abolished: 1949. Became part of Lanarkshire
Strength: *Initial* 11 [1859]   *Final* 59
1859   Alexander Scott
1860   1876   James S Cullen
1876   1882   *Cmdr* Wallace B McHardy
1882   1919   John Millar
1919   1922   John Clark
1922   1933   Charles Cheyne
1933   1949   Thomas G Smith
Notes:
McHardy was also CC of Lanarkshire

Hamilton	**1958-1967**

Re-formed: 1958, from part of Lanarkshire
Abolished: 16 Aug 1967. Became part of Lanarkshire
Strength: *Initial* 67   *Final* 92
Chief Officer:
1958   1967   Robert B Gordon

Hampshire	**1839**	📖

Formed: Dec 1839
Strength: *Initial* 106   *Current* 3562

Chief Officer:

1839 (Dec)	1842	*Capt* George Robbins
1843 (3 Jan)	1856	*Capt* William C Harris
1856	1891 (Mar)	*Capt* John H Forrest
1891	1893 (30 Nov)	*Capt* Peregrine H T Fellowes ✝
1894 (26 Feb)	1928 (Dec)	*Major* St Andrew B Warde
1929 (1 Jan)	1942 (May)	*Major* Ernest R Cockburn
1942 (1 Jun)	1962	[*Sir*] (Richard) Dawnay Lemon
1962 (14 May)	1977	[*Sir*] Douglas Osmond
1977 (1 Jun)	1988	John Duke
1988 (1 Sep)	1999 (20 Sep)	[*Sir*] John C Hoddinott
1999 (21 Sep)	2008 (15 Oct)	Paul Kernaghan
2008 (16 Oct)		Alex Marshall

Notes:
Absorbed Andover Borough, 1846
Absorbed Lymington Borough, 1852
Absorbed Romsey Borough, 1865
Absorbed Basingstoke and Newport Boroughs, 1 Apr 1889
Isle of Wight set up separate force, 1 Apr 1890
Fellowes died of injuries after trying to stop a runaway horse
Absorbed Isle of Wight and Winchester, 1 Apr 1943
Named Hampshire and Isle of Wight, 1943-67
Bournemouth set up separate force, 1 Apr 1948
Absorbed Portsmouth and Southampton, 1 Apr 1967
Part of area transferred to Dorset, 1 Apr 1974

Hanley	1870-1910	🖿

Formed: 30 Sep 1870, from part of Staffordshire
Abolished: 31 Mar 1910. Became part of Stoke-on-Trent
Strength: *Initial* 31   *Final* 66   ● 1889
Chief Officer:

1870 (30 Sep)	1872 (14 Dec)	Stanford Alexander
1873 (11 Jan)	1875 (Jun)	George Williams
1875 (25 Jun)	1901 (May)	Herbert Windle
1901 (31 Aug)	1910 (31 Mar)	Roger J Carter

Hartlepool	1851-1947	🖿

Formed: 1851, from part of Durham
Abolished: 1 Apr 1947. Became part of Durham
Strength: *Initial* ?   *Final* 28   ● 1902
Chief Officer:

1853	1870	James Waters
1871	1875	John Shiels
1875	1897	John Metcalfe
1898 (Mar)	1930	Albert Winterbottom

1930 (Sep)	1939	Henry Piggott
1939 (Sep)	1943	John W Barnett
1943 (Mar)	1947	J E Robinson

Harwich	1836-1857	🗁

Formed: 4 Jan 1836
Abolished: 1 Feb 1857. Became part of Essex
Strength: *Initial* 13   *Final* 5
Chief Officer:

1836 (4 Jan)	1838	William Burton
1838	1842	Thomas Wilding
1842		James Pain
1848 (Jan)	1857 (31 Jan)	George Coleman

Notes:
Force were initially paid in accordance with duties performed. Became full-time with a strength of CC and 3 constables, 1 Jan 1848

Hastings	1836-1943	📖

Formed: 1 Jun 1836
Abolished: 1 Apr 1943. Became part of Sussex Combined
Strength: *Initial* 13   *Final* 114   ♥ 1889
Chief Officer:

1836 (6 May)	1854 (Oct)	John Campbell
1854 (9 Nov)	1857 (5 Jun)	Charles T Battersby
1857 (27 Jun)	1894 (15 Dec)	William M Glenister ♱
1895 (24 Jan)	1907	Charles F Baker
1907 (Apr)	1933 (31 May)	Frederick James
1933 (1 Jun)	1942	Joseph Bell
1942 (1 May)	1943 (31 Mar)	Angus G Cargill

Hastings	1947-1968	📖

Re-formed: 1 Apr 1947, from part of Sussex Combined
Abolished: 1 Jan 1968. Became part of Sussex
Strength: *Initial* 123   *Final* 160
Chief Officer:

1947 (1 Apr)	1954 (Sep)	*Lt Col* Angus G Cargill
1955 (1 Feb)	1958 (30 Oct)	James R Archer-Burton
1959 (5 Jan)	1967 (31 Dec)	Donald L Brown

Haverfordwest	1835-1889	📖

Formed: 1835
Abolished: 1 Apr 1889. Became part of Pembrokeshire
Strength: *Initial* 4   *Final* 6
Chief Officer:

1836 (7 May)	1839	Thomas M Lewis
1839	1846	*No Chief Officer*
1846 (9 Dec)	1851 (2 Feb)	Harry E Pyme
1851 (3 Feb)	1861 (15 Jun)	John Robinson
1861 (Jun)	1862 (10 Oct)	Josiah C Bowden
1862 (10 Oct)	1869 (16 Nov)	James Cecil
1869 (16 Nov)	1871 (20 Oct)	Richard Lewis
1871 (9 Nov)	1889 (31 Mar)	John Williams

Notes:

Robinson was dismissed after falsely reporting that he had been attacked
Cecil resigned following *an affair of the heart*

Hawick	1840-1930	📖

Formed: 1840
Abolished: 16 May 1930. Became part of Roxburghshire
Strength: *Initial* 6   *Final* 19
Chief Officer:

1840	1846	John Scott
1846	1854	Charles C Rudd
1854 (12 Oct)	1862 (4 Mar?)	James Thom
1862 (4 Mar)	1866	Daniel Munro *or* Monroe
1866	1868	*No Supt*
1868 (15 Feb)	1879 (14 Jan)	William Morrison
1879 (18 Jan?)	1902	John McDonald
1902 (Jul)	1909	John Morren
1909 (Nov)	1930	David Thom

Notes:

Munro absconded, possibly to the USA, together with about £54 of police funds and a baker's wife with whom he was having an affair

---

Hedon	1836-1859

Formed: 1836
Abolished: 1859. Became part of East Riding
Strength: *Initial* ?   *Final* ?
Chief Officer: Not known

Helensburgh	1846-1875	📁

Formed: 1846
Abolished: 1875. Became part of Dumbartonshire
Strength: *Initial* 7 [1870]   *Final* ?
Chief Officer: Not known

Helston	1836-1889

Formed: 1836

Abolished: 1 Apr 1889. Became part of Cornwall
Strength: *Initial* 5 [1858]   *Final* 1
Chief Officer:
| 1859 | 1874 | James Fitzsimmons |
| 1874 | 1889 | John Wedlock |

Henley	1838-1856

Formed: 1838
Abolished: 1856. Became part of Oxfordshire
Strength: *Initial* 2   *Final* ?
Chief Officer: Not known

Hereford	1836-1947	📖

Formed: 1 Feb 1836
Abolished: 1 Apr 1947. Became part of Herefordshire
Strength: *Initial* 17   *Final* 53   🏭 1189
Chief Officer:
1836	1856 (5 Feb)	George Adams
1856 (20 Mar)	1882 (30 Nov)	John Davies
1882 (4 Dec)	1919	Frank Richardson
1919 (Nov)	1927 (Dec)	*Capt* Thomas Rawson
1927 (16 Dec)	1947 (31 Mar)	Freeman Newton

Notes:
Newton was also CC of Herefordshire, 1929-47

Herefordshire	1857-1967	📖

Formed: 19 Jan 1857
Abolished: 1 Oct 1967. Became part of West Mercia
Strength: *Initial* 45   *Final* 270
Chief Officer:
1857 (19 Jan)	1895	*Capt* James D Telfer
1895 (27 Apr)	1923 (30 Sep)	*Capt the Hon* Evelyn T S Stanhope
1923	1929 (Jan)	*Capt* Horace F M Munro
1929 (Feb)	1958	Freeman Newton
1958 (Jul)	1967 (30 Sep)	Robert McCartney

Notes:
CC was also CC of Radnorshire, 1857-68
Absorbed Leominster Borough, 1889
Newton was also CC of Hereford City, 1929-47
Absorbed Hereford City, 1 Apr 1947

Hertford	1836-1889	📁

Formed: 21 Jan 1836
Abolished: 1 Apr 1889. Became part of Hertfordshire

Strength: *Initial* 6   *Final* 9
Chief Officer:

1836 (Jan)	1836 (Jun)	Henry Bishop
1836	1839	George Duncan
1839	1862	Thomas Knight
1862	1889 (31 Mar)	Alfred H Jarrett

Hertfordshire   1841   📖

Formed: 12 Apr 1841
Strength: *Initial* 71   *Current* 2000
Chief Officer:

1841 (12 Apr)	1880	*Capt [Lt Col]* Archibald Robertson ♱
1880 (22 Oct)	1911	*Major [Lt Col]* Henry S Daniell
1911	1928 (8 Nov)	*Major [Lt Col]* Alfred L Law ♱
1928	1939	George T Knight
1939	1943	*Capt [Col]* Sidney M E Fairman
1945 (1 Apr)	1947	*Col [Sir]* Arthur E Young
1947	1969	*Lt Col* Albert F Wilcox
1969	1977	Raymond N Buxton
1977	1984	A F C Clissitt
1984	1990	*[Sir]* Trefor A Morris
1990	1994	Baden H Skitt
1994	2000 (6 Feb)	Peter S Sharpe
2000 (21 Feb)	2004 (31 Aug)	Paul Acres
2004 (1 Sep)	2011 (30 Apr)	Frank Whiteley
2011 (6 Jun)		Andy Bliss

Notes:
Absorbed Hertford Borough, 1 Apr 1889
Absorbed St Albans City, 1 Apr 1947
Absorbed part of Metropolitan, 1 Apr 2000

High Wycombe   *see* **Wycombe**

Higham Ferrers   1836?-1874?   🗁

Formed: 1836?
Abolished: 1874? Became part of Northamptonshire
Strength: *Initial* ?   *Final* ?
Chief Officer: Not known
Notes:
Force presumed to have existed but no details known

Hove   1858-1943   📖

Formed: 1858, from part of East Sussex
Abolished: 1 Apr 1943. Became part of Sussex Combined

Strength: *Initial* 57   **Final** 91
Chief Officer:

1859	1884	(G) Benjamin Breach
1884	1905	*Major* George J Teevan
1905 (1 Jan)	1907	Thomas Davies
1907 (14 Oct)	1919	William J Cocks
1919 (12 May)	1942	William C Hillier
1942	1943	George E Lovell (*Acting CC*)

Huddersfield	**1848-1968**	📖

Formed: Nov 1848
Abolished: 1 Oct 1968. Became part of West Yorkshire
Strength: *Initial* 31   **Final** 313   ♥ 1889
Chief Officer:

1853	1859	G Beaumont
1859	1862	Samuel S Priday
1863	1867	William Hannan
1867 (Dec)	1874 (12 Dec)	James Withers
1875 (Feb)	1879	Henry Hilton
1879 (28 Feb)	1897 (May)	John Ward
1897 (Jul)	1917 (24 Aug)	John Morton
1917 (3 Dec)	1931 (3 May)	*Capt* John W Moore ⚜
1931 (17 Jul)	1933 (30 Nov)	*Capt* William J Hutchinson
1933 (17 Nov)	1940 (31 Mar)	Herbert C Allen
1940 (1 Apr)	1940 (3 Dec)	John Wells ⚜
1941 (17 Feb)	1958 (16 Apr)	James Chadwick
1958 (16 Apr)	1968 (30 Sep)	David Bradley

Notes:
Morton was required to resign following allegations of *indiscreet conduct with a female member of his staff*

Hull	**1836-1974**	📖

Formed: 2 May 1836
Abolished: 1 Apr 1974. Became part of Humberside
Strength: *Initial* 88   **Final** 754   ♥ 1889 🏛 1897
Chief Officer:

1836 (2 May)	1866 (6 Apr)	Alexander McManus ⚜
1866 (Apr)	1880 (17 Sep)	Thomas Cook
1880 (18 Sep)	1885 (2 Dec)	J Campbell
1886 (28 Jan)	1886 (18 Aug)	*Major* Walter E Gilbert
1886 (7 Oct)	1903 (30 Sep)	*Capt* Francis P Gurney
1903 (16 Dec)	1910 (29 Sep)	*Major* [*Lt Col*] Pulteney Malcolm
1910 (29 Sep)	1922 (1 Oct)	[*Sir*] George Morley
1922 (1 Oct)	1928 (5 Aug)	*Capt* W A Woods ⚜

1928 (9 Nov)	1941	Thomas E Howden
1941 (1 Oct)	1947	Thomas Wells
1948 (17 Jun)	1962	Sydney L Lawrence
1962 (5 Jul)	1974 (31 Mar)	Robert W Walton

Humberside	1974	📖

Formed: 1 Apr 1974, from Hull and parts of Lincolnshire, West Yorkshire and York and North East Yorkshire
Strength: *Initial* ?   *Current* 1941
Chief Officer:
Notes:

1974 (1 Apr)	1976	Robert W Walton
1976	1991	David Hall
1992	1999 (8 Mar)	(D) Anthony Leonard
1999 (9 Mar)	2005 (31 Mar)	David Westwood
2005 (1 Apr)		Tim Hollis

Huntingdon	?-1857	🗁

Formed: ?
Abolished: 1857. Became part of Huntingdonshire
Strength: *Initial* ?   *Final* ?
Chief Officer:

Huntingdonshire	1857-1965	📖

Formed: 13 Apr 1857
Abolished: 1 Apr 1965. Became part of Mid-Anglia
Strength: *Initial* 41   *Final* 140
Chief Officer:

1857 (14 Mar)	1876	*Capt [Admiral]* George Davies
1877 (17 Feb)	1901	*Major* (H) Godolphin Roper
1901 (1 Jul)	1927	*Lt Col* Alan G Chichester
1928 (2 Apr)	1957	*Lt Col* J C T Rivett-Carnac
1957 (2 Apr)	1964	Thomas C Williams

Notes:
CC appointed jointly with Cambridgeshire but forces administered separately, 1857-77
Absorbed Godmanchester and Huntingdon Boroughs, 1857
Chichester was also CC of Cambridge 1915-19
CC appointed jointly with Isle of Ely but forces administered separately, 1931-64

Hyde	1899-1947	🗁

Formed: 1 Apr 1899, from part of Cheshire
Abolished: 1 Apr 1947. Became part of Cheshire
Strength: *Initial* 23   *Final* 40

Chief Officer:

1898 (Oct)	1931	J W A Danby ✝
1932	1943	William H Smith
1943	1947	Thomas M Skelton

Hythe	**1844-1889**	📁

Formed: 1844
Abolished: 1 Apr 1889. Became part of Kent
Strength: *Initial* 3 [1858]   *Final* 3
Chief Officer:

1844	1874	John Friend
1874	1878	George Raymond
1878	1889	John Aedy

Inverkeithing	**?-1885**

Formed: Not known
Abolished: 1885. Became part of Fife
Strength: *Initial* 3 [1863]   *Final* 2
Chief Officer:

1859	1869	James Craig
1870	1879	Charles Dow
1880		George Macintosh
1881	1885	John Macdonald

Inverness	**1840-1975**

Formed: 16 Oct 1840
Abolished: 16 May 1975. Became part of Northern
Strength: *Initial* 19   *Final* 198
Chief Officer:

1840 (16 Oct)	1841 (24 Feb)	Eyre J Powell
1841 (24 Aug)	1857 (31 May)	John MacBean
1857 (1 Jun)	1882 (24 Oct)	William Murray
1882 (26 Dec)	1911 (30 Apr)	Alexander McHardy
1911 (2 Jun)	1936 (2 Jun)	Alexander C MacLean
1936 (1 Dec)	1951 (17 Aug)	William Fraser
1951 (18 Aug)	1962 (28 May)	John R Johnstone
1963 (23 Jun)	1975	Andrew L McClure

Notes:
Named Inverness-shire, 1840-1968
Absorbed Inverness Burgh, 16 Nov 1968

Inverness Burgh	**1847-1968**

Formed: 1847
Abolished: 16 Nov 1968. Became part of Inverness

Strength: *Initial* 14 [1858]   *Final* 64
Chief Officer:

1847 (4 Sep)	1854 (3 May)	David Anderson
1854 (31 Jul)	1872 (13 May)	John Sutherland
1872 (16 Jun)	1880 (8 Jan)	Thomas Wyness
1880 (25 Feb)	1908 (30 Apr)	John Macdonald
1908 (4 May)	1936 (1 Jan)	John McNaughton
1936 (26 Jan)	1942 (19 Oct)	Alexander Neville
1943 (11 Jan)	1946 (10 Aug)	James Stewart
1946 (11 Aug)	1949 (16 May)	Andrew Meldrum
1950 (15 Mar)	1962 (18 Aug)	William Paterson
1963 (4 Feb)	1968 (15 Nov)	Thomas Sorley

Ipswich   1836-1967   📖

Formed: 1 Mar 1836
Abolished: 1 Apr 1967. Became part of Suffolk
Strength: *Initial* 18   *Final* 248   ♥ 1889
Chief Officer:

1836		*Three Insps*
1841 (1 Apr)	1842	John Hatton
1842 (15 Jul)	1844	Joseph *or* James E Smith
1844 (13 Aug)	1878	William Carrington Mason
1879 (4 Jan)	1907	*Lt Col* H R Russell
1907 (1 Jul)	1936	*Capt* Arthur J Schreiber
1936 (1 Apr)	1946	Charles J Cresswell
1946 (1 Dec)	1967 (31 Mar)	James Crawford

Notes:
The entire force was dismissed on 5 Aug 1842 and the borough had no police until Smith and Mason were re-appointed, with others, 5 Sep 1842

Irish Revenue   180?-1857   📖

Formed: early 19th century
Abolished: 1857. Became part of Royal Ulster
Strength: *Initial* ?   *Final* ?
Chief Officer: Not known

Isle of Ely   1841-1965

Formed: 9 Feb 1841
Abolished: 1 Apr 1965. Became part of Mid-Anglia
Strength: *Initial* 37   *Final* 169
Chief Officer:

1841	1858	F B Hampton
1858	1878	*Capt* J W Foster
1878 (Nov)	1906	*Major* [*Col*] (W) Ferris Browne

1906	1919	*Capt* John H Mander
1919 (14 Aug)	1931	*Major* W R Hartcup
1931	1957	*Lt Col* J C T Rivett-Carnac
1957	1964	Thomas C Williams
1964	1965	J W Davis (*Acting CC*)

Notes:
Mander was appointed temporary CC of Norfolk for the duration of the War, 8 May 1915
CC appointed jointly with Huntingdonshire but forces administered separately, 1931-64

| **Isle of Man** | **1863** | 📖 |

Formed: 7 Sep 1863
Strength: *Initial* 37   *Current* 237
Chief Officer:

1863 (21 Oct)	1873	*Capt* George P Goldie ✝
1874 (7 Jan)	1878 (May)	*Capt* [*Sir*] David Monro
1878 (10 May)	1888	*Lt Col* William H Paul
1888 (24 May)	1911 (Jul)	*Lt Col* William Freeth
1911 (6 Jul)	1936 (19 Sep)	*Lt Col* Henry W Madoc
1936 (19 Sep)	1954	*Major* John W Young ✝
1955	1972	Christopher C Beaty-Pownall
1972 (7 Feb)	1986	Frank Weedon
1986	1999 (Sep)	Robin E N Oake
1999 (Dec)	2007 (31 Dec)	Mike Culverhouse
2008 (1 Jan)		Mike Langdon

| **Isle of Wight** | **1890-1943** | 📖 |

Formed: 1 Apr 1890, from part of Hampshire
Abolished: 1 Apr 1943. Became part of Hampshire
Strength: *Initial* 48   *Final* 79
Chief Officer:

1890 (10 Apr)	1898	Thomas O H Lees
1899 (1 Mar)	1935	*Capt* Harry G Adams-Connor
1935 (1 Oct)	1937 (31 Dec?)	*Capt* [*Major*] Colin D Robertson
1938	1943	*Lt Col* Roy G B Spicer

Notes:
Formation of the force was delayed by a year (from 1889) after objections by Hampshire
Absorbed Ryde Borough, 1 Apr 1922

| **Jedburgh** | **1857-1861** |

Formed: 1857
Abolished: 1861. Became part of Roxburghshire

Strength: *Initial* ?   *Final* ?
Chief Officer: Not known

Jersey	1853	📖

Formed: 1853
Strength: *Initial* 10   *Current* 236
Chief Officer:

1952	1964	E H Le Brocq
1964	1966	L E Johnson
1966	1973 (16 Apr)	James Axon ♱
1974	1983	Edward Cockerham
1983	1993	David Parkinson
1994	2000 (31 Dec)	R H Le Breton
2001 (1 Dec)	2010?	Graham Power
2011 (Jan)		Mike Bowron

Notes:
Originally covered only the Parish of St Helier and named St Helier Paid Police
Extended to whole island and re-named Jersey Paid Police, 24 May 1952
Re-named States of Jersey Police, 1960

Johnstone	1857-1930

Formed: 1857
Abolished: 16 May 1930. Became part of Renfrewshire
Strength: *Initial* 6 [1870]   *Final* 16
Chief Officer:

1871	1871	Walter Holmes
1872	1894	John Fraser
1894	1924	Charles Forbes
1924 (22 Sep)	1930	William MacLeod

Kelso	1854-1881

Formed: Feb 1854
Abolished: 16 Feb 1881. Became part of Roxburghshire
Strength: *Initial* 3   *Final* ?
Chief Officer:

1828	1854	John Smith
1854	1881 (15 Feb)	John Moscrop *or* Moscrip

Notes:
An earlier force existed from 1757

Kendal	1836-1947

Formed: 11 Jan 1836
Abolished: 1 Apr 1947. Became part of Westmorland
Strength: *Initial* 4   *Final* 24

Chief Officer:

1876 (1 May)	1882 (12 Jan)	Joseph Wilkinson
1881 (Dec)	1890	Thomas Cotton
1890 (Jun)	1895	Luke Talbot
1895 (Nov)	1899	George Hardy
1899 (May)	1900	James Burrows
1900 (*ca*5 Oct)	1902	Charles E Harris
1902 (Dec)	1908	A M Berry
1908 (May)	1923	(I) Joseph Smith
1923 (1 Jan)	1947	Patrick O'Neill

Notes:
Administered by the CC of Westmorland, 1836-76

Kent	1857	📖

Formed: 14 Jan 1857
Strength: *Initial* 231   *Current* 3641
Chief Officer:

1857 (14 Jan)	1894 (14 Aug)	*Capt* John H H Ruxton
1894 (15 Aug)	1895 (20 Apr)	*Major* Henry H Edwards ✝
1895 (27 May)	1921 (20 Jun)	*Lt Col* Henry M A Warde
1921 (20 Jun)	1940 (18 Feb)	*Major* Henry E Chapman
1940 (19 Feb)	1942 (10 Oct)	*Capt* John A Davison ✝
1943 (1 Mar)	1946 (30 Apr)	*Capt Sir* Percy J Sillitoe
1946 (15 Aug)	1958 (Oct)	*Major* [*Sir*] John F Ferguson
1958 (1 Nov)	1961	Geoffrey C White ✝
1962 (1 Apr)	1974	[*Sir*] (Richard) Dawnay Lemon
1974	1982	Barry N Pain
1982	1989	Francis L Jordan
1989	1993	[*Sir* later *Lord*] Paul L Condon
1993	2003 (Dec)	[*Sir*] (J) David Phillips
2004 (4 Jan)	2010 (1 Apr)	Michael Fuller
2010 (5 Jul)		Ian Learmonth

Notes:
Absorbed Ashford Borough 1857?
Absorbed Romney Marsh, 1888
Absorbed Deal, Faversham, Hythe, Sandwich and Tenterden Boroughs, 1 Apr 1889
Davison committed suicide
Absorbed Canterbury and Rochester Cities, Dover, Folkestone, Gravesend, Maidstone, Margate, Ramsgate and Tunbridge Wells Boroughs, 1 Apr 1943
Fuller was the first black man to appointed CC in the UK

Kidderminster	1835-1947	

Formed: 1835
Abolished: 1 Apr 1947. Became part of Worcestershire
Strength: *Initial* 14 [1858]   *Final* 44

Chief Officer:

1853	1868	James Gifford
1869	1873	*Capt* C J Hampton
1873	1884	George Haigh
1884	1887	George Ebury
1887 (25 Apr)	1918	E Bennett
1918 (3 Sep)	1919	G Smith
1919 (18 Feb)	1928	Frederick Gray
1928 (23 May)	1931	Ernest W Tinkler
1931 (1 Nov)	1932	(T) Mark Watson
1933 (1 Jul)	1947 (Mar)	H Hodgkinson

Kidwelly	1857-1858	📖

Formed: Dec 1857
Abolished: 2 Sep 1858. Became part of Carmarthenshire
Strength: *Initial* 1   *Final* 1
Chief Officer:

1857?	1858	Rowland

Notes:
The borough set up the force in the mistaken belief that it had police powers and disputed the jurisdiction of the County force. The County CC sent 2 men to Kidwelly in Aug 1858 and eventually the borough accepted defeat on 2 Sep 1858

Kilmarnock	1846-1968

Formed: 1846
Abolished: 16 May 1968. Became part of Ayrshire
Strength: *Initial* 12 [1858]   *Final* 119
Chief Officer:

1846	1855	W Blane
1861		Alexander Galt
1869	1897	George Willison
1898	1904	George Hill
1905		John Campbell
1909	1921	Angus Cameron
1921	1947	Charles Roy
1947	1960	John Grant
1960	1968	William D Gammie

Kilsyth	1840-?

Formed: 1840
Abolished: Not known. Became part of Stirlingshire?
Strength: *Initial* 40?   *Final* ?
Chief Officer:

1840	William Hendry

Kincardineshire	1841-1949	📂

Formed: 1841
Abolished: 16 May 1949. Became part of Scottish North-eastern Counties
Strength: *Initial* 21　　　　*Final* 27
Chief Officer:

1841 (Dec)	1885	Alexander Weir
1885 (Nov)	1924 (May)	Charles George
1924 (May)	1949 (15 May)	Robert Mitchell

King's Lynn	1836-1947	📂

Formed: 8 Jan 1836
Abolished: 1 Apr 1947. Became part of Norfolk
Strength: *Initial* 14　　　　*Final* 42
Chief Officer:

1836 (8 Jan)		William Andrews (*Supt*, Night Watch)
1836 (15 Oct)	1850	John Woods (*Supt*, Day Watch) ✝
1850 (16 Mar)	1861 (25 Mar)	Newton F Thornton
1861 (20 Feb)	1866	Cornelius Reeves
1866 (1 Nov)	1898 (May)	George Ware
1898 (28 Jun)	1913 (May?)	Walter G Payne
1913 (21 Jun)	1923	Charles W Hunt
1923 (7 Aug)	1945 (Sep)	Henry W Young
1945 (19 Sep)	1947 (31 Mar)	Fred Calvert

Kington	1841-1850	

Formed: 14 Jun 1841
Abolished: 30 Jun 1850
Strength: *Initial* ?　　　　*Final* ?
Chief Officer:

1841 (17 Apr)	Robert Langdon

Kinning Park	1892-1905	

Formed: 15 Aug 1892
Abolished: 7 Nov 1905. Became part of Glasgow
Strength: *Initial* 14　　　　*Final* 16
Chief Officer:

1892 (15 Aug)	1905 (7 Nov)	*Capt* Charles Harding

Notes:
Harding was also CC of Bute and Renfrewshire

Kinross-shire	1836-1930	📂

Formed: 1836
Abolished: 16 May 1930. Became part of Perthshire & Kinross-shire

Strength: *Initial* 5		Final 8-9
Chief Officer:		
1836	1837 (May)	John Dease?
1837		John MacDougall
1842	1843 (8 Sep)	Peter Robertson
1843		*Various unknown names*
	1855	Henry Buchan
1857	1858	Peter Clark
1858	1868	George Gordon
1869	1891	Peter Clark
1891	1903	*Capt* James F Bremner
1903 (9 Dec)	1930 (15 May)	James T Gordon

Notes:
G Gordon was also CC of Clackmannanshire and Perthshire
Bremner and J T Gordon were also CC of Fife

Kirkcaldy	1840-1845	☐

Formed: 1840
Abolished: 25 Nov 1845. Became part of Fife
Strength: *Initial* ?   Final 2
Chief Officer: Not known

Kirkcaldy	1877-1949	☐

Re-formed: 11 Nov 1877, from part of Fife
Abolished: 16 May 1949. Became part of Fife
Strength: *Initial* 16   Final 64
Chief Officer:

1877 (Nov)	1892	William Chalmers
1892	1924	David Gatherum
1924	1930	Robert Pryde
1930	1933	David Warnock
1933	1949	David Baldie

Notes:
Chalmers was suspended on 19 Sep 1892 after being found *in a helpless state on High Street, apparently intoxicated*. He died in Nov 1892 but it is not clear whether he was still chief officer

Kirkcudbrightshire	1839-1948	

Formed: 1839
Abolished: 16 Feb 1948. Became part of Dumfries & Galloway
Strength: *Initial* 17 [1859]   Final 30
Chief Officer:

1842	1858	J G MacDougal[l]
1858	1866	John Johnston

1866 (10 Apr)	1907?	Alexander Davidson
1907 (17 Dec)	1939	Alexander Donald
1939 (16 Nov)	1948 (15 Feb)	*Lt Col* William Kerr

Notes:
Force re-organised 1842
Absorbed Maxwelltown Burgh, 16 May 1890
Donald was also CC of Wigtownshire, 1922-39

| Kirkintilloch | 1838-1872 | |

Formed: 1838
Abolished: 15 Jan 1872. Became part of Dunbartonshire
Strength: *Initial* 4   *Final* 4
Chief Officer:

1841	1841	Lyon
1841		Pollock
1841		James McLaren
1842		William White
1847		Alexander Martin
1867	1872	Peter McCall

Notes:
Pollock was dismissed for embezzlement
Martin was dismissed, as were 3 other Supts, 1849-50

| Kirriemuir | 1859-1891 | |

Formed: 1859
Abolished: 1891. Became part of Forfarshire
Strength: *Initial* ?   *Final* ?
Chief Officer:

| | 1866 | John Malcolm |

| Knightlow Hundred | 1840-57 | |

Formed: Mar 1840
Abolished: 5 Feb 1857. Became part of Warwickshire
Strength: *Initial* ?   *Final* ?
Chief Officer:

| 1840 | 1841 | *Capt* George Baker |
| 1841 (May) | 1857 (4 Feb) | James Isaac |

| Lanarkshire | 1850-1975 | |

Formed: 1850
Abolished: 16 May 1975. Became part of Strathclyde
Strength: *Initial* 128 [1857]   *Final* 1249
Chief Officer:

1850		Gavin Miller
1857	1875	George McKay
1875 (1 Dec)	1896	*Cmdr* Wallace B McHardy
1896 (6 Mar)	1926	*Capt* Herbert J Despard
1926 (15 Apr)	1945	Andrew N Keith
1945 (24 Mar)	1958	Thomas Renfrew
1957 (Dec)	1966	John Wilson
1967 (16 Aug)	1975 (15 May)	James K McLellan

Notes:

Force orginally covered only Airdrie district

Absrobed Wishaw, 1859

Coatbridge set up separate force, 1886

Motherwell and Wishaw set up separate force, 16 May 1930

Absorbed Hamilton Burgh, 1949

Hamilton Burgh re-established separate force, 1958

Absorbed Airdrie, Coatbridge and Motherwell and Wishaw Burghs and re-absorbed Hamilton Burgh, 16 Aug 1967

Lancashire	**1839**	📖

Formed: 18 Dec 1839

Strength: *Initial* 500 *Current* 3343

Chief Officer:

1839 (18 Dec)	1856 (11 Sep)	*Capt* [*Lt Col*] John Woodford
1856 (11 Sep)	1859 (29 Aug)	*Capt* Thomas W Sheppard
1859 (6 Sep)	1868 (5 Feb)	*Capt* William P Elgee
1868 (6 Feb)	1876 (30 Dec)	*Col* Robert Bruce
1877 (29 Mar)	1880 (31 May)	*The Hon* Charles G Legge
1880 (1 Jul)	1909 (31 Oct)	*Lt Col* Henry M Moorsom
1909 (1 Nov)	1912 (31 May)	Charles V Ibbetson
1912 (1 Jun)	1927 (24 Apr)	[*Sir*] Harry P P Lane ✟
1927 (5 May)	1935 (31 Aug)	Wilfred Trubshaw
1935 (1 Oct)	1950 (17 Apr)	*Capt* [*Sir*] Archibald F Hordern ✟
1950 (1 Oct)	1967	*Col* [*Sir*] (Thomas) Eric St Johnston
1969	1972 (29 Feb)	William J H Palfrey
1972 (1 Mar)	1977 (20 Dec)	Stanley Parr
1977	1978	John W Moody (*Acting CC*)
1978	1983	Albert Laugharne
1983 (18 Mar)	1995 (26 Jul)	(Robert) Brian Johnson
1995 (31 Jul)	2002 (24 Jul)	Pauline A Clare
2002 (25 Jul)	2005 (15 Mar)	[*Sir*] Paul R Stephenson
2005 (16 Mar)		Steve Finnigan

Notes:

Uniform was rifle green, 1839-*ca*1844 and for most of 1865

Ashton-under-Lyne set up separate force, 1848

Blackburn set up separate force, 1 Mar 1852

Bacup, Blackpool, Bootle, Burnley, Clitheroe and St Helens set up separate forces, 1 Jul 1887
Absorbed Accrington, Ashton-under-Lyme, Bacup and Clitheroe Boroughs and Lancaster City, 1 Apr 1947
Absorbed Barrow-in-Furness, Blackburn, Blackpool, Bolton, Burnley. Oldham, Preston, Rochdale, Saint Helens, Southport, Warrington and Wigan Boroughs, 1 Apr 1969
Parts of area transferred to Cheshire, Cumbria, Greater Manchester and Merseyside, 1 Apr 1974
Parr was dismissed for interference in cases at Blackpool (his former force)
Mrs Clare was the first woman to be appointed CC in the UK

Lancaster	1824-1947	📖

Formed: 1824
Abolished: 1 Apr 1947. Became part of Lancashire
Strength: *Initial* 7   *Final* 62   🏭 1937
Chief Officer:

1835	1857	Malcolm Wright
1857	1865	John Allison
1865	1881	Thomas Pye
1881	1883	Frederick T Webb
1884	1902	Frank Ward
1902 (Nov)	1933	Charles E Harriss
1933 (Aug)	1937	Henry J Vann
1937 (Jul)	1947 (31 Mar)	William M Thompson

Langholm	1846-1893	

Formed: 1846
Abolished: 15 May 1893. Became part of Dumfries-shire
Strength: *Initial* ?   *Final* ?
Chief Officer: Not known

Launceston	1836-1883	📁

Formed: 1836
Abolished: Jan 1883. Became part of Cornwall
Strength: *Initial* 1 [1858]   *Final* 1
Chief Officer:

1861	1883	Edward Barrett

Leamington Spa	1825-1947	📖

Formed: 1825
Abolished: 1 Apr 1947. Became part of Warwickshire
Strength: *Initial* 21   *Final* 59
Chief Officer:

		John Palmer
1839		William S Roby
1853	1859 (Apr)	James Thompson
1859	1881	John Lund
1881	1900	Joseph F Brabner
1900	1902	Alexander Thomson
1902	1938	Thomas T Earnshaw ✝
1938	1939	John A T Hanlon
1939	1941	*Col [Sir]* Arthur E Young
1941	1942	*[Sir]* Charles C Martin
1943	1947	William Rees

Leeds	1836-1974	📖

Formed: 2 Apr 1836
Abolished: 1 Apr 1974. Became part of West Yorkshire
Strength: *Initial* 20   *Final* 1413   ♥ 1889 ⚒ 1893
Chief Officer:

1836 (25 Mar)	1837 (27 Oct)	William Heywood
1837 (8 Dec)	1859 (1 Jan)	Edward Read
1859 (Feb)	1862 (Jan)	Stephen English
1862 (Jan)	1866 (15 Aug)	William R Bell ✝
1866 (22 Sep)	1874 (26 Oct)	James Wetherell ✝
1875 (Feb)	1878 (May)	William Henderson
1878 (May)	1881 (Aug)	*Capt [Sir]* (John) William Nott-Bower
1881 (28 Sep)	1890 (Feb)	Arthur B Nott-Bower
1890 (21 Mar)	1899 (17 Nov)	Frederick T Webb
1900 (12 Feb)	1912 (31 Jul)	*Major* George G Tarry
1912 (6 Dec)	1919 (24 Jul)	William B Lindley ✝
1919 (2 Oct)	1922	*Lt Col* Frederick J Lemon
1923 (15 Jun)	1937 (3 Feb)	Robert L Matthews
1937 (26 Feb)	1947 (1 Mar)	Frank Swaby
1947 (7 Feb)	1956 (30 Jun)	John W Barnett
1956 (1 Oct)	1967 (28 Sep)	Alexander J Paterson ✝
1968 (1 May)	1974 (31 Mar)	James Angus

Notes:
Heywood was dismissed for drinking instead of attending a fire
The Nott-Bowers were brothers
Paterson died while addressing an Interpol conference in Japan

Leicester	1836-1967	📖

Formed: 10 Feb 1836
Abolished: 1 Apr 1967. Became part of Leicestershire
Strength: *Initial* 51   *Final* 570   ♥ 1889 ⚒ 1919
Chief Officer:

1836 (19 Jan)	1839 (10 Dec)	Frederick Goodyer

1840 (Jan)	1871 (Oct)	Robert Charters
1871 (27 Oct)	1882 (Feb)	Joseph Farndale
1882 (15 Mar)	1894 (Jun)	James Duns
1894 (18 Jul)	1907 (Jun)	Thomas W Lumley
1907 (Sep)	1913 (Feb)	*Major [Lt Col]* John Hall-Dalwood
1913 (25 Feb)	1928 (Dec)	Herbert Allen
1929 (1 Jan)	1955 (Dec)	Oswald J B Cole
1956 (17 Jan)	1956 (Oct)	Neil Galbraith
1957 (1 Jan)	1967 (31 Jan)	*[Sir]* Robert Mark

Leicestershire   1839   📖

Formed: 21 Dec 1839
Strength: *Initial* 25   *Current* 2192
Chief Officer:

1839 (7 Dec)	1876 (Sep)	Frederick Goodyer
1876	1889	*Capt* Roland V S Grimston
1889 (22 Jun)	1928	Edward Holmes
1928 (1 Oct)	1949	*Major* Cecil E Lynch-Blosse
1950	1972	John A Taylor
1972	1986	Alan Goodson
1986	1993	Michael J Hirst
1993	1997	*[Sir]* Keith Povey
1997 (Jun)	2002 (6 Sep)	David J Wyrko
2002 (9 Dec)	2009 (22 Sep)	Matthew Baggott
2010 (14 Jun)		Simon Cole

Notes:
Absorbed Rutland, 1 Apr 1951
Named Leicestershire and Rutland, 1951-1967
Absorbed Leicester City, 1 Apr 1967
Named Leicester and Rutland, 1967-74

Leith   1859-1920   📖

Formed: 1859
Abolished: 2 Nov 1920. Became part of Edinburgh
Strength: *Initial* 30   *Final* 165
Chief Officer:

1859	1886	James Grant
1886	1906	Alexander Main
1906	1920	John MacLeod

Leominster   1836-1889   📖

Formed: Feb 1836
Abolished: 1 Apr 1889. Became part of Herefordshire
Strength: *Initial* 6   *Final* 8

Chief Officer:

1836 (1 Apr)	1841 (24 Jun)	William S Smith
1841 (7 Aug)	1862 (May)	John McCrohon
1862	1866	Standford Alexander
1866 (7 Aug)	1889 (31 Mar)	George A Johnson

Lerwick	1892-1940

Formed: 1892
Abolished: 29 May 1940. Became part of Zetland
Strength: *Initial* 3   *Final* 6
Chief Officer:

1892	1892	George Mackay
1892	1896	John Wallace
1896	1900	William J Anderson
1900	1905	Leslie E Mitchell
1905	1925	Gordon Emslie
1925	1940	James McWilliam

Lichfield	1856-1889

Formed: From part of Staffordshire
Abolished: 1 Apr 1889. Became part of Staffordshire
Strength: *Initial* 4 [1859]   *Final* 8   🏭 1553
Chief Officer:

1861	1866	John Ryder
1867	1871	D Mynard
1872	1889	William Hernaman

Lincoln	1829-1967

Formed: Sep 1829
Abolished: 1 Apr 1967. Became part of Lincolnshire
Strength: *Initial* 18 [1858]   *Final* 172   ♥ 1889 🏭 1189
Chief Officer:

1842 (Apr)	1856	John Turner
1856	1858	John Mason
1859	1868	James Handley
1869	1901	William Mansell
1901 (Sep)	1912	John T Coleman
1912 (Jan)	1915 (Oct)	Frederick J Crawley
1915 (Oct)	1940	William S Hughes
1940 (Jun)	1958	Charles H Walters
1958 (Mar)	1967	F Sayer

Lincolnshire	1857	📖

Formed: 1 Jan 1857

Strength: *Initial* 207   *Current* 1171
Chief Officer:

1856 (6 Nov)	1902 (31 Jan)	*Capt* Philip B Bicknell
1902 (1 Feb)	1903 (31 Jul)	*Major* Charles M E Brinkley ♱
1903 (29 Oct)	1931 (11 Oct)	*Capt* Cecil Mitchell-Innes
1931 (12 Oct)	1934 (15 Jan)	*Col* Gordon H R Halland
1934 (16 Jan)	1954 (31 Jul)	[*Sir*] Raymond H Fooks
1954 (1 Aug)	1956 (31 May)	*Lt Col* (Herman) Graham Rutherford
1956 (1 Jul)	1969 (Dec)	John W Barnett
1970	1973	[*Sir*] George W R Terry
1973	1977	[*Sir*] Lawrence Byford
1977	1983	James Kerr
1983	1990	S W Crump
1990	1993	N G Ovens
1993	1998 (23 May)	(J) Peter Bensley
1998 (24 May)	2003 (23 Sep)	Richard J N Childs
2003 (24 Sep)	2008 (Jun)	J A [Tony] Lake
2008 (16 Jun)		Richard Crompton

Notes:
Legally, there were three forces (one for each of the Parts of the County) under one CC until 1964
Absorbed Stamford Borough, 1 Apr 1889
Absorbed Louth Borough, 1 Oct 1920
Absorbed Boston and Grantham Boroughs, 1 Apr 1947
Absorbed Grimsby and Lincoln City, 1 Apr 1967

Linlithgowshire	*see* **West Lothian**

Liskeard	**1836-1877**	🗁

Formed: 1836
Abolished: 16 Jul 1877. Became part of Cornwall
Strength: *Initial* 2 [1856]   *Final* 3
Chief Officer:

1859	1877	Richard Humphries

Liverpool	**1836-1974**	📖

Formed: 9 Feb 1836
Abolished: 1 Apr 1974. Became part of Merseyside
Strength: *Initial* 390   *Final* 2851   ♥ 1889 ▟ 1880
Chief Officer:

1836 (9 Feb)	1844 (6 Jan)	Michael J Whitty
1844 (27 Feb)	1844 (26 Oct)	Henry Miller
1844	1852 (Mar)	Matthew M G Dowling
1852	1881	*Capt* [*Major*] John J Greig

1881 (30 Aug)	1902 (21 Mar)	*Capt* [*Sir*] (John) William Nott-Bower
1902	1912	[*Sir*] Leonard Dunning
1912 (Jan)	1925	Francis Caldwell
1925	1931	Lionel D L Everett
1932	1940 (Mar)	Archibald K Wilson
1940	1948 (Apr)	Herbert Winstanley
1948	1958	[*Sir*] Charles C Martin
1958	1964 (Nov)	Joseph W T Smith
1965 (Jun)	1974 (31 Mar)	[*Sir*] James Haughton

Notes:
Absorbed Bootle, 1 Apr 1967
Named Liverpool and Bootle, 1967-74

Londonderry	**1848-1870**	

Formed: 1848   1613
Abolished: 1870. Became part of Royal Irish
Strength: *Initial* ?   *Final* ?
Chief Officer: Not known

Lothian and Borders	**1975**	

Formed: 16 May 1975, by merger of Berwick Roxburgh and Selkirk, Edinburgh City and Lothians and Peebles
Strength: *Initial* 2368   *Current* 2959
Chief Officer:

1975 (16 May)	1983 (12 Jun)	[*Sir*] John H Orr
1983 (12 Jun)	1996 (5 Sep)	[*Sir*] William G M Sutherland
1996 (6 Sep)	2002 (13 Jan)	[*Sir*] (Hugh) Roy G Cameron
2002 (4 Jan)	2007 (28 Mar)	Paddy Tomkins
2007 (29 Mar)		David J R Strang

Lothians and Peebles	**1950-1975**	

Formed: 16 May 1950, by merger of East Lothian, Mid Lothian, Peebles-shire and West Lothian
Abolished: 16 May 1975. Became part of Lothian and Borders
Strength: *Initial* 281   *Final* 633
Chief Officer:

1950 (16 May)	1968 (23 Sep)	William Merrilees
1968 (24 Sep)	1975 (15 May)	[*Sir*] John H Orr

Notes:
The four component forces had actually been commanded by one CC since 1894

Louth	**1836-1920**	

Formed: 12 Feb 1836
Abolished: 1 Oct 1920. Became part of Lincolnshire

Strength: *Initial* 8   *Final* 9
Chief Officer:

1837 (9 Jan)	1845 (13 Nov)	John Campbell
1845 (13 Nov)	1866 (9 Feb)	John W Tacey
1866 (10 Feb)	1878 (26 Feb)	William Roberts
1878 (20 Feb)	1886 (16 Sep)	William Lloyd ✟
1886 (19 Oct)	1891 (3 Jun)	James T Enwright
1891 (3 Jun)	1901 (19 Feb)	J W Barham
1901 (19 Mar)	1907 (31 Jan)	Arthur E Danby
1907 (21 Jan)	1920 (30 Sep)	James Sparrow

Notes:
Original force disbanded in 1837 and replaced by a Supt and 3 constables

---

Ludlow   **1836-1889**   🗁

Formed: 1836
Abolished: 1 Apr 1889. Became part of Shropshire
Strength: *Initial* ?   *Final* 5
Chief Officer:

1836	1837 (10 Aug)	William Davies
1851	1855 (Jul)	Robert Jones
1855 (Jul)	1865 (27 Feb)	Henry Biggs ✟
1865 (23 Mar)	1885 (31 Jul)	George [or Charles?] H Brookes
1885 (6 Aug)	1888 (4 Oct)	James C Wheatstone
1888 (11 Oct)	1889 (31 Mar)	John Simcox (*Acting*)

Luton   **1876-1947**   📖

Formed: 30 Sep 1876, from part of Bedfordshire
Abolished: 1 Apr 1947. Became part of Bedfordshire
Strength: *Initial* 22   *Final* 134
Chief Officer:

1876 (30 Sep)	1894 (30 Sep)	David Jaquest
1894 (1 Oct)	1916 (13 Dec)	David Teale ✟
1917 (8 May)	1920 (30 May)	Charles Griffin
1920 (1 Jul)	1936 (23 Jun)	Albert Scott ✟
1936 (1 Sep)	1944 (30 Sep)	[*Sir*] George E Scott
1944 (1 Nov)	1947 (31 Mar)	Ronald Alderson

Luton   **1964-1966**   📖

Re-formed: 1 Apr 1964, from part of Bedfordshire
Abolished: 1 Apr 1966. Became part of Bedfordshire
Strength: *Initial* 239   *Final* 286   ● 1964
Chief Officer:

1964 (1 Apr)	1966 (31 Mar)	Joseph Pessell

Lyme Regis	1829-1860

Formed: 1829
Abolished: 3 Apr 1860. Became part of Dorset
Strength: *Initial* 3   *Final* 2
Chief Officer:
1836   1860   William B Wright

Lymington	1836-1852

Formed: 1836
Abolished: 1852. Became part of Hampshire
Strength: *Initial* 3   *Final* ?
Chief Officer:
              1852   G Waghorn

Macclesfield	1836-1947	📖

Formed: 19 Jan 1836
Abolished: 31 Mar 1947. Became part of Cheshire
Strength: *Initial* 7   *Final* 51
Chief Officer:
1836 (Jan)	1840	William Lockett
1840	1842	Edward Stockwin
1842 (2 Dec)	1860	William Harper
1860	1874	James Etchells
1874	1903	William Sheasby
1903	1907	John Berry
1907 (13 May)	1942	Henry Sheasby
1942 (15 Feb)	1944	Ronald Alderson
1945	1947 (31 Mar)	William G Symmons

Notes:
Henry Sheasby was the son of William Sheasby

Macduff	1859-1870

Formed: 1859
Abolished: 17 May 1870. Became part of Banffshire
Strength: *Initial* ?   *Final* 1
Chief Officer: Not known

Maidenhead	1836-1889	🗁

Formed: 27 Jan 1836
Abolished: 1 Apr 1889. Became part of Berkshire
Strength: *Initial* 4   *Final* 11
Chief Officer:
1836 (27 Jan)   1862   Daniel Sexton

1863	1875	Henry MacGraw
1875	1880	William H Austin
1880 (1 Sep)	1889	James Taylor

Maidstone	**1837-1943**	📖

Formed: 1 Apr 1837
Abolished: 1 Apr 1943. Became part of Kent
Strength: *Initial* 16   *Final* 64
Chief Officer:

1837	1854	Thomas Fancett
1854	1865	John Blundell
1866	1868	John Barnes
1869	1882	W Gifford
1882	1895	Henry Dalton
1895 (May)	1921 (Nov)	Angus C Mackintosh
1921 (29 Nov)	1936	Charles E Butler
1936	1942	Henry J Vann
1942	1943 (31 Mar)	G Beslee (*Acting CC*)

Maldon	**1836-1889**	📖

Formed: 5 Jan 1836
Abolished: 1 Apr 1889. Became part of Essex
Strength: *Initial* 11   *Final* 5
Chief Officer:

1836 (5 Jan)	1840	John Bale *or* Beale
1840		John Raymond
1844	1853?	William Clarke
1853 (15 Aug)		Frederick Chilvers
1863	1878	William King
1878	1888	George Wombwell
1888	1889	Charles Halsey

Notes:
The initial 11 officers included John Bale and John Beale. It is not clear whether Bale, Beale or both became chief constable

Manchester	**1839-1974**	📖

Formed: Jun 1839
Abolished: 1 Apr 1974. Became part of Greater Manchester
Strength: *Initial* 347   *Final* 2433   ♥ 1889 ⚒ 1853
Chief Officer:

1839 (Jun)	1839 (Sep)	Richard Beswick
1839 (17 Oct)	1842 (30 Sep)	*Sir* Charles Shaw
1842 (24 Oct)	1857 (19 Mar)	*Capt* Edward Willis
1857 (Mar)	1881 (Feb)	*Capt* William H Palin

1881 (10 Feb)	1898 (Apr)	Charles M Wood	
1898 (6 Apr)	1926 (18 Nov)	[*Sir*] Robert Peacock ✝	
1927 (Mar)	1943	[*Sir*] John Maxwell	
1943	1958	Joseph Bell	
1959	1966	[*Sir*] John A McKay	
1966 (Jul)	1974 (31 Mar)	William J Richards	

Notes:
The force was controlled by a government-appointed Commissioner because of doubts over the legality of the Borough's charter of incorporation, 1839-42
Absorbed Salford, 1 Apr 1968
Named Manchester and Salford, 1968-74

Margate	**1858-1943**	📖

Formed: 1858
Abolished: 1 Apr 1943. Became part of Kent
Strength: *Initial* 6   *Final* 71
Chief Officer:

{1858	1860	Daniel Shelvey	}
{1858	1868	Henry Saunders	}See Notes
1868 (Mar)	1876	T M Compton	
1876	1888 (Oct)	(R) Wilcocks Romanis	
1889 (10 Mar)	1893 (Jun?)	Charles Buck	
1893	1897	Joseph Farndale	
1897	1902 (Dec)	James H Clegg	
1902 (Nov)	1904	A R Ellerington	
1905 (Mar)	1923	Alfred Appleyard	
1923 (1 Apr)	1930 (May)	Charles J Haycock	
1930 (6 Aug)	1943 (31 Mar)	William Palmer	

Notes:
Published histories differ on the name of the first chief officer
Saunders was required to resign following a discrepancy of £26 in the pension fund

Marine Police	**1798-1839**	🗁

Formed: 26 Jun 1798
Abolished: 1 Sep 1839. Became part of the Metropolitan Police
Strength: *Initial ca*1300   *Final* ?
Chief Officer:

1798 (2 Jul)	1800 (2 Jul)	M Armstrong
1800 (2 Jul)	1821 (6 Jul)	John Gotty
1821 (6 Jul)	1839 (31 Aug)	James Evans

Notes:
Initial strength includes *ca*1000 lumpers and master lumpers (labourers to unload ships). Actual police strength *ca*290, including 220 ship constables paid for by shipowners

Maryhill	1856-1891

Formed: 1856
Abolished: 7 Jul 1891. Became part of Glasgow City
Strength: *Initial* 7 [1858]   *Final* 20
Chief Officer:

1856	1886	George Anderson
1886	1891	James Beddie

Maxwelltown	1863-1890

Formed: 1863
Abolished: 16 May 1890. Became part of Kirkcudbrightshire
Strength: *Initial* 2 [1879]   *Final* 3
Chief Officer:

1879	1890 (15 May)	William F MacKay

Maybole	1859-1861

Formed: 1859
Abolished: 1861. Became part of Ayrshire
Strength: *Initial* ?   *Final* ?
Chief Officer: Not known

Merionethshire	1857-1950

Formed: 30 Sep 1857
Abolished: 1 Oct 1950. Became part of Gwynedd
Strength: *Initial* 19   *Final* 46
Chief Officer:

1857 (5 Jan)	1879	*Capt* H H Lloyd-Clough
1880 (Apr)	1883 (7 Feb)	Thomas Ellis ♱
1883 (Apr)	1907	*Major the Hon* Thomas W Best
1907	1911 (2 Mar)	Thomas Jones ♱
1911 (8 May)	1950	Richard Jones

Merseyside	1974

Formed: 1 Apr 1974
Strength: *Initial* ?   *Current* 4222
Chief Officer:

1974 (1 Apr)	1975	[*Sir*] James Haughton
1976	1989	[*Sir*] Kenneth G Oxford
1989	1998 (20 Oct)	[*Sir*] James Sharples
1998 (16 Nov)	2005 (5 Jan)	[*Sir*] Norman Bettison
2004 (13 Nov)	2009 (4 Oct)	Bernard Hogan-Howe
2010 (1 Feb)		Jon Murphy

Notes:

Bettison was seconded to Centrex and thus overlapped with Hogan-Howe

Merthyr Tydfil	1831-1841	📂

Formed: 18 Nov 1831?
Abolished: 1841. Became part of Glamorgan
Strength: *Initial* 1   *Final* 3
Chief Officer:

1831 (18 Nov)	1832 (*ca* Apr)	T Jamieson
1832	1841	*No Chief officer*

Notes:
Jamieson's services were dispensed with. A force of 3 other officers had already been appointed from a police fund contributed by wealthy inhabitants, Mar 1832

Merthyr Tydfil	1908-1969	📖

Re-formed: 1 Oct 1908, from part of Glamorgan
Abolished: 1 Jun 1969. Became part of South Wales
Strength: *Initial* 85   *Final* 141
Chief Officer:

1908 (15 Aug)	1920	[*Sir*] James A Wilson
1920 (27 Nov)	1937	David M Davies
1937 (13 Jul)	1945	T A Goodwin
1945 (20 Feb)	1963	Melbourne Thomas
1963 (1 Dec)	1969	T K Griffiths

Notes:
The initial strength included 10 officers paid for by private companies (4 sgts, 1 acting sgt and 5 PCs)

Metropolitan	1829	📖

Formed: 29 Sep 1829
Strength: *Initial* *ca*3000   *Current* 31993
Chief Officer:

1829 (7 Jul)	1868 (26 Dec)	[*Sir*] Richard Mayne
1829 (7 Jul)	1850 (5 Jan)	*Col Sir* Charles Rowan
1850 (6 Jan)	1855 (29 Aug)	*Capt* William Hay ✝
1869 (13 Feb)	1886 (26 Mar)	*Col Sir* Edmund Henderson
1886 (29 Mar)	1888 (1 Dec)	*Gen* [*Sir*] Charles Warren
1888 (3 Dec)	1890 (21 Jun)	James Monro
1890 (23 Jun)	1903 (4 Mar)	*Col Sir* Edward Bradford
1903 (5 Mar)	1918 (2 Sep)	[*Sir*] Edward R Henry
1918 (3 Sep)	1920 (14 Apr)	*Gen* [*Rt Hon*] *Sir* C F Nevil Macready
1920 (20 Apr)	1928 (7 Nov)	*Brig Gen* [*Sir*] William Horwood
1928 (8 Nov)	1931 (30 Sep)	*Gen Lord* [*Field Marshal Viscount*] Julian H G Byng of Vimy
1931 (2 Nov)	1935 (11 Nov)	*Marshal of the RAF Lord* [*Viscount*]

		Hugh M Trenchard
1935 (29 Nov)	1945 (31 May)	*Air Vice-Marshal Sir* Philip W Game
1945 (1 Jun)	1953 (13 Aug)	*Sir* Harold R Scott
1953 (14 Aug)	1958 (31 Aug)	*Sir* John R N Nott-Bower
1958 (1 Sep)	1968 (20 Mar)	[*Sir*] Joseph Simpson ✝
1968 (21 Mar)	1972 (16 Apr)	*Sir* John L Waldron
1972 (17 Apr)	1977 (12 Mar)	[*Sir*] Robert Mark
1977 (13 Mar)	1982 (1 Oct)	[*Sir*] David B McNee
1982 (2 Oct)	1987 (1 Aug)	*Sir* Kenneth L Newman
1987 (2 Aug)	1993 (1 Feb)	[*Sir* later *Lord*] Peter M Imbert
1993 (1 Feb)	2000 (31 Jan)	[*Sir* later *Lord*] Paul L Condon
2000 (1 Feb)	2005 (31 Jan)	[*Sir* later *Lord*] John A Stevens
2005 (1 Feb)	2008 (30 Nov)	*Sir* [later *Lord*] Ian Blair
2009 (28 Jan)	2011	*Sir* Paul Stephenson
2011 (26 Sep)		Bernard Hogan-Howe

Notes:
Absorbed Marine Police, 1 Sep 1839
Absorbed Croydon Borough, 12 Jan 1840
Mayne was joint Commissioner with Rowan or Hay until 1855
Col D W P Labalmondière, Asst Commissioner, was appointed Acting Commissioner, 30 Dec 1868-12 Feb 1869
Absorbed part of Essex, 1 Apr 1965
Parts of area transferred to Essex, Hertfordshire and Surrey, 1 Apr 2000

Mid-Anglia	**1965-1974**	📖

Formed: 1 Apr 1965, by merger of Cambridge City, Cambridgeshire, Huntingdonshire, Isle of Ely and Peterborough
Abolished: 1 Apr 1974. Re-named Cambridgeshire
Strength: *Initial* 881   *Final* 1022
Chief Officer:

1965 (1 Apr)	1974 (31 Mar)	Frederick Drayton Porter

Mid Lothian	**1840-1950**

Formed: May 1840
Abolished: 16 May 1950. Became part of Lothians and Peebles
Strength: *Initial* 41 [1858]   *Final* 107
Chief Officer:

1840 (1 May)	1877 (23 Dec)	Alfred J List
1877 (24 Dec)	1878 (26 Apr)	H Stuart Johnson
1878 (27 Apr)	1884 (3 Jun)	*Capt* David Munro
1884 (29 Jul)	1914 (6 Oct)	*Lt Col* Alexander Borthwick ✝
1914 (8 Dec)	1950 (15 May)	*Major* Sholto W Douglas

Notes:
Force originally named Edinburghshire, until *ca*1892
Absorbed Dalkeith, date not known

Absorbed Portobello Burgh, 1859
Johnson and Munro were also CC of West Lothian
From 1894 to 1950, the same CC administered four forces: East Lothian, Mid Lothian, Peebles-shire and West Lothian

Mid-Wales	1948-1968	📁

Formed: 1 Apr 1948, by merger of Breconshire, Montgomeryshire and Radnorshire
Abolished: 1 Apr 1968. Became part of Dyfed-Powys
Strength: *Initial* 132   *Final* 235
Chief Officer:

1948 (1 Apr)	1959	*Capt [Sir]* Humphrey C Lloyd
1959 (1 Apr)	1963	R E G Benbow
1963 (11 Nov)	1968	Richard B Thomas

Middlesbrough	1841-1968	📖

Formed: 24 Jul 1841
Abolished: 1 Apr 1968. Became part of Teesside
Strength: *Initial* 1   *Final* 345   ♥ 1889
Chief Officer:

1841	1844 (Feb)	Richard Ord
1844		John Thomas
1845 (Oct)	1849 (May)	Richard Ord
1849 (Jun)	1850 (Oct)	James Amos
1850	1850?	Richard Ord
1851?	1853 (May)	William Kilvington
1853 (Apr)	1861	William Hannan *or* Hannen
1861 (22 Jul)	1884 (Jul/Oct)	Edward J Saggerson
1884	1902	William Ashe
1902 (24 Jun)	1930 (5 Dec)	(W) Henry Riches
1931 (28 Jan)	1938 (22 Oct)	Donald Heald ✟
1939 (9 Feb)	1956	Alfred E Edwards
1956 (8 Apr)	1968 (31 Mar)	Ralph Davison

Notes:
Ord was appointed 3 times as First (or sole) Police Officer

Mold	1841-?

Formed: May 1841
Abolished: Not known. Became part of Flintshire
Strength: *Initial* 4?   *Final* ?
Chief Officer:

1841 (1 May)	[1844]	Christopher Carnes

Monmouth	1836-1881

Formed: 1836

Abolished: 29 Sep 1881. Became part of Monmouthshire
Strength: *Initial* 4   *Final* 6
Chief Officer:
1857 (12 Oct)   1881   Edmund Wheeldon

Monmouthshire	1857-1967	📖

Formed: 23 Mar 1857
Abolished: 1 Apr 1967. Became part of Gwent
Strength: *Initial* 47   *Final* 536
Chief Officer:

1857 (23 Mar)	1893 (31 Dec)	*Major* Edmund P Herbert
1894 (1 Jan)	1936 (7 Sep)	Victor F Bosanquet
1936 (26 Oct)	1950 (13 May)	*Major [Col]* W R Lucas
1950 (14 May)	1956 (4 Jul)	Ronald Alderson ✟
1956 (18 Dec)	1964	Neil Galbraith
1965	1967	W Farley

Notes:
Absorbed Abergavenny, 23 Mar 1857
Absorbed Trevethin, 1 Apr 1860
Absorbed Monmouth Borough, 29 Sep 1881

Montgomeryshire	1840-1948	📖

Formed: 23 Jul 1840
Abolished: 1 Apr 1948. Became part of Mid-Wales
Strength: *Initial* 15   *Final* 45
Chief Officer:

1840 (23 Jul)	1845 (30 Jun)	*Major* James H Newcombe
1845 (2 Jul)	1863 (14 Apr)	William Baird
1863 (7 Jul)	1868 (28 Mar)	John Hodgson ✟
1868 (13 Jul)	1887 (31 Aug)	John Danily
1887 (1 Sep)	1892 (1 May)	*Major* George A Godfrey
1892 (14 May)	1899 (1 Aug)	Robert W Hughes
1899 (25 Aug)	1925 (30 Sep)	(William) James Holland
1925 (1 Oct)	1927 (22 Sep)	*Capt* Cecil E Lynch-Blosse
1927 (22 Sep)	1931 (30 Sep)	*Capt* James E Lloyd-Williams
1932 (1 Oct)	1936 (30 Jun)	David P Parry
1936 (1 Jul)	1948 (31 Mar)	*Capt [Sir]* Humphrey C Lloyd

Notes:
Force commenced active duties on 14 Sep 1840
Uniform was originally green with white embroidery and buttons
Absorbed Welshpool Borough, 1857
Capt R A Bush was appointed CC but the Home Office refused to approve the appointment, Mar 1932. Parry had been acting CC since the resignation of Lloyd-Williams
Lloyd was also CC of Radnorshire, 1946-8

Montrose		1833-1930

Formed: 11 Nov 1833
Abolished: 16 May 1930. Became part of Angus
Strength: *Initial* 15 [1870]   *Final* 14
Chief Officer:

1833 (11 Nov)	1833 (27 Nov)	Robert Wills
1833 (27 Nov)		James Smith
1871	1873	Patrick Webster
1874	1898	James Wilson
1898	1899	Robert T Birnie
1900	1930	Alexander Marr

Moray and Nairn		1930-1949	📁

Formed: 16 Jun 1930, by merger of Morayshire and Nairnshire
Abolished: 16 May 1949. Became part of Scottish North-eastern Counties
Strength: *Initial* 41   *Final* 56
Chief Officer

1930 (16 Jun)	1949 (15 May)	William Stewart

Morayshire		1890-1930	📁

Formed: 1890, by renaming of Elginshire
Abolished: 16 Jun 1930. Became part of Moray and Nairn
Strength: *Initial* ?   *Final* ?
Chief Officer:

1890	1891	James Pirie
1892 (8 Jan)	1927 (26 Jan)	John B Mair ✟
1927 (27 Apr)	1930 (15 Jun)	William Stewart

Notes:
Absorbed Elgin City, 1 Mar 1893

Motherwell	[1915]

A separate force was due to be formed from part of Lanarkshire in 1915 but the plan was postponed then abandoned because of World War 1

Motherwell and Wishaw		1930-1967

Formed: 16 May 1930, from part of Lanarkshire
Abolished: 16 Aug 1967. Became part of Lanarkshire
Strength: *Initial* 70   *Final* 154
Chief Officer:

1930	1931	William H Welsh
1931	1942	George Lamont
1942	1965	John A R Murray
1965 (1 Feb)	1967 (15 Aug)	James K McLellan

Musselburgh	1835-1841?

Formed: 1835
Abolished: 1841? Became part of East Lothian
Strength: *Initial* ?   *Final* ?
Chief Officer:

1835	1841?	George H List

Nairn	1859-1866

Formed: 1859
Abolished: 1866. Became part of Nairnshire
Strength: *Initial* ?   *Final* 2
Chief Officer: Not known

Nairnshire	1850-1930	🗁

Formed: 1850
Abolished: 16 Jun 1930. Became part of Moray and Nairn
Strength: *Initial* 4   *Final* 9
Chief Officer:

1850		John Wilson
1858	1859	Alexander Macpherson
1859	1866	George Walker
1866 (22 Aug)	1906	James Stirling
1906 (1 Oct)	1930	John Bruce

Notes:
Absorbed Nairn Burgh, 1866

Neath	1836-1947	📖

Formed: 9 Feb 1836
Abolished: 1 Apr 1947. Became part of Glamorgan
Strength: *Initial* 1   *Final* 45
Chief Officer:

1836 (9 Feb)	1837 (Dec)	David Protheroe
1837 (Dec)	1839 (May)	Jenkin Francis
1839	1839? (Nov)	Penry Gwyn
1839 (Nov)	1841 (Dec)	William Rees
1842 (May)	1844 (Feb)	William Morgan
1844 (Mar)	1852 (Mar)	William Rees
1852 (Mar)	1857 (12 Oct)	John Worman
1857	1860 (May)	John Lynn
1860 (14 May)	1888 (Sep)	John Phillips
1888	1899 (Nov)	Evan Evans
1899	1900	Robert Kilpatrick
1900 (Nov)	1906 (Aug)	Evan Lewis
1906 (1 Oct)	1907 (14 Apr)	Richard Jones ✝

1907 (27 May)	1921	William Higgins
1921 (2 Nov)	1926 (May)	*Capt [Lt Col]* Horatio Rawlings
1926 (4 or 7 May)	1943	Percy D Keep
1944 (1 Jan)	1947	W V Doolan

Notes:
Rees remained in the force after the appointment of Worman but resigned, Sep 1852

New Sarum	**1836-1838**	🗁

Formed: 8 Jan 1836
Abolished: 26 Apr 1838. Disbanded and re-organised as Salisbury
Strength: *Initial* 16 　　　　　 *Final* ?
Chief officer: Not known

Newark	**1836-1947**	🗁

Formed: 1836
Abolished: 1 Apr 1947. Became part of Nottinghamshire
Strength: *Initial* 5 　　　　　 *Final* 27
Chief Officer:

1835		Richard Bell
1853		Thomas Watterton
1857	1891	Edward Liddell
1891 (11 Dec)	1907	James Challen
1907 (Mar)	1927 (Mar)	Albert Wright
1927 (Apr)	1933	James McConnach
1933	1933	Henry J Vann
1933	1935	Marshall H Bolt
1935	1939	Harry Barnes
1939 (1 May)	1941 (Oct)	Gerald F Goodman
1941 (14 Oct)	1947 (31 Mar)	Reginald T W Millhouse

Newburgh	**1859-1869**	🗁

Formed: 1859
Abolished: 1869. Became part of Fife
Strength: *Initial* 1 　　　　　 *Final* 1
Chief Officer: Not known

Newbury	**1836-1875**	📖

Formed: 26 Mar 1836
Abolished: 26 Mar 1875. Became part of Berkshire
Strength: *Initial* 8 　　　　　 *Final* 6
Chief Officer:

1836 (1 Mar)	1852 (22 May)	Alfred Milsom ☩
1852 (7 Jul)	1873 (25 Aug)	George Deane ☩
1873 (10 Sep)	1875 (25 Mar)	George Goddard

Newcastle-under-Lyme	1834-1947	📖

Formed: 1 Nov 1834
Abolished: 1 Apr 1947. Became part of Staffordshire
Strength: *Initial* 3   *Final* 78
Chief Officer:

1834 (1 Nov)	1849 (Dec)	Isaac Cottrill
1850 (7 Feb)	1855	John T Blood
1855	1857	Charles Barnes
1857	1861	Charles Booth
1861	1866	John Williams
1866	1870 (21 Sep)	Standford Alexander
1870	1878	Walter Jones
1878	1881 (7 May)	Charles Blyth ♱
1881	1891 (1 Feb)	Frederick Dutton
1891 (19 May)	1898 (19 Apr)	George Taylor
1898 (4 Jun)	1901	John Stirling
1901 (Sep)	1903 (15 Apr)	Alfred H Richardson
1903 (Jun)	1912 (Jun)	George Ingram
1912 (12 Aug)	1932 (13 Apr)	William Forster ♱
1932 (18 Jun)	1936 (22 Mar)	George S Lowe
1936 (23 Mar)	1943 (Feb)	Wesley Bate
1943 (10 May)	1946 (31 Oct)	George S Jackson
1946 (1 Nov)	1947 (31 Mar)	Ernest Lewis (*Acting CC*)

Notes:
Cottrill was dismissed for misappropriating fire brigade funds

Newcastle-upon-Tyne	1832-1833	🗀

Formed: 1832
Abolished: Disbanded Sep 1833
Strength: *Initial* 8   *Final* 8
Chief officer: Not known

Newcastle-upon-Tyne	1836-1969	📖

Re-formed: 2 May 1836
Abolished: 1 Apr 1969. Became part of Northumberland
Strength: *Initial* 85   *Final* 727   ♥1889 🏰 1882
Chief Officer:

1836 (Apr)	1854	John Stephens
1854	1857	[*Sir*] John Dunne
1857	1867	John H Sabbage ♱
1868	1869	*Capt* William C Sylvester
1869	1898 (Dec)	*Capt* Samuel J Nicholls
1899 (Feb)	1925	James B Wright
1925 (Jul)	1944	Frederick J Crawley

1944 (1 Oct)	1948	[*Sir*] George E Scott
1948 (1 Jun)	1964	George S Jackson
1964 (15 Jun)	1969	Frank S Gale

Notes:
Stephens set up the River Tyne Police and commanded it, 1845-84
Nicholls was required to resign after complaints of rough treatment of his men

---

Newport [Isle of Wight]	**1837-1889**

Formed: 1837
Abolished: 1 Apr 1889. Became part of the Isle of Wight
Strength: *Initial* 5   *Final* 10
Chief Officer:

1853	1872	George Grapes
1873	1881	William C Ross
1881 (5 Nov)	1888 (12 Nov)	Henry Blackwell
1888	1889	W Salter (*Acting CC*)

Newport [Monmouthshire]	**1836-1967**	📖

Formed: 1 Feb 1836
Abolished: 1 Apr 1967. Became part of Gwent
Strength: *Initial* 15   *Final* 260
Chief Officer:

1836 (1 Feb)	1837 (21 Nov)	John Redman
1837 (17 Dec)	1848 (4 Feb)	Edward Hopkins
1848 (5 Feb)	1852 (30 Apr)	Stephen English
1852 (1 May)	1875 (8 Nov)	John G Huxtable
1875 (9 Nov)	1912 (31 Jul)	Alan I Sinclair
1912 (1 Aug)	1928 (31 Dec)	*Capt* Charles E Gower
1929 (1 Jan)	1940 (31 Aug)	William H Robinson
1940 (1 Sep)	1952 (29 Feb)	Clifford M Harris
1952 (28 Apr)	1967	Francis H Smeed

Notes:
Harris was required to resign for disciplinary offences

Norfolk	**1839**	📖

Formed: 22 Nov 1839
Strength: *Initial* 133   *Current* 1596
Chief Officer:

1840 (Jan)	1852 (Jul)	*Lt Col* Richard M Oakes
1852 (22 Oct)	1880	George Black
1880 (23 Sep)	1909 (30 Sep)	[*Sir*] Paynton Pigott
1909 (1 Oct)	1915 (7 May)	*Major* Egbert Napier
1915 (8 May)	1927 (9 Dec)	*Capt* John H Mander ✝
1928 (10 Feb)	1956	*Capt* Stephen H Van Neck

1956 (30 Jun)	1975 (Mar)	(Frederick) Peter C Garland
1975 (1 Apr)	1980	(Charles) Gordon Taylor
1980 (1 Mar)	1990	George Charlton
1990	1993 (30 May)	Peter J Ryan
1993 (5 Jul)	2002 (Dec)	Kenneth R Williams
2002	2005 (18 Feb)	Andy Hayman
2005 (19 Feb)	2006 (31 Dec)	Carole Howlett (*Temp CC*)
2007 (2 Jan)	2009 (31 Dec)	Ian McPherson
2010 (22 Mar)		Phil Gormley

Notes:
Absorbed Thetford Borough, 22 Jul 1857
Mander was also CC of Isle of Ely and was appointed temporarily to Norfolk in 1915, permanently from 18 Mar 1916
Absorbed King's Lynn Borough, 1 Apr 1947
Absorbed Great Yarmouth Borough and Norwich City, 1 Jan 1968

North Berwick	**?-1858**	

Formed: by 1844
Abolished: 1858. Became part of Haddingtonshire (East Lothian)
Strength: *Initial* ?   *Final* ?
Chief Officer:

1844	Alexander Hatcheon

North Riding	**1856-1968**	📖

Formed: 14 Oct 1856
Abolished: 1 Jul 1968. Became part of York and North-east Yorkshire
Strength: *Initial* 51   *Final* 781
Chief Officer:

1856 (28 Oct)	1898 (7 Jul)	*Capt* Thomas Hill
1898 (30 Sep)	1929 (13 Jun)	*Major* [*Sir*] Robert L Bower ✞
1929 (1 Oct)	1958	*Lt Col* John C Chaytor
1958 (1 Nov)	1965	*Lt Col* James R Archer-Burton
1965	1968 (30 Jun)	Harold H Salisbury

Notes:
Absorbed Gilling West Division, 14 Oct 1856?
Absorbed Richmond Borough, 1 Apr 1889
Absorbed Scarborough Borough, 1 Apr 1947
Part of area transferred to Teesside, 1 Apr 1968

North Wales	**1974**	📖

Formed: 1 Apr 1974, by renaming of Gwynedd
Strength: *Initial* 1156   *Current* 1531
Chief Officer:

1974 (1 Apr)	1981	[*Sir*] Philip A Myers

1982 (1 Apr)	1994 (31 Mar)	David Owen
1994 (27 May)	2000 (31 Dec)	Michael J Argent
2001 (1 Jan)	2009 (30 Jul)	Richard Brunstrom
2009 (10 Sep)		Mark Polin

North Yorkshire   1974   📖

Formed: 1 Apr 1974, from part of York and North-east Yorkshire
Strength: *Initial* 1277   *Current* 1429
Chief Officer:

1974	1977	R P Boyes
1978	1979	[*Sir*] John Woodcock
1979	1985	K Henshaw
1985	1989	Peter J Nobes
1989	1998 (16 Feb)	David M Burke
1998 (2 Feb)	2002	David R Kenworthy
2002 (14 Oct)	2007 (16 May)	Della Cannings
2007 (16 May)		Grahame Maxwell

Northampton   1836-1966   📖

Formed: 11 Jan 1836
Abolished: 1 Apr 1966. Became part of Northamptonshire
Strength: *Initial* 13   *Final* 212   ♥1889
Chief Officer:

1836 (11 Jan)	1851 (24 Apr)	Joseph Ball
1851 (25 Apr)	1887 (29 Sep)	Henry Keenan
1887 (17 Oct)	1923 (31 Dec)	Frederick H Mardlin
1924 (1 Jan)	1955 (30 Jun)	John Williamson
1955 (1 Jul)	1966 (31 Mar)	Dennis R Baker

Northamptonshire   1840   📖

Formed: Jan 1840
Strength: *Initial* 29   *Current* 1317
Chief Officer:

1840 (25 Apr)	1849 (3 Jan)	Henry Goddard
1849 (12 May)	1875 (Jul)	*Capt* Henry L Bayly
1875 (19 Oct)	1875 (19 Oct)	Charles Pearson
1875 (25 Nov)	1881	Thomas O H Lees
1881 (19 Oct)	1931 (31 May)	James D Kellie-MacCallum
1931 (1 Jun)	1941	Angus A Ferguson
1941 (18 Aug)	1960 (13 Jan)	Robert H D Bolton
1960 (13 Jan)	1972 (3 Sep)	John A H Gott ✝
1973 (1 Jan)	1980 (31 Dec)	Frederick A Cutting
1981 (1 Jan)	1986 (Nov)	Maurice Buck
1986 (Dec)	1993	[*Sir*] David J O'Dowd

1993	1996 (25 Aug)	[*Sir*] Edward M Crew
1996 (2 Dec)	2003 (5 Apr)	[*Sir*] Christopher Fox
2003 (6 May)	2009 (21 Jun)	Peter F Maddison
2009 (12 Oct)		Adrian Lee

Notes:
CC was also CC of Peterborough Liberty, 1857-1931
Absorbed Higham Ferrers, 1874?
Pearson resigned within 3 hours of appointment, because of a disagreement over housing
Absorbed Daventry Borough, 1 Apr 1889
Kellie-MacCallum was the longest serving CC in the UK
Absorbed Northampton Borough, 1 Apr 1966
Named Northampton and County, 1966-74

Northern		**1969**

Formed: 16 May 1969, by merger of Caithness-shire, Orkney and Zetland
Strength: *Initial* 100   *Current* 782
Chief Officer:

1969 (16 May)	1975	Robert F P McNeill
1973 (1 Aug)	1985	Donald B Henderson
1986	1996	Hugh C MacMillan
1996 (Oct)	2001 (31 Aug)	William A Robertson
2001 (24 Sep)	2011 (Sep)	Ian Latimer

Notes:
Absorbed Inverness, Ross and Sutherland and parts of Argyllshire and Scottish North-eastern Counties, 16 May 1975

Northern Ireland		**2001-**

Formed: 5 Nov 2001, by re-naming of Royal Ulster
Strength: *Initial*   *Current* 7271

2001 (5 Nov)	2002 (31 Mar)	*Sir* Ronnie Flanagan
2002 (2 Sep)	2009 (31 Aug)	[*Sir*] Hugh Orde
2009 (23 Sep)		Matthew Baggott

Northumberland		**1857-1974**	📖

Formed: 1 Apr 1857
Abolished: 1 Apr 1974. Became part of Northumbria
Strength: *Initial* 61   *Final* 1902
Chief Officer:

1857 (15 Jan)	1869 (15 Oct)	*Major* Alexander Browne
1869 (1 Nov)	1886 (9 Jan)	*Major Gen* George Allgood
1886 (29 Mar)	1900 (15 Mar)	*Capt* Herbert D Terry
1900 (4 Jul)	1935 (5 Sep)	*Capt* [*Sir*] Fullarton James
1935 (6 Sep)	1943 (30 Jan)	*Capt* [*Sir*] Henry Studdy

1943 (15 Mar)	1946 (30 Nov)	[*Sir*] Joseph Simpson
1946 (1 Dec)	1953 (30 Sep)	Francis J Armstrong
1953 (1 Nov)	1963 (31 Mar)	Alan U R Scroggie
1963 (1 Aug)	1974 (31 Mar)	Clarence H Cooksley

Notes:
Absorbed Berwick-upon-Tweed Borough, 1 Apr 1921
Absorbed Newcastle-upon-Tyne City and Tynemouth Borough, 1 Apr 1969

Northumbria   **1974**   📖

Formed: 1 Apr 1974, from Northumberland and part of Durham
Strength: *Initial* 1902   *Current* 4144
Chief Officer:

1974 (1 Apr)	1975	Clarence H Cooksley
1975	1991	[*Sir*] Stanley E Bailey
1991	1996 (Oct)	[*Sir* later *Lord*] John A Stevens
1998	2005 (31 Mar)	(J) Crispian Strachan
2005 (1 Apr)	2010 (31 Mar)	Michael Craik
2011 (20 Apr)		Sue Sim

Norwich   **1836-1968**   📖

Formed: 22 Jan 1836
Abolished: 1 Jan 1968. Became part of Norfolk
Strength: *Initial* 80   *Final* 271   ♥1889 🏭 1195
Chief Officer:

1836 (18 Jan)	1839 (24 Dec)	William Wright
1839	1851 (31 Jul?)	Peter M Yarrington
1851	1853	[*Sir*] John Dunne
1853 (6 Jul)	1859	Stephen English
1859 (24 Mar)	1897 (30 Apr)	Robert Hitchman
1897 (May)	1917	Edwin F Winch
1917 (25 May)	1943 (31 Dec)	John H Dain
1944 (1 Jan)	1963	Alan F Plume
1964 (1 Jan)	1968	Frank A Brown

Nottingham   **1841-1968**   📖

Formed: 1841
Abolished: 1 Apr 1968. Became part of Nottinghamshire
Strength: *Initial* 49   *Final* 791   ♥1889 🏭 1897
Chief Officer:

1814	1833	Richard Birch
1833	1851	William Barnes
1852?		Thomas Wakefield
1851?	1854	William Reddish
1854	1860	William B Raynor

1860	1865	Joseph Hedington
1865	1869	John Freeman
1869	1872	*Capt* Francis J Parry
1872	1881 (Oct)	*Major* William H Poyntz
1881 (Nov)	1892	Samuel Stevens
1892 (4 Nov)	1912	Philip S Clay
1912 (25 Sep)	1920	Thomas C Clarke
1920 (1 Sep)	1929	*Lt Col* [*Sir*] Frank Brook
1930	1959 (Dec)	*Capt* Athelstan Popkess
1960	1968 (31 Mar)	Thomas Moore

Notes:
Wakefield is named as CC in some historical sources but others list only Barnes, immediately succeeded by Reddish

Nottinghamshire	**1840**	📖
Formed: Apr 1840		
Strength: *Initial* 42	*Current* 2269	
Chief Officer:		
1840 (21 Apr)	1842 (Feb)	*Major* Samuel Walker
1842 (Feb)	1852 (Oct)	R Valentine Hatton
1852 (Oct)	1856 (Jul)	*Capt* John H Forrest
1856 (8 Jul)	1892 (Nov)	*Capt* Henry Holden
1892 (1 Dec)	1922 (12 Oct)	*Capt* [*Sir*] William H Tomasson ✝
1923 (1 Mar)	1949 (Dec)	*Lt Col* Frederick J Lemon
1949 (1 Dec)	1970	John E S Browne
1970	1976	Rex S Fletcher
1976	1987 (May)	Charles MacLachlan
1987	1990	[*Sir*] Ronald Hadfield
1990	1995	[*Sir*] Dan Crompton
1995	2000 (23 Jun)	Colin F Bailey
2000 (24 Jun)	2008 (20 Jun)	Stephen M Green
2008 (23 Jun)		Julia Hodson

Notes:
Absorbed Retford Borough, 1 Jan 1841
Absorbed Newark Borough, 1 Apr 1947
Absorbed Nottingham City, 1 Apr 1968
Named Nottinghamshire Combined, 1968-74
Part of area transferred to South Yorkshire, 1 Apr 1974

Okehampton	**1836-1860**	
Formed: 1836		
Abolished: 1860. Became part of Devon		
Strength: *Initial* 1	*Final* 1	
Chief Officer:		
1836	1860	J Milman

Oldham	1849-1969	📖

Formed: 14 Nov 1849
Abolished: 1 Apr 1969. Became part of Lancashire
Strength: *Initial* 12   *Final* 272   💧1889
Chief Officer:

1849	1858	John Jackson
1858 (18 Nov)	1859 (7 Mar)	Abraham A Hunter
1859 (28 Mar)	1861 (Jul)	Edward Lees
1861 (Aug)	1866 (Sep)	James Wetherell
1866	1892	Charles Hodgkinson
1892	1898 (Mar)	[*Sir*] Robert Peacock
1898 (May)	1917 (Dec)	David H Turner
1917 (1 Nov)	1941 (31 Dec)	Arthur K Mayall
1942 (1 Jan)	1958 (11 May)	Walter E Schofield 🛡
1958 (1 Oct)	1967 (31 Oct)	Fred Berry
1967 (1 Nov)	1968 (31 Mar)	Leslie Palmer (*Acting CC*)

Orford	?-1859

Formed: Not known
Abolished: Jul 1860. Became part of East Suffolk
Strength: *Initial* ?   *Final* 1
Chief Officer:

1858	1859	William Peck

Orkney	1858-1969

Formed: 1858
Abolished: 16 May 1969. Became part of Northern
Strength: *Initial* 21 [1917]   *Final* 27
Chief Officer:

1858	1898	Alexander Grant
1898	1900	Colin Cruickshanks
1900 (Jun)	1907	R Atkin
1907 (May)	1927	Robert Wood
1927 (Apr)	1938	John M Tulloch
1938 (15 Jan)	1944 (15 Jun)	Wilson C Campbell
1944 (19 Jun)	1959	Gathorne H Cheyne
1959 (16 May)	1969	James Cormack

Notes:
The force was not subject to the Police (Scotland) Act 1857 until 15 Jan 1938

Oswestry	1836-1861	🗁

Formed: 12 Feb 1836
Abolished: 1 Apr 1861. Became part of Shropshire
Strength: *Initial* 2   *Final* 4

Chief Officer:

1836 (12 Feb)	1851 (1 Oct)	Jacob Smith
1851 (1 Oct)	1856	John Donald
1857 (Sep)	1861 (31 Mar)	William Sykes

Oxford	1869-1968	📖

Formed: 1 Jan 1869
Abolished: 1 Apr 1968. Became part of Thames Valley
Strength: *Initial* 10   *Final* 315   ♥1889 🏭1542
Chief Officer:

1869 (1 Jan)	1897 (12 Mar)	Charles Head
1897 (13 Mar)	1924 (7 Mar)	Oswald Cole ⚜
1924 (7 Apr)	1956	Charles R Fox
1956 (1 Jul)	1968 (31 Mar)	Clement G Burrows

Oxfordshire	1857-1968	📖

Formed: 25 Mar 1857
Abolished: 1 Apr 1968. Became part of Thames Valley
Strength: *Initial* 10   *Final* 393
Chief Officer:

1857 (27 Feb)	1888 (2 Jul)	(Charles) Mostyn Owen
1888 (3 Jul)	1917 (10 Oct)	*Lt Col the Hon* E A Holmes-à-Court
1917 (11 Oct)	1920 (11 Dec)	*Major* Douglas W Roberts
1921 (28 Feb)	1940 (10 Jul)	*Capt* Ernest K Arbuthnot
1940 (11 Jul)	1944 (31 Dec)	*Col [Sir]* (Thomas) Eric St Johnston
1945 (22 Oct)	1954 (31 Jul)	*Lt Col* (Herman) Graham Rutherford
1954 (1 Aug)	1964	James E Bailey
1964 (Oct)	1968 (31 Mar)	David Holdsworth

Notes:
Absorbed Chipping Norton and Henley Boroughs, 1857
Absorbed Banbury Borough, 1 Oct 1925

Paisley	1806-1967	

Formed: 1806
Abolished: 16 Aug 1967. Became part of Renfrew and Bute
Strength: *Initial* 32 [1858]   *Final* 209
Chief Officer:

1820	1829	James Brown
1829	1830	George Jeffrey
1831	1837	William Murtrie
1837	1851	James Stewart
1851	1876	George Ingram
1876	1900	Donald Sutherland
1900	1922	William Duncan

1922	1930	Alexander Duncan
1931 (9 Feb)	1934 (31 May)	Arthur J McIntosh
1935	1955	James H Goudie
1955	1967	James McAulay

Partick	1858-1912

Formed: 1858
Abolished: 5 Nov 1912. Became part of Glasgow City
Strength: *Initial* 13   *Final* 93
Chief Officer:

1858 (26 Jul)	1860 (10 Dec)	Paul McColl
1860 (10 Dec)	1892	Andrew Edwards
1892 (Apr)	1912	William Cameron

Peebles-shire	1841-1950	🗁

Formed: 1841
Abolished: 16 May 1950. Became part of Lothians and Peebles
Strength: *Initial* 8 [1858]   *Final* 19
Chief Officer:

1841	1866 (11 Nov)	Ninian Notman
1866 (21 Nov)	1891 (11 Mar)	David Watson
1894 (19 Jan)	1914 (6 Oct)	*Lt Col* Alexander Borthwick ⚕
1914 (8 Dec)	1950 (15 May)	*Major* Sholto W Douglas

Notes:
From 1894 to 1950, the same CC administered four forces: East Lothian, Mid Lothian, Peebles-shire and West Lothian

Pembroke	1836-1859	🗁

Formed: 9 Jan 1836
Abolished: 10 Jan 1859. Became part of Pembrokeshire
Strength: *Initial* 2   *Final* 4
Chief Officer:

1836		*No Chief Officer*
1840 (Jul)	1859?	William Rees

Pembrokeshire	1857-1968	📖

Formed: 9 Jun 1857
Abolished: 1 Apr 1968. Became part of Dyfed-Powys
Strength: *Initial* 33   *Final* 183
Chief Officer:

1857 (9 Jun)	1879	*Major* Anthony B A Stokes
1879 (1 Jul)	1906	*Capt* (T) Ince Webb-Bowen
1907 (27 Feb)	1933	Fred T B Summers
1933 (11 May)	1958	*Capt* A T N Evans

1958 (1 Sep)	1965	[*Sir*] George W R Terry
1965 (12 Jul)	1968	Alan Goodson

Notes:
Absorbed Pembroke Borough, 10 Jan 1859
Absorbed Haverfordwest and Tenby Boroughs, 1 Apr 1889

Penryn	**1836-1889**

Formed: 1836
Abolished: 1 Apr 1889. Became part of Cornwall
Strength: *Initial* 4 [1858]   *Final* 2
Chief Officer:

1859	1863	George Merrifield
1863	1868	William White
1869	1886	W H Edwards
1886	1889	James Jennings

Penzance	**1836-1943**	🗁

Formed: 1836
Abolished: 1 Apr 1943. Became part of Cornwall
Strength: *Initial* 5 [1858]   *Final* 24
Chief Officer:

1853	1886	John Olds
1886 (Jan)	1908	R Nicholas
1908 (Apr)	1937	H Kenyon
1937 (Jan)	1941	Robert C M Jenkins
1942 (Jan)	1943 (31 Mar)	F G Beale

Perth	**1811-1964**	🗁

Formed: 1811
Abolished: 16 May 1964. Became part of Perth and Kinross
Strength: *Initial* 28 [1858]   *Final* 81   ⛏ H
Chief Officer:

1818	1832	Thomas Luke
1832	1833	Robertson McKay
1833	1861	Andrew Boyle
1862	1892	John Welsh
1893	1914	James Garrow
1914	1934	John Scott
1934	1943	Charles Stephen
1943	1961	Alister McInnes
1961	1964 (15 May)	Donald A MacInnes

Notes:
MacInnes was also CC of Perthshire & Kinross-shire, 1963-4

Perth and Kinross	1930-1975	📖

Formed: 16 May 1930, by merger of Perthshire and Kinross-shire
Abolished: 16 May 1975. Became part of Tayside
Strength: *Initial* 95   *Final* 291
Chief Officer:

1930 (16 May)	1935 (30 Jun)	Matthew J Martin ✝
1935 (16 Nov)	1949 (14 Dec)	Alexander C Sim ✝
1951 (8 Jan)	1963 (3? Oct)	George R Glendinning
1963	1975 (15 May)	Donald A MacInnes

Notes:
Named Perthshire and Kinross-shire, 1930-64
James Coutts was interim CC, 1949-51
MacInnes was also CC of Perth City, 1963-4
Absorbed Perth City, 16 May 1964

Perthshire	1839-1930	🗁

Formed: 30 Sep 1839
Abolished: 16 May 1930. Became part of Perthshire and Kinross-shire (later Perth and Kinross *qv*)
Strength: *Initial* 22   *Final* 85
Chief Officer:

1839		Alexander Stewart
1842 (11 Apr)	1855 (2 Jun)	*Capt* Joseph J Grove
1855 (Jun?)	1877 (23 Jun)	George Gordon ✝
1877 (14 Aug)	1886 (8 Feb?)	John Dodd
1886 (Feb)	1912 (15 Jul)	John Macpherson
1912 (15 Oct)	1930 (15 May)	Matthew J Martin

Notes:
Gordon was also CC of Clackmannanshire [1861] and Kinross-shire 1858-68

Peterborough City	1836?-1857	

Formed: 1836?
Abolished: Amalgamated into Peterborough Liberty, 10 Mar 1857
Strength: *Initial* 10?   *Final* ?   🏭 1541
Chief Officer:

1836?	1857?	George Bristow

Notes:
Jursidiction was the City and Hamlets

Peterborough City	1874-1947	🗁

Re-formed: 30 Sep 1874, from part of Peterborough Liberty
Abolished: 1 Apr 1947. Became part of Peterborough Combined
Strength: *Initial* 18   *Final* 64   🏭 1541
Chief Officer:

1874 (22 Jul)	1889 (Jan)	James *or* William Hurst
1889 (11 Mar)	1909 (Mar)	John W Lawson
1909 (May)	1915 (30 Apr)	John E Ker Watson
1915 (1 May)	1943 (Oct)	Thomas Danby
1943	1947 (31 Mar)	Francis G Markin

Notes:
CC was also CC of Peterborough Liberty, 1931-47

Peterborough Combined   1947-1965   📖

Formed: 1 Apr 1947, by merger of Peterborough City and Peterborough Liberty
Abolished: 1 Apr 1965. Became part of Mid-Anglia
Strength: *Initial* 74   *Final* 150
Chief Officer:

1947 (1 Apr)	1965	Francis G Markin

Peterborough Liberty   1857-1947   🗁

Formed: 10 Mar 1857
Abolished: 1 Apr 1947. Became part of Peterborough Combined
Strength: *Initial* 21   *Final* 10
Chief Officer:

1857 (10 Mar)	1876	*Capt* Henry L Bayly
1876 (2 Feb)	1881	Thomas O H Lees
1881 (19 Oct)	1931 (31 May)	James D Kellie-MacCallum
1931	1943	Thomas Danby
1943	1947 (31 Mar)	Francis G Markin

Notes:
CC was also CC of Northamptonshire, 1857-1931
Kellie-MacCallum was the longest serving CC in England and Wales
Peterborough City set up separate force, 30 Sep 1874
CC was also CC of Peterborough City, 1931-47

Plymouth   1836-1967   📖

Formed: 1836
Abolished: 1 Jun 1967. Became part of Devon and Cornwall
Strength: *Initial* ?   *Final* 530   ♥ 1889 ⚒ 1928
Chief Officer:

1838	1853?	*Lt* Robert Holman
1853	1863	Edward Codd
1863	1865	John Freeman
1865 (31 Oct)	1866	*Lt Col* John L Vivian
1866	1892	F Wreford
1892 (Jul)	1917	Joseph D Sowerby
1917 (Mar)	1929	H H Sanders
1929	1932	Archibald K Wilson

1932	1936	[*Sir*] William C Johnson
1936 (23 Mar)	1941	George S Lowe
1941 (1 Dec)	1943	W T Hutchings
1943 (21 Jun)	1965	J F Skittery
1965 (1 Jul)	1967	Ronald Gregory

Notes:
Absorbed Devonport and Stonehouse, 9 Nov 1914

Pontefract		1836-1889	📖

Formed: 19 Jan 1836
Abolished: 1 Apr 1889. Became part of West Riding
Strength: *Initial* 4   *Final* 8
Chief Officer:

1836 (19 Jan)		Joseph Foster
1845 (1 Jul?)	1846 (Oct)	Charles Stephens
1847 (1 Jan)	1856 (1 Jun)	Richard Ward
1856 (11 Aug)	1889 (31 Mar)	Edwin Fearnside

Poole	1835-1891

Formed: 1835
Abolished: 11 Nov 1891. Became part of Dorset
Strength: *Initial* 11 [1858]   *Final* 15
Chief Officer:

1835	1862	Benjamin Inkpen
1863	1869	W Gifford
1869	1891	Stephen Hunt

Port Glasgow	1857-1895

Formed: 1857
Abolished: 16 Oct 1895. Became part of Renfrewshire
Strength: *Initial* 8 [1871]   *Final* 12
Chief Officer:

1871	1895	*Capt* James Sloan

Portobello	1858-1859

Formed: 1858
Abolished: 1859. Became part of Mid Lothian
Strength: *Initial* 3   *Final* 3
Chief Officer:

1858	1859	Thomas Anderson

Portsmouth	1836-1967	📖

Formed: 21 Mar 1836

Abolished: 1 Apr 1967. Became part of Hampshire
Strength: *Initial* 31   *Final* 550   ♥1889 ⚓ 1926
Chief Officer:

1836 (21 Mar)	1839 (26 Dec)	(*6 HCs*)
1839 (27 Dec)	1848 (11 Aug)	*Capt* Robert T Elliott
1848 (11 Aug)	1859	William Leggatt ♱
1859 (15 Mar)	1860	Thomas H Chase
1860 (15 Mar)	1875	Richard Barber
1875 (25 Oct)	1880	James Jervis
1880 (7 Dec)	1893	A W Cosser
1893 (30 Aug)	1898	H B Le Mesurier
1898 (19 Sep)	1907	Arthur T Prickett
1907 (27 Aug)	1940	Thomas Davies
1940 (19 Jul)	1958	Arthur C West
1958 (7 Jul)	1964	William N Wilson
1964 (1 Sep)	1967 (31 Mar)	Owen Flynn

Notes:
Force re-modelled in 1839 and 1848

Preston	**1815-1969**	📖

Formed: 1815
Abolished: 1 Apr 1969. Became part of Lancashire
Strength: *Initial* 7   *Final* 283   ♥1889
Chief Officer:

1815	1836	Thomas Walton
1836	1853	Samuel Banister
1853	1863	Joseph Gibbons
1863 (Jan)	1872	James Dunn ♱
1872	1882	Joseph Oglethorpe
1882	1907	*Major* F L Gore-Little
1908 (May)	1912 (Mar)	Lionel D L Everett
1913 (May)	1915	*Capt* John A Unett
1915 (1 May)	1937	John E Ker Watson
1937 (1 Oct)	1956	Henry Garth
1956	1969	Frank Richardson

Pulteneytown	**1845-1902**

Formed: 1845
Abolished: *ca*1890 *or* 2 Dec 1902. Became part of Caithness-shire
Strength: *Initial* 3 [1859]   *Final* 3
Chief Officer:

1859	1864	George McKay
1865	1869	George Bain
1870	1874	George Swanson

1875		Alexander Milne
1876	1889	David Petrie

Notes:
Force established by the British Fisheries Society and controlled by their Commissioners, 1845-58
Police & constabulary almanac 1891 states force had merged with County. CCs' (Scotland) Association centenary booklet gives date as 2 Dec 1902

Pwllheli	**1857-1879**	📁

Formed: Mar 1857
Abolished: Jul 1879. Became part of Caernarvonshire
Strength: *Initial* 1　　　　　*Final* 1
Chief Officer:

1857 (Mar)	1869	Robert Williams
1869	1879	William Hughes

Radnorshire	**1857-1948**	📖

Formed: 8 Jan 1857
Abolished: 1 Apr 1948. Became part of Mid-Wales
Strength: *Initial* 10　　　　　*Final* 22
Chief Officer:

1857 (3 Feb)	1868	*Capt* James D Telfer
1868	1873	*Major* Penry Lloyd
1873 (4 Apr)	1892 (30 Aug)	Joseph T Wheeldon
1892 (30 Sep)	1897 (29 Jun)	John E Lloyd
1897 (30 Jun)	1900 (3 Jul)	*Capt* [*Sir*] Fullarton James
1900 (4 Jul)	1909 (17 Jun)	*Major the Hon* Charles E Walsh ✝
1909 (9 Sep)	1916 (10 Sep)	*Major* Harry H Bromfield ✝
1916	1922 (31 Jul)	Richard Jones
1922 (1 Aug)	1946 (21 Mar)	Arthur S Michael
1946 (1 Aug)	1948 (31 Mar)	*Capt* [*Sir*] Humphrey C Lloyd

Notes:
CC was also CC of Herefordshire, 1857-68
John E Lloyd was the son of Penry Lloyd
Bromfield was killed in action at the Somme
H C Lloyd was also CC of Montgomeryshire

Ramsgate	**1838-1943**	📁

Formed: 1838
Abolished: 1 Apr 1943. Became part of Kent
Strength: *Initial* 6-7 [1844]　　　　　*Final* 63
Chief Officer:

1838	1869	James Livick
1869	1895 (May)	Edward Buss

1895	1898	Roderick Ross
1898 (Oct)	1916	William B Jones
1916 (Jul)	1943 (31 Mar)	Samuel F Butler

Reading	**1836 1968**	📖

Formed: 21 Feb 1836
Abolished: 1 Apr 1968. Became part of Thames Valley
Strength: *Initial* 34   *Final* 251   ❤1889
Chief Officer:

1836		W Shannons *and* J Harris
1839	1855	Henry Houlton
1855	1865	John Peck
1865	1887	(E) James Purchase
1887	1897	George Tewsley
1897 (May)	1923	*Capt* John N S Henderson
1923 (Jun)	1944	Thomas A Burrows ✝
1945 (May)	1948	Sydney L Lawrence
1948 (Jun)	1959	Jesse Lawrence
1959 (Jun)	1966	Arthur Iveson
1966 (Oct)	1968	Leonard C Dolby (*Acting CC*)

Reigate	**1864-1943**	📖

Formed: 25 Mar 1864, from part of Surrey
Abolished: 1 Mar 1943. Became part of Surrey
Strength: *Initial* 12   *Final* 59
Chief Officer:

1864 (25 Mar)	1864 (2 Apr)	George Gifford
1864 (Apr)	1888	George Rogers
1888	1891	William Pearson
1891 (Jun)	1894 (Oct)	William G Morant
1894 (Oct)	1894 (Dec?)	Philip J Woodman
1894 (Dec)	1930 (Dec?)	James Metcalfe
1931 (1 Jan)	1943 (28 Feb)	William H Beacher

Notes:
Woodman was dismissed on being convicted of embezzlement from his previous force (Bradford)

Renfrew	**1857-1930**	

Formed: 1857
Abolished: 16 May 1930. Became part of Renfrewshire
Strength: *Initial* 3 [1859]   *Final* 23
Chief Officer:

1859	1876	James Dobbie
1876	1886	Peter Inglis

1886	1891	Charles Kemp
1891	1906	Gilbert Deans
1906	1911	Duncan McMillan
1911	1930	William Robb

Renfrew and Bute	**1949-1975**

Formed: 16 May 1949, by merger of Renfrewshire and Bute
Abolished: 16 May 1975. Became part of Strathclyde
Strength: *Initial* 210   *Final* 847
Chief Officer:

1949 (16 May)	1954	John Robertson
1954	1967	Robert S Allan
1967 (16 Aug)	1975	David Williamson

Notes:
Absorbed Greenock and Paisley Burghs, 16 Aug 1967

Renfrewshire	**1840-1949**

Formed: 1840
Abolished: 16 May 1949. Became part of Renfrew and Bute
Strength: *Initial* 17   *Final* 196
Chief Officer:

1858 (Mar)	1887	Robert Hunter
1887 (May)	1925	*Capt* Charles Harding
1925 (Nov)	1949 (15 May)	John Robertson

Notes:
Absorbed Port Glasgow Burgh, 16 Oct 1895
Harding was also CC of Bute, 1898-1925 and of Kinning Park, 1892-1905
Robertson was also CC of Bute, 1925-1949
Absorbed Johnstone and Renfrew Burghs, 16 May 1930

Retford	**1836-1841**

Formed: 1 Jan 1836
Abolished: 1 Jan 1841. Became part of Nottinghamshire
Strength: *Initial* 3   *Final* ?
Chief Officer: Not known

Richmond	**1838-1889**

Formed: Nov 1838
Abolished: 1 Apr 1889. Became part of North Riding
Strength: *Initial* 2   *Final* 4
Chief Officer:

1858	1866	J Helmsley
1867	1868	George Mann
1868	1871	J C Peacock

1872	1874	John M Garry
1874	1880	William Campfield
1880	1889	Thomas Graham

Ripon   1848-1887   📖

Formed: 1848
Abolished: 1 Oct 1887. Became part of West Riding
Strength: *Initial* 2   *Final* 4   🏰 1836
Chief Officer:

1856	1861	William Smith
1862	1876	William Burneston
1876	1887	Thomas Metcalfe

River Tyne   1845-1968

Formed: Aug 1845
Abolished: 1 Aug 1968. Became part of South Shields
Strength: *Initial* 32 [1884]   *Final* 73
Chief Officer:

1845	1884	John Stephens
1884	1902	Robert Farmer
1903	1925	Martin Jamieson
1926	1932?	Albert Lea
1932 (1 Apr)	1968 (31 Jul)	D Atkinson

Notes:
Stephens was also Supt of Newcastle-upon-Tyne, 1836-54

River Wear   1840-1961   📖

Formed: 1 Sep 1840
Abolished: 30 Sep 1961. Became part of Sunderland
Strength: *Initial* See Notes   *Final* 16
Chief Officer:

1840 (1 Sep)	1855 (17 Feb	William Brown
1855 (2 May)	1858 (Mar)	Robert Gifford
1858 (Mar)	1878 (Mar)	Joseph Stainsby
1878 (17 Mar)	1885 (15 Nov)	John Nicholson ♱
1885 (Nov)	1897 (Aug)	William Huntley
1897 (9 Sep)	1915 (Jul)	William Carter
1915 (12 Oct)	1925	Frederick J Crawley
1925 (13 Jul)	1937	John Ruddick
1937 (19 Jun)	1955 (Oct)	George H Cook
1955 (1 Nov)	1961 (30 Sep)	William Tait

Notes:
The Chief Officer was always the CC of Sunderland Borough

Until 1859, the number of constables was increased in winter (Sep-Apr). The initial strength comprised the Chief Officer, 1 Insp and 4 Captains (later Sgts), plus the variable number of boatmen (constables). In 1849 this number was 10-17

Rochdale	1857-1969	📖

Formed: 13 Apr 1857
Abolished: 1 Apr 1969. Became part of Lancashire
Strength: *Initial* 17   *Final* 212   ☙ 1889
Chief Officer:

1857 (11 Mar)	1863 (30 Jan)	John H Callender
1863	1866 (Oct)	*Lt [Capt]* William C Sylvester
1867	1869	*Capt* Roland Davies
1869	1881	Samuel Stevens
1882 (13 Jan)	1893 (31 Jul)	Joseph Wilkinson
1893 (Jun)	1898 (9 Apr)	Charles Buck ♱
1898 (May)	1917 (30 Jun)	Leonard C Barry
1917 (12 Jul)	1945 (31 Dec)	Henry Howarth
1946 (1 Apr)	1958	*Major* Sydney J Harvey
1958 (1 Oct)	1964	Frank S Gale
1964 (1 Jul)	1967	P Ross

Rochester	1837-1943	📖

Formed: Sep 1837
Abolished: 1 Apr 1943. Became part of Kent
Strength: *Initial* 25   *Final* 59   🏰 1211
Chief Officer:

1837 (Sep)	1842 (Dec)	Thomas Cork
1842	[1862]	John Tuff
1863	1877 (May)	J H Radley ♱
1877	1902 (Oct)	W Broadbridge ♱
1903 (9 Jan)	1931 (Feb)	Alfred S Arnold
1931 (18 Feb)	1933 (Nov)	Herbert C Allen
1934	1937 (Sep)	Horace P Hind
1937 (Dec)	1940	*Cmdr* William J A Willis
1940 (Apr)	1943 (31 Mar)	Kenneth A Horwood

Notes:
Cork was dismissed for failing to pay over tolls collected at the cattle market

Romney Marsh	1840-1888	

Formed: 25 Mar 1840
Abolished: 1888. Became part of Kent
Strength: *Initial* ?   *Final* ?
Chief Officer: Not known

Romsey		1836-1865

Formed: 1836
Abolished: 1865. Became part of Hampshire
Strength: *Initial* 4   *Final* 2
Chief Officer:

1853	1865	William Sivyer

Ross		1858-1889

Formed: 1858
Abolished: 29 Aug 1889. Became part of Ross and Cromarty
Strength: *Initial* 20 [1858]   *Final* 62
Chief Officer:

1858	1867	George Cumming
1867 (Aug)	1889	Donald Munro
1889	1889 (28 Aug)	James Gordon

Notes:
Munro and Gordon were also CC of Cromarty County

Ross and Cromarty		1889-1963

Formed: 29 Aug 1889, by merger of Ross and Cromarty
Abolished: 16 May 1963. Became part of Ross and Sutherland
Strength: *Initial* 64   *Final* 83
Chief Officer:

1889 (29 Aug)	1898	James Gordon
1898 (21 Jul)	1905	Malcolm Macauley
1905 (4 Aug)	1935	*Capt* Duncan Finlayson
1935 (11 May)	1953	William MacLean
1953 (1 Mar)	1962	Finlay Munro

Ross and Sutherland		1963-1975

Formed: 16 May 1963, by merger of Ross and Cromarty and Sutherland
Abolished: 16 May 1975. Became part of Northern
Strength: *Initial* 116   *Final* 164
Chief Officer:

1963 (16 May)	1975	Kenneth Ross

Rotherham		1882-1967	📖

Formed: 1 Jul 1882, from part of West Riding
Abolished: 1 Jun 1967. Became part of Sheffield and Rotherham
Strength: *Initial* 35   *Final* 174   ♥1902
Chief Officer:

1882	1888	John Pollard
1888	1891	*Capt* Lindsay R Burnett

1891 (4 Jun)	1907	James T Enwright
1907 (Nov)	1932	Edwin Weatherhogg
1932 (Mar)	1955	Robert Hall
1955 (Dec)	1961	James E Cotton
1961 (Jul)	1967	*Major* Stanley W Morris

Rothesay 1846-1923

Formed: 1846
Abolished: 1923. Became part of Bute
Strength: *Initial* 6 [1870]   *Final* 14
Chief Officer:

1858	1867	Daniel Duncan
1867	1876	Angus McAlpine
1878	1896	Matthew Waters
1896	1920	William McKay
1921	1923	William David

Roxburghshire 1840-1948

Formed: Mar 1840
Abolished: 16 May 1948. Became part of Berwick, Roxburgh and Selkirk
Strength: *Initial* 26 [1858]   *Final* 59
Chief Officer:

1839 (20 Nov)		William Cleaver
1850	1861 (Nov)	William Everitt
1861 (19 Nov)	1865	James McMaster
1865	1884 (3 Jun)	Richard Boultbee
1884	1909	Alex Porter
1909 (16 Nov)	1933	John Morren
1933	1948 (15 May)	David W S Brown

Notes:
Absrobed Jedburgh Burgh, 1861
Boultbee was also CC of Selkirkshire
Absorbed Kelso Burgh, 16 Feb 1881
Porter was also CC of Berwickshire, 1893-1909 and of Selkirkshire, 1904-9
Morren and Brown were also CC of Berwickshire and Selkirkshire
Absorbed Hawick Burgh, 16 May 1930

Royal Irish 1822-1922

Formed: 1822
Abolished: 31 Aug 1922. Divided into Garda Siochana and Royal Ulster
Strength: *Initial* 5325   *Final* ca 16,000
Chief Officer:
Munster

| 1822 | 1827 | *Sir* Richard Willcocks |

1827		*Major* William Miller
Leinster		
1822	1827	*Major* Thomas Powell
1827		*Sir* John Harvey
Connaught		
1822		*Major* JohnWarburton
Ulster		
1822		*Major* Thomas D'Arcy
		Sir Frederick Stovin
IC/RIC		
1836	1838	*Lt Col* [*Lt Gen*] James Shaw Kennedy
1838	1838 (30 Jun)	*Major* George Warburton
1838 (1 Jul)	1858	*Gen Sir* Duncan McGregor
1858 (19 Oct)		*Sir* Henry J Brownrigg
1865 (8 May)		*Col Sir* John S Wood
1876 (19 Sep)		*Lt Col* George E Hillier
1882 (12 May)	1885	*Col* Robert Bruce
1885 (21 Sep)	1900 (Aug)	[*Sir*] Andrew Reed
1900 (1 Sep)	1916	*Col Sir* Neville F F Chamberlain
1916 (1 Aug)	1920 (Jan)	*Brig Gen* [*Sir*] Joseph A Byrne
1920 (11 Mar)	1920 (5 Dec)	*Sir* Thomas J Smith
1920 (15 May)	1922	*Major Gen* [*Sir*] (H) Hugh Tudor

Notes:
Established as 4 separate forces, one for each Province and collectively named the County Constabulary
Forces merged and named Irish Constabulary, 1836
Absorbed Belfast, 31 Aug 1865
Renamed Royal Irish Constabulary, 6 Sep 1867
Absorbed Londonderry, 1870

Royal Ulster	**1922-2001**	📖

Formed: 1 Jun 1922, from part of Royal Irish
Abolished: 4 November 2001. Re-named [Police Service of] Northern Ireland
Strength: *Initial* 3000   *Final ca*12690
Chief Officer:

1922 (Jun)	1945 (Jul)	*Lt Col Sir* Charles G Wickham
1945 (Aug)	1961 (Jan)	*Capt* [*Sir*] Richard P Pim
1961 (Jan)	1969 (Feb)	*Sir* Albert H Kennedy
1969 (Feb)	1969 (Oct)	(J) Anthony Peacocke
1969 (Nov)	1970 (Nov)	*Col* [*Sir*] Arthur E Young
1970 (Nov)	1973 (Oct)	[*Sir*] Graham R E Shillington
1973 (Nov)	1976 (Apr)	*Sir* James Flanagan
1976 (1 May)	1979 (Dec)	[*Sir*] Kenneth L Newman
1980 (1 Jan)	1989 (31 May)	[*Sir*] John Hermon
1989 (1 Jun)	1996 (3 Nov)	[*Sir*] Hugh Annesley

1996 (4 Nov)   2001 (4 Nov)   [*Sir*] Ronnie Flanagan
Notes:
Force awarded the George Cross, Nov 1999

Rutland		1848-1951	📖

Formed: 29 Jun 1848
Abolished: 1 Apr 1951. Became part of Leicestershire
Strength: *Initial* 2   *Final* 30
Chief Officer:

1848	1855	T Garton
1855 (5 Jul)	1871	R F Mitchell
1871 (6 Apr)	1908	William Keep
1908 (30 Jun)	1921	William Wilson
1921 (30 Mar)	1937	Frederick W Golder
1937 (5 May)	1940	*Major* William S Flower
1940 (7 Sep)	1951	Alan Bond

Ryde		1869-1922

Formed: 15 Feb 1869
Abolished: 1 Apr 1922. Became part of Isle of Wight
Strength: *Initial* 11   *Final* 15
Chief Officer:

1868	1880	John H Burt
1880	1903	George Hinks
1903 (Nov)	1922	Charles Greenstreet

Rye		1838-1889

Formed: 1838
Abolished: 1 Apr 1889. Became part of East Sussex
Strength: *Initial* 1   *Final* 3
Chief Officer:

1838		William H Henley
1853	1876	Parker Butcher
1878	1889	James Bourne

Saffron Walden		1836-1857	📖

Formed: Jan? 1836
Abolished: 1 Nov 1857. Became part of Essex
Strength: *Initial* 2 or 3   *Final* ?
Chief Officer:

1836 (Jan)		John Mynott *and/or* Jeremiah Stock
1836 (*ca*Jul)		Joseph Kent
1848	1849 (9 Nov)	William Campling ✞
1852 (Mar)	1852 (Jul)	James Goss

1852 (Jul)	1856 (Jun)	Benjamin Judd
1856 (Aug)		Oliver Kirby *or* Kerbey
1856 (Sep)	1857 (Oct)	Richard Harvey

Notes:
Watch Committee records refer to a Head Constable but are unclear whether this was Mynott, Stock or another man
Campling was murdered

St Albans	**1836-1947**	🗀

Formed: 23 Jul 1836
Abolished: 1 Apr 1947. Became part of Hertfordshire
Strength: *Initial* 4   *Final* 67   🏛 1877
Chief Officer:

1859	1883	W J Pipe
1883	1889	A Pellant
1889	1893	Jacob Wood
1893	1901	A F Blatch
1901 (Aug)	1905	William H Smith
1905 (4 Jul)	1916 (Apr)	George Whitbread
1919 (19 Jul)	1929	John E Harrison
1929 (13 Oct)	1933 (May)	Nelson Ashton
1934 (23 Jul)	1947 (31 Mar)	H W Thorpe

Notes:
Whitbread was required to resign for drunkenness. As a result, the force was temporarily amalgamated with Hertfordshire, 1 May 1916-*ca*1918

St Andrews	**1858?-1859?**	🗀

Formed: 1858?
Abolished: After 1859? Became part of Fife
Strength: *Initial* ?   *Final* ?
Chief Officer: Not known
Notes:
This force may not have existed. The Town Council paid for a county constable from 1842 until at least 1858

St Helen's	**1887-1969**	

Formed: 1 Jul 1887, from part of Lancashire
Abolished: 1 Apr 1969. Became part of Lancashire
Strength: *Initial* 65   *Final* 237   ♥ 1889
Chief Officer:

1887	1905	James Wood
1905 (12 Jan)	1939	A R Ellerington
1939 (9 Mar)	1947	A Cust
1947	1964	William G Symmons

1964	1969	A Atherton

St Ives	**1836-1889**	📁

Formed: 1836
Abolished: 1 Apr 1889. Became part of Cornwall
Strength: *Initial* 1   *Final* 1
Chief Officer:

1841 (Jan)		Henry Armitage
1853	1889	James Bennetts

Salford	**1844-1968**	📁

Formed: 12 Aug 1844
Abolished: 1 Apr 1968. Became part of Manchester and Salford
Strength: *Initial* 40   *Final* 420   ♥1889 🏭 1926
Chief Officer:

1844	1845	John Diggles
1845	1848	*Capt* E Shepherd
1848	1852	Stephen Neale
1852	1866	James Taylor
1866 (Oct)	1868	*Capt* William C Sylvester
1869	1880	*Capt* R W Torrens
1880	1889	William L Marshall
1889	1898	*Cmdr* Charles T Scott
1898 (Nov)	1908	John W Hallam
1908 (Jul)	1947	*Major* C V Godfrey
1947 (Aug)	1948	A Aberdein
1948	1956 (Sep?)	Alexander J Paterson
1956	1961	F R Gray
1961	1967	J E Cotton
1967	1968	F Richards (*Acting CC*)

Salisbury	**1838-1943**	📖

Formed: 27 Apr 1838, on disbandment of New Sarum
Abolished: 1 Apr 1943. Became part of Wiltshire
Strength: *Initial* 15   *Final* 38   🏭1189
Chief Officer:

1838		John Bunter
1839 (Sep)	1840	Joseph Cooper
1840 (Jan)	1857	Thomas Blake
1857	1860 (14 Mar)	Richard Barber
1861	1867	Edmund Caldow
1867	1874	James White
1874	1903	A Mathews
1903 (Oct)	1929	Frank A R Richardson

| 1929 | 1943 (31 Mar) | Robert F Nixon |

Notes:
Cooper was required to resign for spending the PCs' wages on drink

| **Sandwich** | ***ca*1856-1889** | 🗁 |

Formed: *ca*1856
Abolished: 1 Apr 1889. Became part of Kent
Strength: *Initial* 3   *Final* 2
Chief Officer:

1856	1868	John D Warren
1868	1869?	Edward Buss
1870	1875	John Brothers
1875	1877	John Cuthbertson
1877	1889	William Page

| **Scarborough** | **1836-1947** | 🗁 |

Formed: Jan 1836
Abolished: 1 Apr 1947. Became part of North Riding
Strength: *Initial* 6   *Final* 78
Chief Officer:

1836	1836	W Robinson
1836	1839	J Ramsden
1839 (6 Dec)	1863	Richard Roberts
1865 (15 Sep)	1898	William Pattison
1898	1902	(W) Henry Riches
1902	1913 (Mar)	William Basham
1913 (Apr)	1929 (Apr)	Henry Windsor
1929 (Apr)	1941 (Sep)	Walter Abbott
1941 (Oct)	1943 (31 Dec)	Gerald F Goodman
1944 (Mar)	1947 (31 Mar)	John E S Browne

| **Scilly Isles** | **1836-1947** | 🗁 |

Formed: 1836
Abolished: 1 Apr 1947. Became part of Cornwall
Strength: *Initial* 1   *Final* 3
Chief Officer:

| 1836 | 1865? | James Hicks |
| 1865 | 1875 | Horatio Nelson |

Notes:
The force comprised 1 paid parish constable until 1942, when 2 officers were lent by Cornwall County as reinforcements

| **Scottish North-eastern Counties 1949-1975** | 📖 |

Formed: 16 May 1949, by merger of Aberdeenshire, Banffshire, Kincardineshire

and Moray and Nairn
Abolished: 16 May 1975. Became part of Grampian
Strength: *Initial* 258   *Final* 383
Chief Officer:

1949 (16 May)	1957 (6 Jul)	George I Strath
1957 (7 Jul)	1961 (16 Jul)	William Hunter
1961 (Sep?)	1973 (21 Aug)	Thomas W Chasser ✝
1973 (17 Sep)	1975 (15 May)	Alexander G Lynn

Selkirkshire	**1842-1948**

Formed: 13 Sep 1842
Abolished: 16 May 1948. Became part of Berwick, Roxburgh and Selkirk
Strength: *Initial* 8 [1859]   *Final* 30
Chief Officer:

1842 (13 Sep)	1866	James Fraser
1866	1884	Richard Boultbee
1884	1904	James Milne
1904 (20 Jul)	1909	Alex Porter
1909 (16 Nov)	1933	John Morren
1934 (16 May)	1948 (15 May)	David W S Brown

Notes:
Boultbee was also CC of Roxburghshire, 1866-71
CC was also CC of Berwickshire and Roxburghshire, 1904-48
Absorbed Galashiels Burgh, 16 May 1930

Sheffield	**1844-1967**	📖

Formed: 12 Mar 1844
Abolished: 1 Jun 1967. Became part of Sheffield and Rotherham
Strength: *Initial* 82   *Final* 1233   ♥1889 ⚒ 1893
Chief Officer:

1844	1858	Thomas Raynor
1859 (1 Jan)	1898	John Jackson ✝
1898 (Dec)	1912	*Cmdr* Charles T Scott
1913 (Jul)	1926 (7 Jan)	*Major [Lt Col]* John Hall-Dalwood
1926 (May)	1931 (Nov)	*Capt [Sir]* Percy J Sillitoe
1931 (1 Dec)	1941	*Major* F S James
1941 (1 Dec)	1948	George S Lowe
1948	1959	*[Sir]* George E Scott
1959	1963 (20 Nov)	Eric V Staines
1964	1967 (31 May)	Edward Barker

Sheffield and Rotherham	**1967-1974**

Formed: 1 Jun 1967, by merger of Sheffield and Rotherham
Abolished: 1 Apr 1974. Became part of South Yorkshire

Strength: *Initial* 1406   *Final* 1448
Chief Officer:

1967	1972	Edward Barker
1972	1974 (31 Mar)	[*Sir* later *Lord*] Philip D Knights

Shetland	*see* **Zetland**

Shrewsbury	**1836-1947**	📁

Formed: 5 Feb 1836
Abolished: 1 Apr 1947. Became part of Shropshire
Strength: *Initial* 13   *Final* 56
Chief Officer:

1836	1844	Samuel Farlow
1844 (Nov)	1845 (Nov)	Edward J Blake
1845 (10 Nov)	1854	William Harper
1854 (24 Mar)	1856 (22 Feb)	Joseph Shackell
1856 (29 Feb)	1870 (6 May)	John Hughes
1870 (13 May)	1881 (7 May)	John Davies
1881 (1 Jun)	1887 (27 May)	Joseph Harrop
1887 (Jun)	1888 (Oct)	George W Whitfield
1888 (19 Nov)	1906 (31 Jan)	(G) Henry Blackwell
1906 (31 Jan)	1915 (7 Nov)	Arthur Baxter
1915 (9 Nov)	1918 (1 Mar)	Herbert F Harries *(Hon. CC)*
1918 (1 Mar)	1940 (31 Mar)	Frank Davies
1940 (1 Apr)	1947 (31 Mar)	George H MacDivitt

Notes:
Force reorganised in 1844
Blake was dismissed as an economy measure
Harper was demoted to Chief Supt on the appointment of Shackell
Harries was Chairman of the Watch Committee and appointed temporarily

Shropshire	**1840-1967**	📖

Formed: 9 Mar 1840
Abolished: 1 Oct 1967. Became part of West Mercia
Strength: *Initial* 23   *Final* 555
Chief Officer:

1840 (6 Feb)	1859	*Capt* Dawson Mayne
1859 (7 Mar)	1864 (30 Jul)	*Capt* Philip H Crampton
1864 (17 Oct)	1866 (Jan)	*Lt Col* Edward B Cureton
1866 (12 Apr)	1889 (26 Nov)	*Col* Richard J Edgell ✝
1890 (23 Jan)	1905 (26 Dec)	*Capt* George C P Williams-Freeman ✝
1906 (2 Mar)	1908 (5 Jul)	*Maj* [*Col Sir*] Llewellyn W Atcherley
1908 (2 Sep)	1915 (7 Aug)	*Capt* Gerald L Derriman ✝
1915 (19 Oct)	1918 (24 Mar)	Augustus Wood-Acton (*Hon. CC*) ✝

1918 (25 May)	1935 (30 Sep?)	*Major* [*Sir*] Jack Becke
1935 (3 Oct)	1945 (31 Dec)	*Major* [*Lt Col*] Harold A Golden
1946	1962 (13 May?)	[*Sir*] Douglas Osmond
1962	1967 (30 Sep)	Robert G Fenwick

Notes:
Uniform was rifle green, 1840-
Mayne was the younger brother of Sir Richard Mayne, first Commissioner, Metropolitan Police
Absorbed Wenlock Borough, 4 Jan 1841
Absorbed Oswestry Borough, 30 Oct 1877
Absorbed Bridgnorth and Ludlow Boroughs, 1 Apr 1889
Derriman was recalled to his Regiment, 1 Jan 1915, and died of wounds
Wood-Acton was Vice-Chairman of the Standing Joint Committee and appointed for the duration of the War
Golden returned to the Army, 1 Nov 1943
Absorbed Shrewsbury Borough, 1 Apr 1947

Somerset	**1856-1974**	

Formed: 21 May 1856
Abolished: 1 Apr 1974. Became part of Avon and Somerset
Strength: *Initial* 267   *Final* 1260
Chief Officer:

1856 (1 Jul)	1884 (30 Jun)	Valentine Goold
1884 (1 Jul)	1908 (31 May)	*Capt* Charles G Alison
1908 (1 Jun)	1939 (30 Jun)	*Capt* [*Lt Col*] Herbert C Metcalfe
1939 (28 Aug)	1955 (Jan)	J E Ryall
1955 (10 Jan)	1974 (31 Mar)	Kenneth W L Steele

Notes:
Absorbed Glastonbury Borough, 21 May 1856
Absorbed Wells Borough, 14 Oct 1856
Absorbed Yeovil Borough, Apr 1859
Absorbed Chard Borough, 1 Apr 1889
Metcalfe returned to his Regiment, 1 Dec 1914-Jun 1919
Absorbed Bridgwater Borough, Oct 1940
Absorbed Bath City, 1 Jan 1967
Named Somerset and Bath, 1967-74

South Molton	**1836-1877**

Formed: 1836
Abolished: 16 Oct 1877. Became part of Devon
Strength: *Initial* 2 [1858]   *Final* 2
Chief Officer:

1853	1877	W H Fisher

South Shields		1834?-1968	📖

Formed: 1834?
Abolished: 1 Oct 1968. Became part of Durham
Strength: *Initial* 5   *Final* 203   🛡1889
Chief Officer:

1834		James Robb
1839	1846	Joseph Robb
1846	1855 (Dec)	James Buglass
1855?	1860?	Joseph Heddington
1860?	1880	Thomas Richardson
1881	1881	*Capt* A F Adams
1881	1884	*Major* George J Teevan
1883 (Jun)	1894	Frank [*or* Frederick?] G M Moorhouse
1894	1902 (14 Dec)	William G Morant
1902	1928	William Scott
1929 (Apr)	1936	William R Wilkie
1936 (Sep)	1939	Alexander D Wilson
1939 (Oct)	1957	Thomas B Humphrey
1957 (15 Apr)	1966	Stanley Grey
1966 (1 Oct)	1968	Thomas Barnes

Notes:
Buglass was dismissed after *defalcations of fees payable to the Corporation*
Absorbed River Tyne, 1 Aug 1968

South Wales		1969	📖

Formed: 1 Jun 1969, by merger of Cardiff, Glamorgan, Merthyr Tydfil and Swansea
Strength: *Initial* 2581   *Current* 3014
Chief Officer:

1969 (1 Jun)	1971	Melbourne Thomas
1971	1979	[*Sir*] (Thomas) Gwilym Morris
1979	1983	[*Sir*] John Woodcock
1983	1988	David A East
1989	1996 (21 May)	(William) Robert Lawrence
1996 (21 Nov)	2003 (31 Dec)	[*Sir*] Anthony T Burden
2004 (1 Jan)	2009 (31 Dec)	Barbara Wilding
2010 (1 Jan)		Peter Vaughan

Notes:
Absorbed parts of Dyfed-Powys and Gwent, 1 Apr 1974
Mrs Wilding was the first woman CC in Wales

South Yorkshire		1974	📖

Formed: 1 Apr 1974, by merger of Sheffield and Rotherham, parts of Nottinghamshire and parts of West Yorkshire

Strength: *Initial* 2752   *Current* 2882
Chief Officer:

1974 (1 Apr)	1975 (31 Jul)	[*Sir* later *Lord*] Philip D Knights
1975	1978	[*Sir*] Richard S Barratt
1979	1982	James H Brownlow
1983	1990	Peter Wright
1990	1998 (8 Aug)	Richard B Wells
1998 (10 Aug)	2004 (31 Aug)	Michael I I Hedges
2004 (1 Sep)		Meredydd Hughes

Southampton   1836-1967   📖

Formed: 6 Mar 1836
Abolished: 1 Apr 1967. Became part of Hampshire
Strength: *Initial* 25   *Final* 499   ♥1889 ⚓ 1964
Chief Officer:

1836 (6 Mar)	1868 (Jan)	John T Enright
1868 (20 Jan)	1889 (6 May)	Thomas Breary
1889 (Jun)	1892 (3 Oct)	Philip S Clay
1892	1907 (Sep)	William Berry ☗
1907 (Dec)	1926 (29 Mar)	William E Jones ☗
1926 (1 Nov)	1939 (Nov)	John T McCormac
1940 (1 Apr)	1941 (Sep)	Herbert C Allen
1941 (Sep)	1946 (Dec)	Frederick T Tarry
1947 (Mar)	1960 (31 Mar)	Charles G Box
1960 (1 Apr)	1967 (31 Mar)	Alfred T Cullen

Notes:
Allen was injured in a road accident and retired from ill health. Tarry was appointed
Acting CC during his illness, Dec 1940-Sep 1941

Southend-on-Sea   1914-1969   📖

Formed: 1 Apr 1914, from part of Essex
Abolished: 1 Apr 1969. Became part of Essex
Strength: *Initial* 101   *Final* 398   ♥1914
Chief Officer:

1914 (1 Apr)	1935 (Apr)	Henry M Kerslake
1935 (1 May)	1938 (31 Dec)	George R Crockford
1939 (20 Jan)	1953 (Nov)	Arthur J Hunt
1953 (7 Nov)	1965	William A McConnach
1965	1969	Henry J Devlin (*Acting CC*)

Notes:
McConnach was convicted and imprisoned for using force funds for private
entertaining

Southport		1870-1969	📖

Formed: 23 Mar 1870, from part of Lancashire
Abolished: 1 Apr 1969. Became part of Lancashire
Strength: *Initial* 7   *Final* 203   ♥1905
Chief Officer:

1870 (23 Mar)	1896 (May)	Samuel Kershaw
1896 (18 May)	1906 (Aug)	William Elliott
1907 (1 Apr)	1919 (May)	*Capt [Lt Col]* Charles L Armitage
1919 (May)	1920 (Jun)	*Lt Col [Sir]* Frank Brook
1920 (1 Sep)	1942 (31 Aug)	*Major* Michael J Egan
1942 (16 Nov)	1946 (Jul)	*[Sir]* Charles C Martin
1946 (1 Oct)	1960 (Nov)	*Lt Col* Harold Mighall
1961 (16 Jan)	1964 (Feb)	Joseph Pessell
1964 (6 Jun)	1969 (31 Mar)	*[Sir]* James G C Longhurst

Notes:
Armitage was recalled to his Regiment, Aug 1914-Nov 1918 and never returned to the Force. James Wareing was Acting CC, 1914-19

Southwold		1840-1889

Formed: 1840
Abolished: 1 Apr 1889. Became part of East Suffolk
Strength: *Initial* 1   *Final* 1
Chief Officer:

1859	1874	Spurgeon
1874	1875	Joseph Hedington
1875	1889 (31 Mar)	William H Porter

Stafford		1840-1858

Formed: Oct 1840
Abolished: 1858. Became part of Staffordshire
Strength: *Initial* 4   *Final* 5
Chief Officer:

1840 (16 Nov)		Hugh M Thompson

Staffordshire		1840	📖

Formed: 1840
Strength: *Initial* 210   *Current* 2056
Chief Officer:

1842 (6 Dec)	1856	John Hayes Hatton
1857	1866	*Col* Gilbert Hogg
1866 (2 Jul)	1888	*Capt* William Congreve
1888	1929	*Capt [Lt Col] the Hon Sir* George A Anson
1929	1950	*Col Sir* Herbert P Hunter
1950 (10 Mar)	1960	*Col* George W R Hearn

1961 (1 Apr)	1964	Stanley E Peck
1964	1977	Arthur M Rees
1977	1996	Charles H Kelly
1996	2006 (2 Apr)	John W Giffard
2006 (3 Apr)	2007 (Sep)	David Swift
2007 (24 Sep)	2009 (31 May)	Christopher Sims
2009 (Sep)		Michael Cunningham

Notes:
Force originally covered only South Staffordshire. Extended to whole County, Oct 1842
Absorbed Tamworth Borough, *ca*1857
Absorbed Stafford Borough, 1858
Absorbed Lichfield City, 1 Apr 1889
Absorbed Newcastle-under-Lyme Borough, 1 Apr 1947
Absorbed Stoke-on-Trent Borough, 1 Jan 1968
Named Staffordshire and Stoke-on-Trent, 1968-74
Part of area transferred to West Midlands, 1 Apr 1974

Stalybridge	**1857-1947**	📁

Formed: Aug 1857
Abolished: 1 Apr 1947. Became part of Cheshire
Strength: *Initial* 11   *Final* 35
Chief Officer:

1857 (Aug)	1862	Joseph Sadler
1862 (Feb)	1899	William Chadwick
1899 (Mar)	1924	*Capt* John Bates
1924 (Feb)	1927	*Capt* Roland Y Parker
1927 (Oct)	1929	Frank J May
1929 (1 May)	1947 (31 Mar)	Stanley Pickering

Stamford	**1836-1889**	📁

Formed: 2 Jan 1836
Abolished: 1 Apr 1889. Became part of Lincolnshire
Strength: *Initial* 9   *Final* 10
Chief Officer:

1836 (2 Jan)	1859 (20 Oct)	William Reed ✟
1859 (22 Nov)	1885 (21 Nov)	Richard Ward
1885 (26 Nov)	1886 (29 Sep)	Alfred Palmer
1886 (30 Sep)	1889 (11 Mar)	John W Lawson

Stirling	**1857-1938**	

Formed: 1857
Abolished: 16 Nov 1938. Became part of Stirlingshire
Strength: *Initial* 12 [1858]   *Final* 31

Chief Officer:

1857	1869	Henry Buchan
1869	1871	John Stuart
1872	1874	Walter Reid
1874	1910	Thomas Ferguson
1910	1933	George Nicol
1933	1938	William Whyte

Stirling and Clackmannan	1949-1975

Formed: 16 May 1949, by merger of Clackmannanshire and Stirlingshire
Abolished: 16 May 1975. Became part of Central Scotland
Strength: *Initial* 231   *Final* 467
Chief Officer:

1949	1958	Peter E Brodie
1958	1969	David Gray
1970	1975	Edward Frizzell

Stirlingshire	1850-1949

Formed: 1850
Abolished: 16 May 1949. Became part of Stirling and Clackmannan
Strength: *Initial* 31 [1859]   *Final* 194
Chief Officer:

1850		David Fleming
1858	1867	Alexander E Meffen
1867	1887	Alexander Campbell
1887 (1 Sep)	1907	John T D Sempill
1907 (1 Sep)	1938	Charles Middleton
1938 (1 Sep)	1949 (15 May)	William Whyte

Notes:
Absorbed Kilsyth, date not known
Absorbed Stirling Burgh, 16 Nov 1938
Named Stirling County, 1938-49

Stockport	1870-1967	🗀

Formed: 23 Mar 1870
Abolished: 1 Jul 1967. Became part of Cheshire
Strength: *Initial* 15   *Final* 347   ♥1889
Chief Officer:

1859	1874?	Isaac Moores
1875	1889	*Capt* [*Lt Col*] Frederick B Sharples
1889 (Dec)	1902	W H Jones
1902 (Jun)	1922	F Brindley
1922 (May)	1942	G W Rowbotham
1943 (Mar)	1947	John W Barnett

| 1947 (May) | 1961 | W Rees |
| 1962 (1 Oct) | 1967 | *Major* L Massey |

| Stoke-on-Trent | 1910-1968 | 📖 |

Formed: 1 Apr 1910, by merger of Hanley and part of Staffordshire
Abolished: 1 Jan 1968. Became part of Staffordshire
Strength: *Initial* 177   *Final* 507   🛡1910 ⚒ 1925
Chief Officer:

1910 (1 Apr)	1936 (13 Apr)	Roger J Carter ✝
1936 (1 Sep)	1955 (31 May)	Frank L Bunn
1955 (1 Jun)	1967 (31 Dec)	William E Watson

| Stonehouse | 1836-1914 |

Formed: 1836
Abolished: 9 Nov 1914. Became part of Plymouth
Strength: *Initial* ?   *Final* ?
Chief officer: Not known

| Stranraer | 1857-1870 |

Formed: 1857
Abolished: 1 Aug 1870. Became part of Wigtownshire
Strength: *Initial* 5 [1859]   *Final* 5
Chief Officer:

| 1859 | 1865 | Thomas Fisher |
| 1866 | 1870 | John Henderson |

| Stratford-on-Avon | 1835-1889 |

Formed: 1835
Abolished: 1 Apr 1889. Became part of Warwickshire
Strength: *Initial* 5 [1858]   *Final* 8
Chief Officer:

1853	[1861]	Thomas Taylor
1862	1868	W Richardson
1869	1889	T Rowley

| Strathclyde | 1975 | 📖 |

Formed: 16 May 1975, by merger of Argyllshire, Ayrshire, Dumbartonshire, Glasgow, Lanarkshire, Renfrew and Bute and part of Stirlingshire
Strength: *Initial* 6992   *Current* 8290
Chief Officer:

1975 (16 May)	1977 (12 Mar)	[*Sir*] David B McNee
1977	1985	[*Sir*] Patrick Hamill
1985	1991	[*Sir*] Andrew K Sloan

1991	1995	[*Sir*] Leslie Sharp
1996	2001 (30 Jun)	[*Sir*] John Orr
2001 (1 Jul)	2007 (Oct)	[*Sir*] William Rae
2007		Stephen House

Sudbury 1835-1889 📂

Formed: 1835
Abolished: 1 Apr 1889. Became part of West Suffolk
Strength: *Initial* 4?   *Final* 6
Chief Officer:

1835		James French
by 1855		Stephen Scott
	1859?	Thomas Whitcomb
1859	1889 (31 Mar)	William E Sach

Suffolk 1967 📖

Formed: 1 Apr 1967, by merger of East Suffolk, Ipswich and West Suffolk
Strength: *Initial* 996   *Current* 1242
Chief Officer:

1967 (1 Apr)	1968 (31 Mar)	[*Sir*] Peter J Matthews
1968	1976	Arthur Burns
1976	1989 (Apr)	Stuart L Whiteley
1989 (Apr)	1998 (1 Oct)	Anthony T Coe
1998 (2 Oct)	2002 (20 Sep)	[*Sir*] Paul J Scott-Lee
2003 (17 Feb)	2007 (31 Mar)	Alastair McWhirter
2007 (4 Jun)		Simon Ash

Sunderland 1837-1967 📖

Formed: 5 Oct 1837
Abolished: 1 Apr 1967. Became part of Durham
Strength: *Initial* 53   *Final* 347   ● 1889
Chief Officer:

1837 (17 Sep)	1855 (17 Feb)	William Brown
1855 (2 May)	1858 (Mar)	Robert Gifford
1858 (Mar)	1878 (Mar)	Joseph Stainsby
1878 (17 Mar)	1885 (15 Nov)	John Nicholson ✝
1885 (Nov)	1897 (Aug)	William Huntley
1897 (9 Sep)	1915 (Jul)	William Carter
1915 (12 Oct)	1925	Frederick J Crawley
1925 (13 Jul)	1937	John Ruddick
1937 (19 Jun)	1955 (Oct)	George H Cook
1955 (1 Nov)	1967 (31 Mar)	William Tait

Notes:
Absorbed River Wear, 30 Sep 1961

Surrey	1851	📖

Formed: 1 Jan 1851
Strength: *Initial* 71   *Current* 1847
Chief Officer:

1851 (1 Jan)	1899 (31 Aug)	*Capt* H C Hastings
1899 (1 Sep)	1930 (18 Dec)	*Capt* Mowbray L Sant
1930 (19 Dec)	1946 (30 Nov)	*Major* Geoffrey C Nicholson
1946 (1 Dec)	1956 (31 May)	[*Sir*] Joseph Simpson
1956 (1 Jun)	1968 (31 Mar)	*Lt Col* (Herman) Graham Rutherford
1968 (1 Apr)	1982	[*Sir*] Peter J Matthews
1982 (25 Dec)	1991 (Mar)	[*Sir*] Brian Hayes
1991 (May)	1997 (Oct)	David J Williams
1998 (12 Jan)	2000 (31 Jan)	[*Sir* later *Lord*] Ian Blair
2000 (10 Apr)	2004 (3 Oct?)	[*Sir*] Denis O'Connor
2004 (Nov)	2008 (1 Mar?)	Robert F Quick
2009 (12 Mar)		Mark Rowley

Notes:
Absorbed Guildford Borough, 17 Feb 1851
Guildford set up separate force, 16 Oct 1854
Godalming set up separate force, 1 Apr 1857
Reigate set up separate force, 25 Mar 1864
Absorbed Godalming Borough, 1 Apr 1889
Absorbed Reigate Borough and re-absorbed Guildford Borough, 1 Feb 1943
Part of area transferred from Metropolitan, 1 Apr 2000
Rowley had been temporary CC since Quick left

Sussex	1968	📖

Formed: 1 Jan 1968, by merger of Brighton, East Sussex, Eastbourne, Hastings and West Sussex
Strength: *Initial* 2355   *Current* 3111
Chief Officer:

1968 (1 Jan)	1972 (9 Sep)	Thomas C Williams ✝
1973	1983	[*Sir*] George W R Terry
1983	1993	[*Sir*] Roger Birch
1993	2001 (25 Sep)	Paul C Whitehouse
2002 (7 Jan)	2005	[*Sir*] Ken Jones
2006 (17 Feb)	2007 (30 Sep)	Joe Edwards
2007 (1 Oct)		Martin Richards

Sussex Combined	1943-1947	🗁

Formed: 1 Apr 1943, by merger of Brighton, East Sussex, Eastbourne, Hastings, Hove and West Sussex
Abolished: 1 Apr 1947. Separate forces re-formed, except that Hove became part of East Sussex

Strength: *Initial* 1171   *Final* 1182
Chief Officer:

1943 (1 Apr)	1945 (Nov)	*Major* [*Sir*] John F Ferguson
1945 (Nov)	1947 (31 Mar)	*Capt* William J Hutchinson (*Acting CC*)

Sutherland   1850-1963   📖

Formed: 1850
Abolished: 16 May 1963. Became part of Ross and Sutherland
Strength: *Initial* 10 [1862]   *Final* 27
Chief Officer:

1850		Philip McKay
1862	1865	Peter Ewan
1866	1884	Alexander McHardy
1884	1887	Roderick MacLean
1887 (14 Jun)	1906	Malcolm MacDonald
1906 (1 May)	1933	Hugh Chisholm
1933 (5 Jun)	1962	Douglas G Ross
1962 (6 Apr)	1963 (15 May)	Kenneth Ross

Swansea   1836-1969   📖

Formed: 4 Apr 1836
Abolished: 1 Jun 1969. Became part of South Wales
Strength: *Initial* 7   *Final* 390   ♥ 1889 1969
Chief Officer:

1836 (21 Mar)	1851 (Jan)	William Rees
1851 (14 Feb)	1857	Henry Tate
1857	1863	James Dunn
1863 (4 Mar)	1865	*Lt Col* John L Vivian
1865 (29 Nov)	1877	John Allison
1877 (Nov)	1913 (27 Jul)	*Capt* Isaac Colquhoun
1913	1921 (16 May)	*Capt* Alfred H Thomas ✝
1921	1927 (2 Aug)	Richard D Roberts ✝
1927 (Dec)	1931 (Mar)	*Capt* Thomas Rawson
1931	1941	Frank J May
1941 (3 Sep)	1962	David V Turner
1962 (1 Mar)	1969	Sydney Roberts

Tamworth   1840-1857

Formed: 1840
Abolished: 1857. Became part of Staffordshire
Strength: *Initial* ?   *Final* 2
Chief Officer: Not known

Tavistock		1837-1857?	📂

Formed: Sep 1837
Abolished: Before 1858. Became part of Devon
Strength: *Initial* 2?   *Final* ?
Chief Officer:

1840	1844	Mark Merritt

Tayside		1975

Formed: 16 May 1975, by merger of Angus, Dundee City and Perth and Kinross
Strength: *Initial* 923   *Current* 1236
Chief Officer:

1975 (16 May)	1980	John R Little
1980	1984	Robert S Sim
1984	1995 (31 Mar)	Jack W Bowman
1995 (1 Apr)	2000 (18 Nov)	William A Spence
2000 (19 Nov)	2008 (6 Jul)	John Vine
2008 (7 Jul)	2009 (10 Aug)	Kevin Mathieson
2010 (4 Feb)		Justine Curran

Teesside		1968-1974	📂

Formed: 1 Apr 1968, by merger of Middlesbrough and parts of Durham and North Riding
Abolished: 1 Apr 1974. Became part of Cleveland
Strength: *Initial* 777   *Final* 1074   🛡1968
Chief Officer:

1968 (1 Apr)	1974 (31 Mar)	Ralph Davison

Tenby		*ca*1840-1889	📂

Formed: *ca*1840
Abolished: 1 Apr 1889. Became part of Pembrokeshire
Strength: *Initial* 1   *Final* 3
Chief Officer:

1840	1860	Evan Howells
1860?	1861	James Thomas
1862	1867	R Harrison
1867	1877 (*ca*Oct)	Thomas Thomas
1877 (7 Oct)	1886 (30 Apr)	William H Hodges
1886 (30 Apr)	1889 (31 Mar)	James Carr

Tenterden		*ca*1835-1889	📂

Formed: 1835
Abolished: 1 Apr 1889. Became part of Kent
Strength: *Initial* 4   *Final* 4

Chief Officer:

1856	1881	James Barns
1881	1889	Benjamin T Goldsmith

Tewkesbury	1836-1854

Formed: 29 Jan 1836
Abolished: 1854. Became part of Gloucestershire
Strength: *Initial* ?   *Final* 7
Chief Officer:

1836	1838	Henry Rackham
1838?	1846	John Martin
1846	1854	J Herbert

Thames Valley	1968	📖

Formed: 1 Apr 1968, by merger of Berkshire, Buckinghamshire, Oxford City, Oxfordshire and Reading
Strength: *Initial* 2960   *Current* 4335
Chief Officer:

1968 (1 Apr)	1970	Thomas C B Hodgson
1970	1978	David Holdsworth
1979	1985	[*Sir* later *Lord*] Peter M Imbert
1985	1991	Colin R Smith
1991	2002 (31 Jan)	[*Sir*] Charles Pollard
2002 (1 Feb)	2006 (15 Jan)	Peter Neyroud
2006 (16 Jan)		Sara Thornton

Notes:
Ms Thornton was originally appointed Acting CC and confirmed in post, Apr 2007

Thetford	1836-1857	📂

Formed: 11 Feb 1836
Abolished: 22 Jul 1857. Became part of Norfolk
Strength: *Initial* 1   *Final* 4
Chief Officer:

1836 (29 Feb)	1841 (Feb)	John Nixon
1841 (26 Feb)	1845 (Nov)	Philip P Wilson
1845 (2 Dec)	1846 (18 Jun)	Henry Drake
1846 (15 Jun)	1846 (*ca*Dec)	Charles Utting
1846	1856 (15 Nov)	John C Tyler
1857 (16 Jan)	1857 (21 Jul)	Bernard Andrews

Notes:
Drake and his sole assistant were dismissed for *continual disagreements* with each other

Thurso		1841-1858	
Formed: 1841			
Abolished: 1858. Became part of Caithness-shire			
Strength: *Initial*?		*Final*?	
Chief Officer:			
1841	1842	John Bain	
1842	1846	William Swanson	
1846	1856	John Swanson	
1856	1858	George Swanson	

Tiverton		1836-1943	🕮
Formed: 1836			
Abolished: 1 Jan 1943. Became part of Devon			
Strength: *Initial* 7 [1858]		*Final* 11	
Chief Officer:			
1853	1863	E Harford	
1863	1898	John B Crabbe	
1898	1901	Henry C Rawle	
1901 (Dec)	1926	Thomas Mercer	
1925 (2 Nov)	1942 (31 Dec)	(B) Mervyn Beynon	

Torquay		1835-1870	
Formed: 3 Aug 1835			
Abolished: 1870. Became part of Devon			
Strength: *Initial* 3		*Final*?	
Chief officer:			
1835 (3 Aug)		Charles Kilby	

Torrington		1836-1870	🗁
Formed: 1836			
Abolished: Oct 1870. Became part of Devon			
Strength: *Initial* 1		*Final* 2	
Chief Officer:			
1853	[1862]	William Cole	
1863	1870	Philip Blake	

Torrington		1878-1889	🗁
Re-formed: 1878, from part of Devon			
Abolished: 1 Apr 1889. Became part of Devon			
Strength: *Initial* 2		*Final* 2	
Chief Officer:			
1878	1889	John Quick	

Totnes	1836-1884	📁

Formed: 1836
Abolished: 1 Jul 1884. Became part of Devon
Strength: *Initial* 2 [1858]   *Final* 3
Chief Officer:

1853	1876	John Bishop
1876	1884	James Clark

Trevethin	1836-1860	📖

Formed: 1836
Abolished: 1 Apr 1860. Became part of Monmouthshire
Strength: *Initial* 2   *Final* 6
Chief Officer:

1836	1860	John Roberts

Truro	1838-1921	📁

Formed: Dec 1838
Abolished: 1 Mar 1921. Became part of Cornwall
Strength: *Initial* 6 [1858]   *Final* 13   🏭 1887
Chief Officer:

1838 (Dec)	1859	George Paine
1859	1864	W J Nash
1865	1872	William Woodcock
1873	1894	Richard Angel
1894	1897	Edwin F Winch
1897	1901	J T Coleman
1901 (Oct)	1920	Frank Pearce

Tunbridge Wells	1835-1943	📁

Formed: 1835
Abolished: 1 Apr 1943. Became part of Kent
Strength: *Initial* 6   *Final* 67
Chief Officer:

1835	1840 (Nov)	John A Thompson
1840?	1844?	Thomas Barton
1844?	1847 (May)	William Plumb ⚕
1847 (Jun)	1847 (Oct)	Charles Bailey
1847 (25 Oct)	1853 (Apr)	William Morten
1853 (Jun)	1862	Cyril W Onslow
1862 (Aug)	1891	John J Embury
1891	1893 (28 Jul)	John C Allison
1893 (Aug)	1921	Charles Prior
1921 (May)	1927	*Capt* Stanley A Hector
1927 (May)	1943 (31 Mar)	Guy Carlton

Notes:
Bailey was dismissed after failing to return from compassionate leave
Morten was dismissed after absence from duty and allegations of defrauding his men of expenses
Allison *left the country hurriedly*

Tynemouth		1850-1969	📖

Formed: 1 Jan 1850
Abolished: 1 Apr 1969. Became part of Northumberland
Strength: *Initial* 12   *Final* 172   ♥ 1904
Chief Officer:

1850 (1 Jan)	1856 (19 Dec)	Robert Mitchell
1857 (Feb)	1871 (18 Jan)	John W Hewitt ♱
1871	1878	George Stewart
1878	1893 (28 Nov)	Alexander Anderson ♱
1893 (19 Dec)	1920 (Apr)	John H Huish
1920 (26 May)	1946 (31 Aug)	Tom Blackburn
1946 (1 Sep)	1952 (31 Dec)	Donald Lockett
1953 (1 Jan)	1963 (16 Apr)	James J Scott
1963 (17 Apr)	1969 (31 Mar)	Walter Baharie

Notes:
Mitchell was dismissed on suspicion of forgery (claiming expenses for his men which they did not receive). He disappeared

Wakefield		1848-1968	📖

Formed: 23 May 1848
Abolished: 1 Oct 1968. Became part of West Yorkshire
Strength: *Initial* 19   *Final* 127   ♥ 1915 ▲ 1888
Chief Officer:

1848 (3 Jul)	1868 (Jun)	James McDonald ♱
1868 (29 Jul)	1877 (30 Nov)	James A Chipstead
1877 (Dec)	1889 (May)	Charles T Clarkson
1889 (12 Jun)	1920 (30 Jun)	Thomas M Harris
1920 (1 Aug)	1942 (31 Mar)	Robert Yelloly
1942 (Apr)	1965	Alfred E Godden
1965	1968 (30 Sep)	Clifford A Jarratt (*Acting CC*)

Notes:
Clarkson was dismissed after being absent from a visit by the HMI
John C Huxtable was offered appointment as CC, but declined it, Jun 1920

Walcot		1793-1836	📁

Formed: 1793
Abolished: 1836. Became part of Bath
Strength: *Initial* ca50 [1825]   *Final* ?

Chief Officer:
1825?   *Four Insps*
Notes:
Established as a force of night-watchmen under a local Act of Parliament, 1793
A further local Act empowered the watchmen to act as day-time constables, 1825
Re-modelled on the lines of the Metropolitan Police, 1830

Wallasey	1913-1967	📖

Formed: 1 Apr 1913, from part of Cheshire
Abolished: 1 Jul 1967. Became part of Cheshire
Strength: *Initial* 90   *Final* 225   ♥1913
Chief Officer:

1913 (1 Apr)	1930 (6 Nov)	Percy L Barry
1931 (9 Jan)	1959 (30 Sep)	John Ormerod
1959	1967 (30 Jun)	Walter Marshall

Wallingford	1836-1856	🗁

Formed: 13 Jan 1836
Abolished: 28 Jul 1856. Became part of Berkshire
Strength: *Initial* 3   *Final* 3
Chief Officer:

1836 (1 Feb)		William Argyle
	1856 (8 Sep)	Alfred Clarke?

Walsall	1832-1966	📖

Formed: 6 Jul 1832
Abolished: 1 Apr 1966. Became part of West Midlands
Strength: *Initial* 4   *Final* 244   ♥1889
Chief Officer:

1832 (6 Jul)	1834 (Dec)	F H West
1834?		Ryder
1842 (3 Jan)	1849	John Rofe
1849	1850	Burton
*ca*1852		John Armishaw [*preceded or succeeded by another man*]
1850	1855	*Two successive Supts*
1855 (Aug)	1885	John W Cater
1885 (26 Oct)	1887	George Tewsley
1887	1900	Christopher Taylor
1901	1901	Nicholson R Gardiner
1902	1921	Alexander Thompson
1921 (Apr)	1932	G H Ballance
1932 (Nov)	1952	(T) Mark Watson
1953 (Jan)	1958 (12 Jan?)	Donald Lockett

1958	1964	K M Wherly
1964	1966 (31 Mar)	Edwin Solomon

Notes:
Rofe was dismissed after complaints about the efficiency of the force
Burton was dismissed for neglect of duty (spending time at race meetings)

Wantage **1828-1856** 📁

Formed: 19 Jun 1828
Abolished: 9 Feb 1856. Became part of Berkshire
Strength: *Initial* ? *Final* ?
Chief Officer: Not known

Warrington **1847-1969**

Formed: 1847
Abolished: 1 Apr 1969. Became part of Lancashire
Strength: *Initial* 5 *Final* 180 💧1889
Chief Officer:

1852	1866	J S MacMichael
1868	1895	Samuel Hunt
1895 (Nov)	1907	Luke Talbot
1907 (Jul)	1937	Martin Nicholls
1937 (1 Jul)	1950	Francis L Summers
1950 (20 Mar)	1963	Alexander Jeffrey
1963	1969	*Lt Col* Ronald E Rowbottom

Warwick **1846-1875** 📖

Formed: 26 Sep 1846
Abolished: 30 Sep 1875. Became part of Warwickshire
Strength: *Initial* 12 [1858] *Final* 11
Chief Officer:

1846	1851	Thomas Bellerby ✝
1852 (18 Feb)	1875 (30 Sep)	William C Hickling

Warwickshire **1857** 📖

Formed: 5 Feb 1857
Strength: *Initial* 133 *Current* 893
Chief Officer:

1857 (5 Feb)	1875	James Isaac
1875 (Dec)	1892	R H Kinchant
1892	1928 (14 Dec)	*Capt* John T Brinkley ✝
1929	1948	*Cmdr* E R B Kemble ✝
1948 (19 Oct)	1958	*Lt Col* Geoffrey C White
1958 (1 Nov)	1964	Peter E Brodie
1964 (1 Apr)	1976	Richard B Matthews

1977	1978	Albert Laugharne
1978	1983	[*Sir*] Roger Birch
1983	1998 (Oct)	Peter D Joslin
1998 (Oct)	2000 (9 Feb)	Andrew C Timpson
2000 (Aug)	2006 (Jul)	John Burbeck
2006 (Jul)		Keith Bristow

Notes:
Absorbed Warwick Borough, 30 Sep 1875
Absorbed Stratford-on-Avon Borough, 1 Apr 1889
Kemble commited suicide
Absorbed Leamington Spa Borough, 1 Apr 1948
Absorbed Coventry City, 1 Oct 1969
Named Warwickshire and Coventry, 1969-74
Part of area transferred to West Midlands, 1 Apr 1974

Wells	**?-1856**

Formed: Not known
Abolished: 14 Oct 1856. Became part of Somerset
Strength: *Initial* ?   *Final* ?   1205
Chief Officer: Not known

Welshpool	**1835?-1857**

Formed: Sep 1835?
Abolished: 1857. Became part of Montgomeryshire
Strength: *Initial* ?   *Final* ?
Chief Officer:

1835 (Sep?)	1842 (Dec)	John Armishaw

Wenlock	**1836-1841**

Formed: 1836
Abolished: 4 Jan 1841. Became part of Shropshire
Strength: *Initial* ?   *Final* 4
Chief Officer: Not known

West Lothian	**1840-1950**	🗁

Formed: 1840
Abolished: 16 May 1950. Became part of Lothians and Peebles
Strength: *Initial* 14 [1859]   *Final* 91
Chief Officer:

1840	1877 (4 Sep)	Adam Colquhoun
1877 (24 Dec)	1878 (26 Apr)	H Stuart Johnson
1878 (27 Apr)	1884 (3 Jun)	*Capt* David Munro
1884 (29 Jul)	1914 (6 Oct)	*Lt Col* Alexander Borthwick ♱
1914 (8 Dec)	1950 (15 May)	*Major* Sholto W Douglas

Notes:
Force originally named Linlithgowshire
Johnson, Munro and Borthwick were also CC of Mid Lothian
From 1894 to 1950, the same CC administered four forces: East Lothian, Mid Lothian, Peebles-shire and West Lothian

West Mercia	1967	📖

Formed: 1 Oct 1967, by merger of Herefordshire, Shropshire, Worcester City and Worcestershire
Strength: *Initial* 1746   *Current* 2213
Chief Officer:

1967 (1 Oct)	1974 (31 Dec)	[*Sir*] John A Willison
1975 (1 Jan)	1981 (23 Jan)	Alexander A Rennie
1981 (Jan)	1985	Robert W Cozens
1985 (May)	1991	(Aidan) Anthony Mullett
1991 (28 Aug)	1999 (28 Feb)	David C Blakey
1999 (6 Apr)	2003 (23 Feb)	Peter Hampson
2003 (1 Aug)		Paul West

Notes:
Parts of area transferred to West Midlands, 1 Apr 1974 and Apr 1995

West Midlands	1966	

Formed: 1 Apr 1966, by merger of Dudley, Walsall, Wolverhampton and parts of Staffordshire and Worcestershire
Strength: *Initial* 1962   *Current* 8068
Chief Officer:

1966	1967	Norman W Goodchild
1967	1974	Edwin Solomon
1974 (1 Apr)	1975 (30 Jun)	*Sir* (William) Derrick Capper
1975 (1 Aug)	1985 (7 Apr)	[*Sir* later *Lord*] Philip D Knights
1985 (8 Apr)	1990	[*Sir* later *Lord*] Geoffrey J Dear
1990	1996 (31 Jul)	[*Sir*] Ronald Hadfield
1996 (26 Aug)	2002 (Aug)	[*Sir*]Edward M Crew
2002 (Sep)	2009 (30 Apr)	[*Sir*] Paul J Scott-Lee
2009 (1 Jun)		Christopher Sims

Notes:
Absorbed Birmingham City and part of Warwickshire, 1 Apr 1974
Absorbed part of West Mercia, Apr 1995

West Riding	1856-1968	📖

Formed: 29 Nov 1856
Abolished: 1 Oct 1968. Became part of West Yorkshire
Strength: *Initial* 466   *Final* 3512
Chief Officer:

1856 (14 Nov)	1869 (16 Jun)	*Lt Col* C A Cobbe
1869 (21 Jul)	1876 (30 Jun)	*Capt* Duncan McNeill
1876	1905 (Oct)	*Capt* (T) Stuart Russell
1906 (2 Jan)	1908 (28 May)	*Capt* [*Lt Col*] Herbert C Metcalfe
1908 (6 Jul)	1919 (31 Jan)	*Major* [*Col Sir*] Llewellyn W Atcherley
1919 (4 Mar)	1929 (17 Sep)	*Col* Jacynth d'E F Coke
1929 (1 Nov)	1935 *(17 Sep)*	*Lt Col* [*Sir*] Frank Brook
1935 (4 Nov)	1944 (16 Feb)	George C Vaughan
1944 (1 Aug)	1959	*Capt* [*Sir*] Henry Studdy
1959 (1 Nov)	1968 (30 Sep)	[*Sir*] George E Scott

Notes:
Rotherham set up separate force, 1 Jul 1882
Absorbed Ripon Borough, 1 Oct 1887
Absorbed Pontefract Borough, 1 Apr 1889

West Suffolk	**1845-1967**	📖

Formed: 7 Jan 1845
Abolished: 1 Apr 1967. Became part of Suffolk
Strength: *Initial* 41   *Final* 275
Chief Officer:

1845 (1 Feb)	1846 (Jun)	*Major* George D Griffiths ✝
1846 (14 Jul)	1851 (23 Oct)	*Col* George W Eyres
1852 (17 Feb)	1869 (21 Apr)	*Capt* Edwin C Syer
1869 (4 May)	1898 (2 Dec)	*Major* Clement H J Heigham ✝
1899 (20 Feb)	1902 (30 Sep)	*Major* [*Lt Col*] Arthur F Poulton
1902 (28 Oct)	1906 (1 Jan)	*Capt* [*Lt Col*] Herbert C Metcalfe
1906 (1 Jan)	1932 (31 Mar)	*Major* Edward P Prest
1932 (1 Apr)	1937 (1 Oct)	*Col* Jacynth d'E F Coke
1938 (1 Jan)	1945 (7 May)	*Capt* [*Major*] Colin D Robertson
1945 (24 Sep)	1967 (31 Mar)	William J Ridd

Notes:
Absorbed Bury St Edmunds Borough, 1 Jan 1857
Heigham commanded both East Suffolk and West Suffolk from 1869 to 1898
Absorbed Sudbury Borough, 1 Apr 1889

West Sussex	**1857-1943**	📖

Formed: 26 Feb 1857
Abolished: 1 Apr 1943. Became part of Sussex Combined
Strength: *Initial* 71   *Final* 308
Chief Officer:

1857 (5 Mar)	1879 (Oct?)	*Capt* Frederick Montgomerie ✝
1879 (5 Dec)	1912	*Capt* George R B Drummond [apptd 16 Oct]
1912 (18 Sep)	1934 (31 Dec)	*Capt* Arthur S Williams
1935 (1 Jan)	1943 (31 Mar)	Ronald P Wilson

Notes:

Absorbed Arundel Borough and Chichester City, 1 Apr 1889

West Sussex	1947-1968	📖

Re-formed: 1 Apr 1947, from part of Sussex Combined
Abolished: 1 Jan 1968. Became part of Sussex
Strength: *Initial* 418   *Final* 840
Chief Officer:

1947 (1 Apr)	1964	Ronald P Wilson
1964 (13 Apr)	1967 (31 Dec)	Thomas C Williams

West Yorkshire	1968	📖

Formed: 1 Oct 1968, by merger of Barnsley, Dewsbury, Doncaster, Halifax, Huddersfield, Wakefield and West Riding
Strength: *Initial* 4663   *Current* 5529
Chief Officer:

1968 (1 Oct)	1969 (5 Jun)	*Sir* George E Scott
1969 (6 Jun)	1983 (5 Jun)	Ronald Gregory
1983 (6 Jun)	1989	[*Sir*] Colin Sampson
1989	1993	Peter J Nobes
1993	1998 (4 Jan)	Keith Hellawell
1998 (9 Mar)	2002	Graham Moore
2002 (10 Nov)	2006 (28? Nov)	Colin Cramphorn
2007 (30 Jan)		*Sir* Norman Bettison

Notes:
Parts of area transferred to Cumbria, Greater Manchester, Humberside, Lancashire, North Yorkshire and South Yorkshire, 1 Apr 1974
Absorbed Bradford and Leeds Cities, 1 Apr 1974
Named West Yorkshire Metropolitan Police, 1974-86

Wester Ross	1850-1853	

Formed: 1850
Abolished: 1853. Became part of Ross
Strength: *Initial* ?   *Final* ?
Chief officer: Not known

Westmorland	1857-1963	

Formed: 6 Jan 1857
Abolished: 1 Sep 1963. Became part of Cumberland, Westmorland and Carlisle
Strength: *Initial* 14   *Final* 108
Chief Officer:

1856	1902	[*Sir*] John Dunne
1902 (1 Sep)	1920	Charles de C Parry
1920 (1 Aug)	1925	*Lt Col* [*Sir*] Hugh S Turnbull
1926 (4 Mar)	1951	*Capt* Philip T B Browne

1952	1959	John S H Gaskain
1959	1963	Henry Watson

Notes:
CC appointed jointly with Cumberland but forces administered separately

---

Weymouth and Melcombe Regis 1846-1921

Formed: 1846
Abolished: 1921. Became part of Dorset
Strength: *Initial* 10   *Final* 35
Chief Officer:

1853	1868	C Lidbury
1869	1891	Samuel A Vickery
1891 (Jun)	1915	Frank Eacock
1915	1921	Walter Day

Whitehaven   1843-?

Formed: 27 Nov 1843
Abolished: Before 1858. Became part of Cumberland
Strength: *Initial* 12   *Final* ?
Chief Officer:

1843 (27 Nov)		Charles Fletcher

Wick   1841-1858

Formed: 1841
Abolished: 1858. Became part of Caithness-shire
Strength: *Initial* 1   *Final* ?
Chief officer: Not known

Wick   1863-73

Re-formed: 1863, from part of Caithness-shire
Abolished: 1873. Became part of Caithness-shire
Strength: *Initial* 2   *Final* ?
Chief officer: Not known

Wigan   1836-1969   📖

Formed: 6 Jan 1836
Abolished: 1 Apr 1969. Became part of Lancashire
Strength: *Initial* 7   *Final* 189   🛡 1889
Chief Officer:

1836 (6 Jan)	1840	John Whittle
1840	1852	Thomas Latham
1852	1875 (31 Mar)	William Simm
1875	1879	George Williams

1879 (20 Mar)	1880	*Capt* Charles G Alison
1880 (12 Aug)	1883	*Capt* T Robert Kennion
1883	1890	Frederick T Webb
1890	1898 (Dec)	*Capt* Alexander Bell
1899 (Mar)	1914	George Hardy
1914 (6 Apr)	1921 (31 Mar)	John S Percival
1921 (1 Apr)	1946 (Feb)	Thomas J Pey
1946 (13 Jun)	1957 (25 Jan)	Paul Foster ✞
1957 (9 May)	1968 (31 Mar)	David Aitken
1968 (1 Apr)	1969 (31 Mar)	William H Taylor (*Acting CC*)

Notes:
Whittle was dismissed for being drunk and indecently assaulting a woman

Wigtownshire 1838-1948 🕮

Formed: 1 Nov 1838
Abolished: 16 Feb 1948. Became part of Dumfries and Galloway
Strength: *Initial* 19 *Final* 31
Chief Officer:

1838	1841?	McDougal [*Stranraer*]
1838		John McClelland [*Wigtown*]
1841?		James Stewart [*Stranraer*]
1858 (24 Feb)	1860	John Haining
1860 (29 Mar)	1886 (13 Nov)	Cornelius Murphy
1886 (13 Nov)	1922 (15 May)	Brooke S Cunliffe
1922 (15 May)	1939 (15 Nov)	Alexander Donald
1939 (16 Nov)	1943 (15 Nov)	George Scott
1944 (16 Jun)	1948 (15 Feb)	(Wilson) Colin Campbell

Notes:
Until 1858, the force had 2 Supts, based at Stranraer and Wigtown
Absorbed Stranraer Burgh, 1 Aug 1870
Donald was also CC of Kirkcudbrightshire

Wiltshire 1839 🕮

Formed: 28 Nov 1839
Strength: *Initial* 201 *Current* 1071
Chief Officer:

1839 (28 Nov)	1870	*Capt* Samuel Meredith
1870 (5 Apr)	1908	*Capt* Robert Sterne
1908 (5 May)	1945 (2 Apr)	*Capt* [*Col Sir*] Hoel Llewellyn ✞
1946 (1 Jan)	1963	*Lt Col* Harold A Golden
1963 (4 Oct)	1979	George R Glendinning
1979 (1 Oct)	1983 (Sep)	Kenneth Mayer
1983	1988 (Jun)	Donald Smith
1988	1997 (31 Mar)	Walter R Girven
1997 (1 Apr)	2004 (17 Sep)	[*Dame*] Elizabeth A Neville

2004 (20 Sep)   2007 (30 Sep)   Martin Richards
2008 (1 Jan)   Brian Moore
Notes:
Llewellyn returned to the Army, 14 Sep 1914-18 Jan 1919. R J Buchanan was appointed acting CC
Absorbed Salisbury City, 1 Apr 1943

Winchester	1832-1943	

Formed: 28 Jul 1832
Abolished: 1 Apr 1943. Became part of Hampshire
Strength: *Initial* 8   *Final* 38   ▲ 1189
Chief Officer:

1832	1833	Robert Buchanan
1833	1851	William Shepherd
1851	1873	Henry Hubbersley
1873	1892	William Morton
1892 (Apr)	1909	William Felton
1909 (1 Oct)	1924	John Sim
1924 (1 Oct)	1942	William G Stratton
1942 (1 Apr)	1943	Harry R Miles

Windsor	1836-1947	🗁

Formed: 5 Mar 1836
Abolished: 1 Apr 1947. Became part of Berkshire
Strength: *Initial* 11   *Final* 45
Chief Officer:

1836 (29 Feb)	1853	William H Gillman
1853	1868	Fred Eager
1869	1870	John M Davis
1870 (1 Apr)	1889	George Hayes
1889 (11 Mar)	1898	Andrew W Armour
1898 (31 Aug)	1901	Roger J Carter
1901 (1 Sep)	1907	Martin Nicholls
1907 (30 Sep)	1939	James T Carter
1939 (1 Dec)	1947	Ralph N Wellings

Notes:
Also known as New Windsor

Wisbech	1835-1889	

Formed: 1835
Abolished: 1 Apr 1889. Became part of Isle of Ely
Strength: *Initial* 10   *Final* 11
Chief Officer:

1853	1859	Samuel Taylor

1860	1863	(W) Martin Burke
1863	1869	B Eason
1869	1889	William Sharpe

Wishaw	?-1859

Formed: Not known
Abolished: 1859. Became part of Lanarkshire
Strength: *Initial*?   *Final*?
Chief Officer: Not known

Wolborough	?-*ca*1859

Formed: Not known
Abolished: *ca*1859. Became part of Cornwall
Strength: *Initial*?   *Final*?
Chief Officer: Not known

Wolverhampton	1837-1966

Formed: 3 Aug 1837
Abolished: 1 Apr 1966. Became part of West Midlands
Strength: *Initial* 7   *Final* 300   ♥1889
Chief Officer:

1848	1857	*Lt Col* Gilbert Hogg
1857 (14 Apr)	1878	*Capt* Henry Segrave
1878 (13 Sep)	1887	*Major* R D D Hay
1887 (Dec)	1916	*Capt* L R Burnett
1916 (5 Jun)	1929	David Webster
1930 (15 Jan)	1943	Edwin Tilley
1944 (16 Aug)	1966 (31 Mar)	Norman W Goodchild

Worcester	1833-1967	📖

Formed: 18 Jan 1833
Abolished: 1 Oct 1967. Became part of West Mercia
Strength: *Initial* 14   *Final* 140   ♥1889 🏰1189
Chief Officer:

1833 (18 Jan)	1835 (24 Apr)	Henry Sharpe ♔
1835 (24 Apr)	1840 (24 Jan)	James Douglas
1840 (6 Mar)	1849 (Jul)	John Phillips ♔
1850 (18 Jan)	1861 (Mar)	Thomas Chipp ♔
1861 (1 Jun)	1884 (7 Feb)	Matthew Power ♔
1884 (15 Feb)	1892 (May)	Arthur E Sommers
1892 (10 Jun)	1923 (Mar)	Thomas W Byrne
1923 (1 May)	1928	Oswald J B Cole
1929 (1 Jan)	1931 (Jul)	*Capt* William J Hutchinson
1931 (1 Dec)	1955 (Jan)	Ernest W Tinkler

| 1955 (1 Feb) | 1958 (6 Jun) | Glyn Davies |
| 1958 (1 Oct) | 1967 | Eric A Abbott |

Notes:
Davies was convicted of fraud and dismissed

Worcestershire	**1839-1967**	📖

Formed: 13 Dec 1839
Abolished: 1 Oct 1967. Became part of West Mercia
Strength: *Initial* 41   *Final* 701
Chief Officer:

1839 (16 Dec)	1871 (3 Apr)	Richard R Harris
1871 (3 Apr)	1903 (29 Jan)	*Lt Col* George L Carmichael ✝
1903 (4 Apr)	1931 (30 Sep)	*Lt Col* Herbert S Walker
1931 (1 Oct)	1958 (Apr)	*Capt* James E Lloyd-Williams
1958 (8 Apr)	1967 (30 Sep)	[*Sir*] John A Willison

Notes:
Absorbed Evesham Borough, 14 Oct 1850
Absorbed Droitwich Borough, 1 Aug 1881
Absorbed Bewdley Borough, Apr 1882
Absorbed Kidderminster Borough, 1 Apr 1947

Wycombe	**1836-1947**	📖

Formed: Feb 1836
Abolished: 1 Apr 1947. Became part of Buckinghamshire
Strength: *Initial* 3   *Final* 46
Chief Officer:

1836	1839 (May)	Thomas Skull
1839 (6 Apr)	1879 (Apr?)	George Davis
1879	1886 (Feb?)	Thomas Collins
1886	1891	John G Fraser
1891 (23 Feb)	1913 (4 Aug)	Oscar D Sparling
1913 (Aug)	1918 (Sep)	George P Stephens
1919 (10 Feb)	1947 (31 Mar)	William T Jones

Notes:
Area also known as Chepping Wycombe or High Wycombe

Yeovil	**?-1859**

Formed: Not known
Abolished: Apr 1859. Became part of Somerset
Strength: *Initial* ?   *Final* 5
Chief Officer: Not known

York	**1836-1968**	📖

Formed: 28 Apr 1836

Abolished: 1 Jul 1968. Became part of York and North East Yorkshire
Strength: *Initial* 12   *Final* 219   ♥1889 🏭1189
Chief Officer:

1836	1836	Daniel Smith
1836	1841	William Pardoe
1841 (4 Nov)	1861	Robert T H Chalk
1862	1888	S Haley
1888 (Oct)	1894 (Aug)	George W Whitfield
1894	1897	E T Lloyd
1897	1900	Joseph Farndale
1900 (Aug)	1918	James Burrows
1918 (1 Jun)	1929	Henry Woolnough ✞
1929 (10 Jun)	1955	Harry H Herman
1954 (1 Sep)	1968	Cyril T G Carter

York and North East Yorkshire   1968-1974

Formed: 1 Jul 1968, by merger of East Riding, North Riding and York City
Abolished: 1 Apr 1974. Became part of Cleveland, Durham, Humberside and North Yorkshire
Strength: *Initial* 1213   *Final* 1218
Chief Officer:

1968 (1 Jul)	1972	Harold H Salisbury
1973	1974	R P Boyes

Zetland   1883-1969

Formed: 1883
Abolished: 15 May 1969. Became part of Northern
Strength: *Initial* 4 [1894]   *Final* 21
Chief Officer:

1883	1889	Peter Urquhart
1889 (3 Dec)	1940	Gifford Gray
1940	1950	Thomas Stuart
1950	1967	Robert Bruce
1967	1969	John Johnston (*Acting CC*)

Notes:

The force was not subject to the Police (Scotland) Act 1857 until 15 Jan 1938
Named Shetland until 1940
Absorbed Lerwick Burgh, 29 May 1940

6 Index of Chief Police Officers 1829-2012:

An alphabetical list of the chief officers of British police forces

The index lists all the chief officers named in chapter 5, including those who only held acting or temporary appointments. The arrangement is by surname, then by initials. Entries with the same surname and initials are then arranged chronologically by the year of appointment. This allows you to see the progress of a chief officer who held more than one of the top posts

However, it means that, in a few cases, two officers with the same surname and initials and serving at around the same time may have their index entries interfiled. Please check the full names in chapter 5 to distinguish them. In the case of the two men named Joseph Farndale (uncle and nephew), we have noted them in the index as 1 and 2

Abbott	EA	1959	1967	Worcester
Abbott	W	1929	1941	Scarborough
Aberdein	A	1947	1948	Salford
Acres	P	2000	2004	Hertfordshire
Adams	AF	1881	1881	South Shields
Adams	G	1836	1856	Hereford
Adams	W	1912	1926	Doncaster
Adams-Connor	HG	1899	1935	Isle of Wight
Adamson	R	1839	1860	Fife
Adamson	R	1886	1900	Forfarshire
Adamson	R	1950	1951	Ayr
Adamson	R	1951	1968	Ayrshire
Adcock	A	1900	1918	Boston
Aedy	J	1878	1889	Hythe
Aitken	D	1957	1968	Wigan
Alderson	JC	1973	1982	Devon & Cornwall
Alderson	R	1942	1944	Macclesfield
Alderson	R	1944	1947	Luton
Alderson	R	1950	1956	Monmouthshire
Aldous	DW	1995	1999	Dorset
Alexander	R	1836	1839	Aberdeen
Alexander	S	1862	1866	Leominster
Alexander	S	1866	1870	Newcastle-under-Lyme
Alexander	S	1870	1872	Hanley
Alison	CG	1879	1880	Wigan
Alison	CG	1884	1908	Somerset
Allan	RS	1954	1967	Renfrew & Bute
Allan	WD	1919	1920	Bootle
Allan	WD	1920	1927	Argyllshire
Allbutt	H	1894	1906	Bristol
Allen	H	1913	1928	Leicester
Allen	HC	1931	1933	Rochester
Allen	HC	1933	1940	Huddersfield
Allen	HC	1940	1941	Southampton
Allgood	G	1869	1886	Northumberland
Allison	J	1857	1865	Lancaster
Allison	J	1865	1877	Swansea
Allison	JC	1891	1893	Tunbridge Wells
Ambler	H	1957	1973	Bradford
Amos	J	1849	1850	Middlesbrough
Anderson	A	1878	1893	Tynemouth
Anderson	D	1847	1854	Inverness Burgh
Anderson	D	1858	1859	Dumfries
Anderson	G	1856	1886	Maryhill
Anderson	J	1893	1911	Coatbridge
Anderson	T	1858	1859	Portobello

Anderson	T	1862	1865	Alloa
Anderson	W	1840	1841	Banffshire
Anderson	W	1840	1858	Aberdeenshire
Anderson	W	1903	1932	Aberdeen
Anderson	WJ	1896	1900	Lerwick
Anderton	CJ	1976	1991	Greater Manchester
Andrews	B	1857	1857	Thetford
Andrews	W	1836		King's Lynn
Angel	R	1873	1894	Truro
Angus	J	1962	1967	Grimsby
Angus	J	1968	1974	Leeds
Angus	JW	1886	1913	Greenock
Anley	FR	1918	1941	Derbyshire
Annesley	H	1989	1996	Royal Ulster
Anson	GA	1888	1929	Staffordshire
Anson	I	1853	1859	Grimsby
Appleyard	A	1905	1923	Margate
Arbuthnot	EK	1921	1940	Oxfordshire
Archer-Burton	JR	1955	1958	Hastings
Archer-Burton	JR	1958	1965	North Riding
Argent	MJ	1994	2000	North Wales
Argyle	W	1836		Wallingford
Armishaw	J	1835	1842	Welshpool
Armishaw	J	1852		Walsall
Armitage	CL	1907	1919	Southport
Armitage	H	1841		Saint Ives
Armour	AW	1889	1898	Windsor
Armstrong	A	1971	1979	Bedfordshire
Armstrong	FJ	1946	1953	Northumberland
Armstrong	M	1798	1800	Marine Police
Arnold	AS	1903	1931	Rochester
Arnold	DCJ	1948	1963	Cambridgeshire
Arrowsmith	JP	1885	1887	Dewsbury
Arrowsmith	JP	1887	1888	Bootle
Arrowsmith	JW	1869	1871	Bedford
Arrowsmith	JW	1878	1881	Cheshire
Arton	W	1836	1850	Evesham
Arundale	IB	2008		Dyfed-Powys
Ash	S	2007		Suffolk
Ashe	W	1884	1902	Middlesbrough
Ashton	N	1929	1933	Saint Albans
Ashton	N	1933	1937	Bath
Aston	J	1961	1969	Barrow-in-Furness
Atcherley	LW	1906	1908	Shropshire
Atcherley	LW	1908	1919	West Riding
Atherton	A	1964	1969	Saint Helens

Atkin	R	1900	1907	Orkney
Atkins	R	1959	1967	Flintshire
Atkinson	D	1932	1968	River Tyne
Austin	WH	1875	1880	Maidenhead
Axon	J	1966	1973	Jersey
Bacon	RRM	1947	1961	Devon
Baggott	M	2002	2009	Leicestershire
Baggott	M	2009		Northern Ireland
Baharie	W	1963	1969	Tynemouth
Bailey	AR	1976	1982	Guernsey
Bailey	C	1847	1847	Tunbridge Wells
Bailey	CC	1842	1853	Cambridge
Bailey	CF	1995	2000	Nottinghamshire
Bailey	JE	1954	1964	Oxfordshire
Bailey	SE	1975	1991	Northumbria
Bain	G	1865	1869	Pulteneytown
Bain	J	1841	1842	Thurso
Bain	J	1842	1851	Wick
Bain	W	1858	1873	Haddington
Bainbridge	E	1937	1958	Gateshead
Baird	C	1818	1822	Aberdeen
Baird	W	1845	1863	Montgomeryshire
Baker	CF	1895	1907	Hastings
Baker	DR	1955	1966	Northampton
Baker	FM	1839		Bolton
Baker	G	1840	1841	Knightlow
Baker	M	2005		Dorset
Baker	R	2005	2009	Essex
Baldie	D	1933	1949	Kirkcaldy
Bale	J	1836	1840	Maldon
Ball	J	1836	1851	Northampton
Ballance	GH	1921	1932	Walsall
Ballance	S	1944	1961	Barrow-in-Furness
Banister	S	1836	1853	Preston
Banwell	GE	1942	1946	East Riding
Banwell	GE	1946	1963	Cheshire
Barber	R	1857	1860	Salisbury
Barber	R	1860	1875	Portsmouth
Barclay	R	1839	1854	Aberdeen
Barham	JW	1891	1901	Louth
Barker	E	1957	1964	Bolton
Barker	E	1964	1967	Sheffield
Barker	E	1967	1972	Sheffield & Rotherham
Barker	JB	1876	1898	Birkenhead
Barker-McCardle	J	2009		Essex
Barnard	W	1859	1859	Norwich

Barnden	I	1877	1881	Brighton
Barnes	C	1855	1857	Newcastle-under-Lyme
Barnes	H	1935	1939	Newark
Barnes	H	1939	1942	Burnley
Barnes	H	1942	1958	Blackpool
Barnes	J	1866	1868	Maidstone
Barnes	RT	1858	1863	Aberdeenshire
Barnes	T	1966	1969	South Shields
Barnes	W	1833	1851	Nottingham
Barnett	GA	1893	1909	Bridgwater
Barnett	JW	1939	1943	Hartlepool
Barnett	JW	1943	1947	Stockport
Barnett	JW	1947	1956	Leeds
Barnett	JW	1956	1969	Lincolnshire
Barns	J	1856	1881	Tenterden
Barraclough	S	1914	1930	Dewsbury
Barratt	G	1872	1877	Abingdon
Barratt	RS	1975	1978	South Yorkshire
Barrett	E	1861	1883	Launceston
Barry	L	1898	1917	Rochdale
Barry	PL	1913	1930	Wallasey
Barton	T	1840	1844	Tunbridge Wells
Barton	W	1845	1846	Chipping Norton
Basham	W	1902	1913	Scarborough
Bate	W	1936	1943	Newcastle-under-Lyme
Bates	J	1899	1924	Stalybridge
Battersby	CT	1854	1857	Hastings
Battty	B	1827	1831	Carlisle
Baxter	A	1906	1915	Shrewsbury
Baxter	M	2001	2007	Cumbria
Bayley	HL	1849	1875	Northamptonshire
Bayley	HL	1857	1876	Peterborough Liberty
Beacher	WH	1931	1943	Reigate
Beale	FG	1941	1943	Penzance
Beard	W	1861	1868	Durham City
Beard	W	1871	1873	Glossop
Beaton	J	1864	1872	Galashiels
Beattie	E	1861		Annan
Beattie	J	1884	1903	Accrington
Beaty-Pownall	CC	1955	1972	Isle of Man
Beaumont	G	1853	1859	Huddersfield
Bebbington	BN	1944	1963	Cambridge
Becke	J	1918	1935	Shropshire
Becke	J	1935	1946	Cheshire
Beddie	J	1886	1891	Maryhill
Beech	T	1867	1877	Bolton

Beesley	AS	1923	1941	Folkestone
Bell	A	1890	1898	Wigan
Bell	J	1933	1942	Hastings
Bell	J	1943	1958	Manchester
Bell	R	1835		Newark
Bell	T	1926	1949	Bootle
Bell	W	1860	1863	Fife
Bell	WR	1862	1866	Leeds
Bellamy	H	1875	1894	Boston
Bellerby	T	1846	1851	Warwick
Benbow	REG	1959	1963	Mid-Wales
Bennett	E	1887	1918	Kidderminster
Bennett	S	1948	1958	Bournemouth
Bennetts	J	1853	1889	Saint Ives
Bensley	JP	1993	1998	Lincolnshire
Bent	GE	1857	1873	Carlisle
Bent	T	1873	1886	Exeter
Benyon	BM	1925	1942	Tiverton
Berkins	T	1850		Clackmannanshire
Berry	AM	1902	1908	Kendal
Berry	F	1959	1967	Oldham
Berry	G	1873	1892	Gravesend
Berry	J	1903	1907	Macclesfield
Berry	J	1907	1939	Barrow-in-Furness
Berry	SA	1948	1965	Dumfries & Galloway
Berry	W	1887	1892	Guildford
Berry	W	1892	1907	Southampton
Beslee	G	1942	1943	Maidstone
Best	TW	1883	1907	Merionethshire
Beswick	F	1863	1869	Birkenhead
Beswick	R	1839	1839	Manchester
Bettison	N	1998	2005	Merseyside
Bettison	N	2007		West Yorkshire
Bibby	RR	1958	1969	Blackburn
Bicknell	PB	1856	1902	Lincolnshire
Biddlecombe	WH	1841	1850	Godalming
Biggs	H	1855	1865	Ludlow
Birch	R	1814	1833	Nottingham
Birch	R	1978	1983	Warwickshire
Birch	R	1983	1993	Sussex
Birnie	J	1855	1863	Birkenhead
Birnie	RT	1899	1899	Montrose
Birnie	RT	1900	1928	Forfarshire
Birnie	RT	1928	1929	Angus
Bishop	H	1836	1836	Hertford
Bishop	J	1836	1838	Bristol

Bishop	J	1853	1876	Totnes
Black	G	1852	1880	Norfolk
Black	W	1909	1932	Dumfries
Black	W	1932	1948	Dumfries-shire
Blackburn	T	1920	1946	Tynemouth
Blackwell	GH	1888	1906	Shrewsbury
Blackwell	H	1881	1888	Newport [Isle of Wight]
Blair	D	1825	1843	Greenock Harbour
Blair	I	1998	2000	Surrey
Blair	I	2005	2008	Metropolitan
Blake	EJ	1844	1845	Shrewsbury
Blake	P	1863	1870	Torrington
Blake	T	1840	1857	Salisbury
Blakey	D	1991	1999	West Mercia
Blanchard	T	1862	1872	Barnstaple
Blandy	A	1863	1902	Berkshire
Blane	W	1846	1855	Kilmarnock
Blatch	AF	1893	1901	Saint Albans
Bliss	A	2011		Hertfordshire
Blood	JT	1850	1855	Newcastle-under-Lyme
Blundell	J	1854	1865	Maidstone
Blyth	C	1878	1881	Newcastle-under-Lyme
Bohanna	J	1853	1876	Congleton
Bolt	MH	1934	1935	Newark
Bolt	MH	1935	1941	Dover
Bolton	RHD	1941	1960	Northamptonshire
Bond	A	1940	1951	Rutland
Bond	AM	1924	1935	Dover
Bond	E	1874	1876	Cardiff
Bond	E	1876	1881	Birmingham
Booth	C	1857	1861	Newcastle-under-Lyme
Boothby	EJ	1981	1988	Durham County
Borne	R	1874	1889	Falmouth
Borthwick	A	1884	1914	Mid Lothian
Borthwick	A	1884	1914	West Lothian
Borthwick	A	1894	1914	East Lothian
Borthwick	A	1894	1914	Peebles-shire
Bosanquet	VF	1894	1936	Monmouthshire
Boughey		1839	1844	Birkenhead
Boultbee	EM	1840	1871	Bedfordshire
Boultbee	R	1865	1871	Roxburghshire
Boultbee	R	1866	1884	Selkirkshire
Bourne	J	1878	1889	Rye
Bowden	JC	1861	1862	Haverfordwest
Bower	HJ	1872	1899	East Riding
Bower	RL	1898	1929	North Riding

Bowman	JW	1984	1995	Tayside
Bowron	M	2007	2010	City of London
Bowron	M	2011		Jersey
Box	CG	1940	1947	Great Yarmouth
Box	CG	1947	1960	Southampton
Box Stockdale	JB	1836	1870	Cardiff
Boyd		1839	1842	Bolton
Boyd		1848	1850	Deal
Boyd	J	1888	1902	Glasgow
Boyd	JM	1984	1989	Dumfries & Galloway
Boyes	RP	1973	1974	York & North East Yorkshire
Boyes	RP	1974	1977	North Yorkshire
Boyle	A	1833	1861	Perth
Brabner	JF	1877	1881	Abingdon
Brabner	JF	1881	1900	Leamington Spa
Bradford	E	1890	1903	Metropolitan
Bradford	T	1829		Brecon
Bradley	D	1958	1968	Huddersfield
Bradshaw	J	1850	1877	Denbighshire
Brain	T	2001	2010	Gloucestershire
Bray	W	1859	1865	Bodmin
Breach	G	1859	1884	Hove
Breary	M	1872	1889	Faversham
Breary	T	1868	1889	Southampton
Brechin	J	1893		Broughty Ferry
Breffit	RE	1936	1943	East Sussex
Breffit	RE	1947	1965	East Sussex
Bremner	J	1842	1843	Banffshire
Bremner	JF	1863	1903	Fife
Bremner	JF	1891	1903	Kinross-shire
Brindley	F	1902	1922	Stockport
Brinkley	CME	1902	1903	Lincolnshire
Brinkley	JT	1892	1928	Warwickshire
Bristow	G	1836	1857	Peterborough City
Bristow	K	2006		Warwickshire
Broadbridge	W	1877	1902	Rochester
Brodie	PE	1949	1958	Stirling & Clackmannan
Brodie	PE	1958	1964	Warwickshire
Brogden	W	1881	1894	Great Yarmouth
Bromfield	HH	1909	1916	Radnorshire
Brook	F	1919	1920	Southport
Brook	F	1920	1929	Nottingham
Brook	F	1929	1935	West Riding
Brookes	GH	1865	1885	Ludlow
Broome	RF	1983	1989	Avon & Somerset
Brothers	J	1870	1875	Sandwich

Brown	A	1867	1898	Dorset
Brown	AG	1998	2004	Grampian
Brown	DL	1959	1967	Hastings
Brown	DWS	1933	1948	Berwickshire
Brown	DWS	1933	1948	Roxburghshire
Brown	DWS	1934	1948	Selkirkshire
Brown	DWS	1948	1952	Berwick Roxburgh & Selkirk
Brown	FA	1963	1968	Norwich
Brown	GW	1950	1950	Anglesey
Brown	J	1812	1822	Edinburgh
Brown	J	1820	1829	Paisley
Brown	R	1831	1839	Carlisle
Brown	R	1840		Derwent
Brown	W	1837	1855	Sunderland
Brown	W	1840	1855	River Wear
Brown	WL	1966	1968	Barnsley
Browne	A	1857	1869	Northumberland
Browne	GB	1837	1858	Dublin Metropolitan
Browne	JES	1944	1947	Scarborough
Browne	JES	1949	1970	Nottinghamshire
Browne	P	1857	1888	Flintshire
Browne	PTB	1920	1926	Bootle
Browne	PTB	1926	1951	Cumberland
Browne	PTB	1926	1951	Westmorland
Browne	WF	1878	1906	Isle of Ely
Browne-Edwardes	DI	1871	1876	Carmarthen
Brownlow	JH	1978	1982	South Yorkshire
Brownrigg	HJ	1858		Royal Irish
Bruce	G	1902	1927	Dunfermline
Bruce	J	1906	1930	Nairnshire
Bruce	R	1868	1876	Lancashire
Bruce	R	1882	1885	Royal Irish
Bruce	R	1920	1930	Brechin
Bruce	R	1950	1967	Zetland
Brunstrom	R	2001	2009	North Wales
Buchan	H	1836	1855	Kinross-shire
Buchan	H	1857	1869	Stirling
Buchanan	R	1832	1833	Winchester
Buchanan	RJ	1918	1919	Wiltshire
Buck	C	1889	1893	Margate
Buck	C	1893	1898	Rochdale
Buck	M	1981	1986	Northamptonshire
Buckley	M	1858	1860	Ashton-under-Lyne
Buglass	J	1846	1855	South Shields
Bunn	FL	1930	1934	Gravesend
Bunn	FL	1934	1936	Grimsby

Bunn	FL	1936	1955	Stoke-on-Trent
Bunter	J	1838		Salisbury
Bunyard	RS	1978	1987	Essex
Burbeck	J	2000	2006	Warwickshire
Burden	AT	1993	1995	Gwent
Burden	AT	1996	2003	South Wales
Burgess	F	1839	1842	Birmingham
Burgess	N	1997	2002	Cheshire
Burke	DM	1989	1998	North Yorkshire
Burke	WM	1860	1863	Wisbech
Burneston	W	1862	1876	Ripon
Burnett	JA	1919	1922	Boston
Burnett	LR	1887	1916	Wolverhampton
Burnett	LR	1888	1891	Rotherham
Burns	A	1968	1976	Suffolk
Burrough	T	1853	1861	Faversham
Burrow	JH	1988	1998	Essex
Burrows	CG	1956	1968	Oxford
Burrows	J	1899	1900	Kendal
Burrows	J	1900	1919	York
Burrows	TA	1923	1944	Reading
Burt	G	1891	1909	Airdrie
Burt	JH	1865	1868	Godalming
Burt	JH	1868	1880	Ryde
Burton		1849	1850	Walsall
Burton	W	1836	1838	Harwich
Buss	E	1868	1869	Sandwich
Buss	E	1869	1895	Ramsgate
Butcher	P	1853	1876	Rye
Butler	AJP	1993	2001	Gloucestershire
Butler	CE	1921	1936	Maidstone
Butler	CE	1936	1962	Grimsby
Butler	GH	1898	1939	Barnsley
Butler	SF	1916	1943	Ramsgate
Buxton	RN	1969	1977	Hertfordshire
Byford	L	1973	1977	Lincolnshire
Byng	JHG	1928	1931	Metropolitan
Byrne	JA	1916	1920	Royal Irish
Byrne	TW	1892	1923	Worcester
Caldow	E	1861	1867	Salisbury
Caldwell	F	1912	1925	Liverpool
Callender	J	1857	1863	Rochdale
Callingham	J	1838	1840	Croydon
Calvert	F	1945	1947	King's Lynn
Calvert	R	1877	1888	Cambridgeshire
Cameron	A	1909	1921	Kilmarnock

Cameron	A	2000	2008	Central Scotland
Cameron	R	1994	1996	Dumfries & Galloway
Cameron	R	1997	2002	Lothian & Borders
Cameron	W	1889		Broughty Ferry
Cameron	W	1892	1912	Partick
Campbell	A	1867	1887	Stirlingshire
Campbell	A	1965	1984	Dumfries & Galloway
Campbell	J	1836	1854	Hastings
Campbell	J	1837	1845	Louth
Campbell	J	1860	1879	Grimsby
Campbell	J	1880	1885	Hull
Campbell	J	1905		Kilmarnock
Campbell	JN	1913	1914	Clitheroe
Campbell	JN	1914	1920	Bacup
Campbell	JN	1920	1946	Dudley
Campbell	N	1864		Brechin
Campbell	WC	1938	1944	Orkney
Campbell	WC	1944	1948	Wigtownshire
Campfield	W	1874	1880	Richmond
Campling	W	1848	1849	Saffron Walden
Caney	R	1836	1845	Bury Saint Edmunds
Cann	J	1906	1914	Bristol
Cannings	D	2002	2007	North Yorkshire
Capper	WD	1963	1974	Birmingham
Capper	WD	1974	1975	West Midlands
Capps	HB	1877	1889	Deal
Cargill	AG	1942	1943	Hastings
Cargill	AG	1947	1954	Hastings
Carlton	BHA	1917	1923	Canterbury
Carlton	G	1927	1943	Tunbridge Wells
Carmichael	A	1873	1875	Alloa
Carmichael	GC	1871	1903	Worcestershire
Carmichael	J	1909	1931	Dundee
Carnes	C	1841	1844	Mold
Carpenter	JE	1918	1928	Beverley
Carr	J	1886	1889	Tenby
Carroll	W	1836	1849	Bath
Carter	CTG	1954	1968	York
Carter	JT	1907	1939	Windsor
Carter	RJ	1898	1901	Windsor
Carter	RJ	1901	1910	Hanley
Carter	RJ	1910	1936	Stoke-on-Trent
Carter	T	1894	1901	Brighton
Carter	W	1897	1915	River Wear
Carter	W	1897	1915	Sunderland
Carter	WH	1857	1867	Buckinghamshire

Casburn	JR	1898	1937	Grantham
Cater	JW	1855	1885	Walsall
Cavey	WT	1963	1967	Brighton
Cavey	WT	1968	1980	Cumbria
Cecil	J	1862	1869	Haverfordwest
Chadwick	J	1941	1958	Huddersfield
Chadwick	W	1862	1899	Stalybridge
Chalk	RTH	1841	1861	York
Challen	J	1891	1907	Newark
Chalmers	W	1877	1892	Kirkcaldy
Chamberlain	NFF	1900	1916	Royal Irish
Chanter	W	1836		Barnstaple
Chapman	HE	1921	1940	Kent
Chapman	R	1822	1830	Aberdeen
Chapman	R	1878	1883	Bideford
Charles	J	1855	1865	Arbroath
Charlton	G	1980	1990	Norfolk
Charsley	CC	1899	1918	Coventry
Charters	R	1840	1871	Leicester
Chase	TH	1844	1853	Brighton
Chase	TH	1859	1860	Portsmouth
Chasser	TW	1961	1973	Scottish North-eastern Counties
Chaytor	JC	1929	1958	North Riding
Cheney	BH	1839	1845	Boston
Cheney	JN	1946	1953	East Riding
Cheney	JN	1953	1967	Buckinghamshire
Chester-Master	RC	1910	1917	Gloucestershire
Cheyne	C	1922	1933	Hamilton
Cheyne	GH	1944	1959	Orkney
Chichester	AG	1901	1927	Huntingdonshire
Chichester	AG	1915	1919	Cambridgeshire
Childs	C	1887	1889	Bridgnorth
Childs	RJN	1998	2003	Lincolnshire
Chilvers	F	1853		Maldon
Chipp	T	1850	1861	Worcester
Chipstead	JA	1868	1877	Wakefield
Chisholm	H	1906	1933	Sutherland
Christian	H	1865	1910	Gloucestershire
Christie	AW	1909	1933	Airdrie
Christie	DC	1930	1939	Angus
Christie	EN	1923	1930	Congleton
Christie	EN	1930	1947	Bedford
Christie	J	1913	1945	Greenock
Churchill	C	1836	1846	Grantham
Clare	PA	1995	2002	Lancashire
Clark	J	1825	1833	Gorbals

Clark	J	1876	1884	Totnes
Clark	J	1919	1922	Hamilton
Clark	P	1855	1858	Kinross-shire
Clark	P	1869	1891	Kinross-shire
Clark	RM	1951	1967	Airdrie
Clarke	A	1856		Wallingford
Clarke	TC	1912	1920	Nottingham
Clarke	W	1844	1853	Maldon
Clarke	W	1951	1953	Derbyshire
Clarkson	CT	1872	1876	Halifax
Clarkson	CT	1877	1889	Wakefield
Clay	PS	1887	1889	Brecon
Clay	PS	1889	1892	Southampton
Clay	PS	1892	1912	Nottingham
Clayton	J	1926	1940	Doncaster
Clayton	JM	1879	1886	Caernarvonshire
Clayton	W	1893	1913	Clitheroe
Cleaver	W	1839		Roxburghshire
Clegg	JH	1897	1902	Margate
Clements	J	1836	1860	Canterbury
Clissett	AFC	1977	1984	Hertfordshire
Coathupe	EW	1876	1894	Bristol
Cobbe	CA	1856	1869	West Riding
Cockburn	ER	1919	1928	Ayrshire
Cockburn	ER	1929	1942	Hampshire
Cockerham	E	1974	1983	Jersey
Cocks	WJ	1907	1919	Hove
Codd	E	1853	1863	Plymouth
Coe	AT	1989	1998	Suffolk
Coggan	R	1968		Doncaster
Coke	JDF	1919	1929	West Riding
Coke	JDF	1933	1937	West Suffolk
Cole	J	1857	1887	Bridgnorth
Cole	J	1873	1877	Bideford
Cole	O	1897	1924	Oxford
Cole	OJB	1923	1928	Worcester
Cole	OJB	1929	1955	Leicester
Cole	S	2010		Leicestershire
Cole	TF	1887	1889	Blandford
Cole	W	1853	1862	Torrington
Cole-Hamilton	CG	1912	1947	Breconshire
Coleman	DF	2001	2007	Derbyshire
Coleman	G	1848	1857	Harwich
Coleman	JT	1897	1901	Truro
Coleman	JT	1901	1912	Lincoln
Coleridge	FRC	1892	1907	Devon

Coles	R		1842	Daventry
Colley	J	1874	1881	Droitwich
Collins	T	1879	1886	Wycombe
Colquhoun	A	1840	1877	West Lothian
Colquhoun	I	1877	1913	Swansea
Compton	TM	1868	1876	Margate
Condon	PL	1989	1993	Kent
Condon	PL	1993	2000	Metropolitan
Congreve	W	1866	1888	Staffordshire
Cook	GH	1937	1955	River Wear
Cook	GH	1937	1955	Sunderland
Cook	T	1866	1880	Hull
Cooksley	CH	1963	1974	Northumberland
Cooksley	CH	1974	1975	Northumbria
Coombs	RO	1883	1902	Colchester
Coombs	W	1836	1852	Bedford
Cooper	G	1859	1865	Forfar
Cooper	J	1839	1840	Salisbury
Coram	J	1851	1872	Dover
Cork	T	1837	1842	Rochester
Cormack	J	1959	1969	Orkney
Cormack	WK	1912	1952	Caithness-shire
Cormie	W	1843	1844	Banffshire
Correll	E	1839	1847	Dover
Corstorphan	D	1839	1844	Dundee
Cosser	AW	1880	1893	Portsmouth
Cotton	JE	1955	1961	Rotherham
Cotton	JE	1961	1967	Salford
Cotton	T	1881	1890	Kendal
Cottrill	I	1834	1849	Newcastle-under-Lyme
Coulson	RD	1840	1843	Belfast
Coutts	J	1949	1951	Perth & Kinross
Coward	C	1871	1889	Dorchester
Cox	SS	1856	1867	Dorset
Cozens	RW	1981	1985	West Mercia
Crabbe	JB	1863	1898	Tiverton
Craig	J	1859	1869	Inverkeithing
Craik	M	2005	2009	Northumbria
Cramphorn	C	2002	2006	West Yorkshire
Crampton	PH	1859	1864	Shropshire
Crawford	J	1946	1967	Ipswich
Crawley	FJ	1912	1915	Lincoln
Crawley	FJ	1915	1925	River Wear
Crawley	FJ	1915	1925	Sunderland
Crawley	FJ	1925	1944	Newcastle-upon-Tyne
Creedon	M	2007		Derbyshire

Cresswell	CJ	1936	1946	Ipswich
Crew	EM	1993	1996	Northamptonshire
Crew	EM	1996	2002	West Midlands
Crockford	ER	1935	1938	Southend-on-Sea
Crompton	D	1990	1995	Nottinghamshire
Crompton	R	2008		Lincolnshire
Crosoer	H	1836		Dover
Crowhurst	O	1876	1877	Brighton
Cruickshank	A	1911	1921	Dunbarton
Cruickshanks	C	1898	1900	Orkney
Crump	SW	1983	1990	Lincolnshire
Cullen	AT	1960	1967	Southampton
Cullen	JS	1860	1876	Hamilton
Culverhouse	M	1999	2007	Isle of Man
Cumming	G	1858	1867	Ross
Cumming	H	1836	1847	Exeter
Cumming	J	1887	1891	Bacup
Cumming	JT	1891	1905	Bootle
Cumming	T	1876	1882	Dunbarton
Cunliffe	BS	1886	1922	Wigtownshire
Cunning	W	1832	1835	Dunfermline
Cunningham	M	2009		Staffordshire
Cureton	EB	1864	1866	Shropshire
Curran	J	2010		Tayside
Cust	A	1939	1947	Saint Helens
Cuthbertson	J	1875	1877	Sandwich
Cutting	FA	1973	1980	Northamptonshire
Cuyler	A	1836	1837	Dublin Metropolitan
Dain	JH	1913	1917	Canterbury
Dain	JH	1917	1943	Norwich
Dalgliesh	G	1860	1888	Ashton-under-Lyne
Dalton	H	1882	1895	Maidstone
Danby	AE	1901	1907	Louth
Danby	AE	1907	1909	Bedford
Danby	JWA	1898	1931	Hyde
Danby	T	1912	1914	Congleton
Danby	T	1915	1943	Peterborough City
Danby	T	1931	1943	Peterborough Liberty
Daniell	HS	1880	1911	Hertfordshire
Danily	J	1868	1887	Montgomeryshire
D'Arcy	T	1822		Royal Irish
Davey	WJ	1909	1922	Bridgwater
David	W	1921	1923	Rothesay
Davidson	A	1866	1907	Kirkcudbrightshire
Davies	DM	1920	1937	Merthyr Tydfil
Davies	E	1832	1841	Dowlais

Davies	F	1918	1940	Shrewsbury
Davies	G	1851	1876	Cambridgeshire
Davies	G	1857	1876	Huntingdonshire
Davies	G	1955	1958	Worcester
Davies	J	1856	1882	Hereford
Davies	J	1870	1881	Shrewsbury
Davies	JI	1909	1918	Flintshire
Davies	R	1867	1869	Rochdale
Davies	RP	1862	1881	Canterbury
Davies	RY	1918	1942	Flintshire
Davies	T	1905	1907	Hove
Davies	T	1907	1940	Portsmouth
Davies	W	1836	1837	Ludlow
Davies	WS	1898	1912	Birkenhead
Davis	G	1838	1859	Blandford
Davis	G	1839	1879	Wycombe
Davis	JM	1869	1870	Windsor
Davis	JW	1964	1965	Isle of Ely
Davis	WT	1957	1968	Doncaster
Davison	JA	1940	1942	Kent
Davison	R	1956	1968	Middlesbrough
Davison	R	1968	1974	Teesside
Davison	R	1974	1976	Cleveland
Dawson	AC	1923	1942	Birkenhead
Day	W	1915	1921	Weymouth & Melcombe Regis
De Courcy Hamilton	G	1856	1891	Devon
De Schmid [Spence]	EH	1912	1913	Exeter
De Schmid [Spence]	EH	1913	1928	Carlisle
Deane	G	1852	1873	Newbury
Deans	G	1891	1906	Renfrew
Dear	GJ	1985	1990	West Midlands
Dease	J	1836	1837	Kinross-shire
Delacombe	WA	1876	1898	Derby
Denman	J	1840	1850	Denbighshire
Denman	J	1857	1877	Denbighshire
Denovan	FG	1832	1833	Glasgow
Denson	J	1878	1881	Buckingham
Derham	HE	1919	1935	Blackpool
Derham	JC	1887	1911	Blackpool
Derriman	GL	1908	1915	Shropshire
Despard	HJ	1893	1896	Dewsbury
Despard	HJ	1896	1926	Lanarkshire
D'Espiney	A	1888	1890	Bootle
Devlin	HJ	1965	1969	Southend-on-Sea
Dewar	D	1863	1876	Greenock
Dewar	D	1876	1909	Dundee

Diggles	J	1844	1845	Salford
Dingwall	JJ	1955	1966	Angus
Diston	H	1938	1947	Ashton-under-Lyne
Dobbie	J	1859	1876	Renfrew
Dodd	EJ	1945	1963	Birmingham
Dodd	J	1877	1886	Perthshire
Dodds	J	1859		Brechin
Dodds	R	1876		Durham City
Dods	J	1886	1893	Coatbridge
Dolby	LC	1966	1968	Reading
Donald	A	1907	1939	Kirkcudbrightshire
Donald	A	1922	1939	Wigtownshire
Donald	J	1851	1856	Oswestry
Doolan	WV	1944	1947	Neath
Douglas	J	1835	1840	Worcester
Douglas	SW	1914	1950	East Lothian
Douglas	SW	1914	1950	Mid Lothian
Douglas	SW	1914	1950	Peebles-shire
Douglas	SW	1914	1950	West Lothian
Dove	D	1857	1861	Beverley
Dow	C	1870	1879	Inverkeithing
Dowling	MMG	1845	1852	Liverpool
Downes	O	1858	1873	Colchester
Downie	A	1824	1825	Dundee
Drake	H	1836	1839	Boston
Drake	H	1845	1846	Thetford
Drake	JCT	1867	1896	Buckinghamshire
Drummond	GRB	1879	1912	West Sussex
Drummond	J	1834	1839	Dundee
Duke	J	1979	1988	Hampshire
Dunbar	T	1850	1858	Dunbartonshire
Duncan	A	1922	1930	Paisley
Duncan	D	1858	1867	Rothesay
Duncan	G	1836	1839	Hertford
Duncan	W	1900	1922	Paisley
Dunk	LT	1907	1913	Canterbury
Dunlop	WH	1899	1924	East Riding
Dunn	J	1854	1857	Colchester
Dunn	J	1857	1863	Swansea
Dunn	J	1863	1872	Preston
Dunn	W	1911	1921	Durham City
Dunne	J	1851	1853	Norwich
Dunne	J	1854	1857	Newcastle-upon-Tyne
Dunne	J	1856	1902	Westmorland
Dunne	J	1857	1902	Cumberland
Dunning	L	1902	1912	Liverpool

Duns	J	1876	1882	Durham City
Duns	J	1882	1894	Leicester
Duthie	J	1861	1868	Aberdeen
Dutton	F	1881	1891	Newcastle-under-Lyme
Dyer	A	1985	1995	Bedfordshire
Eacock	F	1891	1915	Weymouth & Melcombe Regis
Eager	F	1853	1868	Windsor
Earnshaw	TT	1902	1938	Leamington Spa
Eason	B	1863	1869	Wisbech
East	DA	1982	1983	Devon & Cornwall
East	DA	1983	1988	South Wales
Ebury	G	1884	1887	Kidderminster
Eddy	R	1893	1905	Barnstaple
Eddy	RS	1905	1921	Barnstaple
Eden	JH	1892	1902	Durham County
Edgell	RJ	1866	1889	Shropshire
Edgeworth-Johnstone	W	1915	1923	Dublin Metropolitan
Edmunds	W	1866	1868	Daventry
Edwards	A	1860	1892	Partick
Edwards	AE	1937	1939	Burnley
Edwards	AE	1939	1956	Middlesbrough
Edwards	HH	1894	1895	Kent
Edwards	J	1860	1862	Devonport
Edwards	J	1887	1893	Clitheroe
Edwards	J	2006	2007	Sussex
Edwards	L	1840	1841	Bridgnorth
Edwards	WH	1869	1886	Penryn
Edwards	WH	1941	1945	Cambridgeshire
Egan	MJ	1920	1942	Southport
Eley	CD	1966	1976	Guernsey
Elgee	WP	1859	1868	Lancashire
Ellerington	AR	1902	1904	Margate
Ellerington	AR	1905	1939	Saint Helens
Elliott	AG	1991	1997	Cumbria
Elliott	D	1984	1988	Devon & Cornwall
Elliott	J	1863	1891	Gateshead
Elliott	RT	1839	1848	Portsmouth
Elliott	W	1896	1906	Southport
Ellis	T	1880	1883	Merionethshire
Else	J	1876	1882	Chesterfield
Embury	JJ	1862	1891	Tunbridge Wells
Emery	E	1883	1900	Chesterfield
Emslie	G	1905	1925	Lerwick
Enfield	TW	1940	1949	Doncaster
English	S	1848	1852	Newport [Monmouthshire]
English	S	1853	1859	Norwich

English	S	1859	1862	Leeds
Enright	JT	1836	1868	Southampton
Enwright	JT	1886	1891	Louth
Enwright	JT	1891	1907	Rotherham
Esson	GA	1989	1994	Dumfries & Galloway
Estcourt	E	1846	1859	Gloucester
Etchells	J	1860	1874	Macclesfield
Etches	W	1841	1861	Doncaster
Evans	ATN	1933	1958	Pembrokeshire
Evans	D	1890	1890	Cardiganshire
Evans	E	1888	1899	Neath
Evans	G	1836		Bridgnorth
Evans	H	1890	1903	Cardiganshire
Evans	J	1821	1839	Marine Police
Evans	J	1831	1832	Carmarthen
Evans	J	1836	1836	Barnstaple
Evans	JS	1989	2002	Devon & Cornwall
Evans	R	1841	1850	Bridgnorth
Evans	S	1889	1893	Devonport
Evans	WH	1918	1947	Carmarthen
Everett	C	1857	1859	Godalming
Everett	C	1859	1867	Chichester
Everett	LDL	1908	1912	Preston
Everett	LDL	1925	1931	Liverpool
Everitt	W	1850	1861	Roxburghshire
Ewan	P	1862	1865	Sutherland
Exelby	FK	1937	1947	Clitheroe
Eyres	GW	1846	1851	West Suffolk
Fahy	P	2002	2008	Cheshire
Fahy	P	2008		Greater Manchester
Fairclough	W	1924	1937	Burnley
Fairman	SME	1939	1943	Hertfordshire
Fancett	T	1837	1854	Maidstone
Farley	T	1842		Daventry
Farley	W	1965	1967	Monmouthshire
Farley	W	1967	1980	Gwent
Farlow	S	1836	1844	Shrewsbury
Farmer	R	1884	1902	River Tyne
Farmery	JW	1892	1907	Canterbury
Farndale	J 1	1870	1871	Chesterfield
Farndale	J 1	1871	1882	Leicester
Farndale	J 1	1882	1899	Birmingham
Farndale	J 2	1893	1897	Margate
Farndale	J 2	1897	1900	York
Farndale	J 2	1900	1931	Bradford
Farquharson	J	1966	1975	Angus

Fawcett		1855	1857	Ashford
Fearnside	E	1856	1889	Pontefract
Fellowes	PHT	1891	1893	Hampshire
Felton	W	1892	1909	Winchester
Fenn	GE	1977	1984	Cheshire
Fenwick	GL	1864	1898	Chester
Fenwick	RG	1962	1967	Shropshire
Ferguson	AA	1931	1941	Northamptonshire
Ferguson	J	1943	1945	Sussex Combined
Ferguson	J	1946	1958	Kent
Ferguson	T	1874	1910	Stirling
Ferrar	WH	1816	1826	Belfast
Findlater	A	1837	1840	Anderston
Finlayson	D	1905	1935	Ross & Cromarty
Finnigan	S	2005		Lancashire
Fisher	H	1838	1856	Bristol
Fisher	J	1869	1882	Bewdley
Fisher	J	1899	1901	Grimsby
Fisher	T	1859	1865	Stranraer
Fisher	WH	1853	1877	South Molton
Fitzsimons	J	1859	1874	Helston
Flanagan	J	1973	1976	Royal Ulster
Flanagan	R	1996	2001	Royal Ulster
Flanagan	R	2001	2002	Northern Ireland
Fleming	D	1850		Stirlingshire
Fletcher	C	1843		Whitehaven
Fletcher	RS	1970	1976	Nottinghamshire
Flower	WS	1937	1940	Rutland
Flynn	O	1964	1967	Portsmouth
Foll	RNC	1881	1907	Barrow-in-Furness
Fooks	RH	1934	1954	Lincolnshire
Forbes	C	1894	1924	Johnstone
Forbes	W	1884	1901	Dunfermline
Forrest	JH	1852	1856	Nottinghamshire
Forrest	JH	1856	1891	Hampshire
Forster	W	1912	1932	Newcastle-under-Lyme
Foster	G	1869	1890	Daventry
Foster	J	1836		Pontefract
Foster	J	1859		Annan
Foster	JW	1858	1878	Isle of Ely
Foster	P	1946	1957	Wigan
Fox	C	1996	2003	Northamptonshire
Fox	CR	1924	1956	Oxford
Fox	DH	1908	1920	Dover
Fox	WG	1857	1873	Derbyshire
Francis	J	1837	1839	Neath

Franklin	S	1853	1861	Basingstoke
Fraser	J	1842	1846	Selkirkshire
Fraser	J	1850	1864	Argyllshire
Fraser	J	1856	1863	Berkshire
Fraser	J	1863	1890	City of London
Fraser	J	1872	1894	Johnstone
Fraser	J	1889	1913	Argyllshire
Fraser	JG	1886	1891	Wycombe
Fraser	JG	1891	1893	Eastbourne
Fraser	W	1921	1939	Dunbarton
Fraser	W	1936	1951	Inverness
Freeman	J	1863	1865	Plymouth
Freeman	J	1865	1869	Nottingham
Freeman	J	1870	1873	Cardiff
Freeman	WC	1844	1876	Cardiganshire
Freeth	W	1888	1911	Isle of Man
French	J	1835		Sudbury
Friend	J	1844	1874	Hythe
Frizzell	E	1970	1975	Stirling & Clackmannan
Frizzell	E	1975	1979	Central Scotland
Frost	N	1944	1947	Boston
Frost	N	1947	1954	Eastbourne
Frost	N	1954	1964	Bristol
Fryer	J	1979	1981	Derbyshire
Fuller	M	2004	2010	Kent
Fyfe	J	1830	1835	Aberdeen
Galbraith	N	1956	1956	Leicester
Galbraith	N	1956	1964	Monmouthshire
Gale	FS	1958	1964	Rochdale
Gale	FS	1964	1969	Newcastle-upon-Tyne
Galt	A	1861		Kilmarnock
Game	PW	1935	1945	Metropolitan
Gammie	WD	1960	1968	Kilmarnock
Garden	J	1872	1899	Berwick-upon-Tweed
Gardiner	NR	1901	1901	Walsall
Garland	FPC	1956	1975	Norfolk
Garrow	J	1893	1914	Perth
Garrow	JM	1941	1951	Derbyshire
Garry	JM	1872	1874	Richmond
Garth	H	1937	1956	Preston
Garton	T	1848	1853	Rutland
Garvin	P	2002	2005	Durham County
Gaskain	JSH	1952	1959	Cumberland
Gaskain	JSH	1952	1959	Westmorland
Gaskain	JSH	1959	1963	Gloucestershire
Gatherum	D	1892	1924	Kirkcaldy

Gauld	J	1920	1946	Aberdeenshire
Gentle	WB	1901	1920	Brighton
George	B	1865	1889	Dunstable
George	C	1885	1924	Kincardineshire
George	JH	1847	1848	Carmarthen
Georgeson	JW	1952	1969	Caithness-shire
Giannasi	M	2008	2011	Gwent
Gibbin	J	1847		Barnstaple
Gibbons	J	1853	1863	Preston
Gibson	D	1866	1881	Annan
Giffard	JW	1996	2006	Staffordshire
Gifford	G	1864	1864	Reigate
Gifford	J	1853	1868	Kidderminster
Gifford	R	1855	1858	River Wear
Gifford	R	1855	1858	Sunderland
Gifford	R	1858	1861	Berwickshire
Gifford	W	1863	1869	Poole
Gifford	W	1869	1882	Maidstone
Gilbert	VL	1977	1981	Cambridgeshire
Gilbert	WE	1886	1886	Hull
Gilbert	WR	1857	1896	Cornwall
Giles	W	1836	1866	Buckingham
Gillies	J	1838		Airdrie
Gillies	J	1844		Haddington
Gilliland	J	1834	1835	Calton
Gillman	WH	1836	1853	Windsor
Girven	WR	1988	1997	Wiltshire
Gleave		1837	1839	Birkenhead
Glendinning	GR	1951	1963	Perth & Kinross
Glendinning	GR	1963	1979	Wiltshire
Glenister	WM	1857	1894	Hastings
Glossop	G	1860	1876	Birmingham
Goddard	G	1873	1875	Newbury
Goddard	H	1840	1849	Northamptonshire
Godden	AE	1942	1965	Wakefield
Godfrey	CV	1908	1946	Salford
Godfrey	GA	1887	1892	Montgomeryshire
Godfrey	GA	1892	1897	Derbyshire
Goff		1854	1854	Guildford
Golden	HA	1935	1945	Shropshire
Golden	HA	1946	1963	Wiltshire
Golder	FW	1921	1937	Rutland
Goldie	GP	1863	1873	Isle of Man
Goldsmith	BT	1881	1889	Tenterden
Goodall	E	1836	1836	Bridgnorth
Goodbrand	J	1859	1861	Cullen

Goodchild	NW	1940	1944	Barrow-in-Furness
Goodchild	NW	1944	1966	Wolverhampton
Goodchild	NW	1966	1967	West Midlands
Goodman	GF	1939	1941	Newark
Goodman	GF	1941	1943	Scarborough
Goodman	GF	1944	1968	Halifax
Goodson	A	1965	1969	Pembrokeshire
Goodson	A	1972	1986	Leicestershire
Goodwin	TA	1937	1945	Merthyr Tydfil
Goodyer	F	1836	1839	Leicester
Goodyer	F	1839	1876	Leicestershire
Goold	V	1856	1884	Somerset
Gordon	DF	1893	1920	Aberdeenshire
Gordon	G	1855	1877	Perthshire
Gordon	G	1858	1868	Kinross-shire
Gordon	G	1859	1868	Clackmannanshire
Gordon	J	1852	1859	Cullen
Gordon	J	1889	1889	Cromarty County
Gordon	J	1889	1889	Ross
Gordon	J	1889	1898	Ross & Cromarty
Gordon	JT	1898	1903	Banffshire
Gordon	JT	1903	1930	Kinross-shire
Gordon	JT	1903	1934	Fife
Gordon	L	1884	1891	Brechin
Gordon	RG	1958	1967	Hamilton
Gordon	W	1891	1932	Dumfries-shire
Gore-Little	FL	1882	1907	Preston
Gormley	P	2010		Norfolk
Goss	J	1852	1852	Saffron Walden
Gott	JAH	1960	1972	Northamptonshire
Gotty	J	1800	1821	Marine Police
Goudie	JH	1935	1955	Paisley
Gower	CE	1912	1928	Newport [Monmouthshire]
Graham	DJ	1984	1993	Cheshire
Graham	J	1825	1832	Glasgow
Graham	J	1839	1844	Carlisle
Graham	N	2008		Fife
Graham	T	1880	1889	Richmond
Graham	W	1803	1805	Glasgow
Grange	T	2000	2007	Dyfed-Powys
Granhan	FW	1859	1874	Bradford
Grant	A	1858	1898	Orkney
Grant	J	1859	1886	Leith
Grant	J	1947	1960	Kilmarnock
Grant	P	1856	1865	Elgin
Granville	D	1898	1924	Dorset

Grapes	G	1853	1872	Newport [Isle of Wight]
Gray	A	1890	1899	Coventry
Gray	D	1955	1958	Greenock
Gray	D	1958	1969	Stirling & Clackmannan
Gray	F	1919	1928	Kidderminster
Gray	FR	1957	1961	Salford
Gray	G	1889	1940	Zetland
Green	C	1920	1924	Dover
Green	EA	1915	1930	Guernsey
Green	J	1853	1859	Chichester
Green	SM	2000	2008	Nottinghamshire
Green	T	1861	1865	Belfast
Green	W	1942	1948	Burnley
Greene	R	1850		Chichester
Greensmith	RC	1929	1941	Glossop
Greenstreet	C	1903	1922	Ryde
Greenwood	N	1968	1969	Burnley
Greenwood	RB	1955	1961	Dorset
Greenwood	RB	1961	1967	Devon
Greenwood	RB	1967	1973	Devon & Cornwall
Gregory	I	1861	1889	Doncaster
Gregory	R	1965	1969	Plymouth
Gregory	R	1969	1983	West Yorkshire
Gregson	H	1932	1937	Ashton-under-Lyne
Greig	JJ	1852	1881	Liverpool
Grey	S	1957	1966	South Shields
Griffin	C	1914	1917	Clitheroe
Griffin	C	1917	1920	Luton
Griffin	C	1920	1933	Brighton
Griffith	DW	1857	1876	Anglesey
Griffith	J	1912	1923	Caernarvonshire
Griffiths	GD	1845	1846	West Suffolk
Griffiths	TC	1837	1839	Birkenhead
Griffiths	TC	1920	1949	Chester
Griffiths	TK	1963	1969	Merthyr Tydfil
Grimston	RVS	1876	1889	Leicestershire
Grove	JJ	1842	1855	Perthshire
Guest	GT	1921	1946	Denbighshire
Gunn	DG	1994	2002	Cambridgeshire
Gurney	FP	1886	1903	Hull
Gwyn	P	1839	1839	Neath
Gwyn	RT	1883	1900	Bath
Gwynne	ER	1857	1904	Breconshire
Hadfield	R	1987	1990	Nottinghamshire
Hadfield	R	1990	1996	West Midlands
Haig	D	1885	1898	Banffshire

Haigh	G	1873	1884	Kidderminster
Haining	J	1858	1860	Wigtownshire
Haining	W	1842	1848	Edinburgh
Haley	S	1862	1888	York
Hall	D	1976	1991	Humberside
Hall	GT	1930	1943	Canterbury
Hall	J	1836		Carmarthen
Hall	J	1877	1902	Congleton
Hall	R	1932	1955	Rotherham
Hallam	JW	1898	1908	Salford
Halland	GHR	1931	1934	Lincolnshire
Hall-Dalwood	J	1907	1913	Leicester
Hall-Dalwood	J	1913	1926	Sheffield
Hallett	JA	1962	1968	Gateshead
Halsey	C	1888	1889	Maldon
Hambleton	A	1962	1967	Dorset
Hambleton	A	1967	1974	Dorset & Bournemouth
Hambleton	A	1974	1980	Dorset
Hambleton	E	1850	1855	Boston
Hamill	P	1977	1985	Strathclyde
Hamilton	J	1819	1833	Calton
Hamilton	JP	1996	2001	Fife
Hamilton	W	1883	1901	Govan
Hammersley	JH	1881	1910	Cheshire
Hampson	P	1999	2003	West Mercia
Hampton	CJ	1869	1873	Kidderminster
Hampton	FB	1841	1858	Isle of Ely
Hancock	PD	2001	2005	Bedfordshire
Handcock	JS	1856	1876	Bristol
Handley	J	1859	1868	Lincoln
Hanlon	JAT	1938	1939	Leamington Spa
Hannan	W	1853	1861	Middlesbrough
Hannan	W	1863	1867	Huddersfield
Hardie	J	1821	1825	Glasgow
Harding	C	1887	1925	Renfrewshire
Harding	C	1892	1905	Kinning Park
Harding	C	1898	1925	Bute
Hardy	G	1895	1899	Kendal
Hardy	G	1899	1914	Wigan
Hare	E	1935	1956	Cornwall
Harford	E	1853	1863	Tiverton
Harland	J	1887	1891	Grantham
Harland	J	1891	1914	Bacup
Harper	W	1842	1860	Macclesfield
Harper	W	1845	1854	Shrewsbury
Harrel	D	1883	1893	Dublin Metropolitan

Harries	HF	1915	1918	Shrewsbury
Harris	CE	1900	1902	Kendal
Harris	CM	1940	1952	Newport [Monmouthshire]
Harris	E	1891	1892	Gateshead
Harris	J	1836		Reading
Harris	J	1843	1867	Bolton
Harris	RR	1839	1871	Worcestershire
Harris	T	1853	1867	Droitwich
Harris	TM	1889	1920	Wakefield
Harris	WC	1843	1856	Hampshire
Harrison	JE	1919	1929	Saint Albans
Harrison	R	1862	1867	Tenby
Harrison	R	1961	1968	Dewsbury
Harriss	CE	1902	1933	Lancaster
Harrop	J	1881	1887	Shrewsbury
Harrop	J	1887	1901	Burnley
Hart	J	2002	2006	City of London
Hartcup	WR	1919	1931	Isle of Ely
Harvey	DW	1839	1863	City of London
Harvey	J	1827		Royal Irish
Harvey	R	1856	1857	Saffron Walden
Harvey	SJ	1945	1958	Rochdale
Harvey	SJ	1958	1967	Birkenhead
Hastings	HC	1851	1899	Surrey
Hatcheon	A	1844		North Berwick
Hatcher	FHL	1900	1913	Banbury
Hatton	J	1841	1842	Ipswich
Hatton	J	1843	1869	East Suffolk
Hatton	J	1844		Beccles
Hatton	JH	1840	1842	East Suffolk
Hatton	JH	1842	1856	Staffordshire
Hatton	RV	1842	1852	Nottinghamshire
Haughton	J	1965	1974	Liverpool
Haughton	J	1974	1975	Merseyside
Hawkins	P	1941	1947	Glossop
Hay	RDD	1878	1887	Wolverhampton
Hay	W	1844	1870	Elginshire
Hay	W	1850	1855	Metropolitan
Haycock	CJ	1923	1930	Margate
Haydon	R	1853	1863	Bradninch
Hayes	B	1982	1991	Surrey
Hayes	G	1870	1889	Windsor
Hayman	A	2002	2005	Norfolk
Haywood	WHM	1898	1926	Derby
Head	C	1869	1897	Oxford
Heald	D	1931	1938	Middlesbrough

Hearn	GWR	1950	1960	Staffordshire
Hector	SA	1921	1927	Tunbridge Wells
Hector	SA	1927	1946	Coventry
Hedges	GE	1997	2002	Durham County
Hedges	MII	1998	2004	South Yorkshire
Hedington	J	1855	1860	South Shields
Hedington	J	1860	1865	Nottingham
Hedington	J	1874	1875	Southwold
Heigham	CHJ	1869	1898	East Suffolk
Heigham	CHJ	1869	1898	West Suffolk
Hellawell	K	1990	1993	Cleveland
Hellawell	K	1993	1998	West Yorkshire
Helmsley	J	1858	1866	Richmond
Hemingway	W	1873	1876	Carlisle
Hemingway	W	1876	1889	Cardiff
Henderson	DB	1973	1985	Northern
Henderson	E	1869	1886	Metropolitan
Henderson	J	1866	1870	Stranraer
Henderson	J	1881	1883	Alloa
Henderson	J	1882	1910	Dunbarton
Henderson	JNS	1897	1923	Reading
Henderson	W	1875	1878	Leeds
Henderson	W	1878	1900	Edinburgh
Hendry	W	1840		Kilsyth
Henley	WH	1838		Rye
Henn	WF	1937	1959	Gloucestershire
Henry	ER	1903	1918	Metropolitan
Henshaw	K	1979	1985	North Yorkshire
Herbert	EP	1857	1893	Monmouthshire
Herbert	J	1846	1854	Tewkesbury
Herman	HH	1929	1955	York
Hermon	J	1980	1989	Royal Ulster
Hernaman	W	1872	1889	Lichfield
Hewitt	JW	1857	1871	Tynemouth
Heywood	W	1836	1837	Leeds
Hibbert	E	1868	1869	Salford
Hibbert	M	1862	1889	Basingstoke
Hickling	WC	1853	1875	Warwick
Hicks	J	1836	1865	Scilly Isles
Higgins	W	1907	1921	Neath
High	T	1860	1865	Godalming
High	T	1870	1879	Godalming
Hill	A	1852	1860	Belfast
Hill	G	1898	1904	Kilmarnock
Hill	G	1904	1913	Carlisle
Hill	J	1836	1864	Chester

Hill	J	1839	1861	Bridgwater
Hill	RM	1896	1909	Cornwall
Hill	T	1856	1898	North Riding
Hillier	GE	1876		Royal Irish
Hillier	WC	1919	1942	Hove
Hilton	G	1859	1876	Derby
Hilton	H	1874	1875	Glossop
Hilton	H	1875	1879	Huddersfield
Hilton	H	1918	1918	Carmarthen
Hinchey	M	1856	1863	Forfarshire
Hind	HP	1934	1937	Rochester
Hind	HP	1937	1957	Bath
Hinks	G	1880	1903	Ryde
Hirst	MJ	1986	1993	Leicestershire
Hitchcock	A	2010		Bedfordshire
Hitchman	R	1854	1859	Devonport
Hitchman	R	1859	1897	Norwich
Hockett	J	1845		Bury Saint Edmunds
Hoddinott	JC	1988	1999	Hampshire
Hodges	WH	1877	1886	Tenby
Hodgkinson	C	1866	1892	Oldham
Hodgkinson	H	1933	1947	Kidderminster
Hodgson	J	1863	1868	Montgomeryshire
Hodgson	JG	1899	1922	Glossop
Hodgson	TCB	1959	1968	Berkshire
Hodgson	TCB	1968	1970	Thames Valley
Hodgson	WH	1876	1899	Glossop
Hodson	C	1914	1931	Blackburn
Hodson	J	2008		Nottinghamshire
Hogan-Howe	B	2004	2009	Merseyside
Hogan-Howe	B	2011		Metropolitan
Hogg	G	1848	1857	Wolverhampton
Hogg	G	1857	1866	Staffordshire
Hoile	G	1836	1848	Deal
Holden	H	1856	1892	Nottinghamshire
Holden	JH	1855	1857	Beverley
Holdsworth	D	1964	1968	Oxfordshire
Holdsworth	D	1970	1978	Thames Valley
Holgate	J	1877	1911	Bolton
Holland	CE	1891	1894	Grantham
Holland	CE	1894	1918	Cambridge
Holland	HC	1897	1916	Derbyshire
Holland	WJ	1899	1925	Montgomeryshire
Hollingsworth	S	1836	1853	Chesterfield
Hollington	C	1841	1850	Guildford
Hollis	T	2005		Humberside

Holman	R	1838	1853	Plymouth
Holmes	E	1889	1928	Leicestershire
Holmes	EH	1928	1936	Accrington
Holmes	EH	1936	1942	Blackpool
Holmes	W	1871	1871	Johnstone
Holmes-a-Court	EA	1888	1917	Oxfordshire
Home	J	1825	1834	Dundee
Hope	W	1904	1931	Banffshire
Hopkins	E	1837	1848	Newport [Monmouthshire]
Hopkinson	G	1865	1870	Beverley
Hordern	AF	1926	1934	East Riding
Hordern	AF	1934	1935	Cheshire
Hordern	AF	1935	1950	Lancashire
Horne	T	1872	1876	Chesterfield
Horwood	KA	1940	1943	Rochester
Horwood	WTF	1920	1928	Metropolitan
Houlton	H	1839	1855	Reading
House	S	2007		Strathclyde
Howard	EA	1965	1966	Guernsey
Howard	J	1846	1863	Grantham
Howard	WJ	1931	1957	Bolton
Howarth	H	1917	1945	Rochdale
Howden	TE	1928	1941	Hull
Howe	J	1866	1878	Buckingham
Howells	E	1840	1860	Tenby
Howlett	C	2005	2006	Norfolk
Hubbersley	H	1851	1873	Winchester
Hughes	A	1852	1868	Bath
Hughes	GWB	1877	1877	Anglesey
Hughes	J	1856	1870	Shrewsbury
Hughes	M	2004		South Yorkshire
Hughes	RW	1892	1899	Montgomeryshire
Hughes	W	1869	1879	Pwllheli
Hughes	WS	1915	1940	Lincoln
Huish	JH	1893	1920	Tynemouth
Hulme	FG	1959	1961	Dewsbury
Hulme	FG	1961	1967	Derby
Humphrey	TB	1939	1957	South Shields
Humphries	R	1859	1877	Liskeard
Hunt	AJ	1939	1953	Southend-on-Sea
Hunt	C	1913	1923	King's Lynn
Hunt	S	1868	1895	Warrington
Hunt	S	1869	1891	Poole
Hunter	A	1946	1949	Aberdeenshire
Hunter	AA	1858	1859	Oldham
Hunter	HP	1929	1950	Staffordshire

Hunter	R	1858	1877	Renfrewshire
Hunter	W	1957	1961	Scottish North-eastern Counties
Huntley	W	1885	1897	River Wear
Huntley	W	1885	1897	Sunderland
Hurst	J	1874	1889	Peterborough City
Hutchings	HW	1886	1890	Chard
Hutchings	WT	1941	1943	Plymouth
Hutchinson	WJ	1929	1931	Worcester
Hutchinson	WJ	1931	1933	Huddersfield
Hutchinson	WJ	1933	1943	Brighton
Hutchinson	WJ	1945	1947	Sussex Combined
Hutchinson	WJ	1947	1956	Brighton
Huxtable	JC	1917	1934	Clitheroe
Huxtable	JG	1852	1875	Newport [Monmouthshire]
Hynd	A	1884	1891	Airdrie
Ibbetson	CV	1909	1912	Lancashire
Imber	W	1918	1927	Coventry
Imbert	PM	1979	1985	Thames Valley
Imbert	PM	1987	1993	Metropolitan
Inch	JR	1942	1949	Dunfermline
Inch	JR	1949	1955	Fife
Inch	JR	1955	1975	Edinburgh
Ingles	H	1908	1912	Congleton
Inglis	P	1876	1886	Renfrew
Ingram	G	1851	1876	Paisley
Ingram	G	1855	1858	Dumfries
Ingram	G	1903	1912	Newcastle-under-Lyme
Inkpen	B	1835	1862	Poole
Innes	CES	1889	1894	Cambridge
Innes	J	1836	1837	Arbroath
Irving	J	1931	1938	Coatbridge
Isaac	J	1841	1857	Knightlow
Isaac	J	1857	1878	Warwickshire
Iveson	A	1954	1959	Dewsbury
Iveson	A	1959	1966	Reading
Jack	CL	1962	1968	Ayr
Jackson	GS	1943	1946	Newcastle-under-Lyme
Jackson	GS	1946	1948	Coventry
Jackson	GS	1948	1964	Newcastle-upon-Tyne
Jackson	J	1849	1858	Oldham
Jackson	J	1859	1898	Sheffield
Jaffray	G	1833	1839	Gorbals
Jaggard	W	1856	1857	Cambridge
James	F	1897	1900	Radnorshire
James	F	1900	1935	Northumberland
James	F	1907	1933	Hastings

James	FS	1925	1931	Chesterfield
James	FS	1931	1941	Sheffield
James	G	1877	1887	Carmarthen
James	RW	1934	1947	Congleton
Jamieson	M	1903	1925	River Tyne
Jamieson	T	1831	1832	Merthyr Tydfil
Jaquest	D	1876	1894	Luton
Jarlett	R	1836		Guildford
Jarratt	CA	1965	1968	Wakefield
Jarrett	AH	1862	1889	Hertford
Jeffrey	A	1950	1963	Warrington
Jeffrey	G	1829	1830	Paisley
Jeffries	B	1861		Bewdley
Jelliff	CF	1947	1967	Great Yarmouth
Jenkins	J	1859	1884	Dunbartonshire
Jenkins	RCM	1937	1941	Penzance
Jenkins	RCM	1941	1943	Folkestone
Jennings	J	1886	1889	Penryn
Jervis	J	1875	1880	Portsmouth
Jervis	J	1881	1882	Blackburn
Johnson	CW	1946	1966	Dudley
Johnson	GA	1866	1889	Leominster
Johnson	HS	1877	1878	Mid Lothian
Johnson	HS	1877	1878	West Lothian
Johnson	L	1922	1944	Boston
Johnson	LE	1964	1966	Jersey
Johnson	RB	1983	1995	Lancashire
Johnson	WC	1932	1936	Plymouth
Johnson	WC	1941	1945	Birmingham
Johnston	AA	1929	1938	Carlisle
Johnston	J	1858	1866	Kirkcudbrightshire
Johnston	J	1906	1930	Alloa
Johnston	J	1967	1969	Zetland
Johnston	JR	1951	1962	Inverness
Jones	E	1912	1921	Denbighshire
Jones	J	1843	1849	Dumfries
Jones	J	1843	1891	Dumfries-shire
Jones	J	1937	1951	Glamorganshire
Jones	JJC	1893	1901	Dublin Metropolitan
Jones	JM	1994	1997	Cheshire
Jones	JR	1960	1968	Carmarthenshire & Cardiganshire
Jones	JR	1968	1975	Dyfed-Powys
Jones	K	2001	2006	Sussex
Jones	R	1851	1855	Ludlow
Jones	R	1903		Cardiganshire
Jones	R	1906	1907	Neath

Jones	R	1911	1950	Merionethshire
Jones	R	1916	1922	Radnorshire
Jones	S	1922	1939	Cardiganshire
Jones	T	1907	1911	Merionethshire
Jones	W	1870	1878	Newcastle-under-Lyme
Jones	WB	1894	1898	Grantham
Jones	WB	1898	1916	Ramsgate
Jones	WE	1907	1926	Southampton
Jones	WH	1889	1902	Stockport
Jones	WJ	1944	1957	Cardiganshire
Jones	WT	1919	1947	Wycombe
Jordan	FL	1982	1989	Kent
Joslin	PD	1983	1998	Warwickshire
Josselyn	FJ	1880	1910	Bedfordshire
Judd	B	1852	1856	Saffron Walden
Julyan	G	1853	1874	Falmouth
Kane	IH	1981	1993	Cambridgeshire
Keddie	D	1836	1836	Arbroath
Keenan	H	1851	1887	Northampton
Keep	PD	1926	1943	Neath
Keep	W	1871	1908	Rutland
Keith	AN	1926	1945	Lanarkshire
Keith	W	1863	1886	Forfarshire
Kellie-MacCallum	JD	1881	1931	Northamptonshire
Kellie-MacCallum	JD	1881	1931	Peterborough Liberty
Kelly	CH	1977	1996	Staffordshire
Kelly	O	1985	1993	City of London
Kelsall	JA	1932	1934	Congleton
Kelsall	W	1974	1977	Cheshire
Kemble	ERB	1929	1948	Warwickshire
Kemp	C	1886	1891	Renfrew
Kempster	T	1841	1842	Wick
Kennedy	AH	1961	1969	Royal Ulster
Kennion	TR	1880	1883	Wigan
Kent	A	1841	1853	Colchester
Kent	J	1836		Saffron Walden
Kentish	S	1848	1870	Carmarthen
Kenworthy	D	1998	2002	North Yorkshire
Kenyon	H	1908	1937	Penzance
Ker Watson	JE	1909	1915	Peterborough City
Ker Watson	JE	1915	1937	Preston
Kernaghan	P	1999	2008	Hampshire
Kerr	J	1977	1983	Lincolnshire
Kerr	W	1939	1948	Kirkcudbrightshire
Kerr	W	1956	1973	Dunbartonshire
Kershaw	S	1868	1870	Glossop

Kershaw	S	1870	1896	Southport
Kerslake	HM	1907	1911	Durham City
Kerslake	HM	1911	1914	Dewsbury
Kerslake	HM	1914	1935	Southend-on-Sea
Kilby	C	1835		Torquay
Kilpatrick	R	1899	1900	Neath
Kilpatrick	R	1900	1923	Chesterfield
Kilvington	W	1851	1853	Middlesbrough
Kinchant	RH	1869	1875	Birkenhead
Kinchant	RH	1875	1892	Warwickshire
King	GM	1850	1857	Denbighshire
King	W	1863	1878	Maldon
Kirby	O	1856	1856	Saffron Walden
Kirkpatrick	T	1841	1843	Dumfries-shire
Kitching	H	1973	1974	Bradford
Knight	GH	1877	1912	Beverley
Knight	GT	1928	1939	Hertfordshire
Knight	H	1870	1877	Beverley
Knight	T	1839	1862	Hertford
Knights	PD	1972	1974	Sheffield & Rotherham
Knights	PD	1974	1975	South Yorkshire
Knights	PD	1975	1985	West Midlands
Knott	C	1836	1846	Chipping Norton
Knott	HNK	1901	1908	Dover
Lake	HA	1871	1877	Dublin Metropolitan
Lake	JA	2003	2008	Lincolnshire
Lakeman	WH	1938	1961	Carlisle
Laker		1847	1850	Dover
Lamb	G	1836	1836	Anderston
Lambert	T	1847	1854	Dunfermline
Lamont	G	1931	1942	Motherwell & Wishaw
Lamy	AP	1946	1965	Guernsey
Lane	HPP	1912	1927	Lancashire
Lang	HG	1894	1920	East Sussex
Langdon	M	2008		Isle of Man
Langdon	R	1841		Kington
Langmead	A	1942	1942	Guernsey
Latham	T	1840	1852	Wigan
Latimer	I	2001	2011	Northern
Laugharne	A	1977	1978	Warwickshire
Laugharne	A	1978	1983	Lancashire
Laverty	W	1854	1863	Blackburn
Law	AL	1911	1928	Hertfordshire
Law	JH	1863	1887	Guildford
Lawrence	J	1948	1959	Reading
Lawrence	SL	1945	1948	Reading

Lawrence	SL	1948	1962	Hull
Lawrence	WR	1989	1996	South Wales
Lawson	JW	1886	1889	Stamford
Lawson	JW	1889	1909	Peterborough City
Layard	BG	1856	1872	East Riding
Laybourne	JH	1898	1920	Chester
Lazenby	J	1832	1836	Carmarthen
Le Breton	RH	1994	2000	Jersey
Le Brocq	EH	1952	1964	Jersey
Le Mesurier	HB	1888	1893	Exeter
Le Mesurier	HB	1893	1898	Portsmouth
Le Moignan	M	1984	1996	Guernsey
Le Page	G	2003	2010	Guernsey
Lea	A	1926	1931	River Tyne
Leadbetter	TJ	1878	1911	Denbighshire
Lear	TM	1862	1893	Bridgwater
Learmonth	I	2010		Kent
Lee	A	2009		Northamptonshire
Lee	H	1861	1871	Brecon
Lees	E	1859	1861	Oldham
Lees	TOH	1875	1881	Northamptonshire
Lees	TOH	1876	1881	Peterborough Liberty
Lees	TOH	1890	1898	Isle of Wight
Lefroy	AT	1839	1865	Gloucestershire
Legg	HE	1953	1969	Bootle
Leggatt	W	1848	1859	Portsmouth
Legge	CG	1877	1880	Lancashire
Legge	H	1932	1954	Berkshire
Lemon	FJ	1919	1923	Leeds
Lemon	FJ	1923	1949	Nottinghamshire
Lemon	RD	1939	1942	East Riding
Lemon	RD	1942	1962	Hampshire
Lemon	RD	1962	1974	Kent
Lennox	J	1815	1822	Greenock
Leonard	DA	1992	1999	Humberside
Leppard	A	2010		City of London
Leverett	W	1847	1859	Bradford
Lewis	CB	1876	1890	Cardiganshire
Lewis	E	1900	1906	Neath
Lewis	E	1946	1947	Newcastle-under-Lyme
Lewis	FD	1876	1877	Carmarthen
Lewis	IG	1887	1914	Blackburn
Lewis	R	1869	1871	Haverfordwest
Lewis	TH	1940	1958	Carmarthenshire
Lewis	TH	1958	1960	Carmarthenshire & Cardiganshire
Lewis	TM	1836	1839	Haverfordwest

Lewis	TM	1839		Glamorganshire
Lidbury	C	1853	1868	Weymouth & Melcombe Regis
Liddell	E	1857	1891	Newark
Lindley	WB	1912	1919	Leeds
Lindsay	AE	1942	1947	Flintshire
Lindsay	HG	1867	1891	Glamorganshire
Lindsay	LA	1891	1937	Glamorganshire
Linton	T	1851	1878	Edinburgh
Linvell	JH	1869		Arundel
Lipp	GS	1903	1909	Dumfries
List	AJ	1832	1840	East Lothian
List	AJ	1840	1877	Mid Lothian
List	GH	1835	1841	Musselburgh
List	GH	1840	1893	East Lothian
List	GH	1862	1893	Berwickshire
Lister	G	1889	1912	Doncaster
Little	JR	1968	1975	Dundee
Little	JR	1975	1980	Tayside
Livick	J	1838	1869	Ramsgate
Livingston	J	1842	1846	Dunfermline
Llewellyn	H	1908	1945	Wiltshire
Lloyd	ET	1894	1897	York
Lloyd	HC	1936	1948	Montgomeryshire
Lloyd	HC	1946	1948	Radnorshire
Lloyd	HC	1948	1959	Mid-Wales
Lloyd	JE	1892	1897	Radnorshire
Lloyd	P	1868	1873	Radnorshire
Lloyd	T	2002	2005	Cambridgeshire
Lloyd	W	1878	1886	Louth
Lloyd-Clough	HH	1857	1879	Merionethshire
Lloyd-Williams	JE	1927	1931	Montgomeryshire
Lloyd-Williams	JE	1931	1958	Worcestershire
Lloyd-Williams	JJ	1939	1943	Cardiganshire
Lockett	D	1946	1952	Tynemouth
Lockett	D	1953	1958	Walsall
Lockett	D	1958	1967	Bournemouth
Lockett	W	1836	1840	Macclesfield
Lockhart	JEG	1966	1967	Coatbridge
Long	A	1963	1965	East Suffolk
Longhurst	JGC	1964	1969	Southport
Looms	CG	1932	1958	Blackburn
Loosmore	J	1838	1841	Bridgend
Love	BL	1836	1857	Great Yarmouth
Lovell	GE	1942	1943	Hove
Low	J	1824		Dundee
Lowdon	J	1902	1950	Ayr

Lowe	GS	1930	1932	Congleton
Lowe	GS	1932	1936	Newcastle-under-Lyme
Lowe	GS	1936	1941	Plymouth
Lowe	GS	1941	1948	Sheffield
Lucas	WR	1936	1950	Monmouthshire
Luke	T	1818	1832	Perth
Lumley	TW	1894	1907	Leicester
Lund	J	1859	1881	Leamington Spa
Luxford	G	1881	1894	East Sussex
Lyle	R	1832	1838	Greenock
Lynch-Blosse	CE	1925	1927	Montgomeryshire
Lynch-Blosse	CE	1928	1949	Leicestershire
Lynn	AG	1973	1975	Scottish North-eastern Counties
Lynn	AG	1983	1990	Grampian
Lynn	J	1857	1860	Neath
Lynn	J	1862	1889	Devonport
Lyon		1841	1841	Kirkintilloch
Maby	CG	1930	1954	Bristol
McAlpine	A	1867	1876	Rothesay
McAulay	J	1955	1967	Paisley
Macauley	M	1898	1905	Ross & Cromarty
MacBean	J	1841	1857	Inverness
McBean	J	1850	1864	Galashiels
McBean	J	1881	1888	Canterbury
McCall	A	1870	1888	Glasgow
McCall	P	1867	1872	Kirkintilloch
McCallum	TBV	1958	1975	Berwick Roxburgh & Selkirk
McCartney	R	1958	1967	Herefordshire
McClelland	J	1838		Wigtownshire
McClure	AL	1963	1975	Inverness
McColl	P	1858	1860	Partick
McConnach	J	1927	1933	Newark
McConnach	J	1933	1955	Aberdeen
McConnach	WA	1953	1965	Southend-on-Sea
McCormac	JT	1926	1939	Southampton
McCrohon	J	1841	1862	Leominster
McCulloch	MM	1943	1960	Glasgow
MacDivitt	GH	1940	1947	Shrewsbury
McDonald	D	1845	1885	Ayr
McDonald	J	1848	1868	Wakefield
MacDonald	J	1876	1882	Alloa
McDonald	J	1879	1902	Hawick
Macdonald	J	1880	1908	Inverness Burgh
Macdonald	J	1881	1885	Inverkeithing
Macdonald	J	1914	1946	Arbroath
McDonald	J	1931	1936	Dundee

Macdonald	M	1887	1906	Sutherland
McDonald	W	1911	1931	Coatbridge
McDonnell	JA	1923	1930	Canterbury
McDougal		1838	1841	Wigtownshire
MacDougall	A	1837		Kinross-shire
McDougall	J	1844	1850	Dunbartonshire
McDougall	J	1850	1854	Arbroath
MacDougall	JG	1842	1858	Kirkcudbrightshire
McFarlane	J	1862	1867	Forres
MacGraw	H	1863	1875	Maidenhead
McGregor	D	1838		Royal Irish
McHardy	A	1866	1884	Sutherland
McHardy	A	1882	1911	Inverness
McHardy	C	1884	1914	Dunbartonshire
McHardy	H	1876	1907	Ayrshire
McHardy	JBB	1840	1881	Essex
McHardy	WB	1875	1896	Lanarkshire
McHardy	WB	1876	1882	Hamilton
McHarg		1844	1855	Birkenhead
McHendry	R	1808	1816	Gorbals
McIlwraith	J	1822	1832	Greenock
McInnes	A	1943	1961	Perth
MacInnes	DA	1961	1964	Perth
MacInnes	DA	1963	1975	Perth & Kinross
McIntosh	AJ	1931	1934	Paisley
McIntosh	AJ	1934	1956	Dunbartonshire
McIntosh	CA	1957	1966	Coatbridge
Macintosh	G	1880		Inverkeithing
Mackay	A	1840	1850	Argyllshire
Mackay	A	1854	1855	Arbroath
McKay	A	1855	1876	Dunbarton
Mackay	C	1864	1889	Argyllshire
MacKay	DW	1844	1876	Dundee
McKay	G	1844	1846	Anderston
McKay	G	1857	1876	Lanarkshire
McKay	G	1859	1864	Pulteneytown
Mackay	G	1892	1892	Lerwick
Mackay	G	1876	1904	Carlisle
Mackay	H	1840	1840	Argyllshire
Mackay	HF	1840	1881	East Sussex
MacKay	J	1858	1898	Bute
McKay	JA	1958	1966	Manchester
McKay	P	1850		Sutherland
McKay	R	1832	1833	Perth
MacKay	W	1872	1880	Galashiels
McKay	W	1885	1902	Ayr

McKay	W	1896	1920	Rothesay
MacKay	WF	1879	1890	Maxwelltown
McKechnie	WM	1945	1955	Greenock
McKenzie	D	1815	1825	Gorbals
McKenzie	D	1832	1836	Anderston
Mackenzie	W	1889	1912	Cardiff
McKerracher	C	2004		Grampian
McKerrow	A	1839	1840	Gorbals
Mackey	C	2007		Cumbria
Mackinnon	K	1961	1975	Argyllshire
Mackintosh	AC	1895	1921	Maidstone
Mackison	W	1844	1844	Dundee
McLachlan	C	1976	1987	Nottinghamshire
McLaren	J	1841		Kirkintilloch
McLauchlan	DM	1938	1957	Coatbridge
MacLean	AC	1911	1936	Inverness
McLean	D	1836	1837	Anderston
MacLean	R	1884	1887	Sutherland
MacLean	W	1935	1953	Ross & Cromarty
McLellan	JK	1965	1967	Motherwell & Wishaw
McLellan	JK	1967	1975	Lanarkshire
MacLennan		1854	1856	Elgin
McLennan	N	1914	1934	Dunbartonshire
MacLeod	A	1939	1949	Dunbarton
McLeod	J	1866	1869	Alloa
MacLeod	J	1906	1920	Leith
MacLeod	W	1924	1930	Johnstone
McManus	A	1836	1866	Hull
McMaster	J	1861	1865	Roxburghshire
MacMichael	JS	1852	1866	Warrington
McMillan	D	1906	1911	Renfrew
MacMillan	HC	1986	1996	Northern
McNab	W	1849	1855	Dumfries
McNaughton	J	1908	1936	Inverness Burgh
McNee	DB	1971	1975	Glasgow
McNee	DB	1975	1977	Strathclyde
McNee	DB	1977	1982	Metropolitan
McNeil	D	1869	1876	West Riding
MacNeill	D	1884	1914	Arbroath
McNeill	RFP	1969	1973	Northern
McNeill	RFP	1973	1975	Dunbartonshire
Macpherson	A	1858	1859	Nairnshire
McPherson	D	1840	1850	Arbroath
McPherson	I	2007	2009	Norfolk
Macpherson	J	1886	1912	Perthshire
Macready	CFN	1918	1920	Metropolitan

McWhirter	A	2003	2007	Suffolk
McWilliam	J	1925	1940	Lerwick
Maddison	P	2003	2009	Northamptonshire
Madoc	HW	1911	1936	Isle of Man
Main	A	1886	1906	Leith
Mair	JB	1890	1892	Elgin
Mair	JB	1892	1927	Morayshire
Malcolm	J		1866	Kirriemuir
Malcolm	J	1866	1903	Dumfries
Malcolm	P	1903	1910	Hull
Malcolm	P	1910	1934	Cheshire
Mander	JH	1906	1919	Isle of Ely
Mander	JH	1915	1927	Norfolk
Mann	A	1838	1858	Greenock
Mann	G	1867	1868	Richmond
Mansell	W	1869	1901	Lincoln
Mansfield	RW	1938	1939	Middlesbrough
Mardlin	FH	1887	1923	Northampton
Mark	R	1957	1967	Leicester
Mark	R	1972	1977	Metropolitan
Markin	FG	1943	1947	Peterborough City
Markin	FG	1943	1947	Peterborough Liberty
Markin	FG	1947	1965	Peterborough Combined
Marr	A	1900	1930	Montrose
Marsh	J	1836	183?	Gloucester
Marshall	A	2008		Hampshire
Marshall	P	1977	1985	City of London
Marshall	T	1852		Blackburn
Marshall	W	1959	1967	Wallasey
Marshall	WL	1880	1889	Salford
Martin	A	1847		Kirkintilloch
Martin	AG	1923	1930	Gravesend
Martin	CC	1941	1942	Leamington Spa
Martin	CC	1942	1946	Southport
Martin	CC	1948	1958	Liverpool
Martin	J	1838	1846	Tewkesbury
Martin	MJ	1912	1930	Perthshire
Martin	MJ	1930	1935	Perth & Kinross
Martin	W	1857	1872	Folkestone
Mason	J	1856	1858	Lincoln
Mason	WC	1844	1878	Ipswich
Massey	L	1960	1962	Burnley
Massey	L	1962	1967	Stockport
Matheson	AJ	1955	1963	Aberdeen
Mathews	A	1874	1903	Salisbury
Mathieson	K	2008	2009	Tayside

Matters	J	1893	1908	Devonport
Matthew	A	1872	1889	Elgin
Matthews	PJ	1965	1967	East Suffolk
Matthews	PJ	1967	1968	Suffolk
Matthews	PJ	1968	1982	Surrey
Matthews	RB	1956	1964	Cornwall
Matthews	RB	1964	1976	Warwickshire
Matthews	RL	1923	1937	Leeds
Maxwell	G	2007		North Yorkshire
Maxwell	J	1927	1943	Manchester
May	FJ	1927	1929	Stalybridge
May	FJ	1931	1941	Swansea
Mayall	AK	1912	1917	Carmarthen
Mayall	AK	1917	1941	Oldham
Mayer	K	1979	1983	Wiltshire
Mayne	D	1840	1859	Shropshire
Mayne	JG	1899	1933	East Suffolk
Mayne	O	1896	1928	Buckinghamshire
Mayne	R	1829	1868	Metropolitan
Maynerds	PD	1861	1868	Bewdley
Mearns	G	1859	1886	Banff
Meffen	AE	1858	1867	Stirlingshire
Meldrum	A	1946	1949	Inverness Burgh
Meldrum	A	1949	1955	Angus
Meldrum	A	1955	1965	Fife
Melville	T	2010		Gloucestershire
Mercer	G	1873	1883	Colchester
Mercer	T	1901	1926	Tiverton
Meredith	S	1839	1870	Wiltshire
Meredyth	F	1884	1887	Bedford
Merrifield	G	1859	1863	Penryn
Merrilees	W	1950	1968	Lothians & Peebles
Merritt	M	1840	1844	Tavistock
Metcalfe	HC	1902	1906	West Suffolk
Metcalfe	HC	1906	1908	West Riding
Metcalfe	HC	1908	1939	Somerset
Metcalfe	J	1875	1897	Hartlepool
Metcalfe	J	1895	1930	Reigate
Metcalfe	T	1876	1889	Ripon
Michael	AS	1922	1946	Radnorshire
Middleton	C	1907	1938	Stirlingshire
Midgley	SRL	1902	1912	Colchester
Mighall	H	1946	1960	Southport
Miler	J	1851	1858	Wick
Miles	HR	1942	1943	Winchester
Millar	A	1865	1885	Dewsbury

Millar	J	1882	1919	Hamilton
Miller	G	1850		Lanarkshire
Miller	H	1836	1847	Glasgow
Miller	H	1844	1844	Liverpool
Miller	H	1848	1848	Glasgow
Miller	J	1858		Caithness-shire
Miller	W	1827		Royal Irish
Millhouse	RTW	1941	1947	Newark
Milman	J	1836	1860	Okehampton
Milne	A	1875		Pulteneytown
Milne	J	1865	1884	Arbroath
Milne	J	1884	1904	Selkirkshire
Milner	L	1941	1947	Chesterfield
Milsom	A	1836	1852	Newbury
Mitchell	A	1859	1884	Caithness-shire
Mitchell	J	1805	1821	Glasgow
Mitchell	LE	1900	1905	Lerwick
Mitchell	R	1850	1856	Tynemouth
Mitchell	R	1924	1949	Kincardineshire
Mitchell	RF	1855	1871	Rutland
Mitchell	W	1840	1841	Dumfries-shire
Mitchell	W	1859	1866	Dumfries
Mitchell-Innes	C	1903	1931	Lincolnshire
Monro	D	1874	1878	Isle of Man
Monro	J	1888	1890	Metropolitan
Montgomerie	F	1857	1879	West Sussex
Moodie	WM	1984	1996	Fife
Moody	JW	1964	1969	Bolton
Moody	JW	1977	1978	Lancashire
Moore	B	2008		Wiltshire
Moore	G	1998	2002	West Yorkshire
Moore	J	1868	1887	Blandford
Moore	JW	1912	1917	Beverley
Moore	JW	1917	1931	Huddersfield
Moore	T	1960	1968	Nottingham
Moores	I	1859	1874	Stockport
Moorhouse	FGM	1884	1894	South Shields
Moorsom	HM	1880	1909	Lancashire
Moran	M	1854	1862	Barnstaple
Morant	WG	1891	1894	Reigate
Morant	WG	1894	1902	South Shields
Morant	WG	1902	1922	Durham County
More-O'Ferrall	JL	1836	1871	Dublin Metropolitan
Morgan	D	1883	1889	Bideford
Morgan	W	1842	1844	Neath
Moriarty	CCH	1935	1941	Birmingham

Morley	G	1910	1922	Hull
Morley	G	1922	1942	Durham County
Morren	J	1902	1909	Hawick
Morren	J	1909	1933	Berwickshire
Morren	J	1909	1933	Roxburghshire
Morren	J	1909	1933	Selkirkshire
Morren	WBR	1935	1955	Edinburgh
Morris	G	1859	1860	Durham City
Morris	J	1836	1836	Carmarthen
Morris	LH	1931	1946	Devon
Morris	SW	1961	1967	Rotherham
Morris	TA	1984	1990	Hertfordshire
Morris	TG	1963	1969	Cardiff
Morris	TG	1971	1979	South Wales
Morrison	A	1892	1893	Elgin
Morrison	A	1970	1975	Aberdeen
Morrison	A	1975	1983	Grampian
Morrison	W	1868	1879	Hawick
Morten	W	1847	1853	Tunbridge Wells
Morton	J	1897	1917	Huddersfield
Morton	W	1873	1892	Winchester
Moscrop	J	1854	1881	Kelso
Moxey	RJ	1848	1851	Edinburgh
Muir	AA	1950	1970	Durham County
Muir	JSR	1951	1962	Ayr
Mullett	AA	1985	1991	West Mercia
Mullineux	FW	1911	1930	Bolton
Munn	J	1840	1844	Elginshire
Munro	D	1862	1866	Hawick
Munro	D	1866		Forfar
Munro	D	1867	1888	Cromarty County
Munro	D	1867	1889	Ross
Munro	D	1878	1884	Mid Lothian
Munro	D	1878	1884	West Lothian
Munro	F	1953	1962	Ross & Cromarty
Munro	HF	1929	1951	Ayrshire
Munro	HFM	1923	1929	Herefordshire
Murison	RF	1965	1983	Fife
Murphy	C	1860	1886	Wigtownshire
Murphy	J	2010		Merseyside
Murphy	WRE	1923	1925	Dublin Metropolitan
Murray	JAR	1942	1965	Motherwell & Wishaw
Murray	W	1857	1882	Inverness
Murtrie	W	1831	1837	Paisley
Muttlebury	GA	1869	1874	Bath
Myers	PA	1970	1974	Gwynedd

Myers	PA	1974	1981	North Wales
Mynard	D	1867	1871	Lichfield
Mynott	J	1836		Saffron Walden
Napier	C	2011		Gwent
Napier	CF	1841	1867	Glamorganshire
Napier	E	1909	1915	Norfolk
Nash	WJ	1859	1864	Truro
Neale	S	1848	1852	Salford
Needham	AE	1949	1957	Doncaster
Neilans	J	1936	1945	Dundee
Neilson	JC	1882	1883	Airdrie
Nelson	H	1865	1875	Scilly Isles
Neville	A	1936	1942	Inverness Burgh
Neville	EA	1997	2004	Wiltshire
Neville	JA	1836	1837	Colchester
Newcombe	JH	1840	1845	Montgomeryshire
Newing	JF	1990	2000	Derbyshire
Newman	KL	1976	1979	Royal Ulster
Newman	KL	1982	1987	Metropolitan
Newnham	W	1858	1863	Greenock
Newton	F	1927	1947	Hereford
Newton	F	1929	1958	Herefordshire
Newton	R	1848	1858	Ashton-under-Lyne
Neyroud	P	2002	2006	Thames Valley
Nicholas	R	1886	1908	Penzance
Nicholas	WV	1910	1929	Guildford
Nicholls	M	1901	1907	Windsor
Nicholls	M	1907	1937	Warrington
Nicholls	SJ	1869	1898	Newcastle-upon-Tyne
Nicholls	W	1836	1855	Beverley
Nichols	GET	1957	1967	Bath
Nicholson	AF	1913	1930	Exeter
Nicholson	GC	1930	1946	Surrey
Nicholson	J	1878	1885	River Wear
Nicholson	J	1878	1885	Sunderland
Nicholson	W	1899	1920	Berwick-upon-Tweed
Nicol	G	1910	1933	Stirling
Nicol	T	1883	1906	Alloa
Nightingale	JC	1962	1978	Essex
Nixon	J	1829	1841	Thetford
Nixon	RF	1929	1943	Salisbury
Nobes	J	1881	1889	Buckingham
Nobes	PJ	1985	1989	North Yorkshire
Nobes	PJ	1989	1993	West Yorkshire
Noble	A	1905	1922	Galashiels
Noble	RA	1948	1960	Burnley

Noble	RA	1959	1960	Derby
Norbury		1859	1860	Macclesfield
Norris	J	1862	1890	Coventry
North	W	1836	1851	Gravesend
Notman	N	1841	1866	Peebles-shire
Nott-Bower	AB	1881	1890	Leeds
Nott-Bower	JRN	1953	1958	Metropolitan
Nott-Bower	JW	1878	1881	Leeds
Nott-Bower	JW	1881	1902	Liverpool
Nott-Bower	JW	1902	1925	City of London
Nove	P	1998	2002	City of London
Nuttall	T	1915	1923	Congleton
Oake	REN	1986	1999	Isle of Man
Oakes	RM	1840	1852	Norfolk
Oakley	W	1849	1852	Bath
O'Byrne	M	1995	2000	Bedfordshire
O'Connor	D	2000	2004	Surrey
O'Dowd	DJ	1986	1993	Northamptonshire
Ogden	J	1878	1881	Great Yarmouth
Ogilvie	RRK	1939	1949	Angus
Ogilvie	RRK	1946	1949	Arbroath
Ogle	R	1917	1937	Gateshead
Oglethorpe	J	1872	1882	Preston
Oldham	B	1848		Barnstaple
Olds	J	1853	1886	Penzance
Oliver	IT	1979	1990	Central Scotland
Oliver	IT	1990	1998	Grampian
Oliver	W	1929	1943	Guildford
O'Neill	P	1923	1947	Kendal
Onslow	CW	1853	1862	Tunbridge Wells
Ord	R	1841	1844	Middlesbrough
Ord	R	1845	1849	Middlesbrough
Ord	R	1850	1850	Middlesbrough
Orde	H	2002	2009	Northern Ireland
Ormerod	GM	1920	1936	East Sussex
Ormerod	J	1931	1959	Wallasey
Orr	J	1876	1886	Greenock
Orr	J	1996	2001	Strathclyde
Orr	JH	1960	1968	Dundee
Orr	JH	1968	1975	Lothians & Peebles
Orr	JH	1975	1983	Lothian & Borders
Osmond	D	1946	1962	Shropshire
Osmond	D	1962	1977	Hampshire
Otter	S	2007		Devon and Cornwall
Ovens	NG	1990	1993	Lincolnshire
Over	JE	1980	1993	Gwent

Owen	CM	1857	1888	Oxfordshire
Owen	D	1980	1982	Dorset
Owen	D	1982	1994	North Wales
Oxford	KG	1975	1989	Merseyside
Pacey	AH	1987	1993	Gloucestershire
Page	CJ	1971	1977	City of London
Page	W	1877	1889	Sandwich
Pain	BN	1974	1982	Kent
Pain	J	1842		Harwich
Paine	G	1838	1859	Truro
Palfrey	WJH	1940	1947	Accrington
Palfrey	WJH	1969	1972	Lancashire
Palin	WH	1857	1881	Manchester
Palmer		1885	1886	Stamford
Palmer	E	1836		Bideford
Palmer	J	183?		Leamington Spa
Palmer	L	1967	1968	Oldham
Palmer	W	1930	1943	Margate
Pardoe	W	1836	1841	York
Parfitt	G	1944	1966	Barnsley
Parker	E	1913	1923	Birkenhead
Parker	G	2005		Bedfordshire
Parker	RY	1924	1927	Stalybridge
Parker	T	1858	1874	Deal
Parker	WH	1894	1918	Great Yarmouth
Parker	WT	1874	1877	Deal
Parkinson	D	1983	1993	Jersey
Parr	S	1962	1967	Blackpool
Parr	S	1972	1977	Lancashire
Parr	S	2010		Cambridgeshire
Parrish	AS	1981	1985	Derbyshire
Parry	CDC	1900	1902	Bath
Parry	CDC	1902	1920	Cumberland
Parry	CDC	1902	1920	Westmorland
Parry	DP	1932	1936	Montgomeryshire
Parry	FJ	1869	1872	Nottingham
Parry	FJ	1873	1892	Derbyshire
Paterson	AJ	1948	1956	Salford
Paterson	AJ	1956	1967	Leeds
Paterson	W	1950	1962	Inverness Burgh
Pattison	JC	1945	1960	Dundee
Pattison	W	1861	1865	Beverley
Pattison	W	1865	1898	Scarborough
Paul	CJ	1894	1898	Bradford
Paul	WH	1878	1888	Isle of Man
Payne	CF	1976	1990	Cleveland

Payne	WG	1898	1913	King's Lynn
Peacock	J	1860	1864	Arundel
Peacock	JC	1868	1871	Richmond
Peacock	R	1888	1892	Canterbury
Peacock	R	1892	1898	Oldham
Peacock	R	1898	1926	Manchester
Peacocke	JA	1969	1969	Royal Ulster
Pearce	F	1901	1920	Truro
Pearce	FW	1922	1940	Bridgwater
Pearce	W	1847	1848	Glasgow
Pearson	C	1870	1879	Caernarvonshire
Pearson	C	1875		Northamptonshire
Pearson	J	1851	1872	Halifax
Pearson	RJ	1919	1944	Cambridge
Pearson	W	1888	1891	Reigate
Peck	J	1855	1865	Reading
Peck	SE	1960	1964	Staffordshire
Peck	W	1858	1859	Orford
Peel	FRJ	1931	1933	Bath
Peel	FRJ	1933	1962	Essex
Peel-Yates	LW	1924	1955	Dorset
Pellant	A	1883	1889	Saint Albans
Pemberton	J	1876	1887	Grantham
Pendleton	EWC	1948	1969	Coventry
Pennycook	W	1858	1859	Alloa
Percival	JS	1914	1921	Wigan
Pessell	J	1961	1964	Southport
Pessell	J	1964	1966	Luton
Petrie	D	1876	1889	Pulteneytown
Pey	TJ	1921	1946	Wigan
Philipps	W	1875	1908	Carmarthenshire
Philipps	WP	1908	1940	Carmarthenshire
Phillipps	JV	1902	1931	Bath
Phillips	C	1997	2001	Cumbria
Phillips	J	1840	1849	Worcester
Phillips	J	1860	1888	Neath
Phillips	JD	1993	2003	Kent
Pickering	S	1929	1947	Stalybridge
Pickersgill	H	1891	1899	Grimsby
Piggott	H	1930	1939	Hartlepool
Pigott	P	1880	1909	Norfolk
Pilkington	S	1998	2005	Avon & Somerset
Pim	RP	1945	1961	Royal Ulster
Pipe	WJ	1859	1883	Saint Albans
Pirie	J	1870	1890	Elginshire
Pirie	J	1890	1891	Morayshire

Pitts	WE	1949	1953	Bootle
Pitts	WE	1953	1967	Derbyshire
Player	J	1861	1886	Chard
Plumb	H	1893	1900	Eastbourne
Plumb	W	1844	1847	Tunbridge Wells
Plume	AF	1944	1963	Norwich
Pole	C	1873	1876	Grantham
Pole	C	1876	1903	Halifax
Polin	M	2009		North Wales
Pollard	C	1991	2002	Thames Valley
Pollard	J	1882	1888	Rotherham
Pollock		1841	1841	Kirkintilloch
Pond	E	1840	1844	Dunbartonshire
Popkess	A	1930	1959	Nottingham
Port	C	2005		Avon & Somerset
Porter		1841	1843	Birkenhead
Porter	A	1871	1909	Roxburghshire
Porter	A	1893	1909	Berwickshire
Porter	A	1904	1909	Selkirkshire
Porter	FD	1963	1965	Cambridgeshire
Porter	FD	1964	1965	Cambridge
Porter	FD	1965	1974	Mid-Anglia
Porter	FD	1974	1977	Cambridgeshire
Porter	WH	1875	1889	Southwold
Potts	J	1863	1878	Blackburn
Poulton	AF	1899	1902	West Suffolk
Poulton	AF	1902	1932	Berkshire
Pouncy	TS	1853	1871	Dorchester
Povey	K	1993	1997	Leicestershire
Powell	EJ	1840	1841	Inverness
Powell	T	1822	1827	Royal Irish
Power	G	2001	2010	Jersey
Power	M	1861	1884	Worcester
Poyntz	WH	1872	1881	Nottingham
Poyntz	WH	1881	1887	Essex
Pratt	AA	1868	1889	Chichester
Pratt	HR	1953	1971	Bedfordshire
Prest	EP	1906	1932	West Suffolk
Preston	D	1875	1900	Banbury
Price	AW	1877	1878	Denbighshire
Price	BDK	1980	1987	Cumbria
Price	HS	1940	1957	Bradford
Price	S	2003		Cleveland
Price	WJ	1946	1954	Cardiff
Prickett	AT	1898	1907	Portsmouth
Priday	SS	1859	1862	Huddersfield

Priest	RW	1938	1946	Bacup
Pringle	WJ	1912	1919	Blackpool
Prior	C	1893	1921	Tunbridge Wells
Pritchard	FE	1930	1950	Dewsbury
Pritchard	TS	1939	1945	Caernarvonshire
Prosser	TH	1836	1857	Coventry
Prothero	L	1894	1919	Anglesey
Prothero	RH	1919	1949	Anglesey
Protheroe	D	1836	1837	Neath
Protheroe-Smith	HB	1909	1935	Cornwall
Proudfoot	W	1835		Berwick-upon-Tweed
Pryde	R	1924	1930	Kirkcaldy
Puckering	AG	1970	1981	Durham County
Pugh	J	1837	1843	Carmarthen
Purchase	EJ	1865	1887	Reading
Pye	T	1865	1881	Lancaster
Pyme	HE	1846	1851	Haverfordwest
Quick	J	1878	1889	Torrington
Quick	RF	2004	2008	Surrey
Rackham	H	1836	1838	Tewkesbury
Radford	J	1859	1864	Chesterfield
Radley	JH	1863	1877	Rochester
Rae	W	1858	1861	Forres
Rae	W	1996	2001	Dumfries & Galloway
Rae	W	2001	2007	Strathclyde
Rafter	CH	1899	1935	Birmingham
Ramsden	J	1836	1839	Scarborough
Rand	W	1837	1841	Colchester
Rawle	HC	1898	1901	Tiverton
Rawle	HC	1901	1905	Burnley
Rawlings	H	1921	1926	Neath
Rawlings	H	1926	1956	Derby
Rawlins	A	1853	1872	Abingdon
Rawson	T	1919	1927	Hereford
Rawson	T	1927	1931	Swansea
Rawson	T	1931	1940	Bradford
Raymond	G	1874	1878	Hythe
Raymond	J	1840		Maldon
Raynor	T	1844	1858	Sheffield
Raynor	WB	1854	1860	Nottingham
Read	E	1837	1859	Leeds
Reddish	W	1851	1854	Nottingham
Redman	J	1836	1837	Newport [Monmouthshire]
Redsull	H	1850	1858	Deal
Redwood	R	1836	1860	Arundel
Reed	A	1885	1900	Royal Irish

Reed	W	1836	1859	Stamford
Rees	AM	1957	1964	Denbighshire
Rees	AM	1964	1977	Staffordshire
Rees	W	1836	1851	Swansea
Rees	W	1839	1841	Neath
Rees	W	1840	1859	Pembroke
Rees	W	1844	1852	Neath
Rees	W	1943	1947	Leamington Spa
Rees	W	1947	1961	Stockport
Reeve	H	1899	1922	Folkestone
Reeves	C	1853	1859	Durham City
Reeves	C	1861	1866	King's Lynn
Reid	A	1842	1848	Blairgowrie
Reid	W	1872	1874	Stirling
Renfrew	T	1945	1958	Lanarkshire
Rennie	AA	1975	1981	West Mercia
Rice	P	2010		Guernsey
Richards	F	1967	1968	Salford
Richards	M	2004	2007	Wiltshire
Richards	M	2007		Sussex
Richards	WJ	1966	1974	Manchester
Richards	WJ	1974	1976	Greater Manchester
Richardson	AH	1901	1903	Newcastle-under-Lyme
Richardson	AH	1903	1943	Halifax
Richardson	F	1884	1919	Hereford
Richardson	F	1956	1969	Preston
Richardson	FAR	1903	1929	Salisbury
Richardson	J	1840	1846	Gorbals
Richardson	T	1860	1880	South Shields
Richardson	W	1862	1868	Stratford-on-Avon
Riches	WH	1898	1902	Scarborough
Riches	WH	1902	1930	Middlesbrough
Ridd	WJ	1945	1967	West Suffolk
Riddell	C	1858	1859	Dunbartonshire
Ridge	CFW	1956	1957	Brighton
Rivett-Carnac	JCT	1928	1957	Huntingdonshire
Rivett-Carnac	JCT	1931	1957	Isle of Ely
Robb	J	1834		South Shields
Robb	J	1839	1846	South Shields
Robb	W	1911	1930	Renfrew
Robbins	G	1839	1842	Hampshire
Roberts	DW	1917	1920	Oxfordshire
Roberts	J	1858	1860	Trevethin
Roberts	JF	1947	1959	Flintshire
Roberts	R	1839	1863	Scarborough
Roberts	RD	1921	1927	Swansea

Roberts	S	1962	1969	Swansea
Roberts	W	1866	1878	Louth
Robertson		1822	1828	Edinburgh
Robertson	A	1841	1880	Hertfordshire
Robertson	A	1844		Dunbar
Robertson	CD	1935	1937	Isle of Wight
Robertson	CD	1938	1945	West Suffolk
Robertson	D	1932	1949	Clackmannanshire
Robertson	J	1875	1889	Arundel
Robertson	J	1925	1949	Bute
Robertson	J	1925	1949	Renfrewshire
Robertson	J	1949	1954	Renfrew & Bute
Robertson	JA	1960	1971	Glasgow
Robertson	N	1844	1885	Banffshire
Robertson	WA	1996	2001	Northern
Robertson-Glasgow	CC	1911	1919	Ayrshire
Robinson	J	1851	1861	Haverfordwest
Robinson	JE	1943	1947	Hartlepool
Robinson	W	1836	1836	Scarborough
Robinson	WH	1929	1940	Newport [Monmouthshire]
Robotham	O	1881	1889	Abingdon
Roby	WS	1839		Leamington Spa
Rofe	J	1842	1849	Walsall
Rofe	J	1850	1851	Dover
Rogers	G	1864	1888	Reigate
Romanis	RW	1876	1888	Margate
Ronaldson	A	1865	1872	Berwick-upon-Tweed
Ronnie	W	1948	1949	Breconshire
Roper	HG	1877	1901	Huntingdonshire
Ross	DA	1927	1961	Argyllshire
Ross	DG	1933	1962	Sutherland
Ross	G	1855	1857	Bridgnorth
Ross	J	1863	1892	Aberdeenshire
Ross	J	1870	1872	Alloa
Ross	K	1962	1963	Sutherland
Ross	K	1963	1975	Ross & Sutherland
Ross	P	1964	1967	Rochdale
Ross	R	1895	1898	Ramsgate
Ross	R	1898	1900	Bradford
Ross	R	1900	1935	Edinburgh
Ross	WC	1873	1881	Newport [Isle of Wight]
Ross of Bladenburg	JFG	1901	1914	Dublin Metropolitan
Rowan	C	1829	1850	Metropolitan
Rowbotham	GW	1922	1942	Stockport
Rowbottom	RE	1963	1969	Warrington
Rowland		1857	1858	Kidwelly

Rowley	M	2009		Surrey
Rowley	T	1869	1889	Stratford-on-Avon
Rowsell	AE	1941	1958	Exeter
Rowsell	AE	1957	1963	Brighton
Roy	C	1921	1947	Kilmarnock
Ruck	AA	1886	1912	Caernarvonshire
Rudd	CC	1842	1845	Gateshead
Rudd	CC	1846	1854	Hawick
Ruddick	J	1925	1937	River Wear
Ruddick	J	1925	1937	Sunderland
Rudkin	J	1865	1873	Grantham
Russell	HR	1879	1907	Ipswich
Russell	TS	1876	1905	West Riding
Russell	W	1842	1853	Dorchester
Rutherford	HG	1945	1954	Oxfordshire
Rutherford	HG	1954	1956	Lincolnshire
Rutherford	HG	1956	1968	Surrey
Rutter	S	1880	1883	Folkestone
Ruxton	JHH	1857	1894	Kent
Ryall	JE	1934	1939	East Riding
Ryall	JE	1939	1955	Somerset
Ryan	PJ	1990	1993	Norfolk
Rydeheard	A	1967	1969	Blackpool
Ryder		1834		Walsall
Ryder	J	1861	1866	Lichfield
Sabbage	JH	1844	1857	Carlisle
Sabbage	JH	1857	1867	Newcastle-upon-Tyne
Sach	WE	1859	1889	Sudbury
Saddleton	HA	1941	1943	Dover
Sadler	J	1857	1862	Stalybridge
Saggerson	EJ	1861	1884	Middlesbrough
St Johnston	TE	1940	1944	Oxfordshire
St Johnston	TE	1945	1950	Durham County
St Johnston	TE	1950	1967	Lancashire
Salisbury	HH	1965	1968	North Riding
Salisbury	HH	1968	1972	York & North East Yorkshire
Salter	W	1888	1889	Newport [Isle of Wight]
Sampson	C	1983	1989	West Yorkshire
Sanders	HE	1958	1962	Blackpool
Sanders	HH	1917	1929	Plymouth
Sanders	TO	1872	1901	Dover
Sant	ML	1899	1930	Surrey
Saunders	H	1858	1868	Margate
Savi	VG	1935	1949	Fife
Sayer	F	1958	1967	Lincoln
Schofield	WE	1942	1958	Oldham

Schorey	WH	1845	1863	Gateshead
Schreber	AJ	1907	1936	Ipswich
Scott	A	1859		Hamilton
Scott	A	1920	1936	Luton
Scott	CT	1887	1890	Dewsbury
Scott	CT	1889	1898	Salford
Scott	CT	1899	1912	Sheffield
Scott	G	1939	1943	Wigtownshire
Scott	GE	1936	1944	Luton
Scott	GE	1944	1947	Newcastle-upon-Tyne
Scott	GE	1948	1959	Sheffield
Scott	GE	1959	1968	West Riding
Scott	GE	1968	1969	West Yorkshire
Scott	HR	1945	1953	Metropolitan
Scott	J	1840	1846	Hawick
Scott	J	1897	1932	Clackmannanshire
Scott	J	1914	1934	Perth
Scott	J	1923	1924	Galashiels
Scott	JJ	1953	1963	Tynemouth
Scott	RA	1843	1875	Carmarthenshire
Scott	S	1855		Sudbury
Scott	W	1902	1928	South Shields
Scott-Lee	PJ	1998	2002	Suffolk
Scott-Lee	PJ	2002	2009	West Midlands
Scroggie	AUR	1953	1963	Northumberland
Sculpher	WR	1930	1946	Guernsey
Segrave	H	1857	1878	Wolverhampton
Sempill	JH	1909	1913	Broughty Ferry
Sempill	JTD	1887	1907	Stirlingshire
Senior	AF	1942	1957	East Suffolk
Sexton	D	1836	1862	Maidenhead
Shackell	J	1854	1856	Shrewsbury
Shannons	W	1836		Reading
Sharp	L	1988	1991	Cumbria
Sharp	L	1991	1995	Strathclyde
Sharpe	H	1833	1835	Worcester
Sharpe	PS	1994	2000	Hertfordshire
Sharpe	W	1869	1889	Wisbech
Sharples	FB	1875	1889	Stockport
Sharples	J	1989	1998	Merseyside
Shattock	DJ	1986	1989	Dyfed-Powys
Shattock	DJ	1989	1998	Avon & Somerset
Shaw	BDD	1993	2003	Cleveland
Shaw	C	1839	1842	Manchester
Shaw	EM	1860	1861	Belfast
Shaw Kennedy	J	1836	1838	Royal Irish

Shearer	P	2007		Dumfries & Galloway
Sheasby	H	1907	1942	Macclesfield
Sheasby	W	1874	1903	Macclesfield
Shelvey	D	1858	1860	Margate
Shepherd	E	1845	1848	Salford
Shepherd	W	1833	1851	Winchester
Sheppard	TW	1856	1859	Lancashire
Shiells	R	1858	1861	Dunbar
Shiels	J	1871	1875	Hartlepool
Shillington	GRE	1970	1973	Royal Ulster
Shore	HM	1896	1911	Dewsbury
Short	J	1893	1901	Exeter
Showbridge	HW	1878	1880	Blackburn
Showers	EM	1886	1888	Exeter
Showers	EM	1888	1915	Essex
Showers	EM	1915	1919	Colchester
Sillitoe	PJ	1923	1925	Chesterfield
Sillitoe	PJ	1925	1926	East Riding
Sillitoe	PJ	1926	1931	Sheffield
Sillitoe	PJ	1931	1943	Glasgow
Sillitoe	PJ	1943	1946	Kent
Sim	AC	1935	1940	Perth & Kinross
Sim	J	1909	1924	Winchester
Sim	RS	1980	1984	Tayside
Sim	S	2011		Northumbria
Simcox	J	1888	1889	Ludlow
Simm	W	1852	1875	Wigan
Simpson	J	1835	1842	Dunfermline
Simpson	J	1943	1946	Northumberland
Simpson	J	1946	1956	Surrey
Simpson	J	1958	1968	Metropolitan
Simpson	TH	1859	1863	Cupar
Simpton		1839		Bolton
Sims	C	2007	2009	Staffordshire
Sims	C	2009		West Midlands
Sinclair	AI	1875	1912	Newport [Monmouthshire]
Sinclair	G	1903	1928	Accrington
Sinclair	N	1859	1881	Airdrie
Sinclair	T	1884	1912	Caithness-shire
Sivyer	W	1853	1867	Romsey
Skelton	TM	1943	1947	Hyde
Skermer	T	1857	1861	Coventry
Skinner	AM	1833	1840	Belfast
Skinner	CM		1833	Belfast
Skitt	BH	1990	1994	Hertfordshire
Skittery	JF	1943	1965	Plymouth

Skull	T	1836	1839	Wycombe
Sloan	AK	1983	1985	Bedfordshire
Sloan	AK	1985	1991	Strathclyde
Sloan	J	1871	1895	Port Glasgow
Smart	D	1891	1920	Brechin
Smart	J	1835	1846	Calton
Smart	J	1848	1870	Glasgow
Smeed	FH	1952	1967	Newport [Monmouthshire]
Smith	AD	1922	1931	Glasgow
Smith	AO	1985	1990	Derbyshire
Smith	B	1833	1834	Calton
Smith	BW	1918	1940	Great Yarmouth
Smith	CR	1985	1991	Thames Valley
Smith	D	1835	1836	York
Smith	D	1851	1857	Chipping Norton
Smith	D	1870	1875	Arundel
Smith	D	1983	1988	Wiltshire
Smith	G	1918	1919	Kidderminster
Smith	H	1890	1901	City of London
Smith	IJ	1908	1923	Kendal
Smith	J	1828	1854	Kelso
Smith	J	1833		Montrose
Smith	J	1836	1851	Oswestry
Smith	J	1882	1907	Durham City
Smith	JE	1842	1844	Ipswich
Smith	JWT	1958	1964	Liverpool
Smith	K	2008		Central Scotland
Smith	T	1887	1911	Carmarthen
Smith	TG	1933	1949	Hamilton
Smith	TJ	1857	1877	Cheshire
Smith	TJ	1920	1920	Royal Irish
Smith	W	1829	1839	Croydon
Smith	W	1840	1842	Ashford
Smith	W	1856	1861	Ripon
Smith	WH	1901	1905	Saint Albans
Smith	WH	1905	1924	Burnley
Smith	WH	1918	1943	Eastbourne
Smith	WH	1932	1943	Hyde
Smith	WM	1963	1970	Aberdeen
Smith	WS	1836	1841	Leominster
Snell	J	1888	1913	Ashton-under-Lyne
Snowden	RL	1842		Gilling West
Solomon	E	1964	1966	Walsall
Solomon	E	1967	1974	West Midlands
Solomon	H	1838	1844	Brighton
Sommers	AE	1884	1892	Worcester

Songhurst	G	1872	1893	Barnstaple
Soper	LAG	1979	1987	Gloucestershire
Sorley	T	1963	1968	Inverness Burgh
Southey	P	1859	1868	Blandford
Sowerby	JD	1892	1917	Plymouth
Sparling	OD	1891	1913	Wycombe
Sparrow	J	1907	1920	Louth
Spence	J	2005	2010	Cambridgeshire
Spence	WA	1995	2000	Tayside
Spencer	J	1947	1947	Bacup
Spense	W	1903	1903	Forfar
Spicer	RGB	1938	1943	Isle of Wight
Spiers	T	1844	1851	Halifax
Spurgeon		1859	1874	Southwold
Staines	EV	1956	1959	Derby
Staines	EV	1959	1963	Sheffield
Stainsby	J	1858	1878	River Wear
Stainsby	J	1858	1878	Sunderland
Stait	A	1868	1874	Droitwich
Stanhope	ES	1895	1923	Herefordshire
Stanley-Clarke	FL	1918	1937	Gloucestershire
Stansfield	W	1964	1967	Denbighshire
Stansfield	W	1967	1979	Derbyshire
Staunton	GS	1933	1942	East Suffolk
Steel	D	1839		Barnstaple
Steel	D	1847	1873	Exeter
Steele	KWL	1955	1974	Somerset
Steele	KWL	1974	1979	Avon & Somerset
Steer	J	1850	1857	Folkestone
Steer	KE	1958	1967	Exeter
Stenhouse	J	1800	1803	Glasgow
Stennett	R	1852	1869	Bedford
Stephen	C	1934	1943	Perth
Stephens	C	1845	1846	Pontefract
Stephens	GP	1913	1918	Wycombe
Stephens	J	1836	1854	Newcastle-upon-Tyne
Stephens	J	1845	1884	River Tyne
Stephens	RA	1842	1860	Birmingham
Stephenson	P	2002	2005	Lancashire
Stephenson	P	2009	2011	Metropolitan
Sterne	R	1870	1908	Wiltshire
Stevens	DF	1998	2005	Essex
Stevens	FAD	1910	1939	Bedfordshire
Stevens	JA	1991	1996	Northumbria
Stevens	JA	2000	2005	Metropolitan
Stevens	JFJ	1842	1860	Brecon

Stevens	S	1864	1868	Chesterfield
Stevens	S	1869	1881	Rochdale
Stevens	S	1881	1892	Nottingham
Stevens	T	1865	1868	Arundel
Stevenson	JV	1902	1922	Glasgow
Stewart	A	1839		Perthshire
Stewart	A	1873	1883	Brechin
Stewart	DO	1837	1840	Arbroath
Stewart	G	1871	1878	Tynemouth
Stewart	J	1828	1842	Edinburgh
Stewart	J	1837	1851	Paisley
Stewart	J	1841		Wigtownshire
Stewart	J	1906	1919	Bootle
Stewart	J	1943	1946	Inverness Burgh
Stewart	W	1927	1930	Morayshire
Stewart	W	1930	1949	Moray & Nairn
Stichbury	J	1999	2004	Dorset
Stirling	J	1866	1906	Nairnshire
Stirling	J	1867	1903	Forfar
Stirling	J	1898	1901	Newcastle-under-Lyme
Stirling	J	1901	1930	Grimsby
Stock	J	1836		Saffron Walden
Stockwell	HC	1913	1947	Colchester
Stockwin	E	1840	1842	Macclesfield
Stoddart	J	2005		Durham County
Stokes	ABA	1857	1879	Pembrokeshire
Stovin	F	183?		Royal Irish
Strachan	JC	1998	2005	Northumbria
Strang	DJR	2001	2007	Dumfries & Galloway
Strang	DJR	2007		Lothian & Borders
Strath	GI	1931	1949	Banffshire
Strath	GI	1949	1957	Scottish North-eastern Counties
Stratton	WG	1924	1942	Winchester
Stretten	CJD	1888	1915	Cambridgeshire
Stronach	R	1927	1942	Dunfermline
Strugnell	J	1863	1865	Grantham
Stuart	G	1854	1884	Dunfermline
Stuart	J	1869	1871	Stirling
Stuart	T	1940	1950	Zetland
Studdy	H	1935	1943	Northumberland
Studdy	H	1943	1944	Durham County
Studdy	H	1944	1959	West Riding
Sturt	EW	1920	1938	Bacup
Summers	FL	1937	1950	Warrington
Summers	FTB	1907	1933	Pembrokeshire
Sutherland	A	1880	1905	Galashiels

Sutherland	D	1876	1900	Paisley
Sutherland	J	1850	1854	Elgin
Sutherland	J	1854	1872	Inverness Burgh
Sutherland	WGM	1979	1983	Bedfordshire
Sutherland	WGM	1983	1996	Lothian & Borders
Swaby	F	1937	1947	Leeds
Swain	R	1864	1865	Bradninch
Swanson	G	1856	1858	Thurso
Swanson	G	1870	1871	Pulteneytown
Swanson	J	1846	1856	Thurso
Swanson	J	1868	1879	Aberdeen
Swanson	W	1842	1846	Thurso
Swift	D	2006	2007	Staffordshire
Syer	EC	1852	1869	West Suffolk
Sykes	W	1836	1860	Oswestry
Sylvester	WC	1863	1866	Rochdale
Sylvester	WC	1866	1868	Salford
Sylvester	WC	1868	1869	Newcastle-upon-Tyne
Symmons	WG	1945	1947	Macclesfield
Symmons	WG	1947	1964	Saint Helens
Tacey	JW	1845	1866	Louth
Tait	J	1805	1812	Edinburgh
Tait	W	1955	1961	River Wear
Tait	W	1955	1967	Sunderland
Talbot	G	1877	1883	Dublin Metropolitan
Talbot	L	1890	1895	Kendal
Talbot	L	1895	1907	Warrington
Tarry	FT	1930	1940	Exeter
Tarry	FT	1941	1946	Southampton
Tarry	GG	1900	1912	Leeds
Tarttelin	C	1930	1934	Grimsby
Tate	H	1851	1857	Swansea
Taylor	C	1887	1900	Walsall
Taylor	CG	1975	1980	Norfolk
Taylor	FW	1988	1997	Durham County
Taylor	G	1891	1898	Newcastle-under-Lyme
Taylor	J	1852	1866	Salford
Taylor	J	1880	1889	Maidenhead
Taylor	J	1883	1899	Folkestone
Taylor	JA	1950	1972	Leicestershire
Taylor	S	1853	1859	Wisbech
Taylor	T	1853	1861	Stratford-on-Avon
Taylor	W	1994	1998	City of London
Taylor	WH	1968	1969	Wigan
Teale	D	1894	1916	Luton
Teale	EJJ	1900	1918	Eastbourne

264 The British Police: Forces and Chief Officers 1829-2012

Teevan	GJ	1881	1884	South Shields
Teevan	GJ	1884	1904	Hove
Telfer	JD	1857	1868	Radnorshire
Telfer	JD	1857	1895	Herefordshire
Terry	GWR	1958	1965	Pembrokeshire
Terry	GWR	1965	1967	East Sussex
Terry	GWR	1970	1973	Lincolnshire
Terry	GWR	1973	1983	Sussex
Terry	HD	1886	1900	Northumberland
Terry	J	1881	1894	Brighton
Tewsley	G	1857	1878	Great Yarmouth
Tewsley	G	1885	1887	Walsall
Tewsley	G	1887	1897	Reading
Thody	H	1887	1906	Bedford
Thom	D	1909	1930	Hawick
Thom	J	1854	1862	Hawick
Thomas	AH	1913	1921	Swansea
Thomas	J	1844	1845	Middlesbrough
Thomas	J	1860	1861	Tenby
Thomas	J	1862	1865	Dewsbury
Thomas	M	1945	1963	Merthyr Tydfil
Thomas	M	1963	1969	Glamorganshire
Thomas	M	1969	1971	South Wales
Thomas	RB	1963	1968	Mid-Wales
Thomas	RB	1975	1986	Dyfed-Powys
Thomas	T	1867	1877	Tenby
Thomas	WF	1954	1963	Cardiff
Thomas	WH	1877	1894	Anglesey
Thomas	WM	1905	1907	Breconshire
Thompson	A	1900	1902	Leamington Spa
Thompson	A	1902	1921	Walsall
Thompson	GA	1835	1840	Tunbridge Wells
Thompson	HM	1840		Stafford
Thompson	J	1853	1859	Leamington Spa
Thompson	JH	1962	1968	Burnley
Thompson	W	1836	1875	Banbury
Thompson	W	1934	1937	Clitheroe
Thomson	J	1904	1930	Forfar
Thomson	W	1937	1947	Lancaster
Thornton	NF	1850	1861	King's Lynn
Thornton	S	2006		Thames Valley
Thornton	W	1892	1912	Gravesend
Thorpe	HW	1934	1947	Saint Albans
Thurley	HF	1912	1923	Gravesend
Tilley	E	1930	1943	Wolverhampton
Timbrell	F	1910	1930	Bedford

Timpson	AC	1998	2000	Warwickshire
Tinkler	EW	1928	1931	Kidderminster
Tinkler	EW	1931	1955	Worcester
Todd	M	2002	2008	Greater Manchester
Todd	N	1944	1947	Accrington
Tolson	HA	1914	1932	Ashton-under-Lyne
Tomasson	WH	1892	1922	Nottinghamshire
Tomkins	P	2002	2007	Lothian & Borders
Tompkins	P	1946	1957	Denbighshire
Tonge	M	2004	2008	Gwent
Toothill	L	1859	1864	Flint
Torrens	RW	1869	1880	Salford
Toshack	W	1854	1861	Burntisland
Trenchard	HM	1931	1935	Metropolitan
Trotter	J	1892	1917	Gateshead
Trubshaw	W	1927	1935	Lancashire
Tudor	HH	1920	1922	Royal Irish
Tuff	J	1842	1862	Rochester
Tulloch	JM	1927	1938	Orkney
Turnbull	HS	1913	1920	Argyllshire
Turnbull	HS	1920	1925	Cumberland
Turnbull	HS	1920	1925	Westmorland
Turnbull	HS	1925	1950	City of London
Turner	DH	1896	1898	Barnsley
Turner	DH	1898	1917	Oldham
Turner	DV	1941	1962	Swansea
Turner	G	1880	1889	Godalming
Turner	J	1842	1856	Lincoln
Turner	J	1933	1951	Airdrie
Turner	K	1999	2003	Gwent
Turrall	WG	1857	1858	Colchester
Turrall	WG	1858	1889	Cambridge
Twist	G	1964	1974	Bristol
Tyler	JC	1846	1856	Thetford
Tymms	T	1837	1841	Doncaster
Underhill	S	1850		Berwickshire
Unett	JA	1913	1915	Preston
Unett	JA	1915	1932	Essex
Urquhart	P	1883	1889	Zetland
Urquhart	W	1862	1869	Dunbar
Usher	J	1836	1842	Gateshead
Utting	C	1846	1846	Thetford
Van Neck	SH	1928	1956	Norfolk
Vann	HJ	1933	1933	Newark
Vann	HJ	1933	1937	Lancaster
Vann	HJ	1936	1942	Maidstone

Vann	HJ	1942	1958	Birkenhead
Vanstone	W	1853	1873	Bideford
Vaughan	GC	1935	1943	West Riding
Vaughan	P	2010		South Wales
Verey	C	1871	1884	Bedford
Verner	T	1843	1849	Belfast
Vickers	G	1855	1863	Guildford
Vickery	SA	1869	1891	Weymouth & Melcombe Regis
Vine	J	2000	2008	Tayside
Vivian	JL	1863	1865	Swansea
Vivian	JL	1865	1866	Plymouth
Vyvyan	HR	1907	1931	Devon
Waghorn	G	18??	1852	Lymington
Waghorn	G	1855	1875	Boston
Wakefield	T	1852		Nottingham
Waldram	J	1879	1891	Grimsby
Waldron	JL	1954	1958	Berkshire
Waldron	JL	1968	1972	Metropolitan
Walker	G	1859	1866	Nairnshire
Walker	HS	1903	1931	Worcestershire
Walker	J	1882	1884	Accrington
Walker	RW	1950	1954	Dewsbury
Walker	RW	1954	1967	Eastbourne
Walker	S	1840	1842	Nottinghamshire
Wallace	HJ	1924	1930	Galashiels
Wallace	J	1892	1896	Lerwick
Wallen	ADG	1982	1984	Guernsey
Wallis	M	2002	2006	Devon and Cornwall
Walsh	CE	1900	1909	Radnorshire
Walters	CH	1936	1940	Accrington
Walters	CH	1940	1958	Lincoln
Walton	RW	1958	1962	Gateshead
Walton	RW	1962	1974	Hull
Walton	RW	1974	1976	Humberside
Walton	T	1815	1836	Preston
Warburton	G	1838	1838	Royal Irish
Warburton	J	1822		Royal Irish
Ward	F	1884	1902	Lancaster
Ward	J	1879	1897	Huddersfield
Ward	R	1847	1856	Pontefract
Ward	R	1859	1885	Stamford
Ward	W	1882	1887	Blackburn
Warde	AB	1894	1928	Hampshire
Warde	HMA	1895	1921	Kent
Ware	G	1866	1898	King's Lynn
Wareing	J	1914	1919	Southport

Warner	AC	1871	1879	Bedfordshire
Warnock	D	1930	1933	Kirkcaldy
Warnock	D	1943	1943	Glasgow
Warren	C	1886	1888	Metropolitan
Warren	JD	1856	1868	Sandwich
Warren	TRP	1928	1953	Buckinghamshire
Waters	J	1853	1870	Hartlepool
Waters	M	1878	1896	Rothesay
Watkins	CH	1951	1963	Glamorganshire
Watkins	J	1880	1887	Brecon
Watson	D	1894	1914	Peebles-shire
Watson	H	1959	1963	Cumberland
Watson	H	1959	1963	Westmorland
Watson	H	1963	1974	Cheshire
Watson	J	1833	1836	Glasgow
Watson	J	1854	1861	Aberdeen
Watson	JH	1902	1908	Congleton
Watson	JH	1908	1914	Devonport
Watson	JH	1914	1930	Bristol
Watson	TM	1931	1932	Kidderminster
Watson	TM	1932	1952	Walsall
Watson	WE	1955	1967	Stoke-on-Trent
Watterton	T	1853	1859	Newark
Weatherald	T	1890	1893	Dewsbury
Weatherhogg	E	1907	1932	Rotherham
Weatherhogg	W	1937	1947	Grantham
Webb	FT	1881	1883	Lancaster
Webb	FT	1883	1890	Wigan
Webb	FT	1890	1899	Leeds
Webb	SA	1872	1880	Brecon
Webb	WV	1919	1935	Cambridgeshire
Webb-Bowen	TI	1879	1906	Pembrokeshire
Webber	RT	1888	1909	Flintshire
Webster	D	1916	1929	Wolverhampton
Webster	K	1934	1943	Gravesend
Webster	P	1871	1873	Montrose
Wedlock	J	1874	1889	Helston
Weedon	FW	1972	1986	Isle of Man
Weigh	B	1975	1979	Gloucestershire
Weigh	B	1979	1983	Avon & Somerset
Weight	BH	1982	1994	Dorset
Weir	A	1841	1885	Kincardineshire
Wellings	RNW	1939	1947	Windsor
Wells	J	1940	1940	Huddersfield
Wells	RB	1990	1998	South Yorkshire
Wells	T	1932	1941	Chesterfield

Wells	T	1941	1947	Hull
Welsh	J	1862	1892	Perth
Welsh	WH	1930	1931	Motherwell & Wishaw
Wemyss	J	1839	1848	Durham County
West	AC	1940	1958	Portsmouth
West	FH	1832	1834	Walsall
West	P	2003		West Mercia
Westlake	H	1843	1844	Carmarthen
Westwood	D	1999	2005	Humberside
Wetherell	J	1861	1866	Oldham
Wetherell	J	1866	1874	Leeds
Whatton	D	2008		Cheshire
Wheatstone	JC	1885	1888	Ludlow
Wheeldon	E	1857	1881	Monmouth
Wheeldon	JT	1873	1892	Radnorshire
Wheller	J	1859	1860	Godalming
Wherly	KM	1958	1964	Walsall
Wherly	KM	1964	1967	Cornwall
Whitbread	G	1905	1916	Saint Albans
Whitcomb	T		1859	Sudbury
White	C	1862	1871	Faversham
White	EPB	1957	1963	East Suffolk
White	EPB	1963	1975	Gloucestershire
White	F	1851	1873	Gravesend
White	G	1853	1876	Brighton
White	GC	1948	1958	Warwickshire
White	GC	1958	1961	Kent
White	GF	1848	1892	Durham County
White	J	1867	1874	Salisbury
White	J	1868	1897	Clackmannanshire
White	R	1989	2000	Dyfed-Powys
White	W	1842		Kirkintilloch
White	W	1863	1868	Penryn
Whitecross	JS	1901	1912	Govan
Whitehouse	PC	1993	2001	Sussex
Whiteley	F	2004	2011	Hertfordshire
Whiteley	SL	1976	1989	Suffolk
Whitfield	GW	1887	1888	Shrewsbury
Whitfield	GW	1888	1894	York
Whittle	J	1836	1840	Wigan
Whitty	M	1836	1844	Liverpool
Whyte	W	1933	1938	Stirling
Whyte	W	1938	1949	Stirlingshire
Wickham	CG	1922	1945	Royal Ulster
Wilcox	AF	1947	1969	Hertfordshire
Wilding	B	2004	2009	South Wales

Wilding	T	1838	1842	Harwich
Wilkie	WR	1922	1929	Glossop
Wilkie	WR	1929	1936	South Shields
Wilkinson	CB	1874	1882	Bath
Wilkinson	FL	1996	1999	Gwent
Wilkinson	J	1876	1882	Kendal
Wilkinson	J	1882	1893	Rochdale
Willcocks	R	1822	1827	Royal Irish
Williams	AS	1907	1911	Breconshire
Williams	AS	1912	1934	West Sussex
Williams	D	1912	1920	Cardiff
Williams	DJ	1991	1997	Surrey
Williams	E	1904	1922	Cardiganshire
Williams	E	1923	1939	Caernarvonshire
Williams	G	1840	1846	Gloucester
Williams	G	1873	1875	Hanley
Williams	G	1875	1879	Wigan
Williams	H	1840	1856	Forfarshire
Williams	HT	1939	1944	Barnsley
Williams	J	1836		Brecon
Williams	J	1846	1847	Chipping Norton
Williams	J	1861	1866	Newcastle-under-Lyme
Williams	J	1871	1889	Haverfordwest
Williams	KR	1993	2002	Norfolk
Williams	R	1857	1869	Pwllheli
Williams	RL	1901	1911	Exeter
Williams	TC	1957	1964	Huntingdonshire
Williams	TC	1957	1964	Isle of Ely
Williams	TC	1964	1967	West Sussex
Williams	TC	1968	1972	Sussex
Williams	W	1856	1860	Beaumaris
Williams	WJ	1946	1950	Caernarvonshire
Williams	WJ	1950	1970	Gwynedd
Williams-Ellis	TP	1857	1870	Caernarvonshire
Williams-Freeman	GCP	1890	1905	Shropshire
Williamson	D	1958	1967	Greenock
Williamson	D	1967	1975	Renfrew & Bute
Williamson	FE	1961	1963	Carlisle
Williamson	FE	1963	1967	Cumberland Westmorland & Carlisle
Williamson	J	1924	1955	Northampton
Willis	E	1842	1857	Manchester
Willis	WJA	1937	1940	Rochester
Willis	WJA	1940	1953	Bedfordshire
Willison	G	1869	1897	Kilmarnock
Willison	JA	1952	1958	Berwick Roxburgh & Selkirk
Willison	JA	1958	1967	Worcestershire

Willison	JA	1967	1974	West Mercia
Wills	R	1833	1833	Montrose
Wilmot	D	1991	2002	Greater Manchester
Wilshere	J	1873	1880	Folkestone
Wilson	A	1840	1844	Anderston
Wilson	AD	1936	1939	South Shields
Wilson	AK	1928	1929	Carlisle
Wilson	AK	1929	1932	Plymouth
Wilson	AK	1932	1940	Liverpool
Wilson	F	1914	1925	Banbury
Wilson	J	1828	1829	Anderston
Wilson	J	1845	1850	Boston
Wilson	J	1850		Nairnshire
Wilson	J	1869	1874	Durham City
Wilson	J	1874	1898	Montrose
Wilson	J	1957	1966	Lanarkshire
Wilson	JA	1908	1920	Merthyr Tydfil
Wilson	JA	1920	1946	Cardiff
Wilson	N	1800	1815	Greenock
Wilson	PM	2001	2008	Fife
Wilson	PP	1841	1845	Thetford
Wilson	QC	1968	1975	Ayrshire
Wilson	RP	1935	1943	West Sussex
Wilson	RP	1947	1964	West Sussex
Wilson	W	1908	1921	Rutland
Wilson	WJM	1990	2000	Central Scotland
Wilson	WN	1958	1964	Portsmouth
Winch	EF	1894	1897	Truro
Winch	EF	1897	1917	Norwich
Windle	H	1875	1901	Hanley
Windsor	H	1913	1929	Scarborough
Winstanley	H	1940	1948	Liverpool
Winter	W	1935	1941	Cambridgeshire
Winterbottom	A	1898	1930	Hartlepool
Withers	J	1867	1874	Huddersfield
Withers	J	1874	1894	Bradford
Wombwell	G	1878	1888	Maldon
Wood	CM	1881	1898	Manchester
Wood	J	1887	1905	Saint Helens
Wood	J	1889	1893	Saint Albans
Wood	JS	1865		Royal Irish
Wood	R	1907	1927	Orkney
Wood-Acton	A	1915	1918	Shropshire
Woodcock	J	1978	1979	North Yorkshire
Woodcock	J	1979	1983	South Wales
Woodcock	W	1865	1872	Truro

Woodford	J	1839	1856	Lancashire
Woodman	PJ	1894	1894	Reigate
Woods	J	1836	1850	King's Lynn
Woods	WA	1922	1928	Hull
Woolnough	H	1918	1929	York
Worlock	WA	1892	1909	Guildford
Worman	J	1852	1857	Neath
Wreford	F	1866	1892	Plymouth
Wright	A	1907	1927	Newark
Wright	JB	1899	1925	Newcastle-upon-Tyne
Wright	M	1835	1857	Lancaster
Wright	P	1983	1990	South Yorkshire
Wright	W	1836	1839	Norwich
Wright	WB	1836	1860	Lyme Regis
Wyeth	MH	1997	2003	Guernsey
Wyness	T	1865	1872	Elgin
Wyness	T	1872	1880	Inverness Burgh
Wyness	T	1880	1902	Aberdeen
Wyrko	D	1997	2002	Leicestershire
Wyse	JWD	1894	1900	Boston
Yarrington	PM	1839	1851	Norwich
Yates	C	1847	1851	Chipping Norton
Yelloly	R	1920	1942	Wakefield
Young	AE	1939	1941	Leamington Spa
Young	AE	1945	1947	Hertfordshire
Young	AE	1950	1971	City of London
Young	AE	1969	1970	Royal Ulster
Young	D	1864	1883	Govan
Young	E	1844	1847	Carmarthen
Young	HW	1923	1945	King's Lynn
Young	J	1839	1876	Ayrshire
Young	J	1859		Blairgowrie
Young	JW	1936	1954	Isle of Man

7 A Bibliography of British Police Force Histories

Martin Stallion

Introduction - This bibliography lists only histories of a single specific force (or a group of forces in the same area, usually those which eventually merged). It excludes general histories and legal or sociological studies of policing, studies of a particular force, descriptions of a force at a particular date, accounts of single events (for example, the murder of an officer) and collections of famous cases.

The geographical area covered is the United Kingdom: England, Wales, Scotland, Northern Ireland, the Isle of Man and the Channel Islands. The period covered is from 1829 to the present.

The term *police force* refers to the uniformed public service supervised by the Home Office or its equivalent in other parts of the UK. I have also included those few specialised forces of which histories have been published, such as military, harbour and railway police. They include the British Transport Police and the police of naval dockyards, which were for many years the responsibility of the Metropolitan Police

Most of the histories were published as independent books or pamphlets and the bibliography should be virtually complete for this type of publication. Others were published as articles in periodicals (such as the force's own magazine), as chapters in more general histories of the area or as duplicated or photocopied handouts for internal training or for external publicity by the force. It is inevitable that I have failed to trace some material of this kind. There are also a few theses, which are therefore not really *published* at all. Finally, there are two histories issued as videos or DVDs (Plymouth and Thames Valley), one CD (Sussex) and one available as a download from the force website (Fife)

Sources of information - Most of the titles listed are held in my own collection. I have also used the following bibliographies and, as far as possible, examined each item in a library that holds it:

Brett, Dennis T. *Police of England and Wales: a bibliography*. 3rd ed. Bramshill: Police Staff College Library, 1979

British national bibliography, 1950 to date
Catalogue of the National Police Library, Bramshill [Online edition]
British Museum Library. *Subject index of modern works acquired at the British Museum Library* [up to 1950]

For periodical articles:
Poole's index to periodical literature, 1802-1906
Annual library index, 1905-10
Athenaeum subject index to periodicals, 1915-22
Subject index to periodicals, 1915-1968
British humanities index, 1968 to date
Royal Historical Society. *Bibliography of British history* [Online edition]

Format of entries - Entries are listed alphabetically under the latest force name covered by the item. For example, a history dealing with a borough force that finishes at (or before) its merger with the county will be listed under the borough name. If it continues the story after that, it will be listed under the county. If there is more than one history for the force, they are arranged by the author's name and then by title.

Histories of a specific area, department or division within the force or of the Special Constabulary follow those for the force as a whole, using the sub-headings **Departments, divisions etc** or **Special Constabulary**. For the large number of entries for the Metropolitan Police, I have used four sub-headings: 1. **Criminal Investigation Department** 2. **Divisions, stations etc** 3. **HQ departments** 4. **Special Constabulary**

Separately published items
Name of force [Name of present-day force]
Author
Title. Edition. Place of publication: Publisher, Date of publication
Collation, ie number of pages, illustrations (either in the text or on separate plates), height*. (Series title). ISBN. Any special notes (eg *Issued to special constables*)
* For items in landscape format, the width is also given after the height

Periodical articles
Name of force [Name of present-day force]
Author
Title of article. *Title of periodical*, Volume and/or issue number (Date) Page numbers, Illustrations. Any special notes

Abbreviations used
b&w - black and white
cm - centimetres
col - colour/ed
ed - edition
fold - folded
illus - illustration/s
Inc - Includes
ISBN - International Standard Book Number
n - number
nd - no date
npl - no place of publication named
npub - no publisher named
p - page/s
pbk - paperback [only for items also published in hardback]
pt - part
v - volume

Aberdeen [Grampian]
Irvine, Hamish
The diced cap: the story of Aberdeen City Police. Aberdeen: The Police, 1972
xv,146p, illus. 23cm. ISBN 0 9502453 0 5

Abingdon [Thames Valley]
Tucker, Roger
Abingdon Borough Police. In: *PICA magazine* (Spring 1984) p9-10, illus

Accrington [Lancashire]
Dobson, R
On the appointed day. In: *Lancashire Constabulary journal* (1967) p349-350, illus

Skellern, A
A history of the Accrington Borough Police Force. 1978
71p, illus. Unpublished typescript

Skellern, Tony
Accrington Borough Police. In: *PICA magazine* (Summer 1986) p23-24, illus

Admiralty [Ministry of Defence]
'Alpha and Omega' 1640-1971: the story of the Admiralty Police. In: *PICA magazine* (Summer 1977) p20-25, illus

Anglesey [North Wales]
Owen, Hugh
History of the Anglesey Constabulary. Bangor: Anglesey Antiquarian Society, [1952]
114p, illus. 23cm

Ashford [Kent]
Bishop, W H
Ashford Borough Police. In: *Bygone Kent* v15 n8 and n9 (Aug-Sep 1994) p480-485, 506-511, illus

Ashton-under-Lyne [Greater Manchester]
Dobson, R
On the appointed day. In: *Lancashire Constabulary journal* (1967) p350-352, illus

Avon and Somerset
Clark, Lewis
A concise history of the English police and the Avon and Somerset Constabulary. Bristol: The Constabulary, [197-?]
30p, illus. 15x22cm

Avon and Somerset - Departments, divisions etc
Foulkes, Stephen
A hundred years in the saddle: the Avon & Somerset Mounted Police 1899-1999. Bristol: Broadcast Books, 1998
202p, illus. 24cm. ISBN 1 874092 85 0

Bacup [Lancashire]
Bacup Borough Police
Bacup Borough Police 1887-1937: jubilee souvenir. Bacup: The Police, 1937
18p. 33cm. Typescript

Bacup Borough Police
Bacup Borough Police 1887-1947: souvenir. Bacup: The Police, 1947
24p, illus. 24cm. An updated version of the previous item

Dobson, R
On the appointed day. In: *Lancashire Constabulary journal* (1967) p352-353, illus

Banbury [Thames Valley]
Richmond, Carol
Banbury constables 1775-1925: 150 years on the beat. Witney: Oxfordshire Black Sheep, 2005
47p, illus. ISBN 0 9546844 7 8. Inc *A brief history of the Banbury Borough Police Force* p2-5

Barnsley [South Yorkshire]
Barnsley County Borough Police
Barnsley Borough. Barnsley: The Police, [1968 or 9]
1p. 27cm. Typescript

Barnsley County Borough Police
County Borough of Barnsley new police headquarters: official opening 21st November 1963. Barnsley: Barnsley County Borough Police, 1963
17p, illus. Inc *History of the force*, 2p

West Yorkshire Constabulary. Public Relations Department
History of police in Barnsley. Wakefield: The Constabulary, nd
2p

Bath [Avon and Somerset]
Wroughton, J (ed)
Bath in the age of reform (1830-1841). Bath: Morgan Books, 1972
xiv,114,[16]p, illus . 23cm. ISBN 0 903044 05 6. Inc Roberts, M *and* Wroughton, J. *Law and order in Bath*, p88-103

Bedford [Bedfordshire]
Hawkey, David *and* Marlow, Alan
Bedford Borough Police 1836-1947. In: *Bedfordshire magazine* v23 n178 (Autumn 1991) p61-67, illus

Bedfordshire
Bedfordshire Constabulary
A history of the police. Bedford: The Constabulary, [ca1965]
10p. 33cm. Typescript

Bedfordshire Police
A history of the police in Bedfordshire. Kempston: The Police, [1988]
11p, illus. 21cm

Emsley, Clive
The Bedfordshire Police 1840-1856: a case study in the working of the Rural constabulary Act. In: *Midland history* v7 (1982) p73-92

Richer, Andrew Francis
Bedfordshire Police 1840-1990. Kempston: Paul Hooley and Associates, 1990
xxiv,260p, illus. 22cm. ISBN 0 905095 27 8

Richer, Andrew F
Early years of policing in Bedfordshire. In: *Bedfordshire magazine* v22 n176 (Spring 1991) p309-316, illus

Bedfordshire - Special Constabulary
The Bedfordshire Special Constabulary in peace and war. Bedford: [The Constabulary?], 1949
32p. 22cm

Belfast [Northern Ireland]
Griffin, Brian
The Bulkies: police and crime in Belfast 1800-1865. Dublin: Irish Academic Press, 1997
x,166p, illus. 25cm. ISBN 0 7165 2670 0
Pbk: 1999. ISBN 0 7165 2695 6

Belfast Harbour
Wilkinson, Dave
The Belfast Harbour Police. In: *PICA magazine* (issue 1/89) p22-23

Berkshire [Thames Valley]
Indge, W
1856-1956: a short history of the Berkshire Constabulary. [Sulhampstead: The Constabulary, 1956]
vii,133p, illus. 22cm. Cover title: *1856-1956: one hundred years, Berkshire Constabulary*

Beverley [Humberside]
Crowther, Jan
Beverley in mid-Victorian times. Beverley: Hutton Press, 1990
135p, illus. ISBN 1 87216 703 9. Inc ch4: *Law and order*, p62-75

Lindley, Ralph
Beverley Borough Police. In: *PICA magazine* (Spring 1981) p3-4, illus

Birkenhead [Merseyside]
Thompson, S P
Maintaining the Queen's peace: a short history of the Birkenhead Borough Police. Birkenhead: [The Police], 1958
112p, illus. 22cm

Birmingham [West Midlands]
Moriarty, C C H
Birmingham City Police centenary, Monday 20th November 1939: the formation of the force and its present organization. [Birmingham: Birmingham City Police], 1939
40p, illus. 22cm

Reilly, John W
Policing Birmingham: an account of 150 years of police in Birmingham. Birmingham: West Midlands Police, 1989
xii,228p, illus. 22cm. ISBN 0 9515152 0 9

Richards, R J
Policing Birmingham: the first policeman. In: *Forward* (Summer 1972) p34-36

Richards, R J
Policing Birmingham: in the beginning. In: *Forward* (Autumn 1972) p37-40

Blackburn [Lancashire]
Hey, Colin
Blackburn Police. In: *PICA magazine* (Winter 1985) p3-6 and (Spring 1986) p17-19, illus

Hey, Colin
A history of the police force in the County Borough of Blackburn.

[Blackburn: The author, 1979]
[*ca*60p], illus. 30cm. Unpublished typescript

Blackpool [Lancashire]
Heaney, D E
Reflections on the passing of the Blackpool Police Force. In: *Lancashire Constabulary journal* (Winter 1969) p148-151

Bolton [Greater Manchester]
Goslin, R J
Duty bound: a history of the Bolton Borough Police Force 1839-1969.
Bolton: Bolton County Borough Council, 1970
144p, illus. 22cm

Bournemouth [Dorset]
Ford, Richard
The history of the Bournemouth Police. [Bournemouth: Bournemouth Borough Police], 1963
44p. 21cm. Typescript

Bradford [West Yorkshire]
Bradford City Police
Annual report of the Chief Constable: year ended 31st December 1973.
Bradford: The Police, 1974
67p. 22cm. Inc notes and illustrations on the history of the Force

Bradford City Police
Summary of the history of the City of Bradford Police. [Bradford]:The Police, 1972
3p

Smith, Gordon
Bradford's police. Bradford: City of Bradford Police, 1974
[6],209p, illus. 22cm. ISBN 0 9503683 0 X

Breconshire [Dyfed-Powys]
Davies, Dewi
Law and disorder in Breconshire 1750-1880. Brecon: D G and A S Evans, [1991]
164p, illus. 21cm. Inc ch2: *The establishment of the County Police Force,* p79-108

Bridgwater [Avon and Somerset]
Johnson, Hugh
Keeping law and order in Bridgwater Borough. In: *Journal of the Police History Society* n21 (2006) p7-8, illus

Brighton [Sussex]
Baines, Gerald W
History of the Brighton Police 1838-1967. Brighton: Brighton Constabulary, 1967
48p, illus. 22cm

Brighton Constabulary
County Borough of Brighton: Police centenary 1838-1938. [Brighton: The Constabulary, 1938]
31p, illus. 23cm

Oakensen, Derek John
Origins and development of policing in Brighton and Hove 1830-1900 with special reference to local political control. npl: The author, 1994
2v. PhD thesis, University of Brighton

Rumble, Mike
The Brighton Police Meritorious Service Medal. In: *PICA magazine* issue 3/1990. 1p, illus

Rumble, Mike
GTN calling: 50 years of police pocket radio. In: *PICA magazine* (Summer 1983) p13-16, illus

Bristol [Avon and Somerset]
A historical review of the Bristol Constabulary 1836-1974. [Bristol: Bristol Constabulary, 1974?]
32p, illus. 30cm. Private circulation

Bristol Constabulary
Bristol Police centenary 1836-1936. Bristol: The Constabulary, 1936
36p, illus. 23cm

Hallett, Penny
150 years policing of Bristol. Bristol: Avon and Somerset Constabulary, 1986

48p, illus. 21x29cm. ISBN 0 9511626 0 8

Howell, Brian
The police in late Victorian Bristol. Bristol: Historical Association, Bristol
Branch, 1989
29p, illus. 21cm. (Local history pamphlets 71). ISBN 0 901388 54 X

Osborne, Michael
Policing Bristol: from the Middle Ages to amalgamation in April 1974.
Bristol: Redcliffe, 1996
109p, illus. ISBN 1 900178 55 9. Cover title: *Policing Bristol: the story of
the Bristol Police Force to 1974*

Walters, Roderick
The establishment of the Bristol Police Force. Bristol: Historical
Association, Bristol Branch, 1975
22p, illus. 22cm. (Local history pamphlets 36). ISBN 0 901388 14 9

British Transport
Appleby, Pauline
A force on the move: the story of the British Transport Police 1825-1995.
Worcester: Images, 1995
288p, illus. 24cm. ISBN 1 89781 767 3

Bowker, Kenneth
The railway police. In: *The Peeler* issue 4 (1999) p14-16, illus

British Transport Police
British Transport Police Force. npl: The Police, 1964?
7p

Gay, William O
The railway police. In: *Police journal* v16 n3 (Jul-Sep 1943) p218-225

Gay, William Owen
Communications and crime. In: *Police journal* v46 (1973) p109-125 and
206-231, illus. Inc *The origin and development of the British Transport
Police*, p109-125
Reprinted: Chichester: Barry Rose, 1974
[2],44p, illus. 24cm. ISBN 0 900500 91 3. Inc *The origin and development
of the British Transport Police*, p1-17

Gordon, Kevin
The British Transport Police: a history of policing the railways. [Tadworth: The author, 1995]
13p. 30cm

Gordon, Kevin
The police dog pioneers: a history of the first British police dog section. Tadworth: The author, 2003. 8p, illus. 30cm

Gordon, Kevin
A time line for policing the railways. npl: The author, 2003. 32p. 30cm

Richards, W B
History and work of the British Transport Commission Police. In: *Proceedings of the British Railways (Western Region) London Lecture and Debating Society* n406 (15 Oct 1953). 19p

Thomas, Colin G
The origins of the British Transport Police. In: *Journal of the Police History Society* n9 (1994) p31-36

Whitbread, J R
The railway policeman: the story of the constable on the track. London: Harrap, 1961
269p, illus. 22cm

British Transport - Departments, divisions etc
Brown, Bernard
The railway police in Kent. In: *Bygone Kent* v12 n11 (November 1991) p659-661

Buckingham [Thames Valley]
Woodley, Leonard
Buckingham Borough Police 1836-1889. [Bletchley]: Woodley, 1989
14p. 21cm
Reprinted in: Journal of the Police History Society n5 (1990) p24-36, illus

Buckinghamshire [Thames Valley]
Hailstone, Alfred G
One hundred years of law-enforcement in Buckinghamshire: an historical survey. [Aylesbury: Buckinghamshire Constabulary], 1957

[6],57p, illus. 22cm. Cover title: *Bucks Constabulary centenary 1857-1957*

Burnley [Lancashire]
Forbes, G J *and* Capstick, G R
The history of the Burnley Police Force. [Burnley]: Burnley County
Borough Council, 1974
[2],iii,64p, illus. 30cm. ISBN 0 9501268 8 8
Reissued: [Preston]: Lancashire County Council, 1980

Bury St Edmunds [Suffolk]
Wheeler, J D
Borough of Bury St Edmunds Constabulary 1836-57. In: *Suffolk review* v2
n6 (1963) p194-197

Bute Docks [British Transport]
Cooke, Harry
Bute's bobbies: the Bute Docks Police. In: *British Transport Police journal*
(Spring 1977) p14-16

Deacon, Brian
Bute Docks Police. In: *PICA magazine* (Winter 1980) p10-12, illus

Caernarvonshire [North Wales]
Jones, J Owen
History of the Caernarvonshire Constabulary 1856-1950. [Caernarvon]:
Caernarvonshire Historical Society, 1963
104p, illus. 22cm

Cambridge [Cambridgeshire]
Malcolm, Lindsay
Cambridge Borough/City Police in the post war years. In: *Journal of the
Police History Society* n22 (2007) p10-12

Cambridgeshire
Cambridgeshire Constabulary
History of the Cambridgeshire Constabulary. npl: The Constabulary, 1975
3p, illus

Watts, Peggy
*The Cambridgeshire Constabulary at the time of its formation 150 years
ago.* In: *Cambridgeshire Local History Society review* new series v10

(2001) p24-32

Watts, Peggy
The formation of the Cambridgeshire Constabulary 150 years ago. Quy:
Peggy Day, 2001
iii,56p, illus. 21cm

Cambridgeshire - Departments, divisions etc
Stevens, T H
Account of the constabulary in Ramsey The author, nd
11p

Canterbury [Kent]
Poole, L
Canterbury City Police 1836-1888. npl: The author, 1974
160p. BA thesis, University of Kent

Cardiganshire [Dyfed-Powys]
The Cardiganshire Constabulary. In: *Police review* (16 Apr 1915) p190-
191, illus

Cardiganshire Constabulary
Rules, orders and guide to constables: also a short history of the force.
Aberystwyth: Gibson, [1897]
Inc *Origin of the police* p75-82; *History of the Cardiganshire Police Force*
p83-115

Evans, Howell
*Retrospect of the nineteenth century relating especially to crime and its
prevention, the administration of justice and the creation of the police force.*
Aberystwyth: Gibson, [1900]
18p. 22cm. Produced as an appendix to the Chief Constable's annual report
for 1900

Carlisle [Cumbria]
Lowther, Bob
*Watching over Carlisle: 140 years of the Carlisle City Police Force 1827-
1967.* Carlisle: P3 Publications, 2011
vi,242p, illus. 30cm. ISBN 978-0955901768

Carlisle - Departments, divisions etc
Brader, Chris
Copperettes and flighty girls: women and policing in Carlisle and the borders during World War 1. In: *North East history* v32 (1998) p1-26

Carmarthen [Dyfed-Powys]
Eyre Evans, G
Carmarthen Borough Constabulary AD1658-1835. In: *Transactions of the Carmarthen Antiquarian Society* v21 pt52 and 53 (1922) p49-51, 62-63

Molloy, Pat
A shilling for Carmarthen: the town they nearly tamed. Llandysul: Gomer Press, 1980
xv,201p, illus. 22cm. ISBN 0 85088 733 X
Pbk: Llandysul: Gomer Press, 1985
xv,201p, illus. 22cm. ISBN 0 86383 182 6

Carmarthenshire [Dyfed-Powys]
Jones, J F
Carmarthenshire rural police force. In: *Carmarthenshire antiquary* v4 n1-2 (1962) p45-48

Chatham Dockyard [Kent]
MacDougall, Philip
The rise and fall of the Dockyard Constabulary: an aspect of policing in nieteenth-century Kent. In: *Bygone Kent* v24 n1 (Jan 2003) p40-47, illus

Salter, A R
The protection of Chatham Dockyard throughout the ages. Chatham: Kent County Library, 1974
22p, illus. 21cm

Cheshire
Cheshire Constabulary
21 years of the Cheshire Police Committee: a record of achievement 1974-1995. Chester: The Constabulary, 1995
87p, illus. 30cm

Cheshire Constabulary
Her Majesty the Queen's Silver Jubilee 1952-1977: a review of the Cheshire Constabulary over the past 25 years. Chester: The Constabulary, 1977

35p, illus. 21cm.

Cheshire Constabulary
A short history of the Cheshire Constabulary. [Chester: The Constabulary, 1984]
8p. 15cm

James, R W
To the best of our skill and knowledge: a short history of the Cheshire Constabulary 1857-1957. [Chester]: The Constabulary, [1957]
128p, illus. 21cm

Chichester [Sussex]
Denyer, Vic
Chichester City Police 1836-1889. In: *PICA magazine* (Summer 1984) p9-11, illus

Chipping Norton [Thames Valley]
Woodley, Leonard
History of the Chipping Norton Borough Police, 1836-1857. [Bletchley]: The author, 2005
29p, illus. 30cm. Private circulation
Reissued: Bramshill: Police History Society, 2007
28p, illus. 21cm. (Police history monographs 6). ISBN 978- 0951253854

City of London
City of London Police
City of London Police: brief history. [London: The Police, 196-]
2p. 33cm. Typescript

Rumbelow, Donald
The City of London Police: 150 years of service 1839-1989. London: City of London Police, [1989]
56p, illus. 30cm

Rumbelow, Donald
I spy blue: police and crime in the City of London from Elizabeth I to Victoria. London: Macmillan, 1971
250p, illus. 24cm. ISBN 0 333 10652 0
Reprinted: Bath: Chivers, 1974
250p, illus. 24cm. ISBN 0 85997 011 6

Stark, John
The Police of the City of London. In: *Police journal* v4 (1931) p5-16 and 197-210, illus

Toet, Wim
The City of London Police: a brief history. In: *PICA magazine* (Spring 1980) p27-34, illus

Wade, Stephen
Square mile bobbies: the City of London Police 1839-1949. Stroud: Sutton, 2008. xii, 144p, illus. 25cm. ISBN 978-0750949521

City of London - Special Constabulary
City of London Police Reserve: a record 1914-1920. London: The Reserve, [1921]
132p, illus. 26cm

Cleveland
On the beat: a pictorial review of Cleveland Constabulary. [Bishop Auckland?]: Printability, [*ca*1998]
39p, illus. 15x21cm. ISBN 1 87223 916 1

Roberts, T E
A short history of policing in Cleveland. [Middlesbrough: Cleveland Constabulary, 1979?]
91p, illus. 21cm

Clitheroe [Lancashire]
Dobson, R
On the appointed day. In: *Lancashire Constabulary journal* (1967) p300, illus

Colchester [Essex]
Blaxill, E Alec
Souvenir of the handing-over parade of the Borough Police Force from the Watch Committee to the Standing Joint Committee under the provisions of the Police Act 1946: 31st March 1947. [Colchester]: Colchester Borough, 1947
7p. 20cm

Stallion, Martin
Our duty has been done: a record of Colchester Borough Police 1836-1947.
In preparation

Colchester - Departments, divisions etc
Fisher, Peter M
The water guard. Brightlingsea: Joyful, 1997
60p, illus. 21cm. ISBN 0 9531262 0 X

Cornwall [Devon and Cornwall]
Hutchings, P
The history of the Cornwall Constabulary 1857-1957. [Bodmin: The
Constabulary, 1957]
59p, illus. 26cm

Searle, Ken
*One and all: a history of policing in Cornwall: the Cornwall Constabulary
1857-1967.* Tiverton: Halsgrove, 2005
192p, illus. 30cm. ISBN 1 84114 451 7

Coventry [West Midlands]
Sheppard, Karen
True as Coventry blue: the history of Coventry Police 1836-1914.
[Coventry: Coventry Evening Telegraph, 2000]
26p, illus. 28cm. ISBN 1 86044 068 1
True as Coventry blue: book 2: the history of Coventry Police Museum.
[Coventry?: West Midlands Police, ca2006]
22p, illus. 30cm

Deal [Kent]
Gillespie, W H
An old force. In: *Police journal* v27 (1954) p306-317

Macfie, A L
Dover and Deal Police 1836-1886. In: *Bygone Kent* v5 n7 (Jul 1984) p403-
406, illus

Denbighshire [North Wales]
Clements, F
Policing Denbighshire 1800-1850. In: *Journal of the Police History Society*
n22 (2007) p21-25, illus

Evans, M W
Turning men into policemen: the history of the Denbighshire Police Force 1850-1880. 1986
60p. 30cm. Dissertation, MA Crime Deviance and Social Policy, Lancaster University. Typescript

Lerry, George G
The policemen of Denbighshire. In: *Denbighshire Historical Society Transactions* v2 (1953) p107-151

Derby [Derbyshire]
Derby County Borough Police
Derby Borough Police. [Derby: The Police, 1966]
2p. 33cm. Typescript

Derbyshire
Derbyshire Constabulary
A short history of the Derbyshire Constabulary. [Ripley]: The Constabulary, [*ca*1981]
[20p], illus. 21cm

International Police Association. Derbyshire Branch
10th anniversary brochure. Derby: The Branch, 1978
?p, illus. 25cm. Inc *History of the Derbyshire Constabulary* p9-13

Devon [Devon and Cornwall]
Devon Constabulary
Annual report of the Chief Constable 1965. Exeter: The Constabulary, 1966
84p. 24cm. Inc *Review of the years 1946-65*, p63-84

Hutchings, Walter J
Out of the blue: history of the Devon Constabulary. [Exeter: The Constabulary], 1956
xii,204p, illus. 22cm

Devon and Cornwall
Dell, Simon Patrick
Policing the peninsula (1850-2000): a photographic celebration of West Country policing over the last 150 years. Newton Abbot: Forest, 2000
144p, illus. 25cm. ISBN 0 9527297 9 2

Devon and Cornwall Constabulary
Devon and Cornwall Constabulary: silver jubilee 1967-1992. Gloucester:
British Publishing, [1992]
72p, illus. 30cm. ISBN 0 7140 2947 5. Cover title: *25 years of service*

Devon and Cornwall - Departments, divisions etc
Dell, Simon
*The beat on western Dartmoor: (a celebration of 150 years of the policing
of Tavistock)*. Newton Abbot: Forest, 1997
192p, illus. 21cm. ISBN 0 9527297 4 1

Dewsbury [West Yorkshire]
Hird, Stanley
Dewsbury Borough Police. In: *PICA magazine* (Summer 1983) p21-24,
illus

Hird, S
A history of the Dewsbury County Borough Police Force 1862-1968.
[Wakefield: West Yorkshire Constabulary. 1969]
4p. 30cm. Typescript

West Yorkshire Constabulary. Public Relations Department
History of police in Dewsbury. npl: The Constabulary, nd
2p

Doncaster [South Yorkshire]
Doncaster County Borough Police
A short history of the Doncaster County Borough Police Force. [Doncaster:
The Police, *ca*1968]
[30]p. 33cm

West Yorkshire Constabulary. Public Relations Department
History of police in Doncaster. npl: The Constabulary, nd
2p

Dorset
Dorset Police. In: *PICA magazine* (Summer 1982) p17-20, (Winter 1982)
p17-19 and (Spring 1983) p16, illus

Dorset Constabulary
Dorset Constabulary 1856-1956. [Dorchester: The Constabulary, 1956]

[6],49p, illus. 26cm

Dorset Police
Policing in Dorset: a short history. [Dorchester: The Police, 198-]
8p, illus. 30cm

Hann, Melvin
Bobbies on the beat 1856-2006: 150 years of policing Dorset. Wimborne
Minster: Dovecote Press, 2006
112p, illus. 24cm. ISBN 1 904349 45 5

Swatridge, Victor
History of the Dorset Constabulary: "a policeman's lot is not an 'appy one".
In: *Dorset: the county magazine* (Aug 1969) p24-29, illus

Dover [Kent]
Harman, J G
The Dover Borough Police Force 1836-1943. In: *Journal of the Police
History Society* n2 (1987) p80-83

Macfie, A L
Dover and Deal Police 1836-1886. In: *Bygone Kent* v5 n7 (Jul 1984) p403-
406, illus

Muskett, Paul
Policing Dover, 1800-1960. In: *Cantium* v2 n4 (Oct 1970) p82-85

Dublin Metropolitan [Garda Siochana]
Blythe, Ernan P
The D M P. In: *Dublin historical record* v20 (1965) p116-126

Herlihy, Jim
*The Dublin Metropolitan Police: a complete alphabetical list of officers and
men 1836-1925.* Dublin: Four Courts Press, 2001
xxii,270p. 24cm. ISBN 1 85182 601 7

Herlihy, Jim
The Dublin Metropolitan Police: a short history and genealogical guide.
Dublin: Four Courts Press, 1999. xv,264p, illus. 24cm. ISBN 1 85182 462 6
Pbk: Dublin: Four Courts Press, 2001
xv,264p, illus. ISBN 1 85182 463 4

Scanlon, Mary
The Dublin Metropolitan Police. London: Minerva, 1998
75p, illus. 20cm. ISBN 1 86106 478 0

Dudley [West Midlands]
Stafford, Leonard
History of the former Dudley Borough Police Force. Brierley Hill: West Midlands Constabulary, 1967
5p

Dumfries [Dumfries and Galloway]
Black, William
Notes on the police of the County and Burgh of Dumfries. Dumfries: Dumfries and Galloway Review, [1947]
30p. 22cm

Dumfries and Galloway
Dumfries and Galloway Constabulary
50 years of caring and protecting 1948-1998. Dumfries: The Constabulary, 1999
39p, illus. 26cm

Dumfries and Galloway Constabulary
60 years of policing in Dumfries and Galloway. In: *Quadrant* issue 18 [2008]
12p, illus. 30cm

Dumfries and Galloway Constabulary
Dumfries and Galloway Constabulary silver jubilee, 1948-1973: a brief history of the first 25 years of the force. Dumfries: S & U N Ltd ("Standard" Office), c1973
76,[iv]p, illus. 23cm

Stewart, Marion M
A policeman's lot: police records in Dumfries and Galloway 1850-1950. In: *Scottish archives* v7 (2001) p25-35

Dumfries-shire [Dumfries and Galloway]
Black, William
Notes on the police of the County and Burgh of Dumfries. Dumfries:

Dumfries and Galloway Review, [1947]
30p. 22cm

Dunbartonshire [Strathclyde]
Macleod, Kenneth
Dunbartonshire Constabulary 1858-1958: a short history of a century's policing with an account of earlier forms of policing employed.
[Dumbarton]: Dunbartonshire Joint Police Committee, 1958
214p, illus. 19cm

Dundee [Tayside]
Buick, C
1824-1974: City of Dundee Police 150th anniversary. [Dundee: The Police, 1974]
[100]p, illus. 30cm

Dundee - Departments, divisions etc
Harris, Stewart
Dundee City Police Pipe Band 1905-1975. Glasgow: Styletype, [1984]
64p, illus. 30cm

Dunstable [Bedfordshire]
Child, Bob *and* Madigan, Tom
Dunstable Borough Police 1865-1889. In: *Bedfordshire magazine* v24 n186 (Autumn 1993) p57-62, illus

Durham City [Durham County]
McManus, Michael
Policing street nuisance in mid-Victorian Durham: Bobby's thoroughly bourgeoisie agency of social control. In: *North East history* v32 (1998) p27-53

Durham County
Durham Constabulary
Durham County Police centenary. Aycliffe: The Constabulary, 1940
39p

Durham Constabulary
Report on the re-organisation of the Constabulary 1945-49. Aycliffe: The Constabulary, 1950
38p, illus, fold chart. 25cm

Durham Police Authority
Official opening: Durham Constabulary headquarters...31st January 1969.
[Aykley Heads]: The Authority, [1969]
24p, illus. 18x23cm. Inc Muir, A A. *The Durham Constabulary, formerly the Durham County Constabulary*, 6p

Watson, Alan S *and* Harrison, Derek
Policing the land of the prince bishops: the history of Durham Constabulary 1840-1990. Exeter: Durham Books, 1990
[8],87p, illus. 23cm. ISBN 1 87290 200 6

Wynne, Harry
Badges, insignia and unfiorm of the North Eastern police forces. v1: Durham County Constabulary, Durham Constabulary including Durham City and Hartlepool. [Sunderland]: Brinkburn Cottage, 2002
47p, illus. 30cm

Durham - Departments, divisions etc
Durham Constabulary
River Division: brief history. [Durham: The Constabulary, 1968]
1p. 33cm. Typescript

Dyfed-Powys
Griffiths, Charles
Heddluoedd Canolbarth a Gorllewin Cymru 1829-1974 = The police forces of Mid and West Wales 1829-1974. Llandybie: Dinefwr, 2008
119p, illus. 19x24cm. ISBN 978-1904323150. Parallel text in English and Welsh. Mainly covers the constituent forces

East Lothian [Lothian and Borders]
Skinner, B C
The police force of East Lothian 1832-1950. In: *Transactions of the East Lothian Antiquarian & Field Naturalists' Society* v12 (1970) p5-21

East Riding of Yorkshire [North Yorkshire]
Clarke, A A
Country coppers: the story of the East Riding Police. Hornsea: Arton Books, 1993
156p, illus. 24cm. ISBN 0 9522163 0 2

East Riding of Yorkshire Constabulary
East Riding of Yorkshire Police 1857-1957. [Beverley: The Constabulary, 1957]
52p, illus. 22cm

Foster, D
The East Riding Constabulary in the nineteenth century. In: *Northern history* v21 (1985) p193-211

East Suffolk [Suffolk]
Reeve, Ronald
When constabulary duty's to be done: the impact of the Great War on the East Suffolk Police. [Darsham]: Darsham Parochial Church Council, 2010
[4],108,[16]p, illus. 25cm. ISBN 978-0953659227

East Sussex [Sussex]
Angel, K
East Sussex Police 1840-1967. Lewes: East Sussex Constabulary, 1967
[15]p. 21cm

Kyrke, R V
History of East Sussex Police 1840-1967. [Lewes]: Sussex Police Authority, 1970
[4],133leaves, illus. 30cm. Private circulation

Eastbourne [Sussex]
Eastbourne County Borough Police
Borough Police: Diamond Jubilee 1891-1951. [Eastbourne: The Police, 1951]
[2],11p. 21cm

Rumble, Mike
Eastbourne Borough Police. In: *PICA magazine* (Spring 1986) p3-6 and (Summer 1986) p15-16, illus

Smith, Alan
The formation of the Eastbourne Borough Police in 1891. npl: [The author, 1994]
38p, illus. 30cm

Edinburgh [Lothian and Borders]
Marwick, *Sir* James D
Sketch of the history of the High Constables of Edinburgh, with notes on the early watching, licensing and other police arrangements of the City.
Edinburgh: [Printed by] John Greig, 1865
300,lxxxivp. 22cm

Robertson, David
A history of the High Constables of Edinburgh, with notes on watching and warding and other subjects. Edinburgh: High Constables of Edinburgh, 1924
ix,191p. 26cm

Edinburgh - Special Constabulary
Steuart, James
The City of Edinburgh Special Constabulary. In: *Police journal* v2 (1929) p485-491
Covers World War 1

Essex
Essex was the first: a force history in brief. In: *Police review* v77 (1969) p965

Essex Constabulary
A brief history of the force. Chelmsford: The Constabulary, 1978
15p, illus. 21cm. Produced for Police Exhibition, Colchester Castle, 2-14 October 1978

Essex Police
A brief history of the force. [Chelmsford: The Police], 1984
15p. 30cm

Essex Police
History notebook. [Chelmsford]: Essex Police Museum, [199?-]. 30cm
Continuing series of 4-page leaflets each on an aspect of the Force's history.
n1 *The murder of Sgt Eves*...n53 *The Borough forces*

Feather, Fred (comp)
The Essex family historian presents Tales from the Essex Police Museum.
[Chelmsford: Essex Society for Family History], 2007. [2],50p, illus. 21cm.
Reprint, with introduction, of 12 leaflets from Essex Police *History*

notebook series. Issued as a supplement to *Essex family historian* (Dec 2007)

Feather, Fred
150 years of service 1840 to 1990: souvenir brochure. [Chelmsford: Essex Police, 1990]
32p, illus. 30cm

Lee, Adrian
Police insignia in Essex - and Southend. In: *Essex countryside* v28 n286 (Nov 1980) p36-37, illus

Lockwood, Martyn
The Essex Police Force: a history. Stroud: History, 2009
127p, illus. 24cm. ISBN 978-0752451671. (Britain in old photographs)

Scollan, Maureen J
The King's peace: studies in Essex police history before 1889. Part 1.
London University and the author, 1970
56p, illus. Thesis?

Scollan, Maureen
Sworn to serve: police in Essex 1840-1990. Chichester: Phillimore, 1993
x,150p, illus. 26cm. ISBN 0 85033 999 5

Tabrum, Burnett
A short history of the Essex Constabulary. Chelmsford: Essex County Chronicle, 1911
62p, illus. 18cm

Woodgate, John
The Essex Police. Lavenham: Dalton, 1985
viii,184p, illus. 24cm. ISBN 0 86138 034 7

Essex - Departments, divisions etc
Essex Police Driving School 50th anniversary 1937-1987. Chelmsford: Essex Police, 1987
12p, illus. 21cm

Beer, Noel
Law and order in 19th century Rayleigh. Rayleigh: Friends of Holy Trinity

Rayleigh, 2000
vi,56p, illus. 21cm. ISBN 0 9537970 1 5

Essex Police
A brief history - Colchester Police Station, Queen Street, Colchester, Essex.
[Colchester: The Police, *ca*1983]
34p, illus. 30cm. Cover title: *Colchester Police Station*

Pawsey, Frederick W
The history of law and order in North Hinckford (north Essex). Halstead:
Halstead and District Local History Society, 1991
92p, illus. 30cm. ISBN 0 9513106 4 X. Inc *Ch7: The police in North Hinckford and Essex*, p47-60

Essex and Southend-on-Sea [Essex]
The Essex and Southend-on-Sea Constabulary. In: *East Briton* v10 n2 (Jan 1973) p7-11, illus

Exeter [Devon and Cornwall]
Newton, Robert
Law and order in Exeter 1837-48. In: *Devonshire Association report and transactions* v94 (1962) p493-530

Exeter - Special Constabulary
Townsend, R W
Exeter City Special Constabulary 1939-1945. [Exeter: npub, 1946]
x,46p, illus. 22cm

Fife
A pictorial history of Fife Constabulary. [Glenrothes: The Constabulary, 1999]
36p, illus. 30cm

Policewomen in Fife Constabulary: 50th anniversary 1945-1995.
Dunfermline: Kingdom, [1995]
20p, illus. 21cm

Brown, William
A history of policing in Fife
203p. Downloadable from *www.fife.police.uk*

Flintshire [North Wales]
Flintshire County Constabulary
Flintshire Constabulary centenary 1856-1956. Holywell: The Constabulary,
[1956]
47p, illus. 25cm

Veysey, A Geoffrey
The early years of the Flintshire Constabulary. In: *Flintshire Historical
Society journal* v35 (1999) p143-166

Folkestone [Kent]
Bishop, W H
Folkestone Borough Police from 1836 to 1943. In: *Bygone Kent* v17 n8
(Aug 1996) p442-446, illus

Gateshead [Northumbria]
Banks, Kenneth B *and* Wynne, Harry
*Badges, insignia and uniforms of the North Eastern police forces v3:
Gateshead, South Shields, Sunderland,* [Sunderland]: Brinkburn Cottage,
2009
iii,83-124p, illus. 30cm

Gatiss, P D
History of the County Borough of Gateshead Police. Gateshead: Gateshead
Constabulary, 1968
36p, illus. 25cm

Glamorgan [South Wales]
Baker, E R
The history of the Glamorgan Constabulary. In: *Glamorgan police
magazine* v1-14 (1954-68)
A series of articles

Glamorgan – Departments, divisions etc
Roderick, Abiah
Clydach police force. In: *Clydach Historical Society newsletter* n38 (Winter
1992) p4-5

Glasgow [Strathclyde]
Goldsmith, Alistair
Glasgow on show and the boys in blue 1888-1938. In: *History today* (Feb

1997) p51-57, illus. Describes the policing of five international exhibitions

Grant, Douglas
The thin blue line: the story of the City of Glasgow Police. London: John Long, 1973
192p, illus. 23cm. ISBN 0 09 114190 7

Ord, John
Origin and history of the Glasgow Police Force. 1906. [Glasgow?: npub, *ca*1906]
31p, illus. 21cm

Pieri, Joe
The big men: personal memories of Glasgow's police. Glasgow: Neil Wilson, 2001
viii,184p, illus. 22cm. ISBN 1 903238 07 2

Gloucestershire
Cratchley, J A
Gloucestershire Constabulary: a short history 1839-1985. [Cheltenham: The Constabulary, 1985]
[2],21p, illus. 21cm

Gloucestershire Constabulary
Birth of the Gloucestershire Constabulary. npl: The Constabulary, 1967

Iliffe-Moon, Peter H
Gloucestershire Constabulary: the first 150 years. Gloucester: British Publishing, 1989
60p, illus. 30cm. ISBN 0 7140 2668 9

Jerrard, Bryan
Early policing methods in Gloucestershire. In: *Transactions of the Bristol and Gloucestershire Archaeological Society* (1982) p221-240

Thomas, Harry
The history of the Gloucestershire Constabulary 1839-1985. [Cheltenham]: The Constabulary, 1987
[v],360p, illus. 23cm

Gloucestershire - Departments, divisions etc
Sindrey, Geoff *and* Heath, Ted
A forest beat: the Forest of Dean police 1839-2000. Lydney: Black Dwarf
Publications, 2000. 168p, illus. 26cm. ISBN 0 9533028 7 3

Gloucestershire - Special Constabulary
Clevely, K G (ed)
The War record book of the Gloucestershire Special Constabulary.
Cheltenham: The editor, [*ca*1945]
128p, illus. 28cm

Godalming [Surrey]
Ford, Richard
Blue coat with silver lace: the history of the Godalming Police. [Guildford]:
Surrey Constabulary, 1969
10p. 20cm. Typescript

Gravesend [Kent]
Deacon, Brian
*The growth and changes in the Gravesend Borough Police from 1836 to
1866.* In: *PICA magazine* (Spring 1977) p27-33, illus

Great Western Railway [British Transport]
Stephens, G
The history and functions of railway police. In: *Proceedings of the Great
Western Railway (London) Lecture and Debating Society* n305 (12 Nov
1936)
12p

Greenock [Strathclyde]
Williamson, D
The organization and history of the Greenock Police Force. Greenock:
Chief Constable, 1961
19p, illus. 21cm

Grimsby [Humberside]
Grimsby Constabulary
*Guardians of the peace 1846-1955: souvenir brochure of the Grimsby
Borough Police exhibition, April 1955.* Grimsby: The Constabulary, 1955
72p, illus. 22cm

Guernsey
The history of the Guernsey Police. In: *PICA magazine* (Winter 1986) p17-24 and (Issue 1/87) p17-23, illus

Bell, William H
I beg to report...: policing in Guernsey during the German occupation.
Guernsey: Guernsey Press, 1995
[vii],408p, illus. 22cm. ISBN 0 9520479 1 8

Lamy, Albert Peter
Policing during the occupation 1940-1945. Guernsey: Guernsey Police,
1991?
26p, illus. 30cm

Le Cocq, Francois
Police of Guernsey. In: *Police world* (Winter 1964) p5-8, illus

Le Poidevin, Stephen E F
History of the Guernsey Police. [St Peter Port: The Police], 1979
15p. 32cm
Another ed: [198-]. 15p. 30cm
Another ed: [ca1993]. 15p, illus. 30cm

Guildford [Surrey]
Ford, Richard
*They guarded Guildford: the history of the Guildford Borough Police
Force, 1836-1947.* [Guildford: Surrey Constabulary?], 1969
[4],26p, illus. 33cm. Typescript

Harris, Des
Guildford Borough Police. In: *PICA magazine* (Spring 1981) p25-27, illus

Gwent
Gwent Constabulary
Report on the development of the force 1964-1968. Abergavenny: The
Constabulary, [1969]
[44]p, illus, 2 fold charts. 25cm

Halifax [West Yorkshire]
West Yorkshire Constabulary. Public Relations Department
History of police in Halifax. npl: The Constabulary, nd

3p

Wild, J
The Halifax Borough Police: a short history. [Halifax: The Police], 1968
[2],28p. 26cm. Typescript

Hampshire
Lee, John (and others)
Policing Hampshire and the Isle of Wight: a photographic history.
Chichester: Phillimore, 2001
x,118p, illus. 29cm. ISBN 1 86077 196 3

Hampshire - Departments, divisions etc
Woodward, Steve
From T-Ford to T5: one hundred years of Hampshire Constabulary transport. New Romney: Bank House Books, 2004
333p, illus. 30cm. ISBN 1 904408 05 2

Hampshire - Special Constabulary
Dixon, Brian (comp)
A very special force: the 175th anniversary of Hampshire Special Constabulary. [Basingstoke: The author, 2007]
i,56p, illus. 24cm

Hampshire and Isle of Wight [Hampshire]
Watt, Ian
A history of the Hampshire and Isle of Wight Constabulary 1839-1966.
Winchester: The Constabulary, 1967
172p, illus. 22cm
New ed: Chichester: Phillimore, 2006
xiii,194p, illus. 26cm. ISBN 1 86077 383 4

Hastings [Sussex]
Banks, Charles
History of the County Borough of Hastings Police 1836-1967. Hastings:
Hastings Constabulary, 1967
84p, illus. 21cm

Haverfordwest [Dyfed-Powys]
Jones, R Winston
The Haverfordwest Borough Police 1835-1889. [Haverfordwest: The

author], 1989
61p, illus. 30cm

Hawick [Lothian and Borders]
Dorward, G B
Border law. Jedburgh: The author, [1990?]
121p, illus. 21cm. Also inc information on Kelso and Roxburghshire

Dorward, George
History of the local police. In: *Hawick Archaeological Society transactions*
(1966) p27-47, (1967) 3-24, (1968) p3-18, (1969) p5-15, illus

Hereford [West Mercia]
Forrest, Gordon *and* Hadley, Ted
Policing Hereford and Leominster: an illustrated history of the City of Hereford Police 1835 to 1947 and Leominster Borough Police 1836 to 1889. Studley: Brewin Books, 1989
[4],92p, illus. 30cm. ISBN 0 947731 55 5

Herefordshire [West Mercia]
Hadley, Vera
Herefordshire Constabulary 1857-1967: a history of the County Constabulary in words and pictures. Hereford: V Hadley, 1999. [9,174]p, illus. 30cm. ISBN 0 9536792 0 9

Herefordshire Constabulary
The first hundred years of the Herefordshire Constabulary 1857-1957. Hereford: The Constabulary, 1957
20p, illus. 22cm

Hertfordshire
Hertfordshire Constabulary
Hertfordshire Constabulary: 1947-1968. npl: The Constabulary, 1969

Hertfordshire Constabulary
Summary of the history and organisation of the Hertfordshire Constabulary. npl: The Constabulary, 1971
var p

Hertfordshire Constabulary. Press and P R Dept
Hertfordshire Constabulary: 150 years of service 1841-1991: souvenir.

[Welwyn Garden City: The Constabulary, 1991]
32p, illus. 30cm

Osborn, Neil
The story of Hertfordshire Police. Letchworth: Hertfordshire Countryside, [1969]
144p, illus. 23cm

Hertfordshire - Departments, divisions etc
Pringle, Nik *and* Treversh, Jim
150 years policing in Watford District. Luton: Radley Shaw, 1991
256p, illus. ISBN 0 9517477 0 3

Workers' Educational Association. Hatfield Branch
Hatfield and its people...: Book 6 Law and disorder. [Hatfield]: The Branch, 1961
28p, illus. 22cm

Horncastle [Lincolnshire]
Davey, B J
Lawless and immoral: policing a country town 1838-1857. Leicester: Leicester UP, 1983
203p, illus. 23cm. ISBN 0 7185 1237 5

Hove [Sussex]
Oakensen, Derek
The police in Victorian Hove: a short history. npl: The author?, 2007
2p, illus. 30cm

Oakensen, Derek
The policing of Hove. In: *PICA magazine* (Spring 1983) p19-20, (Winter 1983) p25-26, (Spring 1984),p17-19,), (Winter 1984) p7-9 and (Summer 1986) p7-12 illus. Article titles vary

Oakensen, Derek
A solution looking for a problem?: women police in the Borough of Hove 1919-1947. In: *PICA magazine* (issue 1/91) p13-17

Oakensen, Derek John
Origins and development of policing in Brighton and Hove 1830-1900 with special reference to local political control. npl: The author, 1994

2v. PhD thesis, University of Brighton

Huddersfield [West Yorkshire]
Holbery, Steve
A pictorial history of the Huddersfield and district police force: from the earliest records to the present day. [Huddersfield?: The author?, *ca*1997]
[2],82p, illus. 21cm

Huddersfield County Borough Council
Official opening of Civic Centre - Phase 2 on Monday 5th February 1968.
Huddersfield: The Council, 1968
?p. 25cm. Inc *Huddersfield County Borough Police: a short history*

West Yorkshire Constabulary. Public Relations Department
History of police in Huddersfield. Wakefield:The Constabulary, nd
2p

Hull [Humberside]
Clarke, A A
The policemen of Hull: the story of Hull Police Force 1836-1974. Beverley:
Hutton Press, 1992
185p, illus. 24cm. ISBN 1 87216 739 X

Hull City Police
A brief history of the police service. Hull: [The Police, 196-?]
3p. 33cm. Typescript. Private circulation to Special Constabulary members

Hull Constabulary
Authentic history of the Hull Police Force in commemoration of its centenary 1836-1936. Hull: The Constabulary, 1936
24p, illus. 26cm. Cover title: *The centenary of the Hull Police Force 1836-1936*

Humberside - Departments, divisions etc
Rogers, Peter *and* Quinney, Sarah
Then and now - Pocklington Police Station 1899 and 1999: a centenary celebration. [Pocklington: The authors?], 1999
16p, illus. 21cm

Wood, Richard
Policing from Wansford Road: a record of policing in Driffield during the

last 100 years. Driffield: Driffield Crime Prevention Panel 1997
[8],128,iiip, illus. 21cm. ISBN 0 9531521 0 3

Huntingdonshire [Cambridgeshire]
Brown, Joanna
The Huntingdonshire constabulary before 1857. In: *Cambridge Antiquarian Society proceedings* v65 pt2 (1974) p102-111
Inc some information on the force established in 1857

Huntingdonshire Constabulary
Police in Huntingdonshire 1734 to 1857, 1857 to 1965. npl: The Constabulary, 1966

Ipswich [Suffolk]
Cross, R L
[*Ipswich Borough Police*] *1836-1967.* Ipswich: Ipswich Corporation, 1967
8p, illus. 23cm. (Ipswich information supplement)

Hodder, Martin
Ipswich Borough Police 1836-1967. Mablethorpe: Police Memorabilia Collectors Club, 2008. 21p, illus. 30cm

Irish Revenue [Northern Ireland/Garda Siochana]
McDonald, Jim
Irish Revenue Police. In: *Journal of the Police History Society* n22 (2007) p3-7, illus

Smith, Simon
The Irish Revenue Police. In: *Journal of the Police History Society* n18 (2003) p24-26, illus

Isle of Man
Draskau, Jennifer Hawley
Keeping the peace in WW1. In: *Journal of the Police History Society* n25 (2010) p15-19, illus

Turnbull, George
The Isle of Man Constabulary: an account of its origin and growth. [Peel]: Mansk-Svenska Publishing, 1984
224p, illus. 22cm. ISBN 0 907715 20 6

Isle of Wight [Hampshire]
Aldred, Chris
Isle of Wight County Council: a centenary souvenir, 1890-1990. Newport:
The County Council, 1990
62p, illus. 30cm. ISBN 0 906328 43 8. Inc *When the island had its own police force*, p51-52, illus

Jersey
Scott Warren, D N M
Bluebottles: the life story of the States of Jersey Police. [Jersey?:] npub,
1999
224p, illus. 21cm

Shutler, G H
The States of Jersey: the island and its police force. In: *Police world* v13 n1
(Spring 1968) p12-19, illus

States of Jersey Police
The history of policing in Jersey. [Rouge Bouillon: The Police, *ca*1984]
[12]p. 30cm

Kent
Ingleton, Roy
Policing Kent 1800-2000: guarding the Garden of England. Chichester:
Phillimore, 2002
xvii,188p, illus. 28cm. ISBN 1 86077 233 1

Kent Constabulary
History of Kent Police. npl: The Constabulary, nd
3,5p

Macfie, A L
The Kent Constabulary: the early years. In: *Journal of Kent local history*
n21 (Sep 1985) p8-9

Thomas, R L
Kent Police centenary: recollections of a hundred years 1857-1957.
[Maidstone]: KCC Centenary Booklet Sub-Committee, 1957
161,42p, illus. 19cm

Kent - Departments, divisions etc
Brown, Bernard
The lost outpost [Knockholt]. In: *Warren: 4 Area Metro Police magazine*
(Summer 1984) p35-40
Expanded ed: In: *Bygone Kent* v20 n11 (Nov 1999) p635-643, illus

Kent County Constabulary. Maidstone and Malling Division
The beat 2000: a millennium collection of articles, anecdotes and pictures.
[Maidstone]: The Constabulary, [1999]. 35p, illus. 30cm

Sevenoaks Society. History Section
100 years' growth in Sevenoaks services: housing, water, hospitals, fire,
libraries, police, recreation etc. [Sevenoaks]: The Society, 1995
113p, illus. 30cm. Inc Lucas, Angela. *Police*, p61-70

Spencer, Diana
Hythe Police Station 1913-1996: a history and personal memoir. Hythe:
Hythe Civic Society, [2000]
8p, illus. 21cm. ISBN 1 900101 25 4

Kidwelly [Dyfed-Powys]
Jones, J Frederick
Kidwelly Borough Police Force. In: *Carmarthenshire antiquary* v4 n3-4
(1963) p152-159

Lancashire
The Force under [*name of Chief Constable and dates of office*]. In:
Lancashire Constabulary journal (Oct 1957-Oct 1959), illus
10 articles each dealing with the period of office of one Chief Constable
1839-1950

History of the uniform of the Lancashire Constabulary. In: *Lancashire*
Constabulary journal (April 1963), illus

Dobson, Bob
Policing in Lancashire 1839-1989. Blackpool: Landy, 1989
99p, illus. 21cm. ISBN 0 9507692 7 4

Dobson, R
A badge of office. In: *Lancashire Constabulary journal* (1966) p244-246,
illus

Hesketh, Peter
Lancon Bus. In: *PICA magazine* (August 1996) p19-24, illus

Trubshaw, W
The Lancashire Constabulary: 80 years ago and today. In: *Police journal* v1 (1928) p487-498

Lancashire and Yorkshire Railway [British Transport]
The unknown force: the Lancashire and Yorkshire Railway Police. In: *British Transport Police journal* (Winter 1977) p13-15

Lancaster [Lancashire]
Dobson, R
On the appointed day. In: *Lancashire Constabulary journal* (1967) p298-299, illus

Leamington Spa [Warwickshire]
Gibbons, W G
Royal Leamington Spa. Part 6: The letter and the law. Coventry: Jones-Sands, 1986
20p, illus. 19x25cm. ISBN 0 947764 45 3. Contents: *The police (and fire brigade)*; *Post Office*

Sutherland, Graham
The Leamington beat 1881-1923. [Warwick]: Warwickshire Constabulary History Society, [198-]
32p. 21cm

Threnody
Passing of the police force from Royal Leamington Spa on 31 March 1947. npl: npub, [1947?]
3p

Leeds [West Yorkshire]
Leeds City Police
Leeds Police centenary 1836-1936: Thursday 2nd April 1936. [Leeds: The Police, 1936]
36p, illus. 22cm

Leeds Police. Research and Planning Dept
The Leeds Police 1836-1974. [Leeds: The Police, 1974?]

[10],181p, illus. 22cm

Leeds - Departments, divisions etc
Thorpe, A
Leeds City Police Fire Brigade. In. *PICA magazine* (Summer 1986) p3-7

Leicester [Leicestershire]
Beazley, Ben
Peelers to Pandas: an illustrated history of the Leicester City Police.
Derby: Breedon, 2001
261p, illus. 26cm. ISBN 1 85983 231 8

Spavold, Janet
The establishment and early years of the Leicester Police Force 1836-1846.
1970
45p. 26cm. Dissertation MA Victorian Studies, Leicester University.
Typescript

Leicestershire
1836 to 1986: celebrating 150 years of policing in Leicestershire. In: *Tally ho!* (1986). [6p]

Leicestershire Constabulary
Leicestershire Constabulary 1839 to 1989: 150 years of service to the community. [Leicester]: The Constabulary, [1990]
28p, illus. 28cm

Stanley, Clifford R
The birth and early history of the Leicestershire Constabulary. In: *Justice of the peace* v118 (1954) p604-606
Another version: In: *Leicestershire historian* v2 (Winter/Spring 1971/72) p21-25

Stanley, Clifford R
How the Leicestershire Constabulary was born. In: *Heart of England* v3 n1 (1973) p7-12

Stanley, Clifford R
Under five commands. In: *Tally Ho!* (Spring 1958-Autumn 1962) various p, illus. Comprises a history from 1839-1951 in 18 parts

Leicestershire - Departments, divisions etc
Elliott, Bernard
A rural police force in 19th century Leicestershire: Oadby. In: *Journal of the Police History Society* n2 (1987) p87-88

Leith [Lothian and Borders]
Wood, Andrew Dick
The High Constabulary of the Port of Leith: a short history. [Leith]: 1972
60p, illus. 22cm. Private circulation

Leominster [West Mercia]
Forrest, Gordon *and* Hadley, Ted
Policing Hereford and Leominster: an illustrated history of the City of Hereford Police 1835 to 1947 and Leominster Borough Police 1836 to 1889. Studley: Brewin Books, 1989
[4],92p, illus. 30cm. ISBN 0 947731 55 5

Lincolnshire
Bedford, William
Birth of the Lincolnshire Constabulary. In: *Lincolnshire poacher* (Winter 2001) p21-23, illus

Pearson, S C
Lincolnshire Constabulary 1857-1957. Lincoln: The Constabulary, 1957
[2],42p, illus. 26cm
Reissued: Lincoln: The Constabulary, 1991
[2],42p, illus. 26cm

Lincolnshire - Departments, divisions etc
Clarke, J N
Watch and ward in the countryside: a review of the development of the County Constabulary from the time of parish constables, watchmen, wardsmen, beadles and bellmen (based on the market town of Horncastle). Horncastle: The author, 1982
80p, illus. 22cm

Gough, Adi
Pros and cons: a history of pre-policing and early policing based on the Alford district of Lincolnshire. Mablethorpe: SBK Books, 1996-98
3v, illus. 21cm. ISBN 1 899881 28 X complete set [v1: 1 899881 23 9. v2: 1 899881 24 7. v3: 1 899881 45 X]

Liverpool [Merseyside]
Bell, S Peter (ed)
Victorian Lancashire. Newton Abbot: David and Charles, 1974
196p, maps. ISBN 0 7153 6213 5. Inc ch7: Cockcroft, W R. *The Liverpool Police Force 1836-1902*, p150 168

Brogden, Mike
On the Mersey beat: policing Liverpool between the wars. Oxford: OUP, 1991
184p. ISBN 0 19 825430 X

Cockcroft, W R
The Albert Dock and Liverpool's historic waterfront. Market Drayton: SB Publications, 1992
88p, illus. 21cm. ISBN 1 85770 016 3. Inc sections on Liverpool City Police docks and river policing
[*New ed*]: Formby: Print Origination, 1994
vii,184p, illus. 25cm. ISBN 0 903348 48 9

Cockcroft, W R
From cutlasses to computers: the police force in Liverpool 1839-1989. Market Drayton: SB, 1991
104p, illus. 21cm. ISBN 1 87070 846 6

Cockcroft, William R
Rise and growth of the Liverpool Police Force in the nineteenth century. The author, 1969
292p. MA thesis, University of Wales

Curran, John A
The lawmen. In: *Liverpool* n34 (1972) p1-5

Liverpool and Bootle Police Orphanage
Police!!: an illustrated and descriptive history of the Liverpool and Bootle Police past and present. Liverpool: The Orphanage, 1910
88p, illus. 25cm

Liverpool City Police
Liverpool City Police 1836-1951. Liverpool: The Police, 1951
16p, illus. 23cm. Souvenir booklet for City Police exhibition

Liverpool Airport
Wilkinson, Dave
The history and badges of the Liverpool Airport Police. In: *PICA magazine* (Summer 1979) p19-21, illus

Liverpool Parks
The history and badges of the Liverpool Parks Police. In: *PICA magazine* (Summer 1978) p5-8, illus

London and North Western Railway [British Transport]
Premier line police: the London and North Western Railway Police. In: *British Transport Police journal* (31 December 1981) p3-8

London and South Western Railway [British Transport]
The London and South Western Railway Police. In: *British Transport Police journal* (Summer 1977) p34-35

London Brighton and South Coast Railway [British Transport]
On the Brighton line. In: *British Transport Police journal* (Autumn 1976) p12

London Transport [British Transport]
Deacon, Brian
The London Transport Police. In: *PICA magazine* (Summer 1976) p15-19, illus

Lothian and Borders
Archibald, T W
A history of the Lothian and Borders Police. [Edinburgh: Archibald, 1990] 184p, illus. 31cm. ISBN 0 9516119 0 9

Luton [Bedfordshire]
Madigan, T J
The men who wore straw helmets: policing Luton 1840-1974 including the development and the story of the Luton Borough Police Force 1876-1947. Dunstable: Book Castle, 1993
viii,268p, illus. 22cm. ISBN 1 87119 981 6. Pbk ISBN 1 87119 911 5

Macclesfield [Cheshire]
Symmons, W G
A short history of the Macclesfield Borough Police Force from its inception

19th January 1836 to amalgamation with the Cheshire Constabulary...1947.
Macclesfield: The Force, 1947
51p, illus. 23cm

Maidstone [Kent]
Hales, Irene
The police in Maidstone. In: *Bygone Kent* v5 n12 (Dec 1984) p698-703, illus

Maldon [Essex]
Scollan, Maureen
Small is beautiful? In: *Police review* (11 Oct 1985) p2070-2071

Manchester [Greater Manchester]
Greater Manchester Police
The police!: 150 years of policing in the Manchester area. Runcorn: Archive Publications, 1989
128p, illus. 28cm. ISBN 0 948946 49 0

Hewitt, Eric J
A history of policing in Manchester. Didsbury: E J Morten, 1979
188p, illus. 23cm. ISBN 0 85972 040 3

Joyce, Peter
The transition from 'old' to 'new' policing in early 19th century Manchester.
In: *Police journal* v66 n2 (Apr 1993) p197-210

Manchester City Police
A short history of the Manchester City Police. Manchester: The Police, 1937
3p. 22cm. From booklet commemorating opening of new HQ

Manchester and Salford [Greater Manchester]
Manchester and Salford Police
A brief history of the English police system. [Manchester: The Police, 1968]
1p. 33cm. Typescript. Inc short note on Manchester and Salford Police history

Margate [Kent]
Bishop, W H
Seaside coppers. In: *Bygone Kent* v14 n4 and n5 (Apr-May 1993) p240-

247, 267-273, illus

Mersey Tunnels
Jenkinson, D and Lloyd, N
The Mersey Tunnels. [Liverpool?]: North West Publications, [*ca*1990]
36p, illus. 26cm. Inc *History of the Mersey Tunnels Police*, p19-25

Wilkinson, Dave
The Mersey Tunnels Police. In: *PICA magazine* (issue 2/91) p5-9, illus

Merseyside - Departments, divisions etc
Atherton, David
Best of the Mersey Mounties. In: *Police review* (29 Aug 1986) p1780, illus

Pollitt, Kenneth
Merseyside Police Band, 125 years, 1868-1993: official commemorative history. [Liverpool: npub, 1993?]
40p, illus. 30cm

Smith, Noel E
Helmets, handcuffs and hoses: the story of the Wallasey police and fire brigade. Part 1: The Wallasey police. Wallasey: The author, [2001?]
76p, illus. 30cm. ISBN 0 9517762 3 1
Part 2: The Wallasey fire brigade. Wallasey: The author, [2001?]
76p, illus. 30cm. ISBN 0 9517762 4 X. Inc the police fire brigade and a list of members of the police force

Merthyr Tydfil [South Wales]
Smith, Eira M
Merthyr Tydfil Borough Police 1908-1938: a brief history. In: *Merthyr historian* v4 (1989) p71-86

Metropolitan
Metropolitan Police centenary celebration: programme, May 25, 1929.
[London: The Police, 1929]. 12p, illus. 21cm. Inc *Historical notes* p3-5 and lists of Commissioners etc p7-9

Scotland Yard: a look back over 25 years. Job silver jubilee special supplement (Oct 1992). 16p, illus. Issued to commemorate the move to Broadway

Scotland Yard: the first 150 years. London: British Tourist Authority. 1979
64p, illus. 30cm. ISBN 0 7095 0346 0

Arden, Michael R, Fletcher, Eleanor *and* Taylor, Christopher
Metropolitan Police images: motor vehicles. Stroud: Phillimore, 2008
xi, 147p, illus. 28cm. ISBN 978-1860775017

Ascoli, David
The Queen's peace: the origins and development of the Metropolitan Police,1829-1979. London: Hamish Hamilton, 1979
xiv,364p, illus. 22cm. ISBN 0 241 10296 0

Ashley, Joe
Short history of the Metropolitan Police. In: *Police world* (Autumn 1969)
p48-50, Winter 1969) p59-60, (Summer 1970) p52-53, (Autumn 1970) p49-50, (Winter 1970) p49-51, (Spring 1971) p45-46,50, (Summer 1971) p37-39, (Autumn 1971) p41-42 and (Winter 1971) p37-38, illus

Bartlett, Robert
The birth of the Met. In: *Police review* (21 Feb 1986) p403-405, illus

Browne, Douglas G
The rise of Scotland Yard: a history of the Metropolitan Police. London: Harrap, 1956
392p, illus. 22cm

Clarkson, Charles Tempest *and* Richardson, J Hall
Police!: a history of the Metropolitan Police. London: Field and Tuer, 1889
380p, illus. 23cm
Reprinted: London: Garland, 1984
xvi,380p, illus. 23cm. (Crime and punishment in England 1850-1922, 17).
ISBN 0 8240 6216 7

Cragoe, Matthew *and* Taylor, Antony (eds)
London politics 1760-1914. Basingstoke: Palgrave Macmillan, 2005
xiii,250p. 23cm. ISBN 1 403 99000 X. Inc Campion, David A. *Policing the Peelers: Parliament, the public and the Metropolitan Police 1829-33*, p38-56

Dilnot, George
The story of Scotland Yard. London: Bles, [1926]

ix,340p, illus. 22cm

Dilnot, George
Scotland Yard: its history and organisation 1829-1929. London: Bles, 1929
xi,351p, illus. 22cm. Revised ed of the previous item

Fido, Martin *and* Skinner, Keith
The official encyclopedia of Scotland Yard. London: Virgin, 1999
320p, illus. 29cm. ISBN 1 85227 712 2
Pbk: [Rev ed]. London: Virgin, 2000
vi,574p, illus. 20cm. ISBN 0 7535 0515 0

Fountain, Michael
'Ello 'ello 'ello: a brief history of the London bobby. In: *Hillingdon Family History Society journal* n60 (Dec 2002) p3-13, illus

Hadaway, D J
A police force at war. In: *Police review* (29 Jan 1998) p230 and 235, illus.
Deals with World War 1

Heron, F E *and* Pike, A R
A brief history of the Metropolitan Police. [London: Metropolitan Police, 1969?]
59p. 21cm

Howe, *Sir* Ronald
The story of Scotland Yard. London: Arthur Barker, 1965
176p, illus. 23cm
Pbk: London: NEL, 1968. 125p. 18cm. ISBN 0 450 00030 3

Howgrave-Graham, H M
The Metropolitan Police at war. London: HMSO, 1947
viii,89p, illus. 23cm

Howgrave-Graham, H M
Police principles and Scotland Yard. In: *Medico-legal journal* v23 pt3 (1955) p74-84

Inwood, Stephen
Policing London's morals: the Metropolitan Police and popular culture, 1829-1850. In: *London journal* v15 n2 (1990) p129-146, illus

Jackson, Louise A
Care or control?: the Metropolitan women police and child welfare 1919-1969. In: *Historical journal* v46 n3 (2003) p623-648

McLagan, Graeme
Bent coppers: the inside story of Scotland Yard's battle against police corruption. London: Weidenfeld and Nicolson, 2003
v,265p, illus. 24cm. ISBN 0 297 83093 7
Pbk: Rev ed. London: Orion, 2004. 453p, illus. BA4-Z5220. ISBN 0 7528 5902 7

Mason, Gary
The official history of the Metropolitan Police: 175 years of policing London. London: Carlton, 2004
160p, illus. 27cm. ISBN 1 84442 602 5

Moylan, J F
"The blue army". In: *Country life* (18 May 1929) p698-700, illus

Price, John
The Metropolitan Police: why it was established and how it was developed.
npl: The author, nd
75p, illus

Shpayer-Makov, Haia
The making of a policeman: a social history of a labour force in metropolitan London 1829-1914. Aldershot: Ashgate, 2002
viii,293p, illus. 23cm. ISBN 0 7546 0337 7

Thomson, *Sir* Basil
The story of Scotland Yard. London: Grayson and Grayson, 1935
[8],347p, illus. 24cm

Wilkes, John
The London police in the nineteenth century. Cambridge: CUP, 1977
48p, illus. 22x21cm. (Cambridge introduction to the history of mankind: topic books). ISBN 0 521 21406 8

Williams, Guy R
The hidden world of Scotland Yard. London: Hutchinson, 1972
270p, illus. 24cm. ISBN 0 09 110570 6

Wood, James Playsted
Scotland Yard. New York: Hawthorn, 1970
xii,211p. 21cm

Woodhall, Edwin T
Secrets of Scotland Yard. London: Bodley Head, 1936
xiii,284p. 22cm

Metropolitan - Criminal Investigation Dept
(inc special units - Flying Squad, Special Branch etc)
Allason, Rupert
The Branch: a history of the Metropolitan Police Special Branch, 1883-1983. London: Secker and Warburg, 1983
xii,180p, illus. 24cm. ISBN 0 436 01165 X

Begg, Paul *and* Skinner, Keith
The Scotland Yard files: 150 years of the CID 1842-1992. London: Headline, 1992
[13],306p, illus. 23cm. ISBN 0 7472 0371 7
Pbk: London: Headline, 1993
306p, illus. 18cm. ISBN 0 7472 3963 0

Cobb, Belton
Critical years at the Yard: the career of Frederick Williamson of the Detective Department and the C.I.D. London: Faber, 1956
251p, illus. 21cm

Cobb, Belton
The first detectives and the early career of Richard Mayne, Commissioner of Police. London: Faber, 1957
214p. 21cm

Darbyshire, Neil *and* Hilliard, Brian
The Flying Squad. London: Headline, 1993
viii,248p, illus. 24cm. ISBN 0 7472 0685 6
Pbk: London: Headline, 1994
ISBN 0 7472 4018 3
Large print: Leicester: Ulverscroft, 1995
22cm. ISBN 0 7089 3234 7

Firmin, Stanley
Men in the shadows: the story of Scotland Yard's secret agents. London:
Hutchinson, 1953
204p, illus. 22cm. Ghost Squad

Gosling, John
The Ghost Squad. London: W H Allen, 1959
206p, illus. 23cm
Pbk: London: Hamilton, 1961
159p. 18cm
Reprinted: London: White Lion, 1974
206p. 21cm. ISBN 0 85617 263 4

Kirby, Dick
Flying high. In: *Police review* v115 n5910 (12 Jan 2007) p24-25, illus
A brief history of the Flying Squad

Kirby, Dick
Scotland Yard's Ghost Squad: the secret weapon against postwar crime.
Barnsley: Wharncliffe, 2011
xvi,224p, illus. 24cm. ISBN 978-184884513

Kirby, Dick
The Sweeney: the first sixty years of Scotland Yard's Flying Squad.
Barnsley: Wharncliffe, 2011
x,226p,, illus. 24cm. ISBN 978-1848843905

Lock, Joan
Dreadful deeds and awful murders: Scotland Yard's first detectives 1829-1878. Lydeard St Lawrence: Barn Owl, 1990
218p, illus. 24cm. ISBN 0 9509057 6 3

Lock, Joan
Scotland Yard casebook: the making of the CID 1865-1935. London: Hale,
1993
223p, illus. 23cm. ISBN 0 7090 4660 X

Lucas, Norman *and* Scarlett, Brian
The Flying Squad. London: Arthur Barker, 1968
199p, illus. 22cm. ISBN 0 213 76224 2

Oram, Gerard (ed)
Conflict and legality: policing mid-twentieth century Europe. London:
Francis Boutle, 2003
217p, illus. 20cm. ISBN 1 903427 20 7. Inc Roodhouse, Mark. *The Ghost
Squad: undercover policing in London 1945-49*, p171-191

Pike, Alan R
*A brief history of the Criminal Investigation Department of the London
Metropolitan Police.* In: *Police studies* (June 1978) p22-30

Porter, Bernard
*The origins of the vigilant state: the London Metropolitan Police Special
Branch before the First World War.* London: Weidenfeld and Nicolson,
1987
xvi,256p, illus. 24cm. ISBN 0 297 79067 6
Reissued: Woodbridge: Boydell, 1991
xvi,256p, illus. 24cm. ISBN 0 85115 283 X

Prothero, Margaret
*The history of the Criminal Investigation Department at Scotland Yard from
earliest times until to-day.* London: Jenkins, 1931
319p, illus. 22cm

Metropolitan - Divisions, stations etc
Vine Street Police Station: a celebration of 168 years of policing. [London:
Metropolitan Police?], 1998
12p, illus

Ashley, J
*Police and the East End of London: a short history of the Metropolitan
Police.* London: Metropolitan Police H Division, 1974
[16]p, illus. 20cm

Beatt, Andrew
Bow Street runs out. In: *Police review* (25 Sep 1992) p1776-1778, illus

Best, William C F
*'C' or St James's: a history of policing in the West End of London 1829 to
1984.* Kingston-upon-Thames: The author, 1985
[5],71p, illus. 22cm. ISBN 0 9510090 0 1

Brown, Bernard [The following 25 items]
A-Z history of the Metropolitan Police divisions. In: *The job* (April 1987-Jan 1989)
Series of 39 articles

Back to the drawing board?: law and order in Bromley. In: *Bygone Kent* v18 no2 (Feb 1997) p67-73, illus

"Damn Yankees" and the Met, 1829-1986: the evolution of the Y District police force. In: *Haringey history bulletin* v29 (1988) p30-33, illus
Juliet Bravo. In: *Journal of the Police History Society* n3 (1988) p36-43, illus

King's Cross: a police connection. In: *3 Area Metro Police magazine* (Autumn 1984) p29
Reprinted in: Journal of the Police History Society n3 (1988) p35

The maritime duties of London's Bobbies. In: *Bygone Kent* v13 n4 (Apr 1992) p211-216, illus
Policing of naval dockyards in Kent

The Metropolitan Police in the County of Surrey. In: *Journal of the Police History Society* n9 (1994) p21-24, illus

The Middlesex constabulary. In: *Journal of the Police History Society* n8 (1993) p64-68

A new baby for Papa. In: *Warren: 4 Area Metro Police magazine* (Autumn/Winter 1983) p31-41. Orpington

Nobody's child: a study in boundaries, transport and policing Penge. In: *Bygone Kent* v13 n9 (Sep 1992) p560-567, illus
Not quite a century: the story of Plumstead Police Station. In: *Bygone Kent* v17 n6 (June 1996) p332-341, illus

The Odd fellow: policing the FCM [Foreign Cattle Market, Deptford]. In: *Bygone Kent* v23 n7 (Jul 2002) p389-392, illus

On the Twickenham beat. In: *Twickenham local history journal* (Sep 1993) [2]p

The only resident of North Woolwich. In: *Warren: 4 Area Metro Police magazine* (Summer 1984) p34
Expanded ed: In: *Bygone Kent* v24 n6 and n8 (Jun and Aug 2003) p349-358, 463-470, illus

The outer limits: policing old Bexley. In: *Bygone Kent* v19 no10 (Oct 1998) p571-580, illus

Patrol Place: policing old Lewisham. In: *Bygone Kent* v21 n4 and n5 (Apr-May 2000) p197-204, 287-296, illus

Policing Metropolitan Kent (1830-1988). In: *Bygone Kent* v9 n8 (Aug 1988) p494-498

Policing old Wickham. In: *Bygone Kent* v15 n12 (December 1994) p751-758, illus

Romeo: law and order in old Greenwich. In: *Bygone Kent* v22 n2 and n3 (Feb-Mar 2001) p103-112, 173-180, illus

Romford Police: the anniversary of a change. In: *3 Area Metro Police magazine* (Spring 1985) p7-13
Reprinted in: *Journal of the Police History Society* n7 (1992) p84-87, illus

The sheriffs of Mottingham. In: *Bygone Kent* v15 n2 (February 1994) p65-75, illus

The topography of the Metropolitan Police district. In: *London Topographical Society newsletter* n35 (Nov 1992) p3-6, illus

Up the creek, or, Policing old Deptford. In: *Bygone Kent* v19 no12 (Dec 1998) p715-720, illus

When Victor bowed out. In: *Police review* (29 Nov 1985) p2424-2425, illus

Z Zulu. In: *Warren: 4 Area Metro Police magazine* (Summer 1981) p45-49

Budworth, Geoffrey
The river beat: the story of London's river police since 1798. London: Historical, 1997
144p, illus. 26cm. ISBN 0 948667 41 9

Bunker, John
Policing the pictures: the Metropolitan Police and the National Gallery. In: *Peeler* issue 2 (1997) p9-12, illus

Elliott, Bryn
A history of Loughton and Chigwell Police. Loughton: Chigwell and Loughton History Society, 1991
36p, illus. 21cm. ISBN 0 902893 03 3

Elliott, Bryn
The Metropolitan Police in the Government arms factories, Enfield Lock - RSAF and Waltham Abbey - RGPF. npl: [The author, 199-?]
6p. 30cm

Elliott, Bryn
Peelers progress: policing Waltham Abbey 1840-2000. npl: [The author?], 1999
*ca*90p, illus. 30cm

[Elliott, Bryn]
Waltham Abbey Police at war 1914-1919; 1939-1945. [Waltham Abbey: The author], 1986
[18]p, illus. 30cm

Elliott, Bryn
Waltham Abbey Police: the early years. In: *Journal of the Police History Society* n4 (1989) p36-41, illus

Fallon, Tom
The River Police: the story of Scotland Yard's little ships. London: Muller, 1956
263p, illus. 21cm

Fallon, Tom
The work of the River Police. In: *Medico-legal journal* v28 pt 4 (1960) p169-183

French, Ivan
Hendon Police. [Hendon: The author, 1984]
152p, illus. 31cm

Hadaway, David
Eltham Police Station: the first hundred years 1839-1939. Sussex: Latter Books, 1984
ii,20p, illus. 21cm

Hadaway, David
Westcombe Park Police Station: centenary 1885-1985. npl: [The author?], 1986
ii,15p, illus. 21cm

Hedgcock, Murray
A slice of old Barnes survives. In: *Barnes and Mortlake History Society newsletter* n162 (Sep 2002) p3-6 and 16, illus
History of Lonsdale Road Police Station

Hobbs, Doris C H
The Croydon Police 1829-1840. In: *Croydon Natural History Society proceedings* v17(6) (Apr 1983) p141-152
Reprinted in: Journal of the Police History Society n2 (1987) p66-79

Jephcote, J R
The Metropolitan Police Dockyard Division. In: *The Peeler* issue 7 (2002) p25-27, illus

Joslin, John H
Early days in forming a police force on the Thames. In: *Lewisham Local History Society transactions* (1979) p1-13, illus. ISBN 0 901637 46 7

Kennison, Peter *and* Swinden, David
Behind the blue lamp: policing north and east London. Upminster: Coppermill Press, 2003
xviii,371p. 21cm. ISBN 0 9546534 0 8

Linwood, Jean
Wealdstone Police Station: a brief history, In: *Stanmore and Harrow Historical Society newsletter* (Autumn 1994). 1p

Metropolitan Police
Metropolitan Police J centenary handbook 1886-1986. London: The Police, 1986. 60p, illus. 24cm

Pink, John (ed)
Past times - how we worked: recollections of policing in Kingston upon Thames 1958-1968. Surbiton: JRP, 1998
18p, illus. 30cm. ISBN 0 9525638 8 6

Trench, G Mackenzie
Metropolitan Police buildings. In: *Police journal* v2 (1929) p91-108, illus

Tyre, Neil
Eight Area Clubs and Vice Unit: a brief history. npl: The author, 1992
40p, illus

Watson, Neil
The history of Pinner Police Station. In: *Pinner Local History Society bulletin* n88 (Summer 2002) p19-23, illus

Metropolitan - HQ departments
Bunker, John
From rattle to radio. Studley: Brewin Books, 1988
viii,272p, illus. 21cm. ISBN 0 947731 28 8. On communications

Fairfax, Norman
From quills to computers: the history of the Metropolitan Police Civil Staff, 1829-1979. [London: The author?, 1980]
158p. 21cm

Fairfax, Norman
A room in Bow Street: the story of the Metropolitan Police Historical Museum. In: *The Peeler* issue 2 (1997) p5-7, illus

Fleming, W
A history of Metropolitan Police transport and driver training. [Hendon: Metropolitan Police Driving School, 196-]
40p, illus. 21cm.

Forester, Chris (ed)
The Mounted Branch: 150 years: a souvenir. [npub: 1986]
64p, illus. Cover title: *Metropolitan Police Mounted Branch: 150th anniversary souvenir*

Gould, Robert W *and* Waldren, Michael J
London's armed police: 1829 to the present. Arms and Armour Press, 1986
222p, illus. 24cm. ISBN 0 85368 880 X

Morris, R M
The Metropolitan Police Receiver in the XIXth century. In: *Police journal*
v47 (1974) p65-74. The Receiver was the chief financial officer for the
force

Paul, Philip
*Murder under the microscope: the story of Scotland Yard's Forensic
Science Laboratory*. London: Macdonald, 1990
368p, illus. 23cm. ISBN 0 356 17902 8
Pbk: London: Futura, 1990
368p, illus. 21cm. ISBN 0 7088 4767 6

Reynolds, John
*The Receiver for the Metropolitan Police District: a short history 1829-
2000*. [London: Metropolitan Police?, 2000]
[2],22p, illus. 30cm

Rivers, K
History of the Traffic Department of the Metropolitan Police. [London?:
npub, 1972]
[4],63p, illus. 25cm

Thomas, O V
The Metropolitan Police Motor Driving School. In: *Police journal* v32 n1
(Jan-Mar 1959) p53-59

Waldren, Michael J
Armed police: the police use of firearms since 1945. Stroud: Sutton, 2007.
xvi, 240p, illus. 24cm. ISBN 978-0750946377

Williams, Paul
A room in Brixton: continuing the story of the Museum. In: *The Peeler* issue
3 (1998) p28-30, illus

Metropolitan - Special Constabulary
Beddington, R
F Division Metropolitan Special Constabulary: a record of three years'

work August 1914-August 1917. [London]: Electric Law Press, 1917

Hadaway, D J
London specials under fire. In: *Police review* (9 Jan 1987) p71-2, illus.
Deals with World War 1

Metropolitan Special Constabulary
Metropolitan Special Constabulary: an illustrated history from 1831 to today. London: The Constabulary, [1989]. 32p, illus. 21cm

Metropolitan Special Constabulary. S Division. Portland Town Sub-Division
The Great War 1914-18. London: Hudson and Kearns, 1919
47p, illus.

Muddock, J E Preston
All clear: a brief record of the London Special Constabulary, 1914-1919.
London: Everett, 1920
122p, illus. 26cm

Pitts, G W
Chronicles of the special Force of the Weald raised in the year 1914.
London: Metropolitan Special Constabulary, 1922
19p, illus. S Division. Wealdstone Sub-Division

Reay, W T
The Metropolitan Special Constabulary: the War force, the Reserve. In:
Police journal v1 (1928) p317-334, illus. Covers World War 1 and later developments

Reay, W T
The Specials: how they served London: the story of the Metropolitan Special Constabulary. London: Heinemann, 1920
xii,223p, illus. 19cm

Swaine, H C (ed)
Metropolitan Special Constabulary: (1914) Croydon Sub-Division, W Division. London: Roffey and Clarke, 1919
23p, illus

Thomson, Victor
Civilians of the King: being a history of the Metropolitan Special Constabulary in Chingford. London: Empire Printing and Publishing, [1919]
80p, illus. 28cm

Witty, Samuel W W
Assisting 1914-1919: some account of the work of the Wood Green Sub-Division of the Metropolitan Special Constabulary. npl: [The Author?], 1919
xii,82p, illus. 19cm

Mid-Anglia [Cambridgeshire]
Cambridgeshire Constabulary
History of the Mid-Anglia Constabulary. npl: The Constabulary, 1975
2p

Mid-Anglia – Departments, divisions etc
Cambridgeshire Constabulary
Police in Huntingdon 1820-1976. npl: The Constabulary, 1976
4p

Middlesbrough [Cleveland]
Lillie, William
The history of Middlesbrough: an illustration of the evolution of English industry. Middlesbrough: Middlesbrough County Borough Council, 1968.
xiv,492p, illus. 21cm. Inc chXXV: *The police and the fire brigade*, p320-334, illus

Middlesbrough County Borough Police
Middlesbrough Constabulary. [Middlesbrough: The Police, 1968]
3p. 33cm. Typescript

Taylor, David
Conquering the British Ballarat: the policing of Victorian Middlesbrough. In: *Journal of social history* v37 n3 (2004) p755-772

Taylor, David
Melbourne, Middlesbrough and morality: policing Victorian new towns in the old world and the new. In: *Social history* v31 n1 (2006) p15-38

Taylor, David
Policing the Victorian town: the development of the police in Middlesbrough c1840-1914. Basingstoke: Palgrave Macmillan, 2002
xv,237p. 23cm. ISBN 0 333 65239 8

Taylor, David
"A well-chosen effective body of men": the Middlesbrough Police Force 1841-1914. [Cleveland]: University of Teesside, 1995
52p. 21cm. (Teesside papers in north eastern history 6). ISBN 0 907350 48 7

Midland Railway [British Transport]
The proud men of the 'MR': the Midland Railway Police. In: *British Transport Police journal* (Autumn 1977) p8-9

Ministry of Defence
Barlow, H E
The history and development of the Ministry of Defence Police from the 17th century. [Wethersfield: Ministry of Defence Police?], nd
12p, illus. 30cm. Cover title: *Ministry of Defence Police then and now*

Barlow, H E *and* Murphy, Lionel
The history and development of the Ministry of Defence Police from the 17th century. [Wethersfield: Ministry of Defence Police?], 1997
12p, illus. 30cm. Cover title: *Ministry of Defence Police then and now*. Updated ed of previous item

Cumberland, Tom
Ministry of Defence Police: a short history. In: *Police world* (Winter 1978/79) p14, illus

Wynne, Harry
Badges and insignia of the Ministry of Defence Police and the former Departmental forces and their histories. [Sunderland: The author], 1996
[8],45p, illus. 30cm
Rev ed: [Sunderland]: Brinkburn Cottage, 1997
[8],50p, illus. 30cm

Ministry of Defence - Departments, divisions etc
Butland, Nigel A
1194-1990, HM Royal Dockyard to HM Naval Base, Portsmouth: the

history and role of the police 1686-1990. [Portsmouth: The author], 1990 46p, illus. 30cm. Inc *History of policing in the Dockyard,* p31-35

Pearse, Tom
Policing Chatham Naval Base. In: *Bygone Kent* v5 n3 (March 1984) p174-180, illus

Monmouthshire [Gwent]
Alderson, R
Monmouthshire: the County and its Constabulary. Abergavenny: Monmouthshire Constabulary, [1952]
19p, illus. 19cm

Baker, W H
The formation of the Monmouthshire Constabulary. In: *Monmouthshire Local History Council bulletin* n4 (1957) p5-6

Monmouthshire Archives Committee
Exhibition of records illustrating the growth of the Constabulary in Monmouthshire, held at County Hall Newport March 25th to April 6th 1957. Newport: The Committee, 1957
[24]p. 22cm

Monmouthshire Constabulary
Monmouthshire Constabulary centenary 1857-1957. Abergavenny: The Constabulary, 1957
47p

Montgomeryshire [Dyfed-Powys]
Lloyd, Humphrey C
Police centenary: address to the members of the Standing Joint Police Committee assembled at Community House, Newtown on 19th April 1940. npl: The Constabulary, 1940
3p. Typescript

Maddox, W C
A history of the Montgomeryshire Constabulary (1840-1948). Carmarthen: Printed by Dyfed-Powys Police, 1982
28p, illus. 30cm

Neath [South Wales]
Taylor, Glen A
History of Neath Borough Police Force. In: *Transactions Neath Antiquarian Society* 2nd ser v7 (1939) p12-17

Newbury [Thames Valley]
Godfrey, Richard
Newbury Borough Police 1836-1875. Newbury: The author, 2008
[14],144p, illus. 21cm. ISBN 978-0956092601

Newcastle-under-Lyme [Staffordshire]
Tunstall, Alf
The Borough men: the story of the Newcastle Borough Police. Leek: Churnet Valley Books, 1995
[4],133p, illus. 25cm. ISBN 1 897949 14 6

Tunstall, Alf
The Newcastle under Lyme Borough Police: a short history. In: *PICA magazine* (Spring 1979) p3-4, illus

Newcastle-upon-Tyne [Northumbria]
Evans, John
The Newcastle-upon-Tyne City Police 1836-1969. In: *Journal of the Police History Society* n3 (1988) p74-80, illus

Newcastle City Police
Newcastle City Police 1836-1969. Newcastle: The Police, 1969
[20]p, illus. 14cm

Newport [Gwent]
Bale, Islwyn
Through seven reigns: a history of the Newport Borough Police. Pontypool: Hughes and Son, [1959]
191p, illus. 25cm

Norfolk
Butcher, Brian David
"A movable rambling police": an official history of policing in Norfolk. Norwich: Norfolk Constabulary, 1989
x,122p, illus. 25cm

Slack, Frank D
The Norfolk Constabulary. [Norwich: Norfolk Constabulary, 1967]
23p, illus. 22cm

Norfolk - Departments, divisions etc
Mason, John
The Norfolk and Norwich river police. In: *Journal of the Police History Society* n13 (1998) p12-15, illus

Neville, David
Whatever happened to old Bill? Harleston: Harleston Heritage Group, 2005
[2],38p, illus. 21cm. ISBN 0 9547372 3 7. An account of policing in Harleston and a short history of the Norfolk Constabulary [cover]

North Eastern Railway [British Transport]
Deacon, B
The North Eastern Railway Police. In: *PICA magazine* (Winter 1976) p11-13

North Riding of Yorkshire [North Yorkshire]
North Riding of Yorkshire Constabulary
1856-1956: the first hundred years of the North Riding of Yorkshire Constabulary. [Northallerton: The Constabulary, 1956]
48p, illus. 23cm
Reissued: [Malton]: KPD Services, 2004
48p, illus. 21cm. ISBN 0 9549339 0 7

North Wales
Birch, H Kenneth
The history of policing in North Wales. Pwllheli: Llygad Gwalch Cyf, 2008
383p, illus. 22cm. ISBN 978-1845240714

North Wales Police
Hanes plismona yng Ngogledd Cymru [*History of policing in North Wales*].
[Colwyn Bay]: North Wales Police, 1991
9p. 21cm. Text in Welsh

North Yorkshire
Milburn, M D
North Yorkshire Police. [Northallerton: The Police], 1987
5p. 30cm. Typescript

North Yorkshire - Departments, divisions etc
East, G C
The constables of Claro. Harrogate: The author, 1996
204p, illus. 20cm. ISBN 0 9529067 0 8. Covers Harrogate

North Yorkshire Police
Open day Divisional Police Headquarters, Fulford Road, York Saturday 3rd May 1986 to celebrate 150 years of policing in York. [Northallerton: The Police, 1986]
16p, illus. 16cm

Whitehead, John
Policing at Ripon. Ripon: Ripon Museum Trust, 2000
12p, illus. (Court House booklet 5)

Northampton [Northamptonshire]
A short history of Northampton Borough Police Force. [Northampton]: Northampton Borough Council, 1990
[20]p, illus. 21cm. Text taken largely from the 1950 and 1966 histories

Northampton County Borough Police
Police Department 1836-1966, (including Chief Constable's annual report...for the year ended 31st December 1965). [Northampton: The Police, 1966]
90p, illus. 25cm. Revised reprint of Williamson, John. *History of the Northampton Borough Police*

Williamson, John
A history of the Northampton Borough Police. [Northampton: The Police], 1950
[4],42p, illus. 22cm. Cover title: *A souvenir of service: a history of the Northampton Borough Police*

Northamptonshire
Cowley, Richard
Guilty m'Lud! the criminal history of Northamptonshire. Kettering: Peg and Whistle Books, 1998
xii,200p. illus. 26cm. ISBN 0 9534095 0 3. Inc *When constabulary duty's to be done: the policing of Northamptonshire* p92-116

Cowley, Richard
A history of the Northamptonshire Police. Stroud: Sutton, 2008
128p, illus. 24cm. ISBN 978-0750949569

Cowley, Richard
Policing Northamptonshire 1836-1986. Studley: Brewin Books, 1986
viii,237p, illus. 21cm. ISBN 0 947731 21 0

Warwick, Lou
Police: old and new. In: *Northampton and County independent* (March 1978) p49-59

Northern Ireland
Trotter, Sam
Constabulary heroes 1826-2009: incorporating the RUC GC/PSNI.
Ballycastle: Impact, [2010?]
xx,487p, illus. ISBN 978-1906689223

Northumberland [Northumbria]
Northumberland County Constabulary
Northumberland County Constabulary 1957-1969. Morpeth: The Constabulary, [ca1969]
51p, illus. 22cm

Northumberland County Constabulary
Northumberland County Constabulary 1857-1957. Morpeth: The Constabulary, [1957]
79p, illus. 22cm. Private circulation

Northumbria
Banks, Ken and Wynne, Harry
Badges, insignia and uniforms of the North Eastern police forces v2: Berwick, Newcastle upon Tyne, Northumberland, Northumbria, Tynemouth.
[Sunderland]: Brinkburn Cottage, 2004
iii,46-83p, illus. 30cm

Moffatt, Frederick C
Constable: a history of Northumbria Police. npl: The author, [ca1991]
94p, illus

Northumbria Police
Northumbria Police 1974-1984. [Ponteland: The Police, 1984]
12p, illus. 21cm

Norwich [Norfolk]
Morson, Maurice
*A force remembered: the illustrated history of the Norwich City Police
1836-1967.* Derby: Breedon Books, 2000
187p, illus. 26cm. ISBN 1 85983 190 7

Nottingham [Nottinghamshire]
Everitt, Geoffrey G
Development of law and order in Nottingham. npl: The author, 1971
40p

Hyndman, David
Nottingham City Police: a pictorial history 1930-1960. [Nottingham: The
author, 197-?]
78p, illus. 30cm
Nottingham City Police: a pictorial history 1960-1968. [Nottingham: The
author, 197-?]
95p, illus. 30cm

Iliffe, Richard *and* Baguley, Wilfred
*Victorian Nottingham: a story in pictures. v19 [Police; Courts and prisons
1837-1901].* Nottingham: Nottingham Historical Film Unit, 1979
99p, illus. 29cm. Inc *The Police*, p5-49

Nottingham Constabulary
Nottingham City Police 1836-1968. npl: The Constabulary, 1967

Popkess, Athelstan
*The archaeologist and the policing of Nottingham: reprint of papers read to
members of the Thoroton Society of Nottinghamshire on 21st April 1945....*
[Nottingham: Nottingham City Police], 1945
[26]p, illus. 22cm

Nottinghamshire
Fry, Terry
The Nottinghamshire Constabulary in the nineteenth cenutry. In:
Nottinghamshire historian v55 (1995) p11-15

Nottinghamshire Constabulary
History of the Nottinghamshire Constabulary. Epperstone: The Constabulary, 1967
10p. 33cm. Typescript

Nottinghamshire Constabulary
Nottinghamshire Combined Constabulary: a historical note. The Constabulary, nd
8p

Nottinghamshire Constabulary
150 years of the British police. [Nottingham]: The Constabulary, 1979
20p, illus. 30cm
Mainly a history of Nottinghamshire Police

Withers, Bill
Nottinghamshire Constabulary: 150 years in photographs. Huddersfield: Quoin, 1989
[96p], illus. 28cm. ISBN 1 85563 008 7

Nottinghamshire - Departments, divisions etc
Jarvis, Malcolm
The history of Stapleford Police. [Ilkeston: The author], 1996
x,195p, illus. 30cm

Oldham [Greater Manchester]
Taylor, Denis R
999 and all that: the story of Oldham County Borough Police Force formed on November 14 1849.... Oldham: Oldham Corporation, 1968
206p, illus. 19cm

Winstanley, Michael
Preventive policing in Oldham c1826-56. [Manchester]: Lancashire and Cheshire Antiquarian Society, 1990
[20p]. 22cm. Reprint from *Transactions of Lancashire and Cheshire Antiquarian Society* v86 (1990)

Oxford [Thames Valley]
Rose, Geoffrey
Pictorial history of the Oxford City Police, or, From Peelers to pandas. Oxford: Oxford Publishing, 1979

iv,100p, illus. 28cm. ISBN 0 86093 094 7

Oxfordshire [Thames Valley]
Oxfordshire Constabulary
Oxfordshire Constabulary: centenary 1857-1957. [Kidlington: The Constabulary, 1957]
40p, illus. 25cm

Pembrokeshire [Dyfed-Powys]
Jones, R W
History of the Pembrokeshire Police Force. Caernarvon: Gwenlyn Evans, [1957]
55p, illus. 22cm

Jones, R Winston
History of the Pembrokeshire Police Force. In: *Police College magazine* v2 n2 (Mar 1952) p121-124

Perth and Kinross
Macfarlane, Willie
The history of the Perthshire and Kinross-shire Constabularies. Perth: Perth and Kinross Libraries, 2011
viii, 71p, illus. 28cm. ISBN 978-0905452609

Peterborough [Cambridgeshire]
Peterborough Combined Police Force
Commemorating 100 years of service of the Peterborough Police 1857-1957 and the official opening of the new police headquarters...23rd May 1957. [Peterborough: The Force, 1957]
32p, illus. 25cm

Plymouth [Devon and Cornwall]
Dickaty, Ernest
From rattles to radio: a history of the Plymouth City Police Force. [Plymouth?: The author], 1977
238,vp. 30cm? Unpublished typescript

Lilley, Phil
Plymouth: policing a city: history of the Plymouth Police force 1850-1967. Plymouth: Aarchive Film, [1996?]
VHS video (col and b&w). 60mins. Also available as DVD

Pontefract [West Yorkshire]
Jackson, Colin
History of the Pontefract Borough Police. Wakefield: Sybil M Jackson, 1984
viii,42p, illus. 21cm

Port of Liverpool
[Marriott, Steve]
A force is born: the Port of Liverpool Police. In: *PICA magazine* (Spring 1978) p6-7

Port of London [Port of Tilbury]
The Port of London Authority Police. In: *PICA magazine* (Spring 1977) p17-22, illus

Bazzone, Alan T
East End dock police. In: *Cockney ancestor* v31 (1986) p2-4

Hardwicke, Glyn
Keepers of the door: the history of the Port of London Authority Police. London: Peel Press for the PLA Police, [1979]
vi,157p, illus. 22cm. ISBN 0 85164 999 8

Portsmouth [Hampshire]
Cramer, James
A history of the police of Portsmouth: the story of the constables, tythingmen, watchmen and other peace officers of the Portsmouth area from c1241 to 1967. Portsmouth: Portsmouth City Council, 1967
22p, illus. 25cm. (Portsmouth papers 2)

Preston [Lancashire]
Preston County Borough Police
Anniversary exhibition 1815-1965: [catalogue of] an exhibition to commemorate the 150th anniversary of the Preston Borough Police Force. Preston: The Police, 1965]
[12]p, illus. 22cm. Inc Lightfoot, L. *History of the police service in Preston*

Rae, Tony
Preston Police: the first force. In: *Lancashire Constabulary journal* (Winter 1993) p8-10, illus

Radnorshire [Dyfed-Powys]
Maddox, Wilfred Charles
A history of the Radnorshire Constabulary. Llandrindod Wells: Radnorshire
Society, 1959
[vi],85p, illus. 23cm
Reissued: Llandrindod Wells: Radnorshire Society, 1981
[vi],85p, illus. 21cm

Ramsgate [Kent]
Bishop, W H
Ramsgate Borough Police Force. In: *Bygone Kent* v13 n10 (Oct 1992)
p576-583, illus

Reading [Thames Valley]
Tucker, Roger
Reading Borough Police. In: *PICA magazine* (Summer 1984) p3-4, illus

Wykes, Alan
The Queen's peace: a history of the Reading Borough Police 1836-1968.
Reading: Reading Corporation, 1968
44p, illus. 23cm

Reigate [Surrey]
Brown, Bernard
The Reigate Police. In: *Journal of the Police History Society* n4 (1989) p69-
71

Ford, Richard
The history of the Reigate Borough Police Force 1864-1947. npl: The
author, 1973. 20p. 21cm

Ripon [North Yorkshire]
Chadwick, Anthony
Ripon Liberty: law and order over the last 300 years. [Ripon]: Ripon
Museum Trust, 1986
60p, illus. 21cm. Inc *The police*, p37-39

River Wear [Northumbria]
Mearns, Neil
*Sentinels of the Wear: the River Wear Watch: a history of Sunderland's
river police and fireboats.* Sunderland: Mearns, 1998

183p. illus. 30cm. ISBN 0 9533377 0 7

Rochdale [Greater Manchester]
Waller, Stanley
Cuffs and handcuffs: the story of Rochdale Police through the years 1252-1957. Rochdale: Rochdale Watch Committee, 1957
[x],141p, illus. 23cm

Waller, Stanley.
One hundred years' protection. In: *Transactions of the Rochdale Literary and Scientific Society* v24 (1950-60) p20-29

Rochester - Departments, divisions etc [Kent]
Gallagher, D F
Policing the Medway. In: *Bygone Kent* v2 no10 (Oct 1981) p615-620, illus

Rotherham [South Yorkshire]
Weston, Peter
Rotherham Borough Police. In: *PICA magazine* (Spring 1984) p5-7, illus

Royal Air Force
75 years of the Royal Air Force Police 1918-1993. Fairford: RAF Benevolent Fund Enterprises, [1993?]
24p, illus. 30cm. Special issue of *Provost parade*

Davies, Stephen R
Fiat justitia: a history of the Royal Air Force Police. London: Minerva, 1997
255p, illus. 21cm. ISBN 1 86106 378 4

Davies, Stephen R
RAF Police: Cape Town to Kabul 1918-2006. Bognor Regis: Woodfield, [2007]
254p, illus. 29cm. ISBN 1 84683 033 8

Davies, Stephen R
RAF Police: operations in Europe 1918-2005. Bognor Regis: Woodfield, 2006
270p, illus. 29cm. ISBN 1 84683 019 2

Davies, Stephen R
RAF Police dogs on patrol. Bognor Regis: Woodfield, 2005
298p, illus. 25cm. ISBN 1 84683 000 1

Hennessey, Patrick
The story of the Royal Air Force Police. [The author?, 1992-5?]
150p, illus. No further details traced

Royal Irish [Northern Ireland and Garda Siochana]
Tales of the R I C. Edinburgh: Blackwood, 1921
[5],314p. 20cm

Bennett, Richard
The Black and Tans. London: Hulton, 1959
228p, illus. 22cm
Pbk: London: Four Square, 1961
192p. 18cm
Reissue of pbk: London: New English Library, 1970
192p. 18cm. ISBN 0 450 00513 5

Brewer, John D
Royal Irish Constabulary: an oral history. Belfast: Inst of Irish Studies, 1990
viii,138p. ISBN 0 85389 340 3

Brophy, Michael
Tales of the Royal Irish Constabulary. v1. Dublin: Bernard Doyle, 1896
xx,192p. No more volumes published

Curtis, Robert
The history of the Royal Irish Constabulary. Simpkin, 1869
2nd ed: Simpkin, 1871
xiv,195p

Fennell, Thomas
The Royal Irish Constabulary: a history and personal memoir. Dublin: University College Dublin Press, 2003
xiv,180p, illus. 19cm. (Classics of Irish history). ISBN 1 904558 00 3

Herlihy, Jim
The Royal Irish Constabulary: a complete alphabetical list of officers and

men 1816-1922. Dublin: Four Courts Press, 1999
xxxi,488p. 25cm. ISBN 1 85182 502 9

Herlihy, Jim
The Royal Irish Constabulary: a short history and genealogical guide with a select list of medal awards and casualties. Dublin: Four Courts Press, 1997
254p, illus. 24cm. ISBN 1 85182 337 9. Pbk ISBN 1 85182 343 3

Herlihy, Jim
Royal Irish Constabulary officers: a biographical and genealogical guide 1816-1922. Dublin: Four Courts Press, 2005
366p, illus. 24cm. ISBN 1 85182 826 5

Leatham, Charles Western
Sketches and stories of the Royal Irish Constabulary. Dublin: Ponsonby, 1909
21p

Malcolm, Elizabeth
The Irish policeman, 1822-1922: a life. Dublin: Four Courts, 2006
266p, illus. 24cm. ISBN 978-1851829200. A "collective biography" of life in the force

O'Sullivan, Donal J
The Depot: the history of the Garda Siochana depot at Phoenix Park, Dublin 8. [Co Kerry]: Navillus, 2007
230p, illus. 21cm. ISBN 978-0955563300

O'Sullivan, Donal
The Irish constabularies 1822-1922: a century of policing in Ireland. Dingle: Brandon, 1999
416p, illus. 25cm. ISBN 086322 257 9

Royal Irish - Departments, divisions etc
Byrne, Brendan
Law, order and the RIC in Waterford 1920-21: a chronology. In: *Decies: journal of the Waterford Archaeological and Historical Society* v55 (1999) p117-126

Desmond, Liam
With the Constabulary in Roscommon. [Ireland]: Annscourt Press, [199?]
70p, illus. 21cm

Desmond, Liam
With the Constabulary in Waterford.
?p, illus. 21cm. No futher details traced

O'Donnell, Stephen
The Royal Irish Constabulary and the Black and Tans in County Louth 1919-1922. [Ireland]: The author, 2004
233p, illus. 22cm. ISBN 0 9547038 0 4

O'Herlihy, Jim
Policing in Blarney: the early years. In: *Old Blarney* v6 (2002) p31-47, illus

Royal Military
Bullock, Humphry
A history of the Provost Marshal and the Provost Service. Aberdeen: Milne and Hutchison, 1929
[5],71p. 18cm

Chappell, Mike
Redcaps: Britain's provost troops and military police. London: Osprey, 1997
64p, illus. 25cm. ISBN 1 85532 670 1

Crozier, S F
The history of the Corps of Royal Military Police. Aldershot: Gale and Polden, 1951
xvi,224p, illus, fold maps. 23cm

Lovell-Knight, A V
The history of the office of the Provost Marshal and the Corps of Military Police. Aldershot: Gale and Polden, 1943
x,174p. 19cm

Lovell-Knight, A V
The story of the Royal Military Police. London: Leo Cooper, 1977
xxi, 360p, illus. 24cm. ISBN 0 85052 222 6

Sheffield, G D
The Redcaps: a history of the Royal Military Police and its antecedents from the Middle Ages to the Gulf War. London: Brassey's, 1994
xvi,263p, illus. 25cm. ISBN 1 85753 029 2

Turnbull, J D
The Ulster watchdogs (1969-1974). Aldergrove: The author, 1975
95p, illus. 21cm
The Ulster watchdogs: Part 2 (1974-1984). [Marple: The author?], 1984
120p, illus. 21cm.

Tyler, R A J
Bloody Provost: an account of the Provost Service of the British Army and the early years of the Corps of Royal Military Police. Chichester: Phillimore, 1980
[10],246p, illus. 23cm. ISBN 0 85033 359 8

Whistler, R J R
The Corps of Royal Military Police: a short history. 2nd rev ed. Leeds: Templar Press, 1963
16p. A summary of Lovell-Knight's 1943 history

Wickes, H L
The Corps of Royal Military Police. In: *Police review* (15 Feb 1980) p306-307

Royal Military - Departments, divisions etc
Boyes, Robert
In glasshouses: a history of the Military Provost Staff Corps. Colchester: Military Provost Staff Corps Association, 1988
x,323p, illus. 22cm. ISBN 0 9513467 0

Phillips, Norman
Guns, drugs and deserters: the Special Investigation Branch in the Middle East. London: Werner Laurie, [1954]
176p

Turnbull, Jack *and* Hamblett, John
The Pegasus patrol: the history of the 1st Airborne Division Provost Company, Corps of Military Police 1942-1945. [Marple]: The author, 1994
200p, illus. 21cm. ISBN 0 9523261 0 8

Royal Ulster [Northern Ireland]
Breathnach, Seamus
The Irish police: from earliest times to the present day. Dublin, Anvil
Books, 1974
230p. 17cm. Inc *The Royal Ulster Constabulary*, p96-115

Cameron, Margaret
*The women in green: a history of the Royal Ulster Constabulary's
policewomen: Golden Jubilee 1943-1993*. Belfast: RUC Historical Society,
1993
120p, illus. 21cm. ISBN 0 948154 75 6

Doherty, Richard
*The thin green line: a history of the Royal Ulster Constabulary GC 1922-
2001*. Barnsley: Pen and Sword, 2004
x,310p, illus. 24cm. ISBN 1 84415 058 5

Ellison, Graham *and* Smyth, Jim
The crowned harp: policing Northern Ireland. London: Pluto, 2000
xix,218p. 23cm. (Contemporary Irish studies). ISBN 0 7453 1398 1
Pbk: 22cm. ISBN 0 7453 1393 0

Griffin, B
A force divided: policing Ireland 1900-60. In: *History today* v49(10) (Oct
1999) p25-31, illus

Hadfield, Brigid (ed)
Northern Ireland: politics and the constitution. Buckingham: Open UP,
1992
xv,183p. 23cm. ISBN 0 335 09963 7. Pbk ISBN 0 335 09962 9. Inc Guelke,
Adrian. *Policing in Northern Ireland*, p94-109

Nagle, John and Kelly, Liam
*We remember: memories of service with the Royal Ulster Constabulary GC
1922 to 1970*. Belfast: RUC GC Foundation, 2010
101p, illus. 21cm. ISBN 978-0955284526. Inc a brief history of the force
1922-69, p9-19

Royal Ulster Constabulary Museum
The Royal Ulster Constabulary Museum: a guide to the collection.
[Belfast]: RUC Historical Society, 1995

[1],40p, illus. 30cm

Ryder, Chris
The fateful split: Catholics and the Royal Ulster Constabulary. London:
Methuen, 2004
xxiii,359p, illus. 24cm. ISBN 0 413 77222 5
Pbk: London: Methuen, 2004. 360p, illus. ISBN 0 413 77223 3

Ryder, Chris
The R U C: a force under fire. London: Methuen, 1989
xvi,381p, illus. 25cm. ISBN 0 413 15340 1
Pbk: London: Mandarin, 1990
xiv,383p, illus. 18cm. ISBN 0 7493 0285 2
Rev ed: London: Mandarin, 1992
xiv,419p, illus. 18cm. ISBN 0 7493 1205 X
[3rd] rev ed: London: Mandarin, 1997
xiv,490p, illus. 20cm. ISBN 0 7493 2379 5
[4th] rev ed: The R U C 1922-2000: a force under fire. London: Arrow,
2000
xviii,536p, illus. 20cm. ISBN 0 09 941099 0

Sinclair, R J K *and* Scully, F J M
Arresting memories: captured moments in Constabulary life. [Belfast]:
RUC Diamond Jubilee Committee, 1982
[137]p, illus. 18x23cm

Royal Ulster - Departments, divisions etc
Dunne, David
Armoured and heavy vehicles of the Royal Ulster Constabulary 1922-2001.
Hersham: Ian Allan, 2007
160p, illus. 28cm. ISBN 978-0711031609. Inc a brief history of the force

Macquigg, J Claude
*A forgotten chapter: history of the Royal Ulster Constabulary Cadet Corps
1970-1986*. [Belfast: Graham and Heslip, 2006]
[1],ii,[1],59p, illus. 30cm

Royal Ulster - Special Constabulary
Clark, Wallace
Guns in Ulster. Belfast: Constabulary Gazette, 1967
127p, illus. 19cm

2nd ed: Upperlands: The author, 2002
152p, illus. ISBN 0 9509042 1 X

Dane, Mervyn
The Fermanagh B Specials. Enniskillen: Wm Trimble, 1970
40p, illus. 25cm
Farrell, Michael
Arming the protestants: the formation of the Ulster Special Constabulary and the Royal Ulster Constabulary 1920-7. London: Pluto, 1983
viii,374p. 20cm. ISBN 0 86104 705 2

Hezlet, *Sir* Arthur
The B Specials: a history of the Ulster Special Constabulary. London: Stacey, 1972
[10],246,[16]p, illus. 24cm. ISBN 0 85468 272 4
Pbk: London: Pan, 1973
xvii,267,[16]p, illus. 18cm. ISBN 0 330 23789 6
Reissued: Belfast: Mourne River Press, 1997
[10],246,[16]p, illus. 20cm. ISBN 1 902090 00 4

Marshall, David
The protected years: a pictorial history of Omagh District Ulster Special Constabulary. Omagh: [printed by] Grahams Printers, 2000
112p, illus. 24cm
The protected years v2: history of Clogher District Ulster Special Constabulary. Omagh: [printed by] Grahams Printers, 2004
[3],232p, illus. 24cm

Morgan, Austen *and* Purdie, Bob (eds)
Ireland: divided nation, divided class. London: Ink Links, 1980
225p. ISBN 0 906133 20 3. Inc Farrell, Michael. *The establishment of the Ulster Special Constabulary*, p125-137

Williams, Peter
The rise and fall of the B Specials. In: *Journal of the Police History Society* n23 (2008) p4-7, illus

Rutland [Leicestershire]
Bailey, Keith
Rutland Constabulary 1848-1951. In: *PICA magazine* (Summer 1982) p3-6, illus

Rutland Local History Society
Services of Rutland: the police of Rutland to 1951.... Oakham: The Society,
1978
111p, illus. 26cm. Pages 1-39 cover the police
Pbk: Soldiers, police and firemen of Rutland. Stamford: Spiegl Press, 1990
111p, illus. 25cm. Reprint of 1978 ed

Stanley, Clifford R
*A different badge: the story of Rutland's police force, England's smallest
county constabulary 1848-1951.* In: *Leicester topic* (July 1974) p41-43

Stanley, Clifford R
Tribute to the Rutland Constabulary 1848-1951. In: *Tally Ho!* (Summer
1968) p7-31

Saffron Walden [Essex]
Rowntree, C B
Saffron Walden, then and now. [Saffron Walden: The author?, 1952]
viii,107p, illus. 21cm. Inc ch11 *Walden Police Force* p75-79

Salisbury [Wiltshire]
Wiltshire Constabulary
History of Salisbury City (Sarum) Police Force. npl: The Constabulary,
1974
2p

Scottish North Eastern Counties [Grampian]
Scottish North Eastern Counties Constabulary
Scottish North East [sic] *Counties Constabulary history: silver jubilee
brochure.* Aberdeen: The Constabulary, [ca1975]
77p, illus. 30cm

Sheffield [South Yorkshire]
Morris, Robert John *and* Trainor, Richard H (eds)
Urban governance: Britain and beyond since 1750. Aldershot: Ashgate,
2000
xiv,254p. 24cm. ISBN 0 7546 0015 2. Inc Williams, Chris. *Expediency,
authority and duplicity: reforming Sheffield's police 1832-40,* p115-127

Shropshire [West Mercia]
Durrell, John *and* Roberts, Victor H

Shropshire Constabulary: the first hundred years 1839-1939. Shrewsbury: The Constabulary, 1963
35p. 25cm. Typescript

Elliott, Douglas J
Policing Shropshire 1836-1967. Studley: Brewin Books, 1984
xii,260,[10]p, illus. 22cm. ISBN 0 947731 00 8. Pbk ISBN 0 947731 01 6

Somerset [Avon and Somerset]
Leach, David E (ed)
A brief history of the Somersetshire Constabulary: 1st September, 1856 to 31st December, 1966. Portishead: Avon and Somerset Constabulary, 2008
40p, illus. 21cm

Somerset Constabulary
History of the Force 1856-1956. [Taunton: The Constabulary, 1956]
[3],48p, illus. 25cm

South Shields [Durham]
History beat! In: *Banks of the Tyne* n4 (1996) p4-7, illus

Banks, Kenneth B *and* Wynne, Harry
Badges, insignia and uniforms of the North Eastern police forces v3: Gateshead, South Shields, Sunderland, [Sunderland]: Brinkburn Cottage, 2009
iii,83-124p, illus. 30cm

Barnes, T
History of the County Borough of South Shields Police. npl: The author, 1968
39p

South Wales
Jones, David J V
Crime and policing in the twentieth century: the South Wales experience. Cardiff: University of Wales Press, 1996
xvi,328p, illus. 22cm. ISBN 0 7083 1366 3

South Wales - Departments, divisions etc
Harris, David
History of the police in Ogmore Vale (1840-2004). In: *Ogmore Valley Local*

History and Heritage Society journal 5 (Dec 2004) p30-33, illus

Westcott, Gordon
A century on the rugby beat: a history of 100 years of police rugby football in the South Wales Constabulary area. [Bridgend]: South Wales Police Rugby Football Club, 1992
xii, 212p, illus. 21cm

South Yorkshire
South Yorkshire Police
Policing and the community: a brief history of policing and its role in society. [Sheffield: The Police, 198-?]
4p, illus. 30cm

Southampton [Hampshire]
Cooke, Anne
S*outhampton police force 1836-1856.* Southampton: City of Southampton, 1972
48p, illus. 25cm. (Southampton papers 8)

Cullen, Alfred Thomas
A history of Southampton City Police 1836-1967. [Southampton: The Police, 1967]
[52]p, illus. 22cm

Southend-on-Sea [Essex]
Essex Police Museum
The Borough men: the police in Southend-on-Sea 1840-1969. [Chelmsford: The Museum, 1992]
23p, illus. 30cm

Williams, B H *and* Doxsey, P
A brief history of the Southend-on-Sea County Borough Constabulary on the occasion of its Golden Jubilee 1914-1964. [Southend: The Constabulary, 1964]
viii,32p, illus. 24cm. Cover title: *1914-1964: Golden jubilee: Southend-on-Sea Constabulary*

Southport [Merseyside]
Darwin, Charles A
Southport County Borough Police 1870-1969. [Southport: Lancashire

Constabulary, 1969]
132p, illus. 25cm. Private circulation

Staffordshire
Staffordshire Police
Staffordshire Police: 150 years of service 1842-1992: commemorative issue. Stafford: The Police, [1992]
44p, illus. 30cm. Cover title

Staffordshire. Education Department
Police in Staffordshire. [Stafford]: The Department, 1974
[1],37leaves, illus. 30cm. ISBN 0 85604 030 4

Stoke-on-Trent [Staffordshire]
Tunstall, Alf *and* Cowdell, Jeff
Policing the Potteries. Leek: TCP Books, 2002
248p, illus. 24cm. ISBN 0 9535239 9 3

Strathclyde
Kenna, Rudolph *and* Sutherland, Ian
In custody: a companion to Strathclyde Police Museum. Glasgow: Strathclyde Police [and] Clutha Books, 1998
[3],96p, illus. 21cm. ISBN 0 952947 13 7

Suffolk
Jacobs, Leslie C
Constables of Suffolk: a brief history of policing in the County. [Ipswich]: Suffolk Constabulary, 1992
99p, illus. 27cm

Prescott, Catherine
The Suffolk Constabulary in the 19th century. In: *Proceedings of the Suffolk Institute of Archaeology* vXXXI pt1 (1967) p1-46, illus

Spencer, H
In days of yore. In: *Constables county* v1 n7 (Autumn 1970) p19-29

Wheeler, J D
Administration of Suffolk and the police. In: *Justice of the peace* v131 (1967) p438-439

Sunderland [Northumbria]
Banks, Kenneth B *and* Wynne, Harry
*Badges, insignia and uniforms of the North Eastern police forces v3:
Gateshead, South Shields, Sunderland,* [Sunderland]: Brinkburn Cottage.
2009
iii,83-124p, illus. 30cm

Conlin, John
History of Sunderland Borough Police. Sunderland: James A Jobling, 1967
96p, illus. 26cm. Private circulation to retired members

Yearnshire, John
*Back on the Borough beat: a brief illustrated history of Sunderland
Borough Police Force.* [Sunderland]: The author, 1987
104p, illus. 20x21cm

Surrey
Durrant, A J
A short centenary history of the Surrey Constabulary 1851-1951.
[Guildford: The Constabulary, 1951]
viii,85p, illus. 23cm. Cover title: *1851-1951: a hundred years of the Surrey
Constabulary*

Ford, R
A guide to the Surrey Constabulary. [Guildford: The Constabulary, *ca*1967]
17p. 19cm

Middleton-Stewart, Geraldine
Surrey Police: a pictorial history 1851-2001. [Guildford, The Police, 2001]
viii,117p, illus. 21x30cm

Middleton-Stewart, Geraldine
*Surrey Police Headquarters 50th anniversary: Mount Browne, Sandy Lane,
Guildford.* [Guildford, The Police, 1999]
39p, illus. 21cm. Cover title: *Mount Browne 50th anniversary 1949-1999*

Sussex
Cook, W Victor
Under the blue helmet in Sussex. In: *Sussex county magazine* (Jan 1946) p6-
9. Covers World War 2

Old Police Cells Museum Society
Policing papers: a selection of documents and histories of policing in Sussex from the Museum's collection. Brighton: The Society, 2009. CD. 43 facsimile documents in pdf format

Poulsom, Neville, Rumble, Mike *and* Smith, Keith
Sussex police forces. Midhurst: Middleton Press, 1987
[152]p, illus. 25cm. ISBN 0 906520 43 6

Sussex - Departments, divisions etc
Lloyd, David *and* Foster, Geoff
Lewes police: a brief history. [Lewes: Sussex Police, 1994]
[10]p, illus. 21cm

Stoner, Peter (comp)
The police in Lewes: a look at some of the more light hearted moments and other reminiscences of the police in Lewes during the second half of the 20th century. Eastbourne: Peter Stoner, 2004
213p, illus. 21cm

Sussex Combined - Departments, divisions etc [Sussex]
Seymour, Victoria
Court in the act: crime and policing in WWII Hastings. [Hastings]: The author, 2004
vi,152p, illus. ISBN 0 9543901 2 1

Sutherland [Northern]
Conner, Dave
Sutherland Constabulary 1850-1963. In: *PICA magazine* (Summer 1985) p21-24, illus

Swansea [South Wales]
Hunt, Walter William
"To guard my people": an account of the origin and history of the Swansea Police. [Swansea: Swansea County Borough Police], 1957
107p, illus. 22cm

Thames Valley
Thames Valley Police
The history of the Thames Valley Police. [Sulhampstead]: The Police, 2004
19p, illus. 21cm

Thames Valley Police
The history of Thames Valley Police. [Sulhampstead: The Police], 2006.
DVD 36min
Contents: 1. *Policing in the Thames Valley.* 2. Reading Borough Police. *The police force* [Educational documentary *ca*1950s]

Thames Valley - Departments, divisions etc
Shaw, Mick
Over 100 years of Hanslope and Castlethorpe village policemen. Milton Keynes: Shaw, [2000?]
92p, illus. 25cm. ISBN 0 9538144 0 8

Tiverton [Devon and Cornwall]
Denyer, Vic
Tiverton Constabulary. In: *PICA magazine* (Winter 1985) p11-13, illus

Trevethin [Gwent]
Babbidge, Adrian
The development of the Constabulary in the Eastern Valley 1830-1890. In: *Gwent Local History* n57 (Autumn 1984) p30-36

Tynemouth [Northumbria]
Fairless, Robert
A brief history of the County Borough of Tynemouth Police 1850-1969. [North Shields: The Police, 1969]
60p, illus. 25cm

Ulverston [Cumbria]
Marsh, J
Policing Ulverston in the 1830s. In: *Police journal* v39 (1966) p287-291

Wakefield [West Yorkshire]
Jackson, Colin
Wakefield City Police 1848-1968. In: *PICA magazine* (Spring 1979) p7-9, illus

Jackson, Colin
Wakefield Constabulary: a history of the borough and city police force 1848-1968. Wakefield: Sybil M Jackson, 1983
xx,127p, illus. 21cm

Wakefield City Police
Brief history of the Wakefield City Police. [Wakefield]: The Police, 1967
7p

Wallasey [Merseyside]
Wallasey County Borough Police
Souvenir handbook to celebrate the golden jubilee of the County Borough of Wallasey Police 1913-1963. [Wallasey: The Police, 1963]
30p(4 fold), illus. 22cm

Walsall [West Midlands]
Collins, James H A
History of the former Walsall Borough Police Force. West Midlands Constabulary, 1967
6p

Woods, David C
The origin of Walsall Borough Police Force. In: *Journal of the Police History Society* n2 (1987) p84-86

Warwick [Warwickshire]
Sutherland, Graham
The Warwick beat 1846-1975. [Warwick]: Warwickshire Constabulary History Society, [1990]
39p. 21cm

Warwickshire
Hinksman, A J
1857-1957: the first hundred years of the Warwickshire Constabulary. [Warwick]: The Constabulary, [1957]
20p, illus. 23cm

Powell, James A, Sutherland, Graham *and* Gardner, Terence
Policing Warwickshire: a pictorial history of the Warwickshire Constabulary. Studley: Brewin, 1997
[8],146p, illus. 15x21cm. ISBN 1 85858 107 9

Sutherland, Graham
Isaac's beat 1840-1875. [Warwick]: Warwickshire Constabulary History Society, [1992?]
33p. 21cm

Sutherland, Graham
The Warwickshire beat 1877-1929. [Warwick]: Warwickshire Constabulary
History Society, [198-]
44p. 21cm

Warwickshire Police
Warwickshire Police 1857-2007. [Warwick]: The Police, 2007
52p, illus. 21cm. Presented to serving and retired officers and staff. Inc
Hinksman, A J. *1857-1957: the first hundred years of the Warwickshire
Constabulary*

Warwickshire - Departments, divisions etc
Powell, J A
*Outline history of the Traffic Department and transport within the
Warwickshire Constabulary.* [Warwick: Warwickshire Constabulary
History Society, 1990?]
21p, illus. 21cm

West Mercia
Hughes, Pat
Hindlip Hall....a dip into history. Hindlip: West Mercia Constabulary,
[1997]
34p, illus. 21cm

Smith, David J
Policing West Mercia 1967 to 1988. Studley: Brewin Books, 1989
[4],188p, illus. 30cm. ISBN 0 947731 46 6

West Mercia Constabulary
*40 years of policing in West Mercia, 1967-2007: policing in Herefordshire,
Shropshire, Telford and Wrekin and Worcestershire.* Hindlip: The
Constabulary, [2007]
21p, illus. 30cm. Cover title

West Mercia Constabulary
Thirty years of policing: Shropshire and Hereford and Worcester. Hindlip:
The Constabulary, [1997]
34p, illus. 30cm. Cover title

West Mercia - Departments, divisions etc
Hereford Police Male Choir: golden jubilee 1957-2007: 50 years of song.
npl: [The Choir, 2007?]
28p, illus. 30cm. Cover title

West Riding of Yorkshire [West Yorkshire]
Short history of the West Riding Police. In: *Yorkshire rose* v3 n1 (1970) p3-6

West Riding Constabulary 1856-1956. In: *White rose* (Winter 1956) p5-57, illus

Alderson, Jack
A history of the West Riding Constabulary 1856-1968. [Holmfirth: The author, 2001]
92,A42,B12p, illus. 30cm

Shaw, Barry
The history of the West Riding Constabulary. Tadcaster: The author, 1970
[3],64p. 30cm. Typescript

West Yorkshire Constabulary. Public Relations Department
History of police in West Riding. npl: The Constabulary, nd
3p

West Riding of Yorkshire - Departments, divisions etc
Bramham, Peter
Policing and the police in an industrial town: Keighley 1856-1870. In: *Local historian* v36 n3 (2006) p175-184

West Suffolk [Suffolk]
West Suffolk Constabulary
West Suffolk Constabulary. Bury St Edmunds: The Constabulary, 1952
12p. Typescript

Wheeler, J D
History of the West Suffolk Constabularies. Bury St Edmunds: The author, 1967
236p, illus. 26cm. Alternative title: *The constabularies of West Suffolk from 1836*

Wheeler, J D
The West Suffolk Constabulary: an outline history. In: *Police journal* v35 (1962) p67-70

Wheeler, J D
West Suffolk Constabulary swords. In: *Suffolk review* v2 n5 (1962) p167-169

West Sussex [Sussex]
West Sussex Constabulary
The West Sussex Constabulary 1857-1957. [Chichester: The Constabulary, 1957]
28p, illus. 22cm

West Yorkshire
West Yorkshire Metropolitan Police: a decade of policing. In: *West Yorkshireman* (Apr 1984). [4p]

Jackson, Colin
The West Yorkshire Constabulary 1968-1974. In: *PICA magazine* (Summer 1984) p5-8

West Yorkshire Metropolitan Police
A short history of the forces that went into the creation of the West Yorkshire Metropolitan Police. Wakefield: The Police, 1979
20p, illus. 25cm

West Yorkshire Police
A history of the police in West Yorkshire. [Wakefield: The Police, 1986-7]
15 leaves in folder, illus. 36cm

West Yorkshire - Departments, divisions etc
Hinton, V M
Chapeltown police station: a history and memories of policing in Leeds 7. [Leeds]: Seven, 2007
[107]p, illus. 17cm. Inc documents and photographs on career of PS George Thompson Cockill 1931-51

Jackson, Colin
Thirty years of driver training: a history of the West Yorkshire Metropolitan Police Driver Training School 1944-1974. Wakefield: West Yorkshire

Metropolitan Police, 1974
54p

Wigan [Greater Manchester]
Fairhurst, James
Policing Wigan: the Wigan Borough Police force 1836-1969. Blackpool: Landy, 1996
[4],86p, illus. 21cm. ISBN 1 872895 29 8

Wigtownshire [Dumfries and Galloway]
Kirkwood, David
Bobbies on the beat. Stranraer: Stranraer and District Local History Trust, 2009
72p, illus. 21cm. ISBN 978-1906737023

Kirkwood, David
The Wigtownshire Constabulary. Stranraer: Stranraer and District Local History Trust, 2008
64p, illus. 21cm. ISBN 978-1906737009

Wiltshire
Sample, Paul
The oldest and the best: the history of Wiltshire Constabulary 1839-1989. Salisbury: No Limit Public Relations, 1989
[48]p, illus. 30cm. ISBN 0 9514949 0 2
2nd ed.: The oldest and the best: the history of Wiltshire Constabulary 1839-2003. [Devizes: Wiltshire Constabulary], 2003
79p, illus. 30cm

Smith, Peter
The origin of the Wiltshire Constabulary. In: *Kewjay* n9 (January 1977) p34-39

Worcester [West Mercia]
Glover, Colin
A history of Worcester City Police 1833-1967. [Worcester: Worcester City Police, 1967]
164p, illus, illus. 22cm

Worcester Constabulary
Police exhibits: civic exhibition, Guildhall, Worcester, September 1957:

souvenir brochure. Worcester: The Constabulary, 1957
8p

Worcestershire [West Mercia]
Pooler, Bob
From fruit trees to furnaces: a history of the Worcestershire Constabulary.
Pershore: Blacksmith, 2002
154p, illus. 30cm. ISBN 0 9543585 0 3

Smith, D J
The establishment and development of the Worcestershire County Constabulary 1839-1843. In: *Journal of the Police History Society* n5 (1990) p3-23

Smith, David Jack
Establishment and development of the Worcestershire County Constabulary 1839 to 1843. West Mercia Constabulary, nd
86p

Worcestershire Constabulary
Brief history of the Worcestershire Constabulary. [Hindlip: The Constabulary, *ca*1963]
8p. 21cm. Typescript

Worcestershire Constabulary
History of the Force. npl: The Constabulary, 1951
31p. Typescript

Wycombe [Thames Valley]
Woodley, Len
The Chepping Wycombe Borough Police: the story of a town's police from 1836 to 1947. [Milton Keynes: The author, 2010]
204p, illus. 30cm

York [North Yorkshire]
Swift, Roger
Police reform in early Victorian York 1835-1856. York: University of York, 1988
48p. 21cm. (Borthwick papers 73)

POLICE HISTORY SOCIETY

The Police History Society (PHS) was formed in 1985 and now has around 400 members world wide. They include serving and retired police officers, academics, librarians, writers, as well as organisations such as police forces and museums. The Society welcomes anybody who has an interest in police history.

Although the PHS is not an official police organisation, it does receive considerable enthusiatic support and encouragement from members of the police service. The Society's Patron is Lord Knights (former Chief Constable of West Midlands) and its President is Her Majesty's Chief Inspector of Constabulary.

The aim of the Society is to promote a general interest in police history and to act as both a focal point and network for anyone with an interest in the subject. Whilst the Society is not primarily interested in family history and has no personnel archive of its own, many of its members do have an interest in genealogy and carry out their own private research.

The Society publishes three *Newsletters* per year and an annual *Journal*, which usually contains between 10 and 15 articles that cover a wide range of police-history related subjects. Special PHS projects have so far included an Open University programme of microfilming old records held by police forces and the re-publication of 19th century *Police Gazettes*.

The Society actively supports research and makes small grants available to its members for approved projects. Furthermore, it encourages the publication of books and articles by its members on relevant subjects.

More information about the Police History Society can be found on its website at www.policehistorysociety.co.uk.

OTHER MONOGRAPHS STILL AVAILABLE

THE POLICE & CONSTABULARY LIST 1844 (Monograph No. 3) This is a reprint of a chance survival of a rare item of police ephemera from the days before there was a police force as we know it. The book purports to be compiled with permission from official documents and contains a royal coat of arms. The contents include a unique collection of names and dates in police history and it is also possible to reconstruct the rank structure, size and organisation of those police forces that existed in 1844. ISBN 978-0951253823. Published 1990. Price £5.50 sterling - overseas orders please add £2.00.

TOWARDS A RECORD MANAGEMENT POLICY FOR PROVINCIAL FORCES IN ENGLAND & WALES (Monograph No. 4). Author: L A Waters. This discussion document was written to assist with the proper record management and archive policies, which are so vital to ensure the survival of the very life blood of future police historians. Chapter headings include *Why do police forces need a policy?*, *Why bother about history?*, *The statutory framework for police archives* and *Objectives for a records management policy*. ISBN 978-0951253830. Published 1992. Photocopy price £2.50 sterling - overseas orders please add £1.00

A HISTORY OF THE CHIPPING NORTON BOROUGH POLICE 1836-1857 (Monograph No: 6). Author: Leonard Woodley. This tiny force started with two officers and finished with only one when it merged with the newly formed Oxfordshire Constabulary in May 1857. ISBN 978-0951253854. Published 2007. Price £5.00 sterling

Prices include postage and packing. Please send orders to Mike Vince, 17 Edmonds Close, Page Hill, Buckingham MK18 1YR. Cheques etc to be payable to *Police History Society*